Women, Technology, and the Myth of Progress

Eileen B. Leonard
Vassar College

Upper Saddle River, New Jersey 07458

Library of Congress Cataloging-in-Publication Data

Leonard, Eileen B.
  Women, technology, and the myth of progress / Eileen B. Leonard.
    p.   cm.
  Includes bibliographical references and index.
  ISBN 0-13-098595-3
    1. Women–Social conditions. 2. Sex role. 3. Progress. 4. Technology and civilization.
5. Technology–Social aspects. I. Title.

HQ 1154 .L48 2002
303.48′3–dc21
                                      2001055165

AVP/Publisher: Nancy Roberts
Production Editor: Cheryl A. Keenan
Copyeditors: Marianne Peters Riordan and Karen Bosch
Editorial Assistant: Lee Peterson
Prepress and Manufacturing Buyer: Mary Ann Gloriande
Marketing Manager: Amy Speckman
Marketing Assistant: Anne Marie Fritzky
Line Art Manager: Guy Ruggiero
Line Art Illustrations: Mirella Signoretto
Cover Art Director: Jayne Conte
Cover Design: Bruce Kenselaar
Cover Photo: Todd Davidson/Stock Illustration Source, Inc.

This book was set in 10/12 Baskerville by DM Cradle Associates
and printed and bound by RR Donnelley & Sons Company.
The cover was printed by Phoenix Color Corp.

© 2003 by Pearson Education, Inc.
Upper Saddle River, New Jersey 07458

Printed in the United States of America
10 9 8 7 6 5 4 3 2 1

ISBN 0-13-098595-3

Pearson Education LTD., London
Pearson Education Australia PTY, Limited, Sydney
Pearson Education Singapore, Pte. Ltd
Pearson Education North Asia Ltd, Hong Kong
Pearson Education Canada, Ltd., Toronto
Pearson Educación de Mexico, S. A. de C.V.
Pearson Education–Japan, Tokyo
Pearson Education Malaysia, Pte. Ltd
Pearson Education, Upper Saddle River, New Jersey

In Memory of Mary

❖ ❖ ❖ ❖ ❖ ❖

Contents

Preface

We live in a time of rapid technological development and, while most assessments of this are decidedly optimistic, some have voiced concern that these changes—as varied as test-tube babies, intelligent robots, smart irons, and genetic engineering—are outstripping our ability to understand or control them. Few would deny that technology has brought improvements in the way many of us live. My own family history offers undeniable evidence of its benefits. As a boy, my father would comb the Brooklyn waterfront for bits of coal to warm his family's small apartment, which lacked centralized heating, while my mother spent years of her childhood bedridden with diseases that my children, given modern antibiotics, wouldn't even know by name. But the belief that technology is purely beneficial needs to be reexamined, not to condemn technology, but to understand more clearly the stereotypical images we have of it, as opposed to its many realities.

This book is an effort to contribute to a critical analysis of technology, offering ways to think about it, make sense of it, and even challenge the direction of technological development. I have been able to draw on a rich and diverse academic literature, bringing together elements that have not been combined previously. I challenge the association of technology and progress by looking at a range of technologies (reproductive, household, and office technologies) and their development and implementation in terms of diverse groups of women. I resist the assessment of technology as either "good" or "bad," perspectives that characterize much public debate about technology and that predominate in media reporting. I insist instead that technology be understood in social terms, as a product of society, developed and utilized in ways that defy such dichotomies. My training as a sociologist has taught me the value of a focus on social inequality and its impact on all dimensions of society, thus including technological development. When viewing technology through a lens of social inequality, it becomes vividly evident that it bestows its benefits differentially, depending on crucial social categories including gender, race, and class. A focus on diverse groups of women and a range of technologies often associated with them, offers one way of demonstrating the varing impacts of technology.

In addition to an emphasis on inequality, the book also offers an analysis of the myth of progress, the pervasive Western belief that connects technological development with continual improvement for all. Reflection on the experiences of women encourages us not only to question the veracity of such claims, but to ask more specifically who benefits from technology and indeed how we define progress. I use the profound insights of sociologist Max Weber, with his concerns about the very meaning of modern technological society, in order to illuminate these issues.

I hope this book will add to a more critical understanding of the role of technology in our society, a rethinking of the myths we hold about it and, more specifically, a keener recognition of the intersections of social inequality and the development and uses of technology. Finally, the book intends to signal that social change is both necessary and possible, but that it will not emerge through a technological fix. If our problems with technology are rooted in social inequality and mythical ideas about technological development, then these must be the targets of social change.

ACKNOWLEDGMENTS

I wish to thank many friends, relatives, and colleagues who encouraged me and provided valuable suggestions throughout this project. In particular, Mona Harrington offered her enthusiasm and her keen insights at an early stage of my writing, and this assistance sustained me throughout. Ben Harris initially got me interested in the significance of issues regarding workplace technology and women, and the project seemed to grow from there. Bill Hoynes, Peter Leonard, Marque Miringoff, Pat Wallace, Deborah Moore, and Beth Weitzman read all or portions of the manuscript and provided invaluable suggestions. Marque Miringoff also assisted with the graphs. Much needed support was also provided by Eleanor Dillon, Jane Parsons-Fein, Eileen Shea, and Jeanne Yglesias. Many Vassar students provided excellent research assistance in preparing this book. I thank, in particular, Rachel Pinsky, as well as Corinne Adams, Rebecca Dudley, Thomas Finni, Sarra Hale-Stern, S. Anne Johnson, Linda Ohman, and Valerie Sobel. I also gratefully acknowledge the constructive and insightful advice offered by the reviewers who commented on the manuscript: Abby L. Ferber, University of Colorado-Colorado Springs; Joan Ferrante, Northern Kentucky University; Claire Renzetti, St. Joseph's University; and Susan Tiano, University of New Mexico. Finally, and most importantly, I thank Pete for his unfailing enthusiasm and constant encouragement.

1

Introduction

❖ ❖ ❖ ❖ ❖ ❖

The aim of an alternative sociology would be to explore and unfold the relations beyond our direct experience that shape and determine it. An alternative sociology would be a means to anyone of understanding how the world comes about for us and how it is organized so that it happens to us as it does in our experience. An alternative sociology, from the standpoint of women, makes the everyday world its problematic.
Dorothy E. Smith

The rhetoric and rules of a society are something a great deal more than sham. . . . They may disguise the true realities of power, but, at the same time, they may curb that power and check its intrusions. And it is often from within that rhetoric that a radical critique of the practice of the society is developed.
E. P. Thompson

Technology is a vital and pervasive feature of modern society. As an integral part of almost every field of activity, it imposes on us daily and in multiple ways, making it virtually inconceivable to get through a day, let alone a lifetime, without experiencing its profound influences.

Despite this centrality, technology has been subjected to relatively little analysis in terms of how it affects the meaning of our lives and the choices or constraints we face. Rather than being reflective, let alone critical, of technology, Americans tend to embrace it as an inherently powerful force, largely for progress. Admittedly, technology is no longer seen as omnipotent: Sophisticated scholarly critiques of it are readily available,[1] as are specific challenges to it, mounted by such social movements as the antigenetic food movement and the antinuclear movement. But these adversarial positions sit largely on the margins of U.S. society and are far from a dominant American perspective. Many of us may have a disquieting sense that things are not as they should be in our "advanced technological society" but remain perplexed as to how to explain this unease. We have been so inundated with the notion that technological development spells progress that the vast majority of us lack even a basic vocabulary to assert a serious critique of it. Even those familiar with such critical analyses often find it difficult to relinquish their confidence in technology. I have found, for example, that many students I teach are able to articulate sophisticated concerns about technology, but as the conversation deepens, one often finds beneath the critical veneer a more powerful acceptance, perhaps even a faith, in technology and its inevitable association with progress.

The belief in technology as progress not only captures the public imagination, it also predominates in business and government circles. The mass media bolsters this idea by regularly featuring dramatic reports of technological developments as varied and intriguing as test-tube babies, self-cleaning houses, and the global computer revolution. Endless scenarios about the millennium assumed this familiar equation of technology and progress. Embedded in all this enthusiasm is the confidence that technology has fundamentally enhanced not only the lives of men but also the status of women in society, emancipating them from drudgery in the home and office, as well as from biological destiny. Consider the vast array of kitchen appliances, electronic office equipment, or new contraceptive devices—and the beneficial results generally attributed to them. In fact, since technology promises to free all of us from menial tasks as well as to expand human choice and potential, it should be a powerful agent of change for women, enabling them increasingly to control their own destinies by easing household labor, enhancing their paid labor, and establishing reproductive choice.

Unfortunately, this optimistic vision tells only part of the story. Technology has indeed provided great benefits for many of us, but the cultural notion that connects technology with progress ultimately obscures more than it reveals. Yes, the situation of U.S. women at home and at work has obviously changed, but more remarkable is the persistent inequality of women despite stunning technological developments. At issue is whether technology has significantly altered the status of women or if, instead, technology itself is largely a product of persistent social inequality.

Although the association of technology and progress is strong and pervasive, a growing uncertainty exists about technology's ability to improve human life, an uncertainty with deep historical roots. My work is grounded in this literature, which interrogates technology, reflects on what it means for our humanity and our future, and envisions remarkably different ways of life. By examining the experiences of women, it is possible to challenge basic American ideas about the nature of technology, specifically three reigning assumptions: the belief that technology is deterministic, that it is beneficent, and that it is apolitical. The deterministic view alleges that technology is an inherently powerful force, a first cause for much social change. Furthermore, it is believed to be beneficent in that this change is predominantly positive for virtually all people. Finally, technology is viewed as a mere tool, developed apart from the pushes and pulls of political constraints and through agents who are neutral and unbiased.[2]

I argue instead that technology is largely an instrument of society, not an independent or neutral force. Created within a social framework, it necessarily has political implications, which shape its ability to be either beneficial or harmful. Thus it must be intensively critiqued regarding its purposes, how and why it is developed, and its relationship to the quality of our lives.

Let me be clear. I am not arguing that technology has done nothing to improve the human condition, to ease our lives, or to increase enjoyment. Of course it has. Many of us relish the freedom of driving a car, the comfort of air conditioning, and the convenience of watching films on a VCR—to say nothing of indoor plumbing and antibiotics. My argument intends to push beyond an unthinking acceptance of the obvious benefits of certain forms of technology, to a deeper analysis of its connections with social inequality. I ask that we consider more seriously *who* benefits from technology and in what terms we judge it as "progressive." An essential part of the scholarly critique of technology has called into question our very definition of progress.[3] Although a fuller analysis of progress will be offered in Chapter 8, a brief introduction here will set the stage for the discussion.

Progress is assumed to be desirable by people who have profoundly different notions about what it could or should entail, or who have, perhaps, never even given it much thought. Often progress is simply defined as continuous development, specifically technological development. The working assumption is that Western civilization moves relentlessly toward social, economic, and political improvement and that technology plays a pivotal role in this by shaping our future in fundamentally beneficial ways—increasing enjoyment, asserting control over nature, and easing our work loads. Even if everyone does not benefit equally, the overall trend is positive. However, a significant body of literature has begun to articulate the need for an analysis of our basic ideas and optimism regarding progress and technology. Critics like Langdon Winner,[4] for example, rightly fear that many of our existing beliefs and premises regarding technology are themselves "pathological." He[5] calls for a critique of technological society itself and challenges the assumption "that the progress of mankind is inextricably linked to new technological apparatus." Instead, he argues that such assumptions "lie at the heart of the trouble." Winner and others are suggesting that we stop and re-think our working assumptions regarding progress and technology, specifically the belief that progress is inevitable, and that it is measured by technological change. These assumptions imply an unquestioning acceptance of technological development with little or no need to examine its point or purpose, since it is, by definition, progressive. But, according to Winner, we need a more thoughtful analysis of the direction of technological development and, equally significant, more concern with a just distribution of its benefits.

The roots of these concerns with technology are found deep in American society. Merritt Roe Smith,[6] for example, aptly observes that Thomas Jefferson revered discovery and invention, but he always kept them in perspective by recognizing that they were the means to a larger social end. "For Jefferson, progress ultimately meant the realization of a republican polity (with its emphasis on liberty and virtue) in a predominantly agrarian society."[7] When Jefferson and his contemporaries spoke of progress, they consequently gave human betterment (intellectual, moral, spiritual) equal weight with material prosperity.[8] But Smith argues that Americans began to lose touch with the nonmaterial dimensions of the belief in progress. Bolstered by seemingly endless triumphs in science and technology, arrogance grew, and the materialistic conception of progress began to dominate. "The old parity between moral and material progress disappeared and with it emerged one of the central dilemmas of our present age, namely, an unbridled enthusiasm for technological innovation and the ascendancy of profit over tradition in the rush to rationalize all aspects of industrial life."[9]

More than anyone, Leo Marx[10] illuminates the Enlightenment vision of progress as one of human liberation—the creation of a democratic, less hierarchical society that technology would enable us to reach. As Marx[11] puts it, "To the republican revolutionaries of the Enlightenment, especially the radical *philosophes*, science and the practical arts were instruments of political liberation, essential tools for arriving at the ideal goal of progress: a more just, peaceful, less hierarchal, republican society based on the consent of the governed." Marx points to Thomas Jefferson's telling rejection of a factory system in America: Jefferson feared that factories would damage the democratic ethos by creating an urban proletariat, and so he advocated the more expensive procedure of shipping materials to England to be assembled and returned to the United States. He "anticipated the viewpoint of the environmentalists and others of our time for whom the test of a technological innovation is its effects on the overall quality of life."[12] Marx also cites Benjamin Franklin's refusal to patent the "Franklin stove" because he believed that inventions are meant to serve others, not for private interest. Marx[13] sees Franklin as representing much of the American character, and as exemplifying a "principled and limited self-interest."

By the mid-nineteenth century, however, technology *itself* was viewed as progressive—not its utility in reaching social or political goals. Marx argues that this type of thinking facilitated the domination of nature and the brutal conquest of Native Americans. By the end of the nineteenth century a thoroughly technocratic idea of progress had emerged, a view which "valued improvements in power, efficiency, rationality as ends in themselves."[14] Currently, according to Marx, the United States is committed to this misguided view: committed to increasing wealth, productivity and technological innovation as the measure of progress. In effect, we have witnessed the appropriation of the belief in progress for the defense of an anti-egalitarian status quo.

Marx argues that we must challenge the assumption that technological development represents progress, we must question our faith in its ability to solve our problems, and we must begin to reassess the purpose of technological development. He offers that technology could mean progress but only if we reflect upon our goals, on what we want to achieve beyond mere development and increased efficiency. Thus, progress is a great myth if we regard it as a historical necessity or an infallible prediction of constant improvement along the lines dictated by a technocratic society. But, as E. P. Thompson keenly observes, the rhetoric of a society may provide the possibility of radical critique. If we treat progress as a possibility, rooted in human choices and human activity, then it can serve as an inspiration. The challenge is to recognize what the dominant myth of technology and progress obscures, to acknowledge that mere technological development does not necessarily mean improvement, and to reassert a focus on social and political goals, such as justice, equality, and democracy—which are the genuine measure of progress.

In an effort to contribute to this rethinking, I aim to challenge the automatic association of technology and progress by exploring a range of technologies often associated with women, highlighting not only problems with these particular technologies, but fundamental forms of inequality that persist regarding women in the United States and globally, despite technological change. While it may be argued that any incremental change that improves the human condition should be defined as progress, I would dispute that notion and argue instead that genuine progress must include more substantive change. Only structural change is capable of undermining gender as well as class and racial inequality and the suffering they necessarily entail. Some, as we will see, contend that technology has already brought this type of progress, or is on the verge of doing so, but the evidence indicates that technology has done little to dislodge inequality and traditional social understandings of women as household laborers, mothers, and secondary workers outside the home. Instead it often serves to fortify the status quo albeit in new guises.

Household technology, for example, has certainly relieved some women from the onerous burdens of housework. Washing machines alone have eased the rigors of hand washing clothes. But technology has not freed women from being largely responsible for housework nor has it decreased the time spent doing housework. Remarkably, full time housewives in the United States spend as much time on household chores as their grandmothers did fifty years ago. Virtually all contemporary research continues to demonstrate that women—even when employed outside the home—do at least twice as much housework as men. Within each category of technology, we will see that extraordinary developments have not resulted in similar social advances for women.

Dramatic developments have occurred in reproductive technology as well, helping a woman have or avoid having a child. Consider *in vitro* fertilization (IVF), which makes it possible for a child to be conceived in a laboratory dish and then implanted in a woman's body. Another process, called embryo transfer, involves washing an embryo from a pregnant woman and transferring it to another woman. Scientists have developed the capability of overriding menopause by impregnating postmenopausal women with the fertilized eggs of younger women. Embryo freezing is also a reality. Australian researchers produced the world's first "freeze-thaw" baby in 1984, so a woman may now conceive a fetus, wash it from her body, freeze it, and reimplant it when she chooses. These developments signal what many understandably refer to as a "revolution" in reproductive technology. But consider some other relevant facts. Since many of these technologies are not covered by insurance, only some women can afford them. Moreover, these women are often deceived by many medical practitioners regarding the success rates of high tech methods of producing a child. Even more crucial, however, is the rhetoric surrounding reproductive technologies that focuses on how they are designed to enable women to bear healthy babies. This stands in striking contrast to the fact that (1) the United States has a worse than average infant mortality rate among rich countries and (2) as of June 2000, the disparity between blacks and whites in the number of infant deaths within the United States had grown to 2.4, despite improvements in infant mortality rates.[15] If technology were truly progressive—increasing equality and ensuring social justice—it would override gender, class, or racial discrimination, but the evidence indicates that instead it serves some groups and not others. This should compel us to ask why technology has *not* been a more powerful agent of social change.

The answer to this apparent paradox lies in the fact that technology is embedded within, and grows out of, fundamental social inequality which profoundly influences its development and use. Unfortunately, the popular discussion of technology is often framed too strictly in terms of whether or not it is progressive, whether it improves human life or diminishes it, whether it has enhanced women's lives or not. Ultimately, these monolithic terms of debate are not helpful. They compel us to decide whether technology is "good" or "bad." On the other hand, many studies of technology leave us mired in confusing details. In these cases, it is impossible to conclude whether technology is good or bad, since it may be either, depending on the specific circumstance.

The terms of my discussion will avoid these dichotomies. Rather than simply praising or damning technology as a whole or arguing that its complexity precludes any conclusions, a sociological analysis illustrates that the development and implementation of technology is not random or incomprehensible, but patterned in terms of gender, class, and racial inequality. Instead of being progressive, as many believe, or its opposite, as some critics would have it, technological development bestows its benefits differentially, depending on these fundamental social categories. Technology has enhanced human life in many ways and may even have quite unanticipated positive outcomes, but it is not "revolutionary"—it does not fundamentally alter basic social divisions. All the developments in the electronic office, for example, have not disrupted the overall gender division of labor, which situates women and men in different and unequal jobs throughout our economy. Women, particularly minority women, still occupy the lowest levels of the office hierarchy. Moreover, women's opportunities for climbing the job ladder in the office have constricted with the development of technology, and office workers are increasingly monitored by computers, which does not serve their interests but the interests of managers. Thus, technology is typically envisioned and implemented *within* the parameters of inequality that fracture our society. In this way, it reflects and even reproduces prevailing social relations, extending rather than eradicating the inequality associated with gender, race, or class.

This analysis reflects a sociology of technology that deals not only with the effects of technology, but also considers how social factors influence the development of technology (what is developed and why). MacKenzie and Wajcman[16] argue that most social scientists have been concerned with "effects," leaving unanswered a prior question: What shapes technological developments in the first place? How do social factors affect technology? Dealing with this question positions social factors at the root of technological development and implementation. It thus illuminates how technology is socially constructed, shaped by both structural and ideological constraints that impede its potential to revolutionize the status of women. Deeply held beliefs and structural inequalities are manifested in the *design* as well as in the *implementation* of the technologies in question. Household technologies, for example, are designed for individual use mainly by women in separate households, thus reinforcing the traditional roles of women and maximizing the number of appliances that will be sold. Moreover, only profit-making items emerge: Little research and development aims at home technologies needed by the disabled, for example, since these tend to be more expensive and less profitable.

Although we are taught to think of more technology, more speed, and more efficiency as ultimate goals, genuine advancement is not equivalent to continuous technological development. Thoreau was right to define technology as "improved means to *unimproved* ends." We need to reflect on the point of our technology. This requires a redefinition of what we mean by progress (if it is not merely technological development), and ultimately far more democratic control of technology for human benefit.

My specific focus is on the experiences of contemporary U.S. women with technology, exploring some of the differences among them across various technologies. Feminist analyses have encouraged serious attention to difference and to varying forms of inequality, rather than assuming that the experiences of all women are alike or that gender equality alone will free women. Gita Sen and Caren Grown[17] capture this understanding when they define feminism as "the struggle against all forms of oppression." In this spirit, I explore differences among women in the United States and also consider some of the connections and implications of Western technology for Third World women.[18] The stories and case studies of Third World women are meant to be comparative—*not* demonstrating universalistic claims, but illustrating global interconnections, signaling the significance of these connections, and encouraging a deeper analysis of them. These case studies are particularly useful since the implications of gender, race, and class inequalities are often heightened to extremes in a global context, and the social construction of technology becomes singularly transparent.

A few words defining technology are in order, especially since it has been characterized in significantly different ways. Most broadly, it may refer to any kind of practical know-how; most restrictively, it may be seen merely as tools or machines. Striking what I believe is a more useful middle ground, I define technology as that part of culture (including knowledge and tools) that involves creating or designing practical solutions to problems. So it is not *any* human skill (like knowing how to pole-vault) nor is it *just* machinery. This definition enables us to explore a variety of developments within reproductive, office, and household technologies.

One further point of clarification. Arguing that technology is profoundly affected by social inequality and thus bestows its benefits differentially does not necessarily imply that problems would be resolved with wider access to all technology. Since what is developed and implemented often works to maintain the current distribution of power and traditional patterns of behavior, many existing technologies may not be in the public interest or that of a humane democratic society. For example, the dilemmas posed by computer monitoring will obviously not diminish if more workers are monitored nor will the profound questions raised by sex selection techniques disappear if working class women have ready access to them. Here again the question of what we mean by "progress" becomes central. What is, and should be, the point of technological development?

Following this Introduction, Chapter 2, *The Social Construction of Technology*, provides a framework for understanding the social nature of technological development and use, and its implications for women. It addresses obstacles to a sociological analysis of technology and discusses various ways of theorizing about technology. I situate and distinguish my analysis from other feminist frameworks: I center on the inequality of women and the implications of this regarding technology, rather than a concern with gender in the wider sense; my focus on women also considers differences among them. Other literature on women and technology does not include a consideration of race and class across various technologies. Focusing on structural patterns of inequality that repeatedly emerge across varying types of technology enables one to see that technology itself is largely an instrument of society's social divisions and inequalities, not independent, neutral, or natural. Rather than being either a pure force for progress or simply pernicious, technology is socially constructed in terms of gender, race, and class, and this profoundly affects what gets developed and who benefits from it. This chapter thus introduces the analytical tools that will be used to understand empirical evidence presented in subsequent chapters on reproductive, office, and household technology.

Chapter 3, *The Wonders of Technology*, then asks us to consider how we learn about technology through the mass media and the messages we absorb. This chapter provides an overview of some recent developments in household, reproductive, and office technology, focusing on how and why they tend to be favorably reported, if not sensationalized, in the media. Chapter 4, *Broken Promises: A Look at the Status of Women*, can be sobering, indeed it may be puzzling to some. It introduces what German sociologist Max Weber might call "inconvenient facts"–facts that challenge prevailing political beliefs–by documenting the dismaying absence of overall improvement in the social and economic status of women in the United States despite technological developments. Women, for example, still maintain a secondary place in the labor market; the segregation of occupations is about the same as it was twenty or thirty years ago. Disproportionately absent from political life and certainly from the financial centers of power, women are still bound by traditional cultural expectations: They remain largely responsible for the housework, for child care, and for the care of the sick and infirm. This chapter also discusses poverty among women in the United States and worldwide. In confirming the persistence of severe inequality, these "inconvenient facts" should spur us to reconsider assumptions about the relationship between technology and "progress."

The next three chapters explore specific problems associated with reproductive, office, and household technology, respectively, illustrating how each may provide some measure of improvement without altering fundamental aspects of women's inequality. Chapter 5, *Reproductive Technology and the Politics of Social Control*, analyzes a range of reproductive technologies, including contraception, *in vitro* fertilization, and embryo transfer. I focus on the considerable problems associated with these developments and the persisting inequality of women despite them. For example, restricted access to conceptive technologies (which aim to promote fertility) bolsters the traditional social order in profound ways. Various government panels have repeatedly recommended that only married women, or women in a stable relationship with a man, be permitted to utilize artificial insemination and *in vitro* fertilization. Single women, lesbians, and people with disabilities are unwelcome at most clinics. Many of the reproductive technologies are also highly commercialized, although women frequently lack knowledge or control regarding them, and deceptive practices have been used to disguise high failure rates.

Chapter 6, *The Electronic Office: A Counterfeit Revolution*, examines both the technological developments that have supposedly "revolutionized" the office and the problems that have ensued in their wake. These problems include threats to job security, concerns about the quality of jobs that remain, the issue of computer monitoring, health risks associated with the technology, and the increasing flexibility of work location (permitting work to be relocated, for example, to the home, to nonunionized parts of the United States, and to the Third World). I discuss why each of these issues poses a serious threat to women workers in particular because they are still concentrated in the lower occupational levels of our work force and promises of retraining at higher levels have not been forthcoming. The current division of labor discourages women from skilled technological occupations, and class and race divisions have left working-class women and black women most in jeopardy of having their jobs automated out of existence.

Chapter 7, *Household Labor and Technology in a Consumer Culture*, briefly examines nineteenth century technological developments in the household, as well as more recent innovations, including "smart" appliances, microwaves, and robots. Improvements in household technology have enhanced the lives of many women, but this chapter documents the more puzzling absence of change in the wake of these developments. This includes empirical studies about the amount of time women still spend doing housework, the understanding that they (not men or older children) do this work often despite full-time employment outside the home and increasing expectations and new tasks in the household. All told, women have not been emancipated from housework. Traditional ideas about the responsibilities of women affect what technology is designed and who uses it in the home, as illustrated by the fact that advertising consistently targets women in private households, and when privileged women work outside the home, household responsibilities are seldom reallocated within the family. Instead, another woman is hired to perform this labor, frequently a minority woman.

Having examined in detail how various forms of social inequality affect reproductive, office, and household technology, Chapter 8, *The Myth of Progress*, helps explain why this information about technology has been marginal to popular debate and why technology has not been subjected to a more intensive critique in a democratic society. Technology has benefited many of us, and this explains part of our reluctance to see other aspects of it. Additionally, Americans have been carefully taught that technology is not only exceedingly powerful, but ultimately beneficent. This chapter considers the continuing power and pervasiveness of this myth. Because many are mesmerized by the idea that technology is progressive, our ability to assess it adequately suffers; so does our understanding of what constitutes authentic improvement.

This chapter adds to the literature on technology and progress by exploring Max Weber's critique of Western civilization and his discussion of the process of rationalization in order to illuminate women's experiences with technology. Weber understood that technological development epitomizes what he termed increasing rationalization—the creation of a less magical, more standardized, and more mechanical world—in that it reflects and promotes efficiency and expert control, as opposed to social concerns and democratic power holding. Modern society values this efficiency and mastery; we emphasize speed and effectiveness rather than sober reflection on more humanitarian goals. Weber argued that rationalization is nothing to cheer about since whatever its merits, it spells the constriction and perhaps death of spontaneity, humane concerns, and democratic control. He thus called into question basic assumptions about technological progress and Western civilization. The three categories of technology (reproductive, office, and household) illustrate the growth and pervasiveness of this particular form of rationality that Weber identified and should lead us to question whether our overemphasis on technological means as opposed to ultimate goals dehumanizes rather than frees us.

Reproductive technology, for example, reflects and imposes upon us a particular world view by raising certain issues and by framing them largely in technological terms. To illustrate: The very development of certain types of reproductive technology, such as prenatal diagnosis, epitomizes a rational society that aims to control the creation and terms of life itself. When this technology presents us with the possibility of detecting and aborting a "defective" fetus, we are then forced to choose whether or not to take advantage of that technology. Our choices are subtly shaped by its very availability and the tendency to view the issue in technological, not ethical, terms.

Pervasive rationality also enhances the power of experts. When problems increasingly come to be viewed as technological, the vast majority of us are suddenly regarded as lacking the expertise to hold opinions, let alone to make decisions. One of the reasons technology is not emancipatory is that women have so little formal or personal control over it. This includes not only an absence of democratic control in terms of its development and implementation, but also a lack of information about the very technologies they use. This was vividly illustrated in the case of Louise Brown, the first "test-tube baby." Mrs. Brown was unaware until she was six months pregnant that she would give birth to the world's first "test-tube baby." She simply assumed that "hundreds of babies" had been born by this procedure. Similarly, Judith Carr did not realize until her pregnancy that she would be the mother of the first "test-tube baby" in North America. When asked why she had not requested information about success rates from her doctors, she replied, "I was too polite to ask that question."

Chapter 9, *Demands and Promises: Implications for Social Change*, considers technology's potential in terms of improving human life. Technologies can serve genuinely progressive goals. As Hopkins[19] notes, they "can open up options for challenging sex-based restrictions, allowing people to 'break out' of proscribed roles and limited spheres of action." But I would argue that improvement will not come through technological change alone, but rather through *social* change. If the problems of technology are indeed rooted in social inequality and misguided notions of "progress," then inequality and our social goals must ultimately be the subjects of discussion and the targets for change. This chapter acknowledges and asserts the potential for change, particularly through social action. Examples of women organizing for social change will highlight the advances that have been made as well as the possibilities. The challenge before us is a political one: a struggle for social and economic justice to ensure that technology serves the common good. The key point is that genuine improvements, such as the results of the women's health movement, most often come from the efforts of individuals organized to confront established power, not from a technological fix.

This analysis of women and technology aims to illuminate several aspects of American society that demand critique and change. By focusing on both structured inequality and our cultural myth of progress we have a framework for understanding the social and political dimensions of technology, who controls it, and why it has been limited in undermining the inequality of women. Most crucially, this analysis emphasizes the manifold forms of inequality that exist and persist in American society, and simultaneously signals that things could be different. Of course there have been improvements in the status of women, and technology has played a part in this. But viewing technology within its larger social context asks us to consider more carefully who benefits? It asks us to question what gets developed and why? What is the point of technology? The central issue is not technological literacy as many would have it, but the far more complex need for genuine democratic control. It remains an open question whether technology will serve the vast majority, and whether it will serve life. But as Louis Mumford has suggested, "Let's make the attempt."

NOTES

1. Critiques of technology will be discussed throughout this book, ranging from general social critiques such as those presented by Ezrahi, Mendelsohn, and Segal (1994), Marx (1994), Noble (1977), Smith and Marx (1994), Weber (1958), and Winner (1972, 1997) to a wide variety of social scientists, philosophers, and historians who have discussed specific technologies.

2. The belief that technology is deterministic has been the most influential theory regarding technology and society, despite the fact that it has been critiqued by many, including a particularly powerful critique by Langdon Winner (1977). Jacques Ellul (1964) epitomizes those who claim that technology is deterministic as well as pernicious. Technological determinism has been espoused in what may be regarded as a feminist text. *Sex Role Changes: Technology, Politics, and Policy* by Lynn Whicker and Jennie Jacobs Kronenfeld (1986). David Noble (1978) observes that technological determinism is politically dangerous since it divorces technology from its social setting and claims that it is bound to have certain effects, thus undermining resistance to it. Albert Borgmann (1984, 10–11) has criticized the notion of technology as apolitical, as a mere tool. He remarks that this assumption is congenial to a liberal democratic tradition, but that it ignores the fact that "A means in a traditional culture is never mere but always and inextricably woven into a context of ends."

3. See, for example, Albany and Schwartz (1982), Dickson (1974), Goldman (1989), Marx (1994), Noble (1993), Richards (1980), and Staudenmaier (1989).

4. Langdon Winner, "On Criticizing Technology." *Public Policy.* 1972: 53.

5. Ibid., 50–51.

6. Merritt Roe Smith, "Technology, Industrialization, and the Idea of Progress in America." In *Responsible Science: The Impact of Technology on Society* (New York: Harper and Row, 1986), 1–30.

7. Ibid., 3.

8. Ibid., 4.

9. Ibid., 10.

10. Leo Marx, "Does Improved Technology Mean Progress?" *Technology Review*, vol. 90 (January 1987): 32–41, 71.

11. Leo Marx, "The Idea of 'Technology' and Postmodern Pessimism." In *Technology, Pessimison, and Postmodernism* (The Netherlands: Kluwer Academic Publishers, 1994), 19.

12. Marx, "Does Improved Technology Mean Progress?" 36.

13. Ibid., 37.

14. Ibid., 39.

15. Leslie Berger, "A Racial Gap in Infants Deaths, and a Search for Reasons," *The New York Times*, 25 June 2000, 13.

16. Donald Mackenzie and Judy Wajcman, *The Social Shaping of Technology* (Philadelphia: Open University Press, 1985).

17. Sen and Grown, *Development, Crises, and Alternative Visions,* (New York: Monthly Review Press, 1987), 19.

18. I am not suggesting that Third World women are a homogeneous category, but I see them as sharing a common fate in that their countries are systematically subordinated and underdeveloped by Western capitalism. Even when they benefit from the creation of jobs by multinationals, this typically occurs in ways that perpetuate their relative inequality. (See Harrington 1977, 16–28.)

19. Patrick D. Hopkins, *Sex/Machine: Readings in Culture, Gender, and Technology* (Bloomington: Indiana University Press, 1998), 6.

2

The Social Construction of Technology

❖ ❖ ❖ ❖ ❖ ❖

*The field of gender and technology can be the lens for a critical assessment
of the late twentieth century.*
Aihwa Ong

The centrality and pervasiveness of technology in modern society is undisputed, and making sense of it—its roots and its effects—is a vital task. Although Americans are inclined to applaud technological development, our discussion aims to persuade the reader that any simple equation of technology with progress is deeply flawed. Granted "progress" may be defined in various ways, but if we accept the ideal that progress should enhance justice and undermine hierarchy, we have yet to succeed in this regard. Who can walk the streets of America's varied urban neighborhoods, enter any of our criminal courts, visit the stock exchange, the U.S. Senate chambers, or a waiting room at social services, and deny the fierce persistence of gender, race, and class inequality? The gap between rich and poor in our advanced technological society is vast and since 1968 it has grown wider than anywhere else in the West; by 1995, the wealthiest 1 percent of U.S. households owned nearly 40 percent of the nation's wealth (twice as much as Britain, which has the greatest inequality in Europe). This concentration of wealth is "essentially double what it has been in the mid-1970s, and back to where it was in the late 1920s, before the introduction of progressive taxation."[1]

A great deal of empirical evidence will be marshalled to demonstrate that technology has not proven to be an autonomous force for social improvement despite popular assertions regarding its progressive nature. The attention paid to its apparent successes has allowed myth to trump evidence in dangerous ways. But, why hasn't technology met expectations of profound social change? What prevents dramatic technological advances from resulting in equally astonishing social advances? And can it be otherwise?

The likelihood of genuine social change is premised on the assumption that we understand the roots of the problems we face. As Langdon Winner[2] asserts, "If it were possible to reflect upon and act intelligently upon patterns in technology as they affect everyday life, it might be possible to guide technocultural forms along paths that are humanely agreeable, socially just, and democratically chosen." This chapter will offer ways to think about technology, introducing frameworks that will be used in later chapters. Attempts to make sense of technology or theorize about it have, however, encountered numerous obstacles. I will begin by reviewing some popular assumptions that hinder a sociological understanding of technology, and then situate the analysis I am offering within the current literature dealing with women and technology. I argue that a consideration of gender as well as class and racial inequality provides a satisfying and coherent way of understanding crucial aspects of technological development and implementation. Moreover, this perspective encourages and even necessitates raising vital questions as to the purpose of technology, who controls it, and who benefits from it.

DETERMINISM AND CHOICE REVISITED

Technology (and indeed science) is commonly regarded as independent, developed, and organized in its own terms quite apart from anything so mundane as politics, economics, or inequality. It is viewed as immune to social divisions and dimensions of power. Given its supposed independence, however, it may affect social relations, compelling us to adapt to it. In this perspective, it is deterministic and a primary causal force, either for good or evil.[3] Alternatively, technology is often viewed as neutral, assuming that it is not good or bad, it simply depends on how you *use* it.[4] Both of these popular viewpoints (determinism and neutrality) miss the sociological significance of technology. Rather than being either an irreducible first cause or simply neutral, technology is largely a secondary phenomenon, a construct of society, socially shaped.[5] In a sense it has been "chosen" and so have its implications since technology is always developed and implemented within a particular social context. Who designs it, who uses it, and why and when they do so are significant factors and have profound effects.

Technology is never a pure creation. Instead, the social position and vantage point of its creators are frequently written into the technology itself, rendering it as something more than an autonomous determining force or a neutral instrument. The automobile offers a useful illustration. This all-American machine reflects and therefore reinforces a range of accepted social relations by being individualized, designed for a small family, and run on fuel. As Albury and Schwartz[6] point out, "Alternatives such as a vastly expanded public transport system, bicycle tracks, and pollution-free vehicles are not considered to be technological priorities." Specific social and economic interests are at work here, including the oil industry, the current automobile industry, and even urban design, affecting the choice and design of our transportation technology.

More than thirty years ago, Paul Goodman[7] observed what remains true today—that technology is largely under political, military, and economic control. How can it be neutral in light of this? He asserted that technology, "in its proliferation, its direction of development, and its intensification of effect . . . has been in the employ of old familiar motives: profits, power, and the aggrandizement of persons or groups . . . I do not see the autonomy." Notions of neutrality and technological determinism ignore this larger context and thus concede all the power to technology. Technology may have unanticipated consequences, but it is naive to view it as an autonomous agent of social change or a neutral tool.

Another popular way to view technology is to reflect upon it in individualistic terms. We are encouraged to believe that we as individuals can decide whether or not to use technology and can use it on our own terms. But reducing the use of technology to a matter of individual choice steadfastly ignores the social and political constraints that shape our "choices" and make them anything but strictly individual. A woman's "individual choice" regarding her use of reproductive technology, for example, may be severely restricted not only by what technology is available but by the social stigma of infertility, the financial expense of these technologies, or her lack of knowledge about them. Rita Arditti et al.[8] put the realities of reproductive "choice" crisply:

> But how can women choose freely in a society where the right to choice must be bought? Where people of color are discriminated against and population 'control' is blatantly racist? Where women are taught to subordinate their interests to those of men? Where a woman isn't 'real' without a husband and child?

In American society, problems are typically defined in individualistic terms, despite the fact that social conditions may be equally or more salient in their creation and solution. *In vitro* fertilization, for example, has been developed to assist individual women who are infertile rather than avoiding the problem of infertility in the first place by providing social policies such as generous work leaves, which would minimize delayed childbearing and the infertility this delay often entails.[9] Instead of acknowledging how larger social patterns influence our lives, our choices, and our technology, we privatize our problems or define them as unchangeable. But the roots of many of our problems with technology are not individual or predetermined but *social*, and best understood (and changed) not solely in terms of private situations but in terms of the connections between our personal lives and larger social structures.

THEORIZING TECHNOLOGY

A sociological perspective challenges familiar notions of technological determinism or neutrality by analyzing technology within its social context. It rejects any tendency to think about technology as either "good" or "bad" as a whole. Moreover, it offers an analysis that can move beyond research that is so focused on details that a larger picture gets lost. Some contend, for example, that it is difficult to pass judgement on office automation because its' outcomes depend on multiple variables—the industry under consideration, the particular equipment being automated, the pace of automation, the office managers involved, and on and on.[10] This allows the details to obscure and prevent an analytical assessment of the larger situation.

Rather than praising or damning technology as a whole or refusing to generalize because we are so mired in particulars, I offer the sociological argument that the development and use of technology is not random or incomprehensible, but patterned along gender as well as class and racial lines. It does not have one fixed set of consequences for all but bestows its benefits differentially in terms of familiar social categories. This analysis permits a deeper and more useful understanding of the multiple ways technology functions in our society, and why it varies so significantly in its effects. It enables us to see that as a product of society, technology is embedded within, and grows out of, fundamental social conditions. A focus on structural inequalities of gender, race, and class is warranted because they are critical to understanding any aspect of American society, including technological development. These inequalities affect what technology is created and how we use it, with the ultimate result that technology often serves to extend, rather than eradicate or disrupt, fundamental social inequality.

FEMINIST FRAMEWORKS

The mainstream study of technology and society tends to ignore gender issues, but an impressive variety of feminist research has developed within the past twenty-five years that illuminates the relationship between gender and technology.[11] The bulk of this work has taken the form of rigorous empirical studies of specific types of technology. This has entailed relatively little comparison of varying types of technology as well as comparatively little theoretical analysis. Although there are different ways of categorizing feminist attempts to analyze technology, eco-feminism, liberal feminism, and socialist feminism are among the primary frameworks.[12]

Briefly, eco-feminism sees technology as essentially male, an example of the male domination of both women and nature. It posits essentialist differences between women and men, and frankly celebrates the woman's side of the equation.[13] Liberal feminists, on the other hand, see technology as neutral and a given in modern society. What concerns them is the unequal relation women and men have to technology. Thus, they advocate policies that would encourage the technological education of women as well as affirmative action in order to permit women to reap the benefits of modern technology. Lastly, socialist feminists argue that technology is both a historical and cultural construction (not essentialist nor the norm). Rooted in a particular cultural and historical setting, it embodies patriarchal as well as capitalistic values, which in turn perpetuate the oppression of women.[14] Recent work has seen a decided shift from an analysis of women and technology to a broader concern with gender and questions about cultural practices and social systems.[15]

Although influenced by this body of work, my approach differs in significant ways. To begin, I do not accept the essentialist differences between women and men posited by eco-feminism nor do I see technology as neutral and technological education as a solution, as the liberal feminists claim. I prefer to center on the inequality of women and the implications of this regarding technology, rather than gender in the wider sense. Thus my focus is not on cultural practices nor a concern with masculinity per se. I believe that a focus on structural inequality illuminates the development and implementation of technology and continues to offer valuable insights. I have been particularly influenced by the socialist feminists' view of technology and their understanding of the need to analyze the impact of both patriarchy and capitalism on women. Those working from a socialist feminist perspective, however, have often ignored race. In fact, most literature on women and technology does not include a consideration of race and class across various technologies. Even critiques of technology often focus on one form of oppression (such as gender or class) while omitting a serious consideration of others (such as class or race). Yet all three categories are among the most significant in structuring the experiences of *all* Americans and to attend to them is merely to acknowledge the power they exert in our lives.

A major thrust of recent American feminist theory has been the analysis of "difference."[16] This resulted, in part, from black and Third-World women's criticisms of Western feminism for ignoring the effects of racism and the very existence of women of color. Excluded, feminists of color "sought to develop methods of analysis that contest the marginalization or absence of questions of racism in much white feminist theory and analysis, offering alternative approaches to the question of difference."[17] Black feminist intellectuals have been at the center of theorizing about race, class, and gender in the United States: Most significant is their "articulation of multiple oppressions."[18] Many argue that one of the great strengths of this theorizing is that it does not simply entail abstract debates but rises directly from the experiences and voices of marginalized women of color in the United States.[19]

The current theoretical work on race, class, and gender is predated by a rich tradition of black women's theorizing and activism, including, for example, the black suffragettes who explicitly called attention to issues of race.[20] The sources of contemporary analyses that acknowledge multiple forms of inequality are found in the experiences of African-American women in the social movements of the 1960s—where they saw issues of race ignored in the feminist movement and their needs as women overlooked in anti-racist activities—and in the curriculum development projects beginning in the 1970s in higher education, organized mainly by Women's Studies faculties.[21] By the early 1980s, several black scholars and activists were developing approaches that explicitly analyzed multiple and interconnecting forms of oppression.[22] Currently, the feminisms of women of color (including U.S.

Third World feminisms, indigenous feminisms, and multicultural feminism) offer varied perspectives, which Zinn and Dill[23] see as evolving largely from socialist feminist thinking and race and ethnic studies.[24] What is clear is that we can no longer imagine and describe the world as if a single perspective on "women" explains their many realities.

Central themes have emerged in this developing literature. Most significant is the emphasis on race as a central category of analysis, and the refusal to see various forms of inequality as discreet and separate. Rather, race, class, and gender are multiple and interactive and, moreover, they represent some, but not all, of the relevant or central factors that shape women's lives. Theorists are insistent that expanding this analysis is welcome.[25] Power relations are also explicitly analyzed in many of these writings. Another crucial aspect is the emphasis on reclaiming the history not only of black women's oppression, but their resistance and agency. Black women are acknowledged to be powerful, independent subjects,[26] and widespread social change is their explicit goal.[27]

The work of Kimberle Crenshaw[28] illuminates several of these themes. She uses the concept of "intersectionality" to indicate the ways in which race and gender interact to shape black women's experiences.[29] Although racism and sexism coexist in the lives of real people, they are often treated analytically, as though they were mutually exclusive, thus failing to capture the many dimensions of women's lives. Crenshaw focuses on the problems that ensue when intragroup differences are ignored, including the fact that analyses are distorted when only a narrow portion of a more complex phenomenon is explored.[30] She offers as an example the way in which feminists describe rape statutes as reflecting *male* control over *female* sexuality. She[31] counters, however, that historically, "there has been absolutely no institutional effort to regulate Black female chastity." Rather, black women were and are sexually vulnerable because of racism. The failure to consider the interaction of racism and sexism thus erases black women.[32] For Crenshaw, ignoring the interaction of multiple forms of oppression also undermines efforts to expand feminist and antiracist analyses and makes the goal of ending inequality that much more difficult.

I have been influenced by these frameworks that argue persuasively that understanding the experiences of women must move beyond considerations of gender to a serious analysis of multiple forms of inequality. For our purposes, then, understanding and assessing the relationship between women and technology demands a serious consideration of categories such as race and class in order to provide a more inclusive analysis of the impact of technology on various groups of women. Gender, class, and race are fundamental organizing principles in our society, and discrimination on the basis of them is an unstated part of all our institutions, including home, office, and the medical establishment—and the technologies associated with these spheres. This analysis is not meant to be exhaustive, but to suggest instead a sociological framework that makes sense of much empirical evidence and that could be expanded in many ways (by considering sexuality, ethnicity, or national origin, for example). This approach also has more to offer than simply understanding the "impact" of particular technologies. It assumes that in a society structured in terms of race, class, and gender, the technology that is developed will bear the earmarks of that setting in terms of who creates it, what gets created, and how it is implemented. More specifically, technology is the creation of a society fractured by inequality, and it frequently serves to reflect and reinforce the social inequality from which it arises. Let me be clear. I am not proposing a meta-analysis of gender, race, and class inequalities in terms of technology. Rather, my focus is on women and the inequalities they endure. In analyzing the situation of women, I include crucial categories of race and class and the ways in which they intersect. Later chapters will document multiple problems with specific technologies and illuminate distinct patterns in technological development and implementation, demonstrating how our technologies reflect and reinforce social inequality.

I also want to emphasize that implied in this perspective is the possibility of challenging these patterns, as feminist theory explicitly advocates and as many women are currently doing. Gender, race, and class are socially constructed and although they constrain our choices, they are not determinative factors. They can and have been confronted and altered. But the first step toward significant social change is to uncover and observe the power and influence of social inequalities and to recognize that technology operates in terms of them.

GENDER INEQUALITY

Let's begin with a consideration of gender inequality and its relationship with technology. Gender is undeniably central to social experience, and feminist scholarship produced over the last twenty-five years has demonstrated this beyond question. Ignoring how gender is located in social practices and institutions distorts or at least limits most analyses in significant ways.[33] The absence of a serious consideration of gender in most discussions of technology has resulted not merely in a partial analysis of technology in our society, but a basic misunderstanding of how profoundly gender inequality is implicated in technological development and implementation. Although technology is often viewed as freeing women, implying that it is a powerful agent of change, a great deal of evidence indicates that the technologies we create and use often reinforce rather than undermine gendered expectations. In other words, gender inequality does more to affect technology than the other way around.

To begin, science and technology are themselves generally viewed as masculine pursuits: Men design, develop, and largely control technology.[34] Although we may ask, along with bell hooks, "*which* men?" Since minorities are systematically steered away from technology, it has become a major instrument of *elite* male domination in terms of education, role models, and job opportunities. Women, on the other hand, are socially conditioned to avoid technology. Cynthia Cockburn[35] refers to this as "technological segregation" and claims that the lack of technological literacy on the part of women is anything but harmless. It bolsters job segregation and all the economic disadvantages this implies in an increasingly mechanized world, including differential earnings and power. Women are seldom employed in occupations that require technological expertise. Webster[36] for example, notes that "the gender segregation of computing work continues, and may even have worsened since the early days of computing." More men than women use the Internet in both public and private settings and, "The frontier nature of the superhighway and the sexist culture of cyberspace are very easy to document. Sexual harassment . . . is rife."[37] Even computer labs and classrooms tend to exhibit a stereotypical masculine culture. Rasmussen and Hapnes[38] document the limited number of women in computer science and demonstrate through their research at the Norwegian Institute of Technology how a small minority of male students (the computer hackers) dominate the culture of computer science in the eyes of female students and marginalized women. Although more women are entering the computer industry, gender bias and hazing are evident not only in Silicon Valley, where women have coined a word for it ("techno-hazing"), but also in New York brokerage firms and West coast law firms.[39]

In the following chapters we will see how reproductive technology as well as office and household technology typically operate within the constraints of gender inequality. These technological developments have not revolutionized traditional understandings of the role of women or their unequal status. When we analyze reproductive technology, for example, we will see the limits of defending it in terms of the "choice" it gives women or the "private" decisions it entails. Instead it often legitimates traditional assumptions that some women, particularly white women, should be wives and mothers, that they are responsible for reproduction and the care of children, and that they have somehow failed if they do not have biological offspring. Likewise, household technology has not released women from domestic labor. Even the tasks done by children are segregated by gender, and daughters are given more housework than sons. Finally, the electronic office operates within the confines of a society that discriminates against women. It has done little to undermine the overall gender division of labor or to enhance the skill of most women workers. In sum, we will see that technology has not undermined gender inequality. On the contrary, it often reflects and even bolsters gendered expectations that women are household laborers, secondary workers in the labor market, and biological mothers.

The relationship between gender inequality and technology is considerably complicated, however, when we turn to other forms of inequality that intersect in the experiences of some women, including race and class inequality.

RACE AND ETHNICITY

Almost 100 years ago, W.E.B. DuBois stated that "the problem of the twentieth century is the problem of the color-line," and racial divisions continue to be a defining American problem. Feminist analyses by women of color are among those that insist on the centrality of race in contemporary America. As Zinn and Dill[40] put it, these analyses "cohere in their treatment of race as a basic social division, a structure of power, a focus of political struggle, and hence a fundamental force in shaping women's and men's lives." To live in a racially divided society not only means that individuals are apt to be prejudiced against certain stigmatized groups, but that our institutions and organizations are patterned in ways that favor some groups while discriminating against others. The inclusion of race creates different questions and new conceptualizations regarding women and technology and helps us make sense of many of the problems with technology, which we will see in the following chapters. More specifically, the differential experiences of women of color and white women with the technologies we will examine indicate how deeply technology is implicated in racial inequality.

Including race as a category of analysis not only supplements but fundamentally changes our understanding of reproductive technology, for example, and signals the necessity of attending to racial inequality within virtually any social analysis. Although birth control may be freeing for *white* women, it has often been a means of coercing and even punishing women of color rather than enhancing their control over reproductive functions. In contrast to our social rhetoric associating the development of reproductive technology with healthy infants, we noted earlier the stark evidence of inequality in infant mortality rates, which are twice as high for black infants in the United States compared to white infants. In Central Harlem, the infant death rate is a staggering 27.6.[41] As Dion Farquhar[42] observes, this makes it clear that "it is not the exceptional sensational case of 'fetal abuse' that is killing black infants but the larger detrimental social effects of poverty and inadequate prenatal care."

The absence of improvement for women in the workplace in the wake of the "electronic revolution" must also be understood on terms of a racially divided society. Historically, women of color have been segregated into labor-intensive, low-technology employment; currently, they are the special targets of automation because they remain located in the more traditional, less-skilled occupations. Racism has also found its way into the organization of our households and household labor. This includes basic access to the household technology and home computers that have been portrayed as transforming households. Discussing computers and communication tools for the home, Julianne Malveaux[43] observes that certain groups simply lack the money to get such equipment. She asks, "With more than a third of white families having home computers, while just 10 percent of Black households and even fewer Latino households have them, exactly how is 'everybody' going to bank by computer if 'everybody' doesn't have access to the technology?"

When we widen our analysis of domestic technology and include *paid* as well as unpaid work in the home, we see that more privileged women are able to shift the burden of housework onto paid domestic workers, typically lower-class minority women. Suddenly, social inequalities, both connected with and beyond gender inequality, become vividly apparent. It is evident that despite technological developments, household labor is structured in our society in terms of racial as well as gender inequality.

CLASS DIVISIONS

Along with race, class divisions are fundamental in making sense of problems regarding women and technological advances.[44] Class inequality means that some are privileged and more advantaged than others in almost every aspect of life imaginable. Class differences have a decided impact on where you "choose" to live, the schools and churches you attend, the clothes you wear, the quality of your medical care, and even the length of your life. Most of us may have relinquished the notion that America is a "classless" society, but many still embrace the idea that it is the "land of opportunity." Numerous sociologists, however, have demonstrated the fallacy of this notion and documented with heartbreaking precision that class boundaries remain remarkably impenetrable for most Americans. An analysis of women and technology illustrates the power and pervasiveness of class inequality and its implications regarding each of the technologies we will examine.

When technology is developed in a capitalist society, it necessarily reflects class interests because only certain groups have the power to determine what is designed and how it is implemented. Capitalists are not neutral agents of progress, but instead have clearly situated political and economic interests. Within capitalism, by definition, the marketplace plays a central role, not public interest. As Karl Marx taught us, the profitability of an item, not its inherent value or necessity, is paramount in terms of what gets produced and sold. Albury and Schwartz[45] provide a disturbing illustration of this. They note that although many people in the Third World suffer from malnutrition, it is not profitable for businesses to devote significant sums of money to the research and development of nutritious food—poor people can't afford it anyway. Instead, corporations research, develop, advertise, and sell useless items to those of us who can afford to buy them, including electric bagel slicers, chocolate-flavored cereal, and vaginal deodorants. "What we eat, drink, wear, and live in are designed and developed not primarily for the benefit we gain from them as consumers, but for the maximisation of profit."[46]

Class inequality plays a profound role in the development and use of reproductive technologies. It affects access to reproductive technology, which can be extremely expensive, but, moreover, the commercialization entailed in selling products at a profit determines *what* will be produced—only products that are profitable. This commercialization has also involved exaggerating the benefits and minimizing the risks of many procedures in order to insure that they are marketable. Some technologies (such as sex selection) were in fact advertised and utilized for years when there was no evidence at all that they worked. Similarly, the electronic revolution might have meant more satisfying jobs and even shorter work weeks for all workers, but these promises did not materialize. Indeed, it should puzzle us that such massive increases in productive capacity did not bring an increase in the quality of life for office workers. The limited improvement women have experienced in the labor force, despite the emergence of the electronic office, has to be understood in terms of the creation and implementation of this technology within an economic system where management has the decision-making power, not workers. Whether or not to automate, or how to proceed, is fundamentally management's decision. As Richardson[47] observes, "Technologies are designed, developed, and implemented with little or no attention to the needs of the workforce or the impact that the technologies might have on the workforce." The very purpose of electronic technology is to increase productivity, reduce costs, and increase profits—which reflects the interests of those in power, not ordinary workers.

Class divisions are also evident when we turn to the development and use of household technology. Whether or not an item can sell at a profit is the central issue: Consumers only get to choose between profitable alternatives.[48] Moreover, our corporate economy does not aim at developing technology to meet household needs but instead fosters a growing consumerism. With the help of advertising, problems are quite deliberately created (like the need to squeeze carrot juice) and new technologies are produced to solve them. Thus it is consumerism and profit-making that fuel the development of many household technologies, not an effort to free women from labor or any genuine human need. The motorizing of all manner of household gadgets (can openers, toothbrushes, knives) serves as an example. Paid household labor illustrates class divisions even more vividly. But whether household labor is paid or unpaid, technology has not freed women; it operates within class constraints and illustrates both hierarchy and interdependence among women.

CONCLUSION

We are told that our technologies are neutral or, even better, that they necessarily improve the situation of women and men. We have been told that they hold power in and of themselves to shape human life and destiny. Even if we are unwitting pawns in a technological universe we cannot control, we are counseled not to worry: It works out to our advantage anyway.

But if we examine the development and implementation of technology through a sociological and feminist lens, we will see that these firmly held beliefs are partial at best. Technology is not neutral nor is it a deterministic force for the good of everyone. Instead, it is rooted in power inequalities and serves some groups of people at the expense of others. We will see that its benefits are not distributed randomly, but structurally patterned in terms of gender, race, and class divisions in our society and beyond. In a world fractured by inequality, technology is confirming rather than altering many of these dimensions.

In one sense, the fundamental issue is not technological at all, but rather a question of power relations: Who has the power to decide what will be developed and how it will be implemented? Who selects the technological "choices" we are offered, and whose interests do these choices serve? As we explore reproductive, household, and office technology, we will consider the larger context of structured inequality, the ways in which the control of technology is decidedly undemocratic, and the repercussions of this. We will consider the extent to which inequality does more to determine the form and direction of technological development rather than the public interest or the interests of women.

This analysis implies that a serious reconstruction of American society is required for technology to genuinely benefit all women and men. This possibility will be addressed more fully in the final chapter as we discuss the efforts of women to subvert technology and to organize for social change. But first we will turn to a discussion of what we typically learn about technology through the mass media. Here we find a strikingly different portrayal of technology compared to the one proposed in this chapter.

NOTES

1. Lester Thurow, "Why Their World Might Crumble," *The New York Times Magazine*, 19 November 1995, 78–79. Income distribution in the U.S. is similarly unequal. Fully three-fourths of income gains during the 1980s and *all* of the increased wealth went to the top 20 percent of families, who now own 80 percent of the nation's wealth (Bradsher, 1995).

2. Langdon Winner, "Technology Today: Utopia or Dystopia?," *Social Research*, Vol. 64 (Fall 1997): 995.

3. See Ellul, *The Technological Society*, as an example of a deterministic and negative vision of technology.

4. See Winner, *Autonomous Technology* for a critique of this perspective.

5. See MacKenzie and Wajcman, *The Social Shaping of Technology* for an early and influential work in this regard.

6. Dave Albury and Joseph Schwartz, *Partial Progress: The Politics of Science and Technology* (London: Pluto Press, 1982), 101.

7. Paul Goodman, "The Morality of Scientific Technology," *Dissent*, January-February 1967, 42.

8. Rita Arditti et al., *Test-Tube Women: What Future for Motherhood?* (London: Pandora Press, 1984), 1.

9. Barbara Drygulski Wright, "Introduction." In *Healing Technology: Feminist Perspectives* (Ann Arbor: University of Michigan Press, 1989), 14.

10. The comprehensive and valuable report of the National Research Council (1986) on computer technology is an example of this.

11. See, for example, the early work of Arditti, Klein, and Minden, eds., *Test-Tube Women*, on reproductive technology; Cowan, *More Work for Mother*, on household technology; and Marschall and Gregory, eds., *Office Automation*, on office technology. Other edited volumes exploring numerous types of technology are Rothschild, *Women, Technology, and Innovation* and *Machina Ex Dea*; and Zimmerman, *The Technological Woman*.

12. Keith Grint and Rosalind Gill, eds., *The Gender-Technology Relation: Contemporary Theory and Research* (London: Taylor and Francis, 1995); Juliet Webster, *Shaping Women's Work: Gender, Employment, and Information Technology* (London: Longman, 1996).

13. It is important to note that eco-feminism has grown increasingly diverse, and many eco-feminists currently reject essentialism (Armbruster, "Ecofeminist Natures," and Sturgeon, *Ecofeminist Natures*).

14. Grint and Gill (*The Gender-Technology Relation*, 1–28) term this perspective the study of technology as masculine culture, and although they subscribe to this particular framework, they offer a thoughtful analysis of various tensions within it.

15. Nina E. Lerman, Arwen Palmer Mohun, and Ruth Oldenziel, "The Shoulders We Stand On and the View from Here: Historiography and Directions for Research," *Technology and Culture*, Vol. 38 (January 1997): 9–30.

16. Ann R. Cacoullos, "American Feminist Theory," *American Studies International*, Vol. 39 (February 2001): 72.

17. Chris Weedon, *Feminism, Theory, and the Politics of Difference* (Oxford: Blackwell Publishers Inc., 1999), 159.

18. Rose M. Brewer, "Theorizing Race, Class, and Gender: The New Scholarship of Black Feminist Intellectuals and Black Women's Labor." In *Theorizing Black Feminism: The Visionary Pragmatism of Black Women* (New York: Routledge, 1993), 13.

19. Cacoullos, "American Feminist Theory."

20. Barbara Christian ("The Race for Theory") observed that people of color always theorized, although this has taken the form of narrative in stories, riddles, proverbs, and in the play with language.

21. Kathleen Daly, "Class-Race-Gender: Sloganeering in Search of Meaning," *Social Justice*, Vol. 20 (1993): 57–72. The Combahee River Collective ("A Black Feminist Statement," 362), an organization formed by black lesbian feminists in the mid-1970s, called for integrated analysis and practice, committing itself to work against "racial, sexual, heterosexual, and class oppression." Its statement on black feminism articulated the need for connecting these forms of inequality.

22. Angela Davis, *Women, Race, and Class* (New York: Random House, 1981); Bonnie Thornton Dill, "Race, Class, and Gender: Prospect for an All-Inclusive Sisterhood," *Feminist Studies*, Spring 1983, 131–150; bell hooks, *Ain't I a Woman?* (Boston: South End Press, 1981); Audre Lorde, *Sister Outsider* (Trumansburg, NY: The Crossing Press, 1984).

23. Maxwell Baca Zinn and Bonnie Thornton Dill, "Theorizing Difference from Multiracial Feminism." In *Gender Through the Prism of Difference* (Boston: Allyn and Bacon, 2000), 25.

24. Zinn and Dill, "Theorizing Difference from Multiracial Feminism," call their framework "multiracial feminism." It moves beyond recognizing differences among women to an exploration of structures of domination.

25. Michele Bograd, "Strengthening Domestic Violence Theories: Intersections of Race, Class, Sexual Orientation, and Gender," *Journal of Marital and Family Therapy*, Vol. 25 (July 1999): 275–289; Kimberle Williams Crenshaw, "Mapping the Margins: Intersectionality, Identity Politics, and Violence against Women of Color." In *Critical Race Theory: The Key Writings That Formed the Movement* (New York: The New Press, 1995), 357–383.

26. Patricia Hill Collins, *Black Feminist Thought: Knowledge, Consciousness, and the Politics of Empowerment* (Boston: Unwin Hyman, 1990); Deborah K. King, "Multiple Jeopardy, Multiple Consciousness: The Context of a Black Feminist Ideology." In *Feminist Social Thought* (New York: Routledge, 1997), 220–242; Weedon, *Feminism, Theory, and the Politics of Difference*.

27. Thus, as Daly ("Class-Race-Gender," 56) summarizes, "Class-race-gender offers a way not only to theorize about social structure, but also to link social-movement politics and struggles with a changed consciousness and analysis of structure and process."

28. Crenshaw, "Mapping the Margins."

29. The work of Patricia Hill Collins (*Black Feminist Thought*, 18) has been profoundly influential in the development of a race, class, and gender analysis. She observes that intersectional analyses remind us that there is more than one form of oppression, but her formulation of the "matrix of domination" refers instead "to how these intersecting oppressions are actually organized. Regardless of the particular intersections involved, structural, disciplinary, hegemonic, and interpersonal domains of power reappear across quite different forms of oppression."

30. Crenshaw ("Demarginalizing the Intersection of Race and Sex," 326–327) notes that by overlooking race, for example, "Feminists thus ignore how their own race functions to mitigate some aspects of sexism and, moreover, how it often privileges them over and contributes to the domination of other women. Consequently, feminist theory remains *white*, and its potential to broaden and deepen its analysis by addressing non-privileged women remains unrealized."

31. Kimberle Williams Crenshaw, "Demarginalizing the Intersection of Race and Sex: A Black Feminist Critique of Antidiscrimination Doctrine, Feminist Theory, and Antiracist Politics." In *Feminism and Politics* (New York: Oxford University Press, 1998), 328.

32. Whelehan (*Modern Feminist Thought*) provides an additional example when she notes that white feminists' complaints about stereotypically feminine constructions of women strikingly ignore different representations of black women, who are denied any access to that feminine "ideal."

33. See Lorber (*Paradoxes of Gender*) for a discussion of parenting, domestic labor, paid labor, and politics.

34. See Ruth Oldenziel (*Making Technology Masculine*) for an exploration of the development of the cultural association of technology with masculinity within the last 100 years.

35. Cynthia Cockburn, *Machinery of Domination: Women, Men and Technical Know-How* (London: Pluto Press, 1985).

36. Webster, *Shaping Women's Work*, 37.

37. Dale Spender, "The Position of Women in Information Technology—or Who Got There First and with What Consequences?," *Current Sociology*, Vol. 45 (April 1997):145.

38. Bente Rasmussen and Tove Hapnes, "Excluding Women from the Technologies of the Future? A Case Study of the Culture of Computer Science," *Futures*, Vol. 23 (December 1991): 1107–1119.

39. Laura Didio, "Look out for Techno-hazing," *Computerworld*, Vol. 31 (September 1997): 72.

40. Zinn and Dill, "Theorizing Difference," 324.

41. Dorothy Roberts, *Killing the Black Body: Race, Reproduction, and the Meaning of Liberty* (New York: Random House, 1997), 184.

42. Dion Farquhar, *The Other Machine: Discourse and Reproductive Technologies* (New York: Routledge, 1996), 74.

43. Julianne Malveaux, "Will Technology Bridge the Gap Between Black and White?" *Black Issues in Higher Education*, Vol. 13 (22 August 1996): 48.

44. See Joan Acker ("Rewriting Class, Race, and Gender") for an astute analysis of the necessity and the difficulties of integrating the concept of class with considerations of gender and race and incorporating the varying effects of the "economic" on the lives of subordinate and dominant women and men.

45. Albury and Schwartz, *Partial Progress*.

46. Ibid., 65.

47. Charley Richardson, "Computers Don't Kill Jobs, People Do: Technology and Power in the Workplace," *The Annals of American Academy of Political and Social Science*, Vol. 544 (March 1996), 170.

48. Ruth Schwartz Cowan, *More Work for Mother: The Ironies of Household Technology from the Open Hearth to the Microwave* (New York: Basic Books, 1983).

3

The Wonders of Technology

❖ ❖ ❖ ❖ ❖ ❖

Despite the wonders of communications technology, the news often seems little more than folklore, a steady stream of nursery tales for adults.
British Journalist Ed Harriman

"Is there any other point to which you would wish to draw my attention?"
"To the curious incident of the dog in the night-time."
"The dog did nothing in the night-time."
"That was the curious incident," remarked Sherlock Holmes.
Sir Arthur Conan Doyle

In the second half of the twentieth century, a wide array of technological developments—from test-tube babies to smart houses—appear to have propelled us to the brink of a futuristic society. We learn about these innovations in various ways, but the bulk of information for many of us comes from the mass media which cover technological change extensively. According to Dorothy Nelkin,[1] for most people, "media is their only contact with what is going on in rapidly changing scientific and technological fields, as well as a major source of information about the implications of these changes for their lives." She cites print media as a primary source in this area.[2]

This chapter examines media coverage of numerous developments in reproductive, household, and office technology. It focuses on print media, mainly popular news magazines, which reach millions of readers on a regular basis. We will see that very different types of technological development receive remarkably similar treatment in the media. Nelkin[3] observes that both simple and attention-seeking imagery of technology often replaces content. Since journalists have to process hugh amounts of scientific and technological information, they are inclined to rely on persistent patterns of selection and presentation.[4] These patterns and the perceptions they foster are not simply determined by the media, but instead the media simultaneously shape, reflect, and reinforce cultural ideas regarding technology. As

Nelkin[5] puts it, "Public beliefs about science and technology tend to correspond with the messages conveyed in the media, though the direction of cause and effect is not clear." What is clear, however, is that the media "promote each new technology as the cutting edge of history, the frontier that will transform lives."[6]

Nelkin does not argue that the media presentation of technology is strictly one-dimensional. Less enthusiastic articles and even doomsday versions of technology can be found, but they are relatively rare compared to the way technology is generally extolled.[7] The essential point is that the predominant portrayal tends to be largely uncritical, with little analysis of potential social and economic problems associated with technology. To understand technology we need to know its social context, but the media seldom provide this type of reporting.

In Sir Arthur Conan Doyle's story, "Silver Blaze," the dog failed to bark in the night-time because he knew the culprit, and his puzzling silence allowed Sherlock Holmes to solve yet another mystery. The absence of a critical analysis of the social context of technology in most media reporting is similarly curious: Exploring this can lead to a deeper understanding of technology and popular attitudes toward it. Although the dominant media representations of technology occur in part because the public is intrigued by stories that reflect and bolster attitudes about the power and beneficence of technology, constraints imposed on journalists by their profession are crucial and need to be outlined before looking in depth at media coverage of technology.

To begin, the emphasis in journalism is on "breaking news," not assessment or analysis. Stories are written quickly, using standard sources, and editors look for drama and controversy in order to insure reader interest.[8] The economic pressures on journalists are significant because these are profit-making enterprises, typically owned by large corporations and intent on pleasing their advertisers. To maintain a sound relationship with advertisers, media reporting avoids being what might be construed as offensive or negative and indeed steers toward what appeals to the mainstream.[9] Increasing emphasis is placed on entertaining rather than informing people in order to secure a large audience and thus make a large profit. Nelkin[10] notes that brilliant examples of reporting *can* be found, but too often reporting is "more a source of entertainment than of information."

Reporting also reflects the relationship between journalists and their sources, who tend to be a relatively few male experts, often scientists, with a stake in emphasizing the benefits of technology. According to Nelkin,[11] the complexity of scientific and technological material reinforces "the tendency of journalists to rely on press releases, press conferences, and other prepackaged sources." So IVF, for example, is discussed with information obtained from a press conference with the scientists who developed it. What is crucial is that this reliance on official sources reduces the chances of critical or probing investigations.

Journalists accept objectivity as a working norm, and also see science as neutral and objective. They rely on authoritative sources and avoid expressing their own political views. Unfortunately, however, this apparent absence of a political perspective inclines them to uncritically accept their scientific sources. As Nelkin[12] puts it,

> Many journalists are, in effect, retailing science and technology rather than investigating them, identifying with their sources rather than challenging them.

Given these institutional constraints and traditions, journalists are not apt to offer a serious social analysis of technology or the ways in which race, class, and gender inequalities interact with technological development and implementation. The potential of the media to fully inform is thus blunted.

With these constraints in mind, we will begin by exploring the media's optimism regarding the direction of technological development, as well as specific innovations. This optimism is expressed in a variety of ways, including an emphasis on the control that technology allows us to exert over our environment and our bodies, its accessibility and affordability, the way it resolves our problems and, perhaps most significant, the way technology benefits all of us: rich, poor, male, female, First and Third World. This is followed by an analysis of a curious formula found in this reporting: Problems regarding technology are briefly raised in most articles, only to be abruptly dismissed. Finally, we explore the typical portrayal of the "experts" in these fields.

We will see throughout this discussion that the popular media seldom provide a coherent critique or analysis of technology. They rarely illuminate the ways in which gender issues or racial factors interact with technological development. Instead, by eschewing such analysis, they permit cultural myths regarding technology (such as technology as a primary determining force or as a-political) to go unchallenged.

OPTIMISTIC VISIONS

In general the media celebrate technology. In their reporting, "writers still convey their fervent conviction that new technology will create a better world."[13] Optimism regarding technology's beneficence is clear regardless of the particular innovation under discussion. In an article on medical technology, for example, *U.S. News and World Report* describes the "wondrous technology" that enables doctors to consult with colleagues around the world and notes that "soon to come will be robots doing some surgery a person can't do at all."[14] In the same issue computer networking is extolled, and we are informed that "analysts of all ideologies claim the network revolution will profoundly change our culture."[15] One finds an undeniable certitude that technology is mainly helpful, increasingly affordable, and accessible to all. In the fall of 1992, for example, *Time* devoted a special issue to what may be expected after the turn of this century, explicitly connecting technological development with progress. The twentieth century is characterized as "astonishing" and as providing a steady pace of progress, thanks to science, industry, and moral philosophy. But now, *Time* claims, this "stately march of progress" has been turned into "a long-distance, free-for-all sprint." Implying all of us, (*Time*[16] reports that, "The underlying drive of all this change is increased human control: over the environment, over other living organisms, over mountains of data, above all over one's psychology and genetics and destiny."

Almost two decades ago, the January 3, 1983 edition of *Time* magazine epitomized media enthusiasm for technology when it heralded the computer as the "Machine of the Year" rather than choosing their traditional "Man of the Year." *Time's* publisher justified the choice of a machine as opposed to a human being on the grounds that "none symbolized the past year more richly, or will be viewed by history with more significance, than a machine." (Israel's Prime Minister Menachem Begin and Britain's Margaret Thatcher were reduced to runners up.) The issue's lead article referred to America's "giddy passion" for the personal computer and emphasized its powerful and pervasive role in daily life. "It predicts the weather, processes checks, scrutinizes tax returns, guides intercontinental missiles and performs innumerable other operations for governments and corporations."[17] Since the computer is readily available to millions, according to *Time*, it promises "dramatic changes in the way people live and work, perhaps even in the way they think."

Nearly a decade later, a cover story in *Newsweek*[18] praised the computer in remarkably similar terms, referring to it as "The Next Revolution." *Newsweek* laments that the "techno-paradise" we had previously anticipated was not forthcoming, but now a new wave of technology is developing "an explosion of new supergadgets and services that could change all our lives."[19] This vast "revolution" is emerging through computerized products, ranging from television systems that select desirable shows to electronic books "that put whole encyclopedias in a briefcase."[20] In the 1980s, many gadgets were too expensive for most consumers, but *Newsweek* claims that this is changing, making the computer revolution of the 1990s bigger than ever simply because it will reach so many. *Newsweek* contends that the most significant change may come through our television screens. Not merely sharper pictures, but virtually a private video store will be at our fingertips: "Call up the program-guide screen–with a preview of selected shows, if you like. Viewers will be able to shop in video 'catalogs'–and probably pay by the credit cards your TV keeps on file."[21]

SMART HOUSES

Part of the appeal of technology has to do with the "control" it gives people. New technologies for the home illustrate this control, and the media have reported on this in great detail. In "smart houses," electrical systems and appliances are operated by computer. "Computers can open and shut doors, windows, or drapes, change the temperature, shop, bank or communicate with others."[22] The smart house typically has a screen with a menu containing information on radio and TV programs, appliances, lights, and alarm systems; the controls can be voice-activated. The technology is portrayed as beneficial for everyone, providing convenience as well as safety. You have the luxury, for example, of turning on your home air conditioner with a phone call when leaving the office. You are also protected against electrical fire hazards: If the oven is about to burn the dinner, for example, the system will reduce the heat or turn it off. In *Forbes* magazine, Jeff Block[23] provides such a scenario when he suggests that, leaving work tonight, you may

> pick up the mobile cellular telephone in your car, dial your house's computerized kitchen and, with a few pushes of buttons, instruct the microwave to start cooking the pot roast, the stove to start boiling the potatoes and the dishwasher to start cleaning the china for use tonight.

In a related development, James Lardner, in *U.S. News and World Report*, extols the possibility of buying groceries over the Internet. The article cites Sandra Charton, a Massachusetts lawyer (married to another lawyer) who "absolutely loves it." With a refrigerator in her garage, Charton no longer has to shop or unpack the groceries: "'It's like having a wife, actually,' she says."[24] Timothy DeMello, the founder and CEO of a major online grocery, claims that it saves customers four hours of shopping with each order. He predicts business will boom. " 'Look at cellular phones,' he says. 'A few years ago they were an expensive novelty. Now my nanny has one.' "[25]

We are told that people with disabilities will also benefit from these household innovations. "An elderly person, with severe arthritis, who has difficulty with conventional controls, can just talk to the appliances, telling them what to do: to make toast, brew coffee, or do the laundry."[26] Cynthia Wagner[27] reported in *The Futurist* on a competition entitled "Search for Computing Applications to Assist Persons with Disabilities," which was sponsored by Johns Hopkins University. The contest attracted more than 700 entries, and a cash prize of $10,000 went to the top winner, Arjan S. Khalsa of Richmond, California, who developed a more accessible keyboard for disabled persons.

Again in terms of accessibility, Bruce Ahnafield, an electronics designer, predicts that computerized household technology will eventually cost no more than regular wiring (presently it is about $1500 extra). He believes these systems will become as familiar and "necessary" to all of us as the TV, toaster, or refrigerator. Similarly, Nobelist Penzias, vice-president of research at AT&T Bell Laboratories, insists that future technology will provide for everyone what only an elite can now afford. "Where the rich now hire chauffeurs to drive them to work, for example, the working stiff of the future will be transported to work in his robocar."[28]

The computerized household was featured in a *Popular Science* report on "The New American Home for 1994," an exhibition in Las Vegas displaying the latest possibilities in home technology. With its Total Home system from Honeywell, high-tech advances are at your command, and the system is easy as well as accessible. As spokesman Jerry Blackman puts it, "it's pretty straightforward—it's not rocket science."[29] The point is that *anyone* can operate and thoroughly enjoy this home. Imagine yourself in this picture: "As you enter and amble through the house toward the master bedroom, wall sensors track your passage and adjust the lighting, along with the heating or air-conditioning and even the music playing softly in the background."[30] An intriguing feature of "The New American Home" is its built-in theater. About the size of a bedroom, it is a comfortably upholstered space to view laser-disc movies.

> The entire room comes to life at the touch of a button: Automatically, curtains on the far wall rise to reveal the screen, as motorized drapes close to block light from the window and doorway. The room lights dim, the air conditioning shifts to occupancy mode, and the Lucasfilm THX Home Theater System starts the show.[31]

A basic system controlling lighting, security, and appliances costs approximately $4,000; other units can be added at additional cost. A zone controller, for example, costs about $1,000 and can be programmed to operate on a budget: "When home electrical use threatens to exceed the budget, the microprocessor determines how and when to shed some of the electrical load, starting with low-priority items."[32] The fully equipped New American Home is yours for $1,900,000.

Household Appliances

Specific household appliances have also been advancing, and they are widely regarded as saving time and labor while producing more effective results. Consider the leap from coal stoves to gas or electric stoves, from beating carpets to using vacuum cleaners, from the misery associated with hand washing and wringing clothes to the ease of electric washing machines and dryers. We now have at our disposal "smart" appliances: Smart dishwashers alert us to a variety of malfunctions, smart irons shut off when left unmoved for a given length of time. Microwave ovens cook automatically based on the weight and type of food. Ovens are self-cleaning, refrigerators are self-defrosting. Darwoo Electronics Company in Seoul, South Korea, created a microwave oven that will open and close with one voice command. Mastervoice, Inc., a California-based company, sells Butler in a Box, a system that permits voice control of as many as thirty-two electrical appliances. GE now has a dishwasher that flashes lights when it needs repair. We are told that home appliances will eventually be able to "speak" electronically to repair centers by telephone: The repair center can then mail the replacement parts to the owner.

In addition to increasingly sophisticated appliances, it is predicted that household robots will soon be available to perform routine tasks such as loading the dishwasher, removing the garbage, and sweeping the floor. Rodney Brooks, robot designer from MIT, describes "tiny insect-like vacuum cleaners that will hang out in dusty corners, scooping up dirt into their bellies. When they hear the big vacuum robot coming, they will scurry to the center of the room, empty their innards and run back under sofa."[33] *U.S. News and World Report*[34] predicts that "mechanical maids will be able to perform most common housekeeping chores. And, yes, they will do windows." Gender stereotypes still prevail, and one household robot is explicitly described as coming "complete with a skirt" and "made small so as not to be intimidating."[35] Computerized robots are envisioned not only for boring jobs, but dangerous ones as well.

Since the depression, each new electrical appliance has promised to transform the home by decreasing labor and increasing efficiency. Media reports of household technology bolster these ideas. *U.S. News and World Report*,[36] for example, contends that today's aspirations regarding household appliances focus on the computer: "The PC promises to make household chores like bill paying easier and to put the world right at your fingertips as well, opening up vast new horizons of information sources." They note that computer manufacturers had to figure out how to sell their computers like an appliance: ready to go, designed for the average person, and affordable. Almost a year later to the day, *Business Week*[37] featured a cover story illustrating how successful computer manufacturers have been in this regard: "Home Computers: Sales Explode as New Uses Turn PCs into All-Purpose Information Appliances." It is estimated that homes will eventually be the biggest market for PCs and that they will be second only to color televisions in terms of consumer electronics. *Business Week* contends that consumers, not business customers, are now driving the evolution of the PC and that these consumers can count on one thing: "The personal computer is going to become a fixture in their living rooms, kitchens, and dens."

The promise of comfort also drives consumer interest in household technologies, and the media highlight many of these luxuries. For example, General Magic Inc., a Silicon Valley company, has software called Telescript which provides "intelligent agents," a digital version of the English butler. *Newsweek*[38] reports that these agents can travel through the computer network and find what "master" desires: "You would list the specifications and send the agent out through the system to find the best price. The next time you turn on your computer, the agent will have drawn up a list of possibilities." The "intelligent agents" can also monitor weather reports, make reservations, sort the electronic mail, or help choose your stereo equipment.

Let us consider for a moment that this reporting on technology contains no mention of gender inequality, no hint of racial discrimination, not a whisper about social class. Rather blithely, buying and delivering groceries through online services is compared to having a wife, an executive brags that even his nanny has a cellular phone, and we are advised that *anyone* can operate a smart house . . . including its theater system. It leaves uncontested assumptions about the autonomous power of technology and the benefits it bestows on virtually everyone. Erased in these accounts is the role of social inequality and how this affects what technology gets developed and who actually benefits from it. In fact, media accounts provide evidence of the assumptions discussed by Leo Marx and Merritt Roe Smith that progress through technology means human betterment and liberation, and a less hierarchal society. Thus it is reported that technology will "change all our lives," including people with disabilities, "the working stiff," and, as we will see in our discussion of reproductive and office technology, women and those in the Third World.

CONTROL OF REPRODUCTION

A counterpart to the control technology exerts in the home is found in the control it reportedly gives people in terms of birth itself: the timing, the means of reproduction, and the health or "quality" of the fetus. Dramatic developments have occurred in reproductive technology, including *in vitro* fertilization (IVF), which makes it possible for a child to be conceived in a laboratory dish and then implanted in a woman's body. The first IVF baby, known as a "test-tube baby," was born in Britain in 1978; within a decade, more than 4,000 IVF births had taken place in the United States alone. Embryo transfer, which involves washing an embryo from a pregnant woman and transferring it to another woman, first took place in 1983 at Harbor/UCLA Medical Center in Torrance, California, when an egg donor was artificially inseminated with the sperm of an infertile woman's husband. Five days later, the embryo was flushed from her body with a nutrient solution and implanted in the infertile woman.

Scientists have developed the capability of overriding menopause by impregnating postmenopausal women with the fertilized eggs of younger women; using this method, doctors at the University of Southern California enabled a 63-year-old woman to give birth to a baby girl.[39] Through embryo freezing, Australian researchers produced the world's first "freeze-thaw" baby in 1984: A woman may now conceive a fetus, wash it from her body, freeze it, and reimplant it when she chooses. Moreover, new technologies allow for embryo screening for gender or for genetic defects: We may test an embryo and abort or only reimplant those that meet our specifications. These developments signal what many understandably refer to as a "revolution" in reproductive technology.

Initially, many of these new technologies treated infertility. The media introduced us to the plight of the infertile and the growing number of American couples experiencing this problem. In articles such as "Anguished Search to Cure Infertility,"[40] we learned about the suffering of couples desperate to conceive. Even the strongest marriage is portrayed as vulnerable to a problem of this magnitude and the grief associated with it, and thus infertility leads to a desperate quest to become pregnant. Dena Kleiman explains that, "At a time when most men and women can decide how many children they want and when, the infertile couple often feel alone, cheated of an option they had long taken for granted, an experience they still regarded as a rite of passage into adulthood. In an era of choice, they have been denied the right to decide." Alongside this overwhelming trauma, the new reproductive technologies are presented as a beacon of hope that has "freed women from the tyranny of the biological clock."[41]

Kleiman[42] specifically discusses the birth of the world's first baby by *in vitro* fertilization as a new chance for "tens of thousands of women" to conceive. The first

IVF birth had caused a worldwide sensation. In July of 1978, even before the actual birth, *Time* magazine highlighted the extensive coverage this event was receiving in the British press with newspaper headlines heralding the "Baby of the Century," "Test-Tube Baby Any Day Now," and "Our Miracle Baby." *U.S. News and World Report*[43] proclaimed "a new and perhaps revolutionary era of human reproduction." A decade later, however, IVF was no longer as newsworthy unless there was a twist to the story. *People* magazine,[44] for example, devoted a cover to the infertility problems of Michele and Raymond L'Esperance who had three children from previous marriages but wanted "a child of their own." The L'Esperances entered an IVF program at the William Beaumont Hospital in Royal Oak, Michigan. After a successful though tumultuous pregnancy, "they found fulfillment beyond their wildest dreams when Michele gave birth to America's first test-tube quintuplets."[45] Pictures of the joyful parents, the five tiny babies (and their three older siblings) complete the story.

A cover story in *Time*[46] described infertility in familiar terms as "The Saddest Epidemic," and once again surveyed three "startling techniques" now available as the "science of conception brings hope to childless couples." Here, and virtually everywhere, the new reproductive technologies were presented as incredible scientific feats, which the infertile were desperate to use. In January of 1986, *Reader's Digest*[47] reported that although infertility has reached "epidemic proportions" in the United States, more than half of infertile couples can now be helped. On its cover September 30, 1991, *Time* announced "How a Dazzling Array of Medical Breakthroughs Has Made Curing Infertility More Than Just a Dream." The lead story ("Making Babies") begins with the familiar assertion that we are in the midst of an "infertility epidemic," but now we have "a reproductive revolution: an explosion of new techniques for overcoming infertility and an unprecedented rush by would-be parents to take advantage of them."[48] The article provides a series of scenarios as to "What Can Go Wrong" (with reproduction) and then "How To Fix It" (with technology). All the solutions described are high tech and involve surgical procedures, hormone treatment, and sophisticated equipment.

Success stories abound in the media's coverage of reproductive technology. A cover story in *Life* magazine,[49] for example, proclaimed the "Miracles of Birth" and alerted us to "The Blessings of a Medical Revolution" and "Healthy Babies Who Ten Years Ago Would Never Have Been Born." We are introduced to Lisa and Kevin Gilbert who chose GIFT, a variation of IVF, when they were unable to conceive a second child, and had triplets through the procedure. *Life* (like *Time*) also covers Arlette Schweitzer, who carried and delivered her daughter's child through IVF because her daughter was born without a uterus.

AND IN THE OFFICE

The twentieth century's "electronic revolution" in the office has been lavishly praised as capable of upgrading jobs and skills, eliminating boredom, and producing better quality work—while simultaneously saving costs and labor. Word processors can record how much time is spent on a terminal, how many pages are typed per day, and how many mistakes are made. Managers claim this motivates employees, makes them more productive, and provides an objective way to rate performance.

Office computers continue to become increasingly powerful, more reliable, and less expensive. The speed of processing information is rapidly increasing along with memory size. The keyboard is still the most common means of data entry, but the optical character reader (OCR) is 40–50 times faster than the keyboard. Speech recognition and voice-activated "typewriters" are also developing. Toshiba's voice-activated telephone is already on the market, boasting its ability to dial a telephone number when given the name of the person being called. Electronic mail, including "automatic calendering," helps office workers keep track of appointments and arrange meetings. Telephone handsets currently have call waiting, call forwarding, and three-way calling; they also serve as terminals for data entry and retrieval. Increasingly, telephone digital lines will transmit data and video material as well as voice.

Thanks to technology, office work is now highly mobile. We are invited to envision the age of the "electronic cottage," where a family works, lives, and plays at home. Given the flexibility of telecommuting, it is frequently seen as enabling women in particular to balance child care and careers.

In "The New Face of Business," *Business Week*[50] discusses the information revolution in the office in glowing terms. Increasingly, cheap information is depicted as "the great equalizer," enabling small as well as big businesses to benefit. Digital technology supposedly breaks down corporate barriers by allowing the sharing of information, cutting waste, and eliminating management layers and employment levels while simultaneously permitting workers to operate from distant locations. *Business Week*[51] also regards new technology as giving workers "unprecedented power to make decisions that once were their managers' province." Workers are now more skilled: They analyze data and make decisions. Secretaries, for example, previously spent all their time answering phones, opening mail, and typing, whereas today "many secretaries are expected to be able to update spreadsheets and judge how best to graphically present data in charts. As time-pressed executives realize their support staff is computer-literate, they hand over more decisions and judgement calls."[52]

U.S. News and World Report[53] specifically claims that more opportunities will be available for women as technology "changes the working environment and lessens the need for human muscle power." They cite Margaret Gayle, assistant vocational-education director in North Carolina, who pointedly claims that, "Technology is equalizing the workplace and is even giving women the edge in some cases."

In a familiar vein, *Business Week* devoted a cover story in March of 1991 to laptop computers and their potential. They state that laptops are already routine and changing work in significant ways. Since the newest laptops can read handwriting, they are more accessible than ever, particularly for those who have never been near a computer. They will reduce the amount of paper work necessary in many jobs and make work outside the office increasingly convenient. In fact, AT&T is experimenting with removing thousands of salespeople from their offices: Laptops permit them to do all their work on the road. AT&T claims that this will vastly increase worker productivity and save the company the costs of overhead.

COMPUTER NETWORKS

Part of the tremendous optimism of the media regarding new technology revolves around the belief that it can and will reshape society—and just about everyone on the planet will benefit. *U.S. News and World Report*[54] discussed, for example, the creation of a computer network in Maryland that connects five school districts. They claim that "The project will put poorer schools on a par with wealthier ones by giving them equal access to large amounts of information and will enable them to bypass dated textbooks and go directly to academic experts." The same type of optimism, expanded to a global stage, is found in *Business Week*[55] which claims that "In the next 20 years, humankind will witness one of history's greatest technological transformations." They predict that "the most dazzling electronic products" will be developed quickly and cheaply anywhere and that the beneficial possibilities for the Third World in particular are endless. *Business Week*[56] informs us that "Using high-speed videoconferencing links, specialists at some large U.S. medical centers, for example, can now diagnose and treat patients at remote locations—from small rural American hospitals to facilities overseas." They[57] contend that "as science itself goes digital and supercomputer speeds migrate down to desktops, all geographical barriers are disintegrating, putting basic science within the reach of smaller and poorer nations." *Business Week*[58] concludes that we have seen the beginning of a revolution that is distributing "fantastically powerful tools across a huge sweep of humanity." And, they predict, it will continue.

In a bonus issue on "The Information Revolution," *Business Week* profiled computer use in various countries around the world. They[59] confidently state that for most Americans the information economy "translates into jobs and prosperity." And, once again, they are especially optimistic about the Third World, predicting that "developing countries will skip past entire stages of technology" and even economic development. Referring to the Third World, they pointedly conclude that, "despite the mistakes they'll make, they'll persist—so that one day they can cruise alongside Americans and Western Europeans on the Information Superhighway." *Working Woman*[60] provides an equally cheerful scenario regarding global technology when they assert that, "Last-minute presentations are written on laptops at 35,000 feet as satellite dishes beam episodes of 'Baywatch' to remote Thai villages."

Technology is thus envisioned as transforming home life, reproduction, and the office, and as benefiting us all—rich and poor, women and men, workers and managers, big and small companies, and the First and Third Worlds. It is the "great equalizer" for small and large companies as well as "equalizing the workplace" for women. It puts "poorer schools on a par with wealthier ones," and basic science "within the reach of poorer nations." Again, the larger social context and all forms of social inequality are not seriously analyzed, leaving the impression that they have relatively little to do with the development and implementation of technology.

THE STANDARD FORMULA

Our review of how technology is treated in weekly magazines is meant to illustrate that it is typically regarded very positively in the media. But let me qualify this since most articles dealing with technology are more multivocal than this assertion indicates. They include different points of view and varying perspectives, but the way alternative perspectives are introduced and framed typically allows an optimistic view of technology to remain firmly in place. For example, most articles include some type of warning about the technology under consideration, essentially an alternative perspective, but this warning is rapidly followed by reassurances that serve to undercut the alternative view. The formula is astonishingly consistent: First, we are given to understand the power and value of whatever technology is under discussion, then (usually about three-fourths of the way through the piece), we are reminded that there may be problems associated with the technology. Finally, we are assured that all will be well. In *Time's* special issue on "What to Expect in the New Millennium," for example, numerous technological advances are reviewed and praised including radios, cars, airliners, and computers. *Time* [61] acknowledges that the implications of these changes may be anxiety producing and cause us to raise questions about the very purpose of our lives (obviously no small matter). Ultimately, however, these concerns are rendered as minor: "Thanks to this amazing age, more people than ever before have the freedom to ask the questions for themselves."

Examples of this curious pattern are endless. Here are a few more:

In a cover story on April 6, 1992, entitled "Computers: The Next Revolution," *Newsweek* discusses home technology and mentions the possibility of a downside to it, including the fact that you may never be able to escape your boss and the worrisome prospect that a small group of people may have privileged access to enormous amounts of data. The idea that Americans may become even more addicted to private television viewing is cited as being the most troubling to many observers. But the article ends on an optimistic note by reiterating that the computer age may finally reach most Americans and that this could spell additional jobs for U.S. workers. "Ultimately," *Newsweek* [62] claims, "we might get all the technology–and the future–we always wanted."

Similarly, a Special 1994 Bonus Issue of *Business Week* [63] on "The Information Revolution" frankly acknowledges that there will be winners and losers as digital technology develops and spreads. Some people will lose jobs. But *Business Week* emphasizes the overwhelmingly positive impact of this revolution: We are assured, for example, that "over the past 200 years or so, there has been no long-term trend toward higher unemployment because of investment in new machines and technology." *Business Week* admits that the less educated are being left behind and that certain types of jobs will decline due to office automation, including computer operators, typists, bank tellers, and telephone operators. But again they quickly add that several occupations requiring a college degree are expected to expand as technology "generates new openings in the info-tech world." *U.S. News and World Report*[64] briefly discusses the possibility of job loss with new technology, as well as the problem of the widening gap between rich and poor. They ultimately assure us, however, that "If such dilemmas are handled wisely, the overwhelming prospect is for new gains for the country." Finally, when *Time* named the computer the "Machine of the Year" in 1983, we were given the same scenario. The possibility of increasing unemployment due to computerization was entertained and dismissed: "The general rule seems to be that new technology eventually creates as many jobs as it destroys, and often more."[65]

Not only job loss but virtually all negative outcomes regarding technology are quickly dispatched. When *Business Week*[66] announced, for example, that digital technology may mean unexpected gains and losses among the nations of the world, they warned of a possible decline in America's commanding lead in basic research. But, ultimately, they claim that "the gains or losses of individual companies or countries are trivial when viewed against the potential scientific breakthroughs ahead." Lack of concern regarding potentially negative effects of technology on the Third World is vividly evident. *Time* magazine[67], for example, acknowledged that the effects of the computer on the Third World are less than certain, but in what has to be regarded as a flight of fancy, they state that "the prophets of high technology believe the computer is so cheap and so powerful that it could enable underdeveloped nations to bypass the whole industrial revolution." *Time* contends that this will be accomplished through robot factories and new industries in the Third World created by microprocessors. Moreover, "an international computer network could bring important agricultural and medical information to even the most remote villages." We are led to believe that we have little to fear regarding the ultimate impact of new technology on the Third World.

Gender concerns regarding new technology are also minimized. When *Business Week*[68] reported on "The Information Revolution," they featured Amy C. Arnott, a 25-year-old analyst with Morningstar Inc. of Chicago. When Arnott's husband was offered a job in Los Alamos, she continued working for Morningstar from Los Alamos by telecommuting from her new home. *Business Week* reports that, thanks to new information technology, she is able to get all her mail, access Morningstar's mutual-fund database and annual reports, do telephone interviews with portfolio managers, and write reports up on her computer and e-mail them to Chicago. Although many observers worry about the isolation involved in working at home, and *Business Week* acknowledges that Arnott misses her co-workers, they conclude by assuring us that she feels "increasingly independent" in her new life.

The weekly media's coverage of reproductive technology follows the same pattern found in discussions of home and office technology: Problems are mentioned and abruptly dismissed. In the earliest reports about Louise Brown, the world's first "test-tube baby," *U.S. News and World Report*[69] notes, for example, that IVF raises troubling legal and moral questions. They quickly add that "Most medical scientists agree, however, that future uses of the embryo-transfer technique–if it works–will be limited to couples who are unable to conceive children any other way." A decade later much had changed, including the clients of IVF clinics (who are no longer limited to couples "unable to conceive in any other way"), but we are still assured that the technology is basically fine. In its lead story of September, 1991, *Time*[70] candidly acknowledges that reproductive technologies are expensive, they can cause emotional turmoil, and they raise serious ethical questions. "But all these issues pale before the newly revealed miracle of fertilization, an event so dizzyingly complex that researchers say the more they know, the more they wonder that it works as often as it does."

When *Newsweek*[71] discussed the fact that women can now carry a fetus to term after menopause, they subtitled this item "a stunning success." They demonstrate the familiar formula when they end by stating

> There are caveats, of course. Childrearing becomes far riskier when attempted by older women (maternal death rates are four times as high in 40-year-olds as in 30-year-olds). And by creating a new class of potential egg recipients, the procedure could encourage the ethically troublesome sale of human tissue ('donors' are typically paid for each set of eggs they provide). Still, it's hard not to marvel at the prospect of postmenopausal women having babies at will.

In a discussion of donor eggs, *Newsweek*[72] asked: "How Far Should We Push Mother Nature?" They noted that people may now wait until retirement before having children. But should they? And should couples be permitted to choose the race of their children? *Newsweek* ultimately brushes aside such questions: "To the millions of American couples on the front lines of infertility, the ethical hypotheticals paled against the excitement of new possibilities." When Lee M. Silver, genetics professor at Princeton, discussed sex selection in *Time*, he noted the concern among some observers that the technology could lead to an imbalance in the sex ratio. He concedes that some parents prefer children of one sex, but optimistically concludes that "such preferences would presumably balance out."[73]

When we turn to birth control technology, the same pattern persists. In a brief piece on Norplant, *Newsweek*[74] asserts that "Norplant has helped nearly a million American women avoid pregnancy since its introduction in 1991." *Newsweek* discusses a class-action suit that has been leveled against Norplant's U.S. marketer, Wyeth-Ayerst Laboratories, by customers who have had painful or damaging experiences extracting Norplant. But the piece concludes by citing Wyeth-Ayerst's claim that the rate of complication has been lower than the 6 percent the company predicted, and women are simply advised to have Norplant inserted by health workers specifically trained for this task.

I would argue that this pattern of reporting reflects an attempt on the part of the media to provide balance and thus objectivity in their stories. But when subjected to other institutional constraints, including entertaining an audience, the prospects of a serious analysis of technology in terms of its social context or its negative implications for some people, fades. We are left with a veneer of objectivity and reporting that is largely uncritical.

THE EXPERTS

Media reports also have a particular slant on those who develop and market new technologies. The image conveyed is favorable, hinting that these people are different from the rest of us, and the work they do is beyond our ken. As Nelkin puts it, science is still "arcane and incomprehensible," and scientists "remote but superior wizards." This portrayal is evident in comments made about scientists and scientific work in general, as well as in profiles of specific people. Here are some examples drawn from the reporting of reproductive and computer technology, and the experts engaged in this work.

In a discussion of infertility treatments in *Time* magazine,[75] the lead story begins with the assertion of an "infertility epidemic," but *Time* finds hope in doctors who are depicted as able to "manipulate virtually every aspect of the reproductive cycle." A cover story in *Life* magazine[76] informs us that not long ago nature was in charge of birth but now, thanks to medical doctors, miracles are possible. In a *Newsweek*[77] cover story on Louise Brown, scientific work itself is unabashedly praised when we are told that "when and if it happens, the delivery will represent a major medical achievement," that the impending birth is "a miracle of modern medicine," as well as a "scientifically assisted blessed event." In similar tones, although on a different topic, *U.S. News and World Report*[78] discussed the future of robotics, and while reporter Paul Recer acknowledges that scientists realize they cannot solve all our technical problems, the image again is highly complimentary, as Recer concludes that scientists "want it known that they are still hard at work, and that American science and engineering still lead the world."

Scientific work is often depicted as fascinating and obscure. When *Time* did their cover story[79] about the first test-tube baby, they claimed it involved an unknown British couple "and the abstruse subject of embryology." Similarly, in a bonus issue on the "Information Revolution," *Business Week*[80] describes the technology comprising this revolution as, "Chips and switches, yes, but also strange materials and stranger ideas—evolving even as you read this."

When the media profile scientists in more depth, their praise and appreciation is vividly evident. *Time*[81] describes gynecologist Patrick Steptoe and physiologist Robert Edwards (the team involved in the birth of the first test-tube baby) as "a highly respected pair of researchers who for more than a decade have been conducting painstaking experiments on *in vitro* . . . fertilization." *Newsweek*[82] claims that "Steptoe's medical credentials are clearly beyond reproach. He has been the major figure in developing the complex methods of manipulating human eggs before and after they are fertilized." Although in a later issue *Time*[83] acknowledges the possibility of problems with the new process of IVF, including malformed babies, high costs, and ethical and legal questions, they cite Steptoe as humbly maintaining: "All I am interested in is how to help women who are denied a baby because their tubes are incapable of doing their small part." *Time*[84] continues its discussion of Steptoe in these terms

> Silver-haired and elegant, Steptoe is a pioneer in the use of laparoscopy, a technique for exploring the abdomen and observing the reproductive tract by means of a long, thin telescope equipped with a fiber optics light. He is also an impeccable dresser, enjoys watching cricket and is a fine organist.

Physiologist Robert Edwards is described[85] in equally flattering terms

> His partner Edwards, the father of five daughters, is no less accomplished in his own field, the physiology of fertilization, and just as dedicated. During early experiments at Cambridge, he often returned to the physiology department at night, scaled a wall, and slipped into his lab to see if fertilized eggs were still alive.

In the same issue, *Time* refuted any possibility of dishonesty on the part of Steptoe and Edwards. They raised this because of a recent, although unrelated, case of scientific fraud in a book claiming that a baby boy had been cloned. *Time*[86] assures us that fraud was not involved in the impending birth of Baby Brown, and they explain why: "The difference was that the test-tube fertilization had been performed by two respected scientists whose accomplishments and progress had been described in many published papers." The birth of Louise Brown was imminent, and in a remarkably sanguine statement, *Time*[87] concludes that "Steptoe and Edwards . . . must surely feel highly confident; otherwise these experienced researchers would never have allowed the pregnancy to go so far."[88]

More than twenty years later, *Time* was discussing these scientists in virtually identical language. Steptoe (who died in 1988) is described as "tall and silver-haired, with softly reassuring blue eyes." Although he looks like he "just stepped out of a Marcus Welby rerun," in fact "the kindly doctor was a medical revolutionary."[89] His partner Edwards is also credited for the "astonishing feat" they achieved, which provide women "a desperately sought service."[90]

Depictions of the experts involved in creating and marketing home and office technology indicate the same respect and awe. In June, 1993, *Time* featured William Gates, characterizing him as "America's richest and most famous computer nerd." Although the article discusses his new system to connect all electronic office equipment into one network, Gates himself is highlighted. He is described as a Harvard dropout who, at 37, "is the most powerful—and most feared—person in the industry. With a personal net worth of $7 billion, he is the richest self-made billionaire in history."[91] Gates is described as unpretentious, but also imperious and able to reduce employees to near tears. According to *Time*, Gates "radiates infectious confidence," and *Time* claims that his record gives him reason to do so.

In an article on home computers, *Business Week* also featured Bill Gates, who had recently "outlined his vision for a brave new world of computer-based consumer electronics." *Business Week* characterized this as developing "at a breathtaking pace . . . luring Americans into a new world of electronic recreation."[92] Gates' personal ambition regarding this project is described in impressive detail: "In recent weeks he has laid out plans to buy Intuit Inc., the top seller of personal-finance software, signed a deal to offer electronic banking with Chase Manhattan Bank, agreed to jointly develop technology for electronic shopping with Visa International, and launched a $100 million advertising blitz."[93] *Business Week* approvingly cites Gate as bragging that: "The PC industry has come a long way, but that's nothing compared with what's going to happen."

U.S. News and World Report featured an article on Gates' new home: Xanadu 2.0, a "pleasure dome and futuristic home" that cost him approximately $100 million to construct. Once again, Gates himself is described as "a symbol of wealth, technology" and "shrewd intelligence."[94]

Similarly, in an article entitled "How Mac Changed the World," *Time* asserts that most of the excitement surrounding the Macintosh is "directly traceable" to Steven Jobs, former chairman of Apple. According to *Time*,[95] Jobs tells his designers that their work will "not only change the world, but also 'put a dent in the universe.'" *Time* claims that Jobs has played a crucial role in making people increasingly comfortable with technology, and in the process he has changed the way people think.

In 1991, *Fortune*[96] described the executives who merely *use* new technology in glowing terms:

> An adventurous breed of top executives and professionals–call them the wired executives–stay on top of business wherever they are, anywhere in the world, with highly portable computers and telecommunications devices that liberate them from the constraints of the office.

The magazine then profiles a number of these executives so "You will discover how these pioneers deploy their supergadgets, and see some of their often spectacular results." One of those profiled is Philippe Kahn, 39, founder and CEO of a software company in California. *Fortune* approvingly describes Kahn as a "French-born mathematician, musician, sailor, and software genius." Although he came to the United States with merely $2000 in 1982, in less than a decade his sales were $500 million annually. *Fortune* notes that this unique man is a "dynamo who gets by on an average of five hours' sleep."

Popular Science recently profiled Vincent Anderson in a report on Whirlpool's production of the most energy-efficient refrigerator available, a machine that should save consumers several hundreds in electric bills. The development is credited in large measure to Anderson whom they claim, "knows as much about refrigerators as anyone–that's why executives chose him to mastermind Whirlpool's effort from Day One."[97] For producing this refrigerator, Anderson's company won $30 million in a fierce competition sponsored by twenty-four utility companies. The winner was announced at a packed conference in Boston, and that evening everyone celebrated at a party . . . everyone, that is, except Anderson. *Popular Science* portrays Anderson as another humble genius: "Slipping away from the spotlight during a break in the festivities, he went to drink beers with an old friend who lived nearby. 'It was nice,' he says, 'to spend time with someone who hadn't even heard of the contest.' "[98]

Thus, the experts associated with new technology, particularly those who have developed it, are regularly portrayed in the media as not only rich and powerful, but dedicated and even eccentric personalities. They obviously control their own destinies as well as ours, and the impression conveyed is that this is basically acceptable since these men are far more knowledgeable than the rest of us, and perhaps even destined to their greatness. Nelkin[99] argues that this promotional reporting of science and technology as beyond our understanding encourages "apathy, a sense of impotence, and the ubiquitous tendency to defer to expertise."

INDICATORS OF STRUCTURAL CONSTRAINTS

Media images of science and technology leave the impression that various technologies are not only progressive but, like the extraordinary individuals who create them, somehow beyond the understanding of ordinary people. This coverage is remarkably consistent and reflects a very limited view of technology. An alert reader can be aware of the constraints under which journalists are working, including the pressure to be entertaining, profitable, and appealing to advertisers and to find evidence of this in their writing. It can be discerned, for example, in the body of an article through the repeated use of attention-getting language to describe new technology: "stunning," "revolutionary," "miraculous," "life-changing." Technology is the "great equalizer" that abolishes "permanent birthrights among individuals and nations." Journalists may also be inclined to "bury the lead": to take what could have been the entire story, albeit a far more serious one, and instead treat it as a minor consideration.[100] The formula that repeatedly emerges in coverage of technological developments entails precisely this: Serious problems are mentioned and then dismissed. The specter of unemployment is raised regarding the electronic office, for example, and then we are assured that there will be no problem if we just handle things wisely. A problematic aspect of technological development that could have been the focus of a story, seldom is.

Headlines may also be scrutinized for evidence of these constraints. Sometimes misinformation is found in a headline, which is most apt to catch a person's eye and shape one's reading of the article. In "Fertility With Less Fuss," for example, *Time*[101] reports the possibility of a cheaper and simpler method of IVF developed by Alan Trounson, an IVF expert at Monash University in Australia. Rather than giving a woman fertility drugs, doctors "simply remove" immature eggs. IVF treatments may cost more than $100,000, "but Trounson says he can slash that figure 80 percent by eliminating drugs, curtailing testing and reducing doctors' fees." *Time* ultimately states, however, that American infertility experts doubt that this method will save much money or even be more effective. Why, then, is the article entitled "Fertility With Less Fuss?"

The public is also poorly informed when significant aspects of a topic are overlooked. Various media reports claim, for example, that robots may be a great boon to people with physical disabilities: Most home chores and many business jobs could be done by disabled people with the assistance of a robot. These reports often neglect to mention, however, that given the price range of robots (from several hundred to thousands of dollars), their availability is severely limited. Moreover, most researchers are not particularly interested in developing robots for the disabled. The contest Johns Hopkins University sponsored to encourage applications of technology for people with disabilities awarded a top prize of $10,000. If we compare this to the $30 million awarded for a commercial refrigerator, we get a more accurate sense of technological priorities. Necessity may drive many inventions for the disabled, as reporter Cynthia Wagner contends in her article on technology for people with disabilities, but more than necessity is at work regarding most (far more profitable) technological developments—such as CDs, microwaves, hair dryers, or smart irons.

Selective reporting is also evident in the coverage of the infertility "epidemic" among professional women, which has been greatly exaggerated by the media. "If you look at the federal fertility/family growth survey, a massive survey polling tens of thousands of women every few years, you find . . . that infertility rates have declined steadily since the '60s and the women that have the least problems with fertility are women who are well-educated and have high income, who can afford good nutrition and good medical care."[102] In fact, low-income black women have the highest rates of infertility, but their infertility problems are not the sort of attention-getting story that the media are inclined to pursue.

Class and race are virtually ignored in reporting on technology, giving the impression that they don't really matter, that perhaps we all share the same concerns and are equally affected by technological developments. When class or race emerges in an article, however, stereotyping can also occur. A *Newsweek*[103] article on infertility, for example, reported that Massachusetts State Representative Ronald Gauch was "stunned" to learn that Medicaid funds paid for infertility drugs for 260 women in Massachusetts the previous year: 58 percent of these women were on AFDC (Aid to Families with Dependent Children), and 63 percent already had children. *Newsweek*[104] reports, in shocked tones, that "two of the women already had *eight children each*." The Governor of Massachusetts, Republican William Weld, immediately banned the drugs from Medicaid's approved list, and Democratic Senator Edward Kennedy readily agreed. But this and similar media reports foster inaccurate stereotypes about women on welfare and their children. According to a Health and Human Services Report, the average number of children in AFDC families is only 1.9–well below our national average.[105] *Newsweek* admits that the amount of money spent on fertility drugs for these women was small, but nonetheless they complain that eleven states still have some form of fertility assistance through Medicaid. According to *Newsweek*,[106] this raises philosophical questions such as: "Is every woman entitled to bear a child, even if she can't afford to raise one?" *Newsweek* apparently answers its own question when it later informs us that "there is now a broad political consensus that welfare recipients should be discouraged from having more children." Apparently the new cures for infertility are not intended to assist women on welfare, just as robots are not developed for people with disabilities. (And who *is* going to buy the $2 million "New American Home"?)

Although media stories about technology are cast as neutral and balanced, the relative absence of contextual information and analysis, combined with a favorable point of view, calls into question the "balance and neutrality." Gender inequality is also evident, in part because men account for the vast majority of news commentators and reporters who have the highest profiles.[107] Top executives in news organizations are overwhelmingly male, as are the sources the mainstream media rely on repeatedly.[108] Women's issues are more likely to be reported now than they were in 1970, "but such stories suffer from two consistent problems: their continued emphasis on upper-middle-class, professional white women; and their segregation, both spatially and conceptually, from other 'hard news' stories. Thus, the interconnections between so-called 'women's issues' and the nation's economic, political and international decisions are overlooked."[109]

Abortion, a heavily covered issue, provides an example of this. "Over a two-year period (1989–1990), close to 1500 articles on abortion appeared in the major papers; the weeklies–*Time*, *Newsweek*, *U.S. News and World Report*–featured stories on abortion more regularly than any other social policy issue."[110] In this reporting, however, abortion is not viewed from the standpoint of those most affected, but from the standpoint of Washington politics. Far more information is available on how abortion affects political candidates than how women with unwanted pregnancies are affected by growing restrictions on funding and counseling. Moreover, it is never acknowledged that women of color accounted for 80 percent of the mortality rates from illegal abortions when it was criminalized.[111]

CONCLUSION

It is challenging to maintain a critical perspective on the media presentation of technology since this requires analyzing things we are not accustomed to viewing critically. Magazine reports and news items are usually regarded, even by journalists themselves, as unbiased, neutral, factual. In reality, they are shaped by the norms of journalism as well as the pressures to be entertaining and profitable. The dominant media message regarding technology (all is well, things are improving for everyone, just leave it to the experts) distracts us from taking a hard look at social reality. Although problems with technology are routinely mentioned, giving an impression of "balance," they are seldom taken seriously. The business arrangements regarding technology are vaguely mysterious, and financing is never mentioned. The *exclusive* focus is on the technology itself–class, race, or gender inequalities that may affect technology or be affected by it, are seldom a serious aspect of these discussions. Technology is thus depicted as separate from the larger social world and apparently unrelated to it. We shall see that this image of technology ignores a great deal of social reality, even as it legitimizes the clout of the "experts."

The following chapter provides empirical data on the inequality of women, particularly in the United States, and it stands in stark contrast to the media portrayal of technology's beneficial effects on everyone, including women. This will be followed by an extensive examination of problems associated with reproductive, office, and household technology, inequalities which the media for the most part overlooks.

NOTES

1. Dorothy Nelkin, *Selling Science: How the Press Covers Science* (New York: W.H. Freeman and Company, 1995), 2.

2. Nelkin's research on media coverage of science and technology included a systematic study of national and local newspapers; national news magazines like *Time*, *Newsweek*, and *U.S. News and World Report*; as well as television evening news.

3. Nelkin, *Selling Science*, 6.

4. Todd Gitlin (*The Whole World*, 7) refers to this as a "frame;" a "persistent pattern of cognition, interpretation and presentation, of selection, emphasis, and exclusion."

5. Nelkin, *Selling Science*, 69.

6. Ibid., 31.

7. The September 1995 issue of *Newsweek*, for example, contains a serious treatment of the difficulties surrounding reproductive technologies (Begley, "The Baby Myth"). A December 2000 issue of *U.S. News and World Report* presents a historical discussion of the pace of technological change, arguing that it is declining (Longman, "The Slowing Pace of Progress").

8. Nelkin, *Selling Science*, 113.

9. David Croteau and William Hoynes, *Media Society* (Thousand Oaks, CA: Pine Forge Press, 2000), 71.

10. Nelkin, *Selling Science*, 162.

11. Ibid., 119.

12. Ibid., 164.

13. Ibid., 163.

14. Charles Petit, "Brave New Medicine: Wondrous Technology Could Bring Back the House Call," *U.S. News and World Report*, 1 December 1977, 82.

15. Susan Gregory Thomas, "1998 Tech Guide," *U.S. News and World Report*, 1 December 1997, 66.

16. *Time*, "Special Issue: Beyond the Year 2000: What to Expect in the New Millennium, Fall 1992, 34.

17. *Time,* "Machine of the Year: The Computer Moves In," 3 January 1983, 14.

18. John Schwartz, "Computers: The Next Revolution," *Newsweek*, 6 April 1992, 42–48.

19. Ibid., 42.

20. Ibid., 44.

21. Ibid., 48.

22. Paul Martin, "Smart Houses: When Houses Take Over," *Social Issues and Health Review*, Vol. 2, No. 1 (1987): 5.

23. Jeff Block, "The Computer Chip as Cook," *Forbes*, Vol. 137 (March 1982): 158.

24. James Lardner, "Please Don't Squeeze the Tomatoes Online: Supermarkets of the Future Have No Aisles," *U.S. News and World Report*, 9 November 1998, 51.

25. Ibid., 52.

26. Martin, "Smart Houses," 5.

27. Cynthia Wagner, "Enabling the Disabled: Technologies for People with Handicaps," *The Futurist*, May–June 1992, 29–32.

28. *Time*, "Special Issue," 41.

29. Michael Morris, "The New American Home '94: An Amazing Adaptable Showcase Proves How Far a House Can Go with Innovative Off-the-Shelf Technology," *Popular Science*, February 1994, 74.

30. Ibid., 73.

31. Ibid., 77.

32. Ibid., 76.

33. *Time*, "Special Issue," 40.

34. Paul Recer, "Yankee Ingenuity: Ways It Will Change Your Life," *U.S. News and World Report*, June 1981, 66.

35. Ursula Huws, *Your Job in the Eighties: A Woman's Guide to New Technology* (London: Pluto Press, 1982), 102.

36. Mary Kathleen Flynn, "Computers: The Newest Appliance," *U.S. News and World Report*, 29 November 1993, 90.

37. *Business Week*, "Home Computers: Sales Explode as New Users Turn PCs into All-Purpose Information Appliances," 28 November 1994, 89–94.

38. *Newsweek*, "How Far Should We Push Mother Nature?" 17 January 1994, 58.

39. Gina Kolata, "Childbirth at 63 Says What About Life?" *The New York Times*, 27 April 1997.

40. Dena Kleiman, "Anguished Search to Cure Infertility," *The New York Times Magazine*, 16 December 1979, 60.

41. Frederic Golden, "Patrick Steptoe and Robert Edward: Brave New Baby Doctors," *Time*, 29 March 1999, 178.

42. Kleiman, "Anguished Search," 64.

43. *U.S. News and World Report*, "England's Test-Tube Baby," 31 July 1978, 24.

44. Julie Greenwalt, "Thankful for Five Tiny Blessings," *People*, 15 February 1988, 92ff.

45. Ibid., 92.

46. *Time*, "The Saddest Epidemic," 10 September 1984, 50.

47. Peggy Mann, "New Help for the Childless," *Readers Digest*, January 1986, 135–140.

48. Philip Elmer-DeWitt, "Making Babies," *Time*, 30 September 1991, 58.

49. Claudia Glenn Dowling, "Miraculous Babies," *Life*, December 1998, 75–84.

50. *Business Week*, "Home Computers," 98–120.

51. Ibid., 112.

52. Ibid., 113.

53. *U.S. News and World Report*, "Jobs of the Future," 23 December 1985, 41.

54. Ibid., 47.

55. *Business Week*, "In the Digital Derby, There's No Inside Lane," 18 November 1994, 146.

56. Ibid., 148.

57. Ibid., 154.

58. Ibid., 154.

59. *Business Week*, "The Information Revolution: How Digital Technology Is Changing the Way We Work and Live," 18 November 1994, 22, 47.

60. *Working Woman*, "Science and Technology," 41.

61. *Time*, "Special Issue," 29.

62. Schwartz, "Computers," 48.

63. *Business Week*, "The Information Revolution," 106.

64. *U.S. News and World Report*, "Jobs of the Future," 41.

65. Otto Friedrich, "The Computer Moves In," *Time*, 3 January 1983, 22.

66. *Business Week*, "In the Digital Derby," 154.

67. *Time*, "Machine of the Year," 14.

68. *Business Week*, "The Information Revolution."

69. *U.S. News and World Report*, "England's Test-Tube Baby," 24.

70. Elmer-DeWitt, "Making Babies," 59.

71. *Newsweek*, "Making Babies after Menopause," 5 November 1990, 75.

72. *Newsweek*, "How Far Should We Push Mother Nature?" 54–57.

73. Lee Silver, "A Quandry That Isn't: Picking a Baby's Sex Won't Lead to Disaster," *Time*, 21 September 1998, 83.

74. *Newsweek*, "Contraceptive Controversy," 18 July 1994, 60.

75. Elmer-DeWitt, "Making Babies."

76. Dowling, "Miraculous Babies."

77. Peter Gwynn, "The First Test-Tube Baby," *Newsweek*, 24 July 1978, 76.

78. Recer, "Yankee Ingenuity," 66.

79. *Time*, "The First Test-Tube Baby," 31 July 1978, 58.

80. *Business Week*, "The Information Revolution," 4.

81. *Time*, "Test-Tube Baby: Conceived in a Laboratory," 24 July 1978, 47.

82. Gwynn, "The First Test-Tube Baby," 76.

83. *Time*, "The First Test-Tube Baby," 62.

84. Ibid., 62.

85. Ibid., 64–65.

86. *Time*, "A Test-Tube Baby Is Not a Clone," 31 July 1978, 65.

87. *Time*, "To Fool (or Not) with Mother Nature," 31 July 1978, 69.

88. Ibid., 69.

89. Golden, "Patrick Steptoe," 178.

90. Ibid., 178.

91. *Time*, "New, Improved, and Ready for Battle," 14 June 1993, 60.

92. *Business Week*, "Home Computers," 90.

93. Ibid., 92, 93

94. Richard Folkers, "Xanadu 2.0: Bill Gates's Stately Pleasure Dome and Futuristic Home," *U.S. News and World Report*, 1 December 1997, 87.

95. Philip Elmer-DeWitt, "How Mac Changed the World," *Time*, 31 January 1994, 93.

96. *Fortune*, "Saving Time with New Technology," 30 December 1991, 98.

97. *Popular Science*, "The $30 Million Refrigerator," January 1994, 66.

98. Ibid., 87.

99. Nelkin, *Selling Science*, 162.

100. Martin A. Lee and Norman Solomon, *Unreliable Sources: A Guide to Detecting Bias in News Media* (New York: Carol Publishing Group, 1990).

101. *Time*, "Fertility with Less Fuss," 79.

102. *Extra!*, "Backing the Backlash: How the Press Promotes Myths About Women. Interview with Susan Faludi," Special Issue (1992): 6.

103. *Newsweek*, "The Infertility Trap," 4 April 1994, 30–31.

104. Ibid., 30.

105. Renu Nahata, "Too Many Kids and Too Much Money: Persistent Welfare Sterotypes," *Extra!*, Special Issue (1992): 12.

106. *Newsweek*, "The Infertility Trap," 30, 31.

107. Laura Flanders, *Real Majority, Media Minority: The Cost of Sidelining Women in Reporting* (Monroe, ME: Common Courage Press, 1997).

108. Martha A. Fineman and Martha T. McCluskey, *Feminism, Media, and the Law* (New York: Oxford University Press, 1997).

109. Susan J. Douglas, "Missing Voices: Women and the U.S. News Media," *Extra!*, Special Issue (1992): 5.

110. Tiffany Devitt, "Abortion Coverage Leaves Women Out of the Picture," *Extra!*, Special Issue (1992): 18.

111. Angela Davis, *Women, Race, and Class* (New York: Random House, 1981).

4

Broken Promises
A Look at the Status of Women

❖ ❖ ❖ ❖ ❖ ❖

If this is the best of all possible worlds, what were the others like?
Candide

Media reports leave the unmistakable impression that technology has dramatically improved the human condition, including the situation of women. Certainly the lives of many women have been enhanced by some technologies, but it is necessary to assess women's current status carefully before accepting the appealing message of virtually universal benefit for women through technological development. While acknowledging improvements that have occurred, this chapter emphasizes troubling evidence of stubborn inequality and even deterioration in the status of women. This information tends to get less attention in the media and in larger society, and yet it calls into question fundamental assumptions regarding the power of technology to change women's lives. A careful consideration of the status of women is necessary in order to challenge notions of progress for all through technology, particularly if progress is defined in terms of equality.

Before we begin, it must be emphasized that women do not share a common experience. A growing body of multicultural and feminist research has taught us to question universalizing assumptions about women and to acknowledge profound differences among them. Women's lives are shaped by numerous factors, including class and race as well as gender, and the interacting effects of these differences influence not only women's status but their access to opportunity, their autonomy, and their experiences with many social phenomena, including technology.

This chapter explores changes in the status of various groups of women over time, as well as their current status in relation to men. Since gender roles are, by definition, relational, a fair assessment of the "progress" of women requires that we consider not only changes in women's social position from one decade to another, but equally significant, women's achievements vis-à-vis those of men at any given time.[1]

Our focus will be on women in the United States, paying careful attention to differences among them; but since the technologies we are discussing have serious implications for women around the world, we will also examine the status of women globally, using a wide range of indicators that have been used to gauge women's status.[2] We will look at economic position as well as health, participation in the centers of power, and educational achievements. We will see that despite increases in women's participation in the labor force, increases in levels of education, and more participation in political offices, women still have fewer opportunities compared to men, less education, and less pay. Although women's status varies enormously from one country to another, nowhere are women equal to men. They are concentrated in the lowest paid occupations, and they continue to do the traditional and demanding unpaid work in the home. The poverty of many women in the Third World as well as in industrialized societies is particularly noteworthy. Worldwide, a stunning 70 percent of women live in poverty.[3]

Many feminist analyses discuss the roots of this inequality, as well as why it persists. Although they vary in their causal explanations, they all explain gender inequality by analyzing social institutions. Marxist-feminists, for example, focus on capitalism, and see gender inequality as rooted in social class inequality. Radical feminists see gender inequality as rooted in a wider range of cultural institutions beyond the economy, including the family, politics, and the media, which are all sites of male privilege and power. Liberal feminists believe that women's inequality stems from a lack of opportunities for women and argue that legal change can increase equality. All these perspectives argue explicitly for change and chart the ways in which this can occur by changing social institutions. The point of this chapter is to document the persisting inequality of women, demonstrating that although technology brought significant improvement for some women, it has not resulted in social equality.

WOMEN AND PAID LABOR

Women's work has changed considerably over the past 200 years. In the United States, women have moved in unprecedented numbers from the household to paid labor in factories, offices, and the professions. In 1890, only 19 percent of U.S. women were in the labor force, by 1950, this had increased to 30 percent.[4] By 1998, 59.8 percent of women participated in the labor force (see Figure 4–1).

This participation varies somewhat among women by race and ethnicity (see Figure 4–2).

Black women are slightly more likely than white women to engage in paid labor: 62.8 percent, and 59.9 percent, respectively. Hispanic women's participation is also rising, but they remain behind their white and black counterparts at 55.6 percent in 1998. Asian women are also active in the labor force with an overall participation rate of 59.2 percent. They have lower participation rates than black and white women within age groups under 45, which is generally attributed to their enrollment rates in postsecondary education.[5] U.S. women in general are among

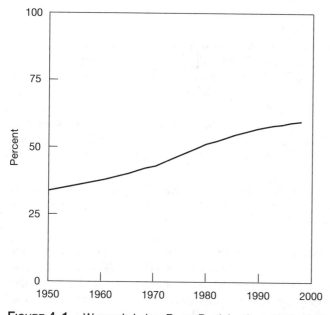

FIGURE 4–1 Women's Labor Force Participation, 1950–1998

Source: Economic Report of the President, 1999

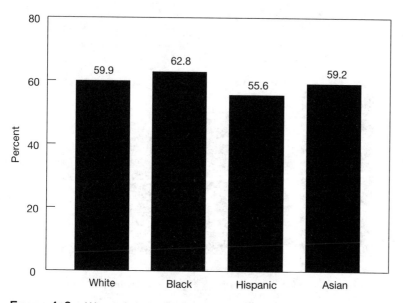

FIGURE 4–2 Women's Labor Force Participation, 1998

Source: U.S. Bureau of Labor Statistics http://www.bis.gov/opub/ted/2000/feb/wk3/art03.htm

the most active in the labor force among the industrialized countries, lagging behind only Sweden and Canada.

Despite this increasing labor force participation, women remain in a decidedly secondary economic position. They are disproportionately represented in the so-called "female professions" (such as secretarial and clerical work), which are characterized by lower-than-average wages.[6] This results in a "wage gap:" Women in the United States make 74 cents for every dollar a man makes.[7] Even within the same occupations, whether marketing or elementary school teaching, men earn more than women.[8] Hilda Scott[9] succinctly captures the irony of the situation women confronted in the 1970s and continue to confront:

> Women had to give up the idea that they were properly dependent on men for their sole support. And yet the nature of the jobs they were offered during the decade was totally incompatible with the eradication of economic dependence.

Currently, most new jobs are in the service sector where women are already highly concentrated.[10] These industries do not pay adequate wages for women to support themselves or their children, and women's economic inequality is thus being institutionalized in the most rapidly expanding sectors of the U.S. economy. The situation is worse for many women of color. Although a white woman earns only 74 cents on every dollar a white man earns, a black woman earns 63 cents, and a Hispanic woman only 53 cents see (Figure 4–3).

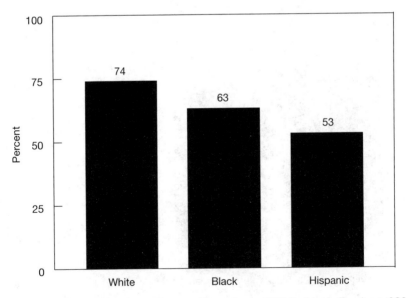

FIGURE 4–3   Women's Earnings as Percentage of White Men's Earnings, 2000
Source: U.S. Bureau of Labor Statistics, 2000

In developing countries, job discrimination and inequality is even more severe for women workers. In Latin American economies, for example, although the participation of women has grown rapidly, their income is still only 50 percent that of males.[11] Women tend to be located predominantly in female-dominated jobs, and often in the informal sectors of the economy.[12]

"Contingent employment" is a term used to refer to non-regular employees, those who supplement the regular labor force. Natividad and Lauth[13] list the inequities found in this workforce as compared to regular employees: They are paid lower wages, generally lack medical coverage as well as job security, have irregular hours, have few opportunities for advancement, and have few legal protections, such as unemployment insurance or a minimum wage. During the last decade, the contingent workforce has grown twice as fast as the total workforce.[14] Significantly, women and minorities are overrepresented in this work, especially in its low-wage segment.

When the Women's Bureau of the U.S. Department of Labor surveyed over a quarter million women in 1994 about being a working woman, they found that the majority of women liked their jobs overall, but they expressed strong agreement about overriding problems. Two critical concerns were a need to improve pay (according to 65 percent of respondents) and a need for adequate health care insurance. "Forty-three percent of women who work part-time and 34 percent of women over 55 years old lack health care insurance. These percentages far exceed the 18 percent of the general population who lack health insurance."[15] Vacation and sick leaves were also regarded as inadequate. Many women believe their work does not get the recognition it deserves nor do they have opportunities to train for more prestigious positions. In fact, more than half the sample reported little or no opportunity to advance. Many noted the difficulties of balancing work and family. Problems with child care, as reported by more than 53 percent of the women, are pervasive: It is difficult to find quality child care and equally difficult to afford it.

The shortage of affordable child care in the United States dramatically affects the composition of the labor force since many women are often relegated to part-time positions in order to meet family responsibilities. Unfortunately, this is precisely the type of employment that has inherent limitations, including "less pay, fewer benefits, and often less respect."[16] Randy Albeda[17] summarizes the "bad news" regarding women's employment in the United States as "the increased impoverishment of women and children accompanied by policies that have exacerbated their poverty, the increasing need for two earners to earn a family wage foisting the 'double day' onto many working parents, and an increased inequality among women and their families."

OCCUPATIONAL SEGREGATION

It is vital to explore the issue of occupational segregation in more depth since it plays a significant role in the continuing inequality of women. Since the Fourth World Conference on Women in 1995, more than sixty countries have changed a variety of laws that discriminated against women.[18] Legislation has been enacted around the world that guarantees women equal pay compared to men for equal work. Unfortunately, however, this applies only to women and men in the *same* jobs, while job segregation in terms of gender is a defining characteristic of the labor force.[19] Thus, the law does not even touch the most fundamental problem of wage inequality since men and women do not work at the same jobs. To illustrate: In 1999, according to the U.S. Department of Labor, ten (of more then 500) occupational categories accounted for almost one-third of all employed women workers, and seven of these ten were at least 75 percent female.[20] Women represented 98.6 percent of secretaries; 91.4 percent of bookkeepers, accounting, and auditing clerks; and 95.5 percent of receptionists; but only 30.5 percent of managers and administrators (see Figure 4–4).

According to the Bureau of Labor Statistics, in 1998 women in managerial positions earned far more than those in jobs in the service sector ($655 weekly median income compared to $296), but women are concentrated in the latter positions.[21] Reskin and Cassirer[22] note that the segregation of women by occupation is so well established that as late as 1990, "53 percent of either men or women would have had to change their occupations in which their sex was underrepresented for the sexes to be integrated across occupations." Women still constitute over 90 percent of: child-care workers, bank tellers, nurses, and private household workers.[23]

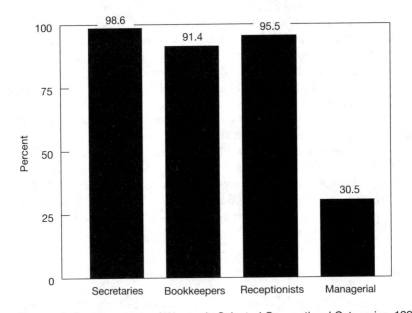

FIGURE 4–4   Percentage of Women in Selected Occupational Categories, 1999

Source: U.S. Department of Labor, Women's Bureau, 1999 http://www.dol.gov/dol/wb/public/wb_pubs/201ead99.htm

If we look at more detailed job descriptions within organizations, we see that job segregation is even more pervasive than the bleak census data initially indicate. In part this is because in some businesses only men or women perform specific jobs.[24] Certain restaurants, for example, have only men (or women) waiting tables, but the national data collapses everyone into one category, and thus gives a false impression of how many men and women actually work together. Both secretaries and production workers are grouped in the "auto industry," but women's work in this industry tends to be more labor intensive with lower levels of pay and unionization.

While women are vastly overrepresented in certain occupations, white men continue to dominate the top of the labor market. Moreover, "most women still work in women-dominated jobs which pay less than men's jobs requiring comparable levels of education and responsibility."[25] Minority women, like white women, work in "female" occupations, but poverty and discrimination often further limit their options. Although different minority groups face very different situations, women of color often shoulder particular burdens related to being female and nonwhite. Considerable disparity in occupational attainment and wages exists among women of color, and yet gender continues to be a significant factor in determining their status and their occupations. Reskin and Cassirer[26] observe that although "gender remains the primary basis by which workers are sorted into occupations," looking at gender in isolation distorts our understanding of labor force segregation. Race plays a crucial role *in combination* with gender. Significantly, they note that "racial differences are more consequential for segregating same-sex than other-sex workers. In terms of occupational outcomes, the importance of sex is unrivaled."

The issue of race is fundamental to understanding the unique place of black women in the labor force. Most women work because of economic necessity, but more black women are under pressure to do so given the reduced earning power of black men. In addition, they are more likely to be unemployed or underemployed than white women. In 1996, for example, 10 percent of black women were unemployed compared to 4.7 percent of white women. Studies have found that only 23 percent of black women have jobs in the preferred job sector as compared to 35 percent of white women. According to Dodoo and Kasari,[27] this "implies a multilayered configuration of poverty in America, where the doubly disadvantaged black woman resides at the bottom end of the spectrum." Compared to Anglo women and men, Hispanic women are also over-concentrated in low-paid jobs, with high rates of poverty and an unemployment rate of 10.2 percent in 1996. This is due to low educational achievement (some of it stemming from the disruptions of migrant labor), as well as the discrimination they face as Spanish-speakers in an Anglo system.[28] Asian women have an occupational distribution more similar to white women and a lower unemployment rate of 4.4 percent in 1996, which reflects in part their high educational attainment.

Occupational segregation has been declining for women, but the pace has been slow, and in some cases, female ghettoes are re-emerging within formally male occupations. For example, bus-driving has become integrated, but women drive the school buses, men drive the city buses.[29] Thus apparent integration does not always mean genuine progress in terms of wages, benefits, or opportunities for advancement.

The continuing gender segregation of occupations might not be as vexing if "female" jobs brought equal pay. But, as we have seen, they do not. In the United States and indeed worldwide, women earn far less for their jobs than men do. The particular jobs women hold bring not only lower wages but less status and few, if any, benefits. According to Bureau of Labor Statistics' data, women's earnings increased by almost 14 percent between 1979 and 1998, while men's earnings declined about 7 percent.[30] This meant greater parity, but women still earned only 76 percent of what men earned in 1998–and the decline for men is obviously problematic. Changes have also been uneven for different groups of women. "Between 1974 and 1995, white women's median annual earnings increased by 18 percent while black and Hispanic women's median income rose by only 9 percent and 3 percent respectively, despite disproportionate educational gains in high school and college educational attainment by black and Hispanic women."[31] White women earn more than black and Hispanic women, but despite the privilege of their race, they continue to earn less than white men. These disparities remain constant despite the improvement in educational levels among women. In fact, United States women have caught up with men in virtually all educational categories, including college graduation,[32] and yet job segregation and unequal pay remain stubborn obstacles to women's equality.

The inequality of women in the United States is exacerbated in part by traditional assumptions that women enter the labor force as secondary workers. This reinforces their segregation in low-paying occupations and legitimizes wage discrimination. Increasingly, however, women depend on their own earnings and cannot count on the earnings of men. Half of all marriages in the U.S. now end in divorce, and in 80 percent of these divorces, children stay with the mother. Significantly, child support payments are a negligible source of income: Many women receive little or no payments at all.[33] According to census data, in 1995 only 39 percent of custodial parents received the full amount they were awarded. The amount of child support received tends to be minimal, barely covering the actual expenses of caring for a child or children. In 1995, for example, the average child support payment was $3732 per year. Perhaps not surprisingly, 32 percent of custodial parents who did not receive child support payments in 1995 were poor.[34]

Financial insecurity often keeps women dependent on men, and it frequently spells poverty when a male is absent. Simply put, women are less able than men to support themselves and their children, and thus their risk of poverty is high. The gender gap in pay, and the traditional responsibility women have for children, is a crucial cause of their poverty. Although more women now have jobs and they can leave unhappy marriages, the economic consequences of this are severe given the pay gap. Women themselves need to earn a living wage, but this will require significant changes in the current labor market.

Hilda Scott perceptively suggests that we reconsider the way we think about the poverty of women. On the one hand, she wants us to acknowledge the tremendous amount of unpaid work women do, arguing that "the vast majority of women are poor in the absolute sense that they carry out an enormous amount of indispensable work without any remuneration whatsoever."[35] But she also contends that the family-based way of counting the poor disguises what really goes on in our society since poverty is about *control* over resources. Many women "who are 'indirectly' *not* in poverty by virtue of the chief breadwinner's status *are* poor in the sense that their own access to resources is limited."[36] For many women, poverty is only a divorce away since they lack the financial clout to support themselves and their children with their own resources.

Wages have increased among well-educated women, although they have declined for high-school dropouts.[37] Francine Blan[38] argues that women have made "substantial progress" toward gender equality, but she also notes that "there still exists a considerable, although reduced, gender wage gap after controlling for measured characteristics, which is often taken as an estimate of discrimination. And the challenges of combining work and family appear to continue to pose serious obstacles and dilemmas for women but, at this point, do not seem to affect men in the same way or at least to the same extent."

WOMEN IN THE PROFESSIONS

It is tempting to assume that this inequality does not affect the women who have "made it," those fortunate enough to have achieved positions of prestige and power. But the reality is considerably more complicated than we might initially assume. It is wise to begin by reminding ourselves how comparatively few in number professional women are. Worldwide they represent a small minority of those in relatively well-paying professional, technical, managerial or administrative jobs. Studies from the United States in the 1980s and 1990s confirm the persistence of patterned inequality in the professions. In an illuminating analysis of United States data from the Department of Labor and the Census Bureau, Harold Benenson[39] examined the "dual career family," which has been regarded as the symbol of modern success. Benenson's analysis demonstrated, however, that the percentage of married women in elite professions was virtually insignificant among married women as a whole: In 1982 married women in law, medicine, or college teaching "constituted *less than three-fourths of 1 percent of all married women in the labor force*."[40] Furthermore, women who do have elite jobs are far more likely than their male counterparts to be single, without children, or divorced. Thus, the popularized concept of the dual career family ignores, as Benenson astutely observes, "the constraints of social class, occupational segregation and female subordination that shape the experience of close to 99 percent of employed adult women."

In 1993, Mary Guy compared the status of women and men in public management positions and found that men hold the overwhelming majority of decision-making positions. Her research indicates that women who do reach high levels of management come from more advanced backgrounds than men in similar positions, both in terms of education and class background. According to Guy,[41] this information tells us that "while the average man is able to climb the bureaucratic ladder, the average woman is shut out. She needs to be above average in order to make it." In line with Benenson's earlier research, Guy[42] confirms that the women who make it to the top tend to live nontraditional lives: As many as 71 percent of female managers had no dependents (compared to 48 percent of the men), and only 50 percent were married (vs. 80 percent of the men).

Increasingly, educated young women are joining certain professions. In 1999, the U.S. Census Bureau documented the progress in terms of graduation from law school and medical school: In 1970, women represented 5.4 percent of law school graduates and 8.4 percent of medical school graduates. By 1996, this had risen to 43.5 percent and 40.9 percent, respectively (see Figure 4–5).

Women are more underrepresented at the top ranks of universities: In 1996, they were only 19.3 percent of full professors.[43] They have made considerably less progress in corporate America: As of 1995, women comprised only 7 percent of the total number of seats on corporate boards in the United States.[44] Currently only three companies of the Fortune 500 are headed by women: Avon, Hewlett-Packard, and Golden West Financial.[45] Women were 4.1 percent of the top earning officers

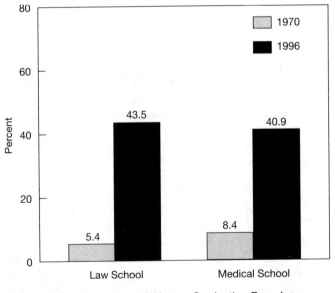

FIGURE 4–5   Percentage of Women Graduating From Law
School and Medical School

Source: U.S. Bureau of the Census, 1999

in the year 2000, and more than 83 percent of the Fortune 500 companies lacked a woman among their five highest earning officers.[46] This pattern is repeated in most industries. For example, although women, such as Geraldine Laybourne of Oxygen have run networks and cable-related companies, they accounted for just 34.4 percent of officials and managers for cable operators in 1999, down from 35.2 percent in 1998. Moreover, women comprised fully 74 percent of the reduction of 1565 positions in cable companies between 1998 and 1999.[47]

Black women have made important gains in the professions in the United States, including a 79 percent increase in managerial and professional specialty occupations from 1986 to 1996 when a total of 1.6 million black women held these jobs. Nonetheless, they remain poorly represented in male-dominated professions and are found largely in the traditional female professions such as nurse, elementary school teacher, and social worker. In 1996, 1.8 million black women also worked in service occupations: 60 percent of these service workers were employed as nursing aides, orderlies and attendants, janitors and cleaners, cooks and maids.[48]

WOMEN AND POVERTY

The economic inequality experienced by women has translated into higher rates of poverty. In 1997, the United Nations' Development Program released its Human Development Report, which revealed that women comprise 70 percent of the world's poor. Rural poor women in particular (approximately half a billion people) have seen little economic progress over the past thirty years. In the United States, women in all age groups have higher poverty rates than men. As of 1999, 13.2 percent of women were below the poverty level compared to 10.3 percent of men.[49] Families maintained by women had a poverty rate of 29.9 percent in 1998, and this has been relatively stable since the mid 1960s despite changes in the economic situation.[50]

Race is a significant factor since poverty is disproportionately concentrated among minorities. Overall in the United States, black, Latina, and Native American women are in lower socioeconomic standing than white and Asian women. Asian women have higher educational levels, and they are more likely to be professionals or to work in their own businesses. However, "women of all racial-ethnic origins earn considerably less, work fewer hours, and are less likely to work in their own businesses than men."[51] Although African Americans make up only 12 percent of the U.S. population, they account for 40.8 percent of single mothers in poverty. The percentage of Hispanics living in poverty was 25.6 percent in 1998.[52] According to the Bureau of Labor Statistics, 14.6 percent of black working women lived below the poverty line in 1997, and 12.6 percent of Hispanic working women.[53]

Although Asian Americans have been labeled the "model minority," implying that they (unlike other minorities) have escaped conditions of poverty, this assumption is erroneous. Often used as an argument against affirmative action, the myth of the model minority serves to mask "the persistence of poverty and self-exploitation among Asians as well as the presence of virulent anti-Asian sentiment."[54] Some Asian Americans have been particularly successful in terms of education: Chinese and Japanese women in the United States have, for example, higher rates of college or advanced degrees as compared to white women: 30 percent, 20 percent, and 13 percent, respectively.[55] This is due in part to a cultural emphasis on education as well as the higher class status of some Asian immigrants. Nonetheless, many Asian Americans remain at the bottom of the economic hierarchy. In 1998, for example, the overall poverty rate for Asian Americans was 12.5 percent compared to 8.2 percent for whites.[56]

CHILDREN AND POVERTY

We have seen that the media devotes a great deal of attention to medical "miracles" that enable women to produce healthy children. In light of this, it is particularly jarring and instructive to examine the status of children and to learn that they are among the most disadvantaged in many societies around the world. According to Census data, a stunning 12.1 million American children lived in poverty in 1999. That is a slight decrease from 1998, but more children are living in poverty in the United States today than twenty years ago.

Racial and ethnic differences play a significant role in child poverty. In 1999, according to the Census Bureau, 9.4 percent of white children were poor, compared to 30.3 percent of Hispanic children, and 33.1 percent of African-American children (see Figure 4–6).

These figures are particularly striking given that the federal poverty line for a family of three in 1999 was a meager $13,290. In addition, it is estimated that approximately 100,000 children in the United States are homeless each night.[57] Economic growth alone has obviously not rescued these children. Many of these impoverished children come from *working* families. According to the Children's Defense Fund (CDF), the percentage of poor children in working families continues to rise—from 61 percent in 1993 to 77 percent in 1999.[58]

The Children's Defense Fund maintains that children need healthy bodies and minds, and to insure this they need education, immunization, comprehensive health care, and mothers who have received adequate prenatal care. In contrast to these goals or—better—*rights*, the CDF notes that "more than 8 million children and half a million pregnant women in the United States have no health insurance and are at risk of not getting the health care they need."[59] One in six American children had no health insurance in the year 2000. Teen mothers are most likely to receive inadequate prenatal care and, as a result, many of them deliver low birth-weight babies (less than 5.5 pounds). Nearly one in ten births to teen mothers, and more than one in eight births to black teen mothers, fall into this category. Low birth-weight is significant because it puts a baby who survives at "much greater risk of such lifelong disabilities as mental retardation,

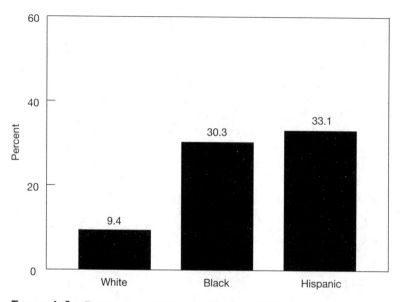

FIGURE 4–6   Percentage of Children in Poverty, 1999

Source: U.S. Bureau of the Census, 1999 http://www.census.gov/hhes/poverty/histpov/hstpov3.html

blindness, deafness, cerebral palsy, and other health problems."[60] Poverty has been closely associated with teen pregnancy—as family income rises, teen births decline.

UNPAID LABOR

Let us consider also the significance of the unpaid work that women do. Hilda Scott contends that what women have in common is that they do most of the unpaid work of the world: "Women's unpaid work, her productive and reproductive labor for which she receives no remuneration, underpins the world's economy, yet it is peripheral to the world's economy as men define it, and therefore has no value."[61] Although the proportion of women in paid employment varies, virtually everywhere women have full responsibility for children and household chores, and work longer hours than men. Empirical studies consistently document that the allocation of hours of housework between husbands and wives is persistently unequal, even when the wife is employed. Women still do the bulk of the housework and child care, as much as 84 percent.[62] Unpaid labor for many older women in their late fifties and sixties continues, since they are likely to be the ones providing care to elderly parents, in-laws, and other relatives.[63]

Various estimates have been made regarding the amount of unpaid work women do and the economic value of it. According to figures from the International

Labor Office,[64] women do two-thirds of the world's work and receive 10 percent of the world's income, while a U.S. Department of Commerce report put the value of American women's unpaid work at $1462 billion a year. Figure 4–7 from the World Health Organization in 1992 vividly illustrates the contributions of women worldwide and their lack of remuneration.

Much of women's work remains invisible and generally unacknowledged, although it is worth a significant amount if someone had to be hired to do it or if it were done commercially. Industry, government, and society as a whole depend on this unpaid and often undervalued labor. Like paid labor, this work varies in terms of different groups of women. In the United States, for example, Hispanic women tend to have larger families, and they and black women are more likely than white women to be single parents with total responsibility for raising children and supporting them. According to the U.S. Department of Labor, in 1992 47 percent of black families were maintained by women, compared to 25 percent of Hispanic families, and 14 percent of all white families.[65]

WOMEN'S HEALTH

Women's health concerns are related to their economic situation. Since they have lower incomes than men and frequently hold part-time jobs, they often have limited health insurance or none at all. Their responsibility for the care of children and the sick and elderly often interferes with employment and adequate insurance coverage. In 1999, 19.2 percent of U.S. women of child-bearing age (15–44 years)

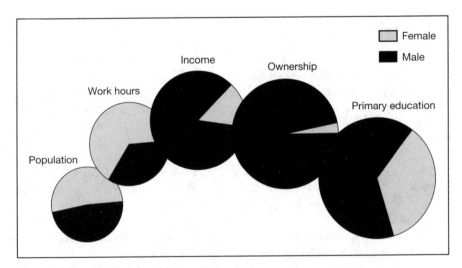

FIGURE 4–7   Gender Differences Worldwide
Source: World Health Organization, Women's Health: Across Age and Frontier, 1992: 22.

had no health insurance, according to the U.S. Census Bureau.[66] More than one-third of Hispanic and Native American women were without health insurance in 1999, compared to 18 percent of white women. In addition, 14 percent of pregnant women lacked insurance in 1997.[67]

Devastating examples of the absence of good health among women of color in the United States have been available for decades. In the 1980s, two government reports on minorities and health documented that minority women experience higher infant mortality rates; increased rates of chronic diseases such as diabetes, hypertension, and cardiovascular diseases; certain types of cancer; and a lower life expectancy of five to seven years compared to their white counterparts.[68] Black and Hispanic women were reported as being at higher risk than women from most other ethnic groups, and insurance coverage was a major problem. "Blacks and Puerto Ricans were twice as likely as whites not to have health insurance. Among Mexican Americans the noninsured rate is three and one-half greater than that of white non-Hispanics."[69] By the early 1990s, black and Hispanic women accounted for more than 70 percent of all women with AIDS; nearly half of black women over age 60 had hypertension; black women had a 40 percent higher rate of strokes, twice the incidence of uterine cancer, and twice the death rate from diabetes as compared to white women.[70] Moreover, black women were four times as likely to die in childbirth compared to their white counterparts.[71] Death from heart disease was 64 percent greater for black women than for white women in 1991;[72] and as of May, 2000 they continue to be at the greatest risk of dying from heart disease compared to other racial and ethnic groups.[73] According to a recent study from the University of Michigan at Ann Arbor, women with high blood pressure, diabetes, or obesity are at greatest risk of early death from heart disease, and black women have the greatest number of these factors.[74] As recently as 1998, the Centers for Disease Control and Prevention reported that low income women are eight times as likely to be uninsured as high-income women.[75] Currently, minority women use fewer health services than white women although they have more health problems.[76]

Because of limited access to affordable health care, many individuals wait until they are very ill before seeking medical attention. As a result, it is far more likely that their illnesses will be in much later stages, and their chances of recovery diminished. Every year deaths are experienced by black women that would not occur if they had the same age-sex rates as whites. These deaths are referred to as "excess deaths."[77] Some of these differences are due to employment in positions that expose them to greater risks from occupational hazards such as physical and mental stress as well as toxic substances. Although health research on women is becoming a priority, research on women of color still lags. The combination of issues that affect them as *both* women *and* members of a minority community have yet to be adequately addressed.

Significant differences also exist between races in terms of prenatal care. Approximately 81 percent of white mothers receive prenatal care, but only 64 percent of black mothers. Moreover, less than three in five Native-American and Mexican-American mothers receive prenatal care.[78]

The health care delivered to women varies dramatically not only within the United States but also globally. Jodi Jacobson[79] characterized women's health care in most developing countries in terms of "four toos"–"too far from home, too few trained birth-attendants, too poorly equipped to identify or handle complications, and too deficient in quality of care." In South Asia and much of Africa, it is esti-mated that a mere 25 percent of women receive adequate prenatal care. "Only about one-third of all births are assisted by trained medical attendants in Africa and South Asia, as opposed to 64 percent in Latin America, 93 percent in East Asia, and virtually 100 percent in North America."[80] Because of access to basic nutrition and medical care, women in the richest countries live almost twice as long as those in the poorest parts of the world.

Discrimination against girls is pervasive in all countries, but it is arguably more profound in some developing countries where female children get less health care, less education, and even less food compared to male children. In some por-tions of the Third World, if a female survives infancy, she will most likely grow up on a diet that does not meet her nutritional needs. In Bangladesh, for example, research indicates that "boys under five years old were given 16 percent more food than girls that age and that girls were more likely to be malnourished in times of famine."[81] Similarly, in India, "boys are given more fatty and milky foods than girls. As a result, girls are four times more likely than boys to be suffering from acute malnutrition, but more than 40 times less likely to be taken to a hospital."[82] As a child, a girl will work several hours each day taking care of siblings and help-ing out around the house. Unlike her brothers, these tasks take precedence over school. She will most likely marry early in her teens, and her main role will be to raise as many children as her husband desires.[83] She will be the first to rise in the morning and the last to go to bed.

Infant mortality is a particularly good indicator of the health of a society since statistics on infant mortality tend to be more readily available than many other health indicators. According to Dr. Reed Tuckson, senior vice-president for the March of Dimes, "It's not only a measure of the medical system, but of the life of women in society during pregnancy."[84] In low-income countries, 113 children per 1000 died before age 5 in 1998. The rate drops to 7 per 1000 for high-income countries. Although infant mortality rates are lower among industrialized coun-tries, the United States has an unworthy record in this regard. Among rich coun-tries, it is worse than average, with a rate of 8 deaths per 1000.[85] As of June 2000, the disparity between blacks and whites within the United States had grown to 2.4 times the number of infant deaths, despite improvement in infant mortality rates.[86] Around the world, more than 35,000 children die each day from preventable dis-eases.[87] The tragically high rates of infant mortality that exist in the Third World are avoidable through simple medical interventions and preventive health meas-ures, such as immunization, better hygiene, and safe drinking water.

REPRODUCTIVE ISSUES

Combined illnesses and deaths from complications of pregnancy, childbirth, unsafe abortion, diseases of the reproductive tract, and the improper use of contraceptive methods top the list of health threats to women of reproductive age worldwide. According to the World Health Organization (WHO),[88] approximately 1600 women die each day from complications during pregnancy or childbirth. These deaths are highest among poor women: Almost 90 percent occur in Asia and sub-Saharan Africa, less than 1 percent in the developed world.[89] Hospital- and community-based data from Latin America point to unsafe abortion as the leading killer of women in their twenties and thirties in six countries, and the second cause of death in another six.[90] A recent study of maternal mortality in seventy-nine less developed countries indicated that women's status, as measured by education relative to men, age at first marriage, and reproductive autonomy, is a strong predictor of maternal mortality.[91] For every woman who dies, many others are left with illnesses or impairments that rob them of their health and productivity. Even within industrialized nations, economically disadvantaged women suffer the highest rates of complications from pregnancy, sexually transmitted diseases (STDs), and reproductive cancers.

In the late 1980s, the Women's Health Movement in Latin America campaigned vigorously against maternal deaths, calling attention to the issue of preventable deaths, the need for safe birth control, and the poverty of many Third World women. The data collected by this movement illuminated the depth of the problems some women confront. In Brazil, for example, only forty-nine public hospital beds were available for a population of over 2 million people in the southern part of San Paulo. As a result, 100 women died per 100,000 births in that city.[92] An appalling example of maternal mortality comes from Peru, where the leading cause of maternal death is hemorrhaging before or after childbirth. Dr. Cervantes, a Peruvian physician, noted that half of women who die of hemorrhage are treated in hospitals with fewer than fifty beds. He continues: "If we ask what these hospitals have in common, it is that they have no blood bank. It is quite simple—the mothers die because they go to hospitals not equipped to give them blood transfusions."[93]

Costa Rica offers an instructive contrast. Its health authorities attempted to end all preventable maternal deaths, and in fact lowered the maternal mortality rate to 22 deaths per 100,000. This is explained by the simple fact that "91 percent of women in this Central American nation receive pre-natal care and give birth in hospitals."[94] In Guatemala, where less than one-fourth of births take place in hospitals, 115 deaths occur per 100,000 women, making the official maternal mortality rate in this country one of the highest in Latin America. Actual figures are likely to be even higher given that many rural deaths are never registered.[95] The key is the medical care pregnant women receive.

Several threats to reproductive health transcend classification solely by economic class. The rapid spread of STDs, the restricted range of contraceptive choices, and the lack of access to safe abortion services are of concern to every woman. For the past decade, well deserved attention has been paid to the global spread of the HIV virus and its deadly consequence—AIDS. Worldwide, women accounted for 42 percent of the 21 million adults living with HIV.[96] The Feminist Women's Health Center reports that AIDS is the leading cause of death among African-American and Hispanic women ages 25 to 44 in the United States. These two groups of women accounted for 76 percent of the new AIDS cases among women in the United States in 1996. Significantly, women are 33 percent more likely to die than men because treatment begins so much later, if at all.[97] This attention to AIDS has, however, obscured what some observers regard as a more widespread, equally devastating epidemic—reproductive tract infections, which cause more deaths among women. The International Women's Health Coalition is calling for attention to this neglected and serious aspect of women's health.[98] Poverty among women contributes to prostitution—and thus sexually transmitted diseases—in many urban areas worldwide. Similarly, poverty, drug problems, and prostitution create high rates of sexually transmitted diseases among low-income U.S. populations. Syphilis is an example of an STD that can be life-threatening if untreated.[99] Although the number of people with syphilis has been decreasing, higher rates prevail among certain U.S. groups including women ages 20 to 24.[100]

Many of these medical problems do not require technological solutions, but instead are connected with inferior social status. Lack of access to basic health care is the fundamental reason women suffer and die from illnesses that could be prevented even in the poorest countries. In many developing countries, health objectives emphasize reducing population growth and the high rates of infant and child mortality, but little attention is paid to the health of women themselves. International agencies have begun to address this issue, but more attention is needed.

SOCIAL INTEGRATION

The status of women may be measured not only by their paid and unpaid labor and by health care issues, but also by their participation in centers of power in the corporation, government, and other decision-making bodies. Our earlier discussion of women in the professions indicates that significant disparity exists between women and men. Here I will elaborate on that. In corporations, women are seldom in the top positions of the boards of directors, law partners, or high-level financiers. Optimistic assessments of women's progress has exaggerated the extent of women's integration and their opportunities in managerial ranks. As mentioned earlier, women comprised only 7 percent of the total number of seats on corporate boards in the United States in 1995, and currently head only three companies of the Fortune 500.

Giscombe and Sims[101] observe that although women of color are 23 percent of the U.S. female workforce, they comprise only 15 percent of women in managerial positions in the private sector. African-American women are the most underrepresented at 12 percent of the female workforce as a whole, but only 7 percent of these select positions. Similarly, Hispanic women are 7 percent of females in the workforce, and 5.2 percent of managers; Asian women 3.6 percent of the female workforce and only 2.5 percent of female managers. This reflects both the racial and gender discrimination that women of color encounter. As Giscombe and Sims[102] point out, all women managers, including white women, earn less than their male counterparts even within their racial subgroups: "For every dollar white male managers in the private sector earn, white women earn 59 cents, men of color earn 75 cents, and women of color, on average, earn 57 cents."

A similar lack of integration is evident in terms of government positions: Of the 192 countries in the United Nations, five are headed by women.[103] Few countries have more than 30 percent female representatives. Sweden is among the highest with 38 percent of its Parliament comprised of women in the year 2000. From 1917 to 1980, thirteen women served in the U.S. Senate and of those, seven were appointed to fill a vacancy. As of 2000, women accounted for only 13 percent of the seats in the House of Representatives and 9 percent in the Senate. With the 2001 elections, women made slight gains of three seats in the House and four in the Senate. The major positions of president, vice president, and speaker of the house have never had female incumbents. In 1999, only three women were among the fifty state governors, and only sixteen women were mayors of the 100 largest U.S. cities.

Women seldom appear in the top levels of labor unions, even though their participation in unions is sizeable, nor are they typically among the decision makers in the large foundations. Although women now account for half of all journalists in the United States, they are rarely editors. They made up 16 percent of television news directors in the top 100 media markets in the United States in 1996.[104] Women writers fared somewhat better, comprising 22 percent of primetime television writing staffs in 1996.[105] As mentioned earlier, women now comprise over 40 percent of graduates from law school.[106] This is genuine progress, but women have remained in middle range positions in law, concentrated in "appropriate" specialties such as family, estate, divorce, and poverty law. They remain a minority of partners in major law firms. In New York, for example, women comprise 41 percent of associates, but fewer than 14 percent of law partners.[107] It was a momentous event when Sandra Day O'Connor was appointed to the Supreme Court, but women accounted for only 20 percent of all federal district court judges in 2001, and only 20 percent of full professors at law schools.[108] They are still underrepresented among full professors at U.S. universities, accounting for 19.3 percent of the total in 2000.[109]

In sum, despite the significant advances women have made on certain fronts, they are effectively excluded from the very centers of power that make decisions concerning their lives. In the United States, for example, power is vested in the hands of a relatively small minority of elite white males who hold the overwhelming majority of key positions in government, the labor market, the educational establishment, and the mass media.

EDUCATION

Throughout the world, women have made some of their greatest gains in terms of an emphasis on their education as well as educational attainment. U.S. women, for example, are on a par with or surpass men in virtually all educational categories, including college graduation.[110] Nonetheless, significant gender differences remain, and some women have fared better than others. In terms of high-school graduation, for example, approximately 80 percent of white women received degrees in 1994, whereas 75 percent of black women achieved this level of education.[111] In major U.S. cities, high-school dropout rates for black and Hispanic females are often high. On the other hand, Asian women have achieved high levels of education, in part because Asian immigrants tend to be from families of high social status in their countries of origin.[112] In 1996, according to the Department of Labor, 80 percent of Asian and Pacific Islander women had a high-school diploma.[113] Great disparities exist between and among nations in terms of education: In Sweden virtually all school-age girls attend school, but in developing countries the majority of girls do not. Indeed millions of girls worldwide are denied the right to education, and this effectively means they are consigned to early marriage and, often, powerlessness.[114]

Despite the increasing educational levels of Western women, these achievements have not had the same impact as they have had for men. In the United States, the financial rewards for women are consistently lower than those of men with similar educational backgrounds. As Taeuber[115] puts it, "Equal educational attainment and job experience do not lead to equal pay for many women." A U.S. woman with a university degree will earn less in her lifetime than a man who does not finish secondary school. Similarly, women with full-time jobs and high-school diplomas earn less than comparable men who had not completed elementary school.[116] According to the Bureau of Labor Statistics, among 1993 college graduates, women earned 73 percent as much as men.[117] Men's and women's jobs require equal amounts of education, but women's jobs tend to provide less training, less mobility, and little supervision of other workers.[118]

Employment within the educational system itself demonstrates gender inequality. In the United States, women represent the large majority of primary school teachers, but they are seldom principals or heads of departments. As we have seen, this discrimination persists even at the highest levels of the educational system. After a five year study, MIT's School of Science concluded that its women professors had lower salaries and less office space than their male counterparts.[119] As a result, MIT raised women's salaries and increased research money and laboratory space for female faculty.

CONCLUSION

Most observers agree that in the past twenty-five years women have made considerable improvements in terms of their legal status throughout the world, they have entered paid labor in unprecedented numbers, and they have in some cases improved their levels of education. Women, however, have yet to achieve economic equality with men in any country, and their representation in the highest seats of government rarely exceeds a small minority. The success of some women in certain countries, the United States among them, has been hailed as a sign of great progress for women. But despite improvements, persisting inequality exists between women and men (and among women themselves) in terms of occupations, wages, power, and education. Women are still socially subordinate to men and are faced with unequal cultural expectations regarding paid and unpaid labor. In some countries (like Norway and Sweden), women have made impressive gains, but the vast majority of the world's women have not. Most U.S. women are still clustered in sales, clerical, or service jobs; race and class often exacerbate this inequality. Ultimately, the most privileged groups maintain their monopoly on prestigious U.S. occupations.[120] Cockcroft[121] summarizes the broader context: "UN and other global estimates show women providing two-thirds of the hours of work, earning one-tenth of the world's income, and possessing less than one-hundredth of the world's wealth."

Major technological developments have yet to alter these blunt facts regarding the social status of women. Economic and political inequality has remained entrenched in crucial respects. These conditions are difficult if not impossible to reconcile with optimistic claims regarding the "revolutionary" impact of technology on women.

We turn now to a more focused analysis of the problems women confront regarding specific technologies.

NOTES

1. Janet Saltzman Chafetz, *Feminist Sociology An Overview of Contemporary Theories* (Itasca, IL: F.E. Peacock Publishers, 1988).

2. Teresa Amott and Julie Matthaei, *Race, Gender, and Work: A Multicultural Economic History of Women in the United States* (Boston: South End Press, 1996); Doris Anderson, *The Unfinished Revolution: The Status of Women in Twelve Countries* (Toronto: Doubleday Canada Limited, 1991); James D. Cockcroft, "Gendered Class Analysis: Internationalizing, Feminizing, and Latinizing Labor's Class Struggle in the Americas," *Latin American Perspectives*, Vol. 25 (November 1998): 42–74; Winnie Hazou, *The Social and Legal Status of Women* (New York: Praeger, 1990).

3. María Patricia Fernandez-Kelly and Kathleen M. Fallon, "How Is Globalization Affecting Inequalities Between Women and Men?" In *Sociology for a New Century* (Boston: Pine Forge Press, 2001), 240.

4. Paula England and Irene Browne, "Trends in Women's Economic Status," *Sociological Perspectives*, Vol. 35 (1992): 18.

5. Howard N. Fullerton, "Labor Force Participation: 75 Years of Change, 1950–98 and 1998–2025," *Monthly Labor Review*, Vol. 122 (December 1999): 3.

6. Randy Albeda, "Improving Women's Employment in the U.S.A.," *Industrial Relations Journal*, Vol. 28 (December 1997): 275–282.

7. U.S. Bureau of Labor Statistics. Usual Weekly Earnings Summary: First Quarter 2000, *Labor Force Statistics from the Current Population Survey* (Washington, D.C.: U.S. Government Printing Office, 2000).

8. Fernández-Kelly and Fallon, "How Is Globalization Affecting Inequalities Between Women and Men?" 259–260.

9. Hilda Scott, *Working Your Way to the Bottom: The Feminization of Poverty* (London: Pandora Press, 1984), 304.

10. Francoise Core, "The Continuing Saga of Labour Market Segregration," *OECD Observer*, March 1999, 42–43.

11. *WIN News*, "Commission on the Status of Women," Vol. 26 (Spring 2000): 2.

12. Fernández-Kelly and Fallon, "How Is Globalization Affecting Inequalities," 260.

13. Irene Natividad and Jenny Lauth, eds., *Contingent Employment of Women Workers in Japan, the Philippines, and the United States* (Washington D.C.: The Philippine American Foundation, 1999), 45.

14. Natividad and Lauth, *Contingent Employment of Women.*

15. U.S. Department of Labor. Women's Bureau, *Working Women Count! A Report to the Nation: Executive Summary* (Washington, D.C.: U.S. Government Printing Office, 1994): 3.

16. Miriam B. Gottesfeld, "The Worker's Paradise Lost: The Role and Status of Russian and American Women in the Workplace," *Comparative Labor Law Journal*, Vol. 14 (Fall 1992): 81.

17. Albeda, "Improving Women's Employment," 275.

18. Fernández-Kelly and Fallon, "How Is Globalization Affecting Inequalities Between Women and Men?" 239.

19. Barbara H. Wootton, "Gender Differences in Occupational Employment," *Monthly Labor Review*, Vol. 120 (April 1997).

20. http://www.dol.gov/dol/wb/public/wb_pubs/20lead99.htm

21. http://www.bis.gov/opub/ted/1999/jun/wk2/art04.htm

22. Barbara Reskin and Naomi Cassirer, "Occupational Segregation by Gender, Race, and Ethnicity," *Sociological Focus*, Vol. 29 (August 1996): 231.

23. Cynthia Taeuber, *Statistical Handbook on Women in America* (Phoenix, AZ: Onyx Press, 1996), 75.

24. England and Browne, "Trends in Women's Economic Status," 23.

25. Amott and Matthaei, *Race, Gender, and Work*, 347.

26. Reskin and Cassirer, "Occupational Segregation," 241.

27. F. Nii-Amoo Dodoo and Patricia Kasari, "Race and Occupational Location in America," *Journal of Black Studies*, Vol. 25 (March 1995): 473.

28. Amott and Matthaei, *Race, Gender, and Work,* 86.

29. England and Browne, "Trends in Women's Economic Status," 26.

30. http://www.bis.gov/opub/mir/1999/12/art2exc.htm

31. Albeda, "Improving Women's Employment," 277.

32. *PS: Political Science and Politics*, "Females Match or Exceed Males in Educational Achievement," Vol. 33 (December 2000): 944.

33. Taeuber, *Statistical Handbook*, 75.

34. http://www.census.gov/Press-Release/www/1999/cb99–77.html

35. Hilda Scott, *"Working Your Way to the Bottom": The Feminization of Poverty* (London: Paudora Press, 1984): 3.

36. Ibid., 14.

37. Francine D. Blau, *Trends in the Well-Being of American Women, 1970–1995* (Cambridge: National Bureau of Economic Research, 1997), 12.

38. Ibid., 50.

39. Harold Benenson, "Women's Occupational and Family Achievement in the U.S. Class System," *The British Journal of Sociology*, Vol. 35 (March 1984): 19–40.

40. Ibid., 21, 35.

41. Mary E. Guy, "Three Steps Forward, Two Steps Backward: The Status of Women. Integration into Public Management," *Public Administration Review*, Vol. 53 (July/August 1993): 290.

42. Ibid., 290.

43. *Annual Report on the Economic Status of the Profession 1999–2000*, American Association of University Professors Survey Database, 2000.

44. *Poughkeepsie Journal*, "More Women Make Leap to Corporate Boards," 19 April 1995, 9A.

45. Fernández-Kelly and Fallon, "How Is Globalization Affecting Inequalities Between Women and Men?" 258.

46. *Research Alert*, "Women Account for Less Than 20% of Executive Positions in Fortune 500 Companies," Vol. 18 (16 February 2001): 8.

47. K.C. Neel, "Still a Man's Club," *Cable World*, Vol. 13 (29 January 2001): 46.

48. http://www.dol.gov/dol/wb/public/wb_pubs/bwlf97.htm

49. http://www.census.gov/hhes/poverty/histpov/hstpov7.html

50. http://www.census.gov/hhes/poverty/poverty98/pv98est1.html

51. Vilma Ortiz, "Women of Color: A Demographic Overview." In *Women of Color in U.S. Society* (Philadelphia: Temple University Press, 1994), 25.

52. http://www.census.gov/hhes/poverty/poverty98/pv98est1.html

53. http://www.bls.gov/opub/ted/1999/sept/wk2/art04.htm

54. Amott and Matthaei, *Race, Gender, and Work,* 249.

55. Ibid., 450.

56. http://www.census.gov/hhes/poverty/poverty98/pv98est1.html

57. Children's Defense Fund (CDF), *CDF Reports: Priority Agenda for Children,* July 1994, 7.

58. http://www.childrensdefense.org/release000926.htm

59. CDF, *CDF Reports: Priority Agenda for Children,* 6.

60. CDF, *CDF Reports: Births to Teens,* December 1994, 9.

61. Scott, "Working Your Way to the Bottom," x.

62. Blau, *Trends in the Well-Being;* Toni Calasanti and Carol Bailey, "Gender Inequality and the Division of Household Labor in the United States and Sweden: A Socialist-Feminist Approach," *Social Problems,* Vol. 38 (February 1991): 34–53; Scott Coltrane and Masako Ishii-Kuntz, "Men's Housework: A Life Course Perspective," *Journal of Marriage and the Family,* Vol. 54 (February 1992): 43–57; Terri L. Orbuch and Sandra L. Eyster, "Division of Household Labor Among Black Couples and White Couples," *Social Forces,* Vol. 76 (September 1997): 301–332; Steven Stark, "Housekeeping Today: Just a Lick and a Promise," *The New York Times,* 20 August 1987, C6.

63. Taeuber, *Statistical Handbook,* 2.

64. *WIN News,* "Counting Women's Unwaged Work," Vol. 19 (Autumn 1993): 78.

65. http://www.dol.gov/dol/wb/public/wb_pubs/wwmfl.htm

66. *Marketing to Women,* "Among U.S. Women of Child-Bearing Age, 19.2% Had No Health Coverage in 1999," Vol. 14 (10 January 2001).

67. *Marketing to Women,* "Among U.S. Women."

68. Ruth E. Zambrana, "A Research Agenda on Issues Affecting Poor and Minority Women: A Model for Understanding Their Health Needs," *Women and Health,* Vol. 12 (1988): 142.

69. Ibid., 149.

70. Judy Scales-Trent, "Women of Color and Health: Issues of Gender, Community, and Power," *Stanford Law Review,* Vol. 43 (July 1991): 1361–1362.

71. Ibid., 1366.

72. Taeuber, *Statistical Handbook,* 5.

73. Saunders, "Atlas of Racial Health Inequalities," *Patient Care,* 15 May 2000, 18.

74. *Jet,* "Why Exercise Should Be Important to Women," 13 March 2000, 46.

75. http://www.cdc.gov/nchs/products/pub/pubd/hus/2010/98chtbk.htm

76. Saunders, "Atlas of Racial Health."

77. Ruth H. Gordon-Bradshaw, "A Social Essay on Special Issues Facing Poor Women of Color," *Women and Health,* Vol. 12 (1988): 250.

78. Taeuber, *Statistical Handbook,* 165.

79. Jodi Jacobson, *Women's Reproductive Health: The Silent Emergency,* Worldwatch Paper 102, Worldwatch Institute (1991), 22.

80. Ibid., 25.

81. U.S. Agency for International Development, "Agency Emphasizes Women in Development," *USAID Highlights,* Vol. 7 (Winter 1990): 3.

82. Ibid., 3.

83. Jacobson, *Women's Reproductive Health,* 17–18.

84. Philip Hilts, "Life Expectancy for Blacks in U.S. Shows Sharp Drop," *The New York Times,* 29 November 1990, B17.

85. York W. Bradshaw, "How Can Sociology Help Us Understand Global Trends?" In *Sociology for A New Century* (Boston: Pine Ridge Press, 2000), 31.

86. Leslie Berger, "A Racial Gap in Infants Death, and a Search for Reasons," *The New York Times*, 25 June 2000, 13.

87. Bradshaw, "How Can Sociology Help Us," 30.

88. World Health Organization (WHO), *World Health Day Highlights Scandal of 600,000 Maternal Deaths Each Year* (New York: World Health Organization, 336 Press Release, 1998).

89. WHO, *World Health Day Highlights Scandal.*

90. Jacobson, *Women's Reproductive Health*, 9.

91. Ce Shen and John B. Williams, "Maternal Mortality, Women's Status, and Economic Dependency in Less Developed Countries," *Social Science and Medicine*, Vol. 49 (July 1999): 197.

92. Regina Rodriguez, "Maternal Mortality and Morbidity: From Tragedy to Prevention," *Women's Health Journal*, Vol. 35 (1990): 37.

93. Ibid., 47.

94. Ibid., 41.

95. Ibid., 43.

96. http://www.avert.org/womenid.htm

97. http://www.fwhc.org/hiv.htm

98. Peggy Antrobus et al., "Challenging the Culture of Silence: Building Alliances to End Reproductive Tract Infections," *WIN News*, Vol. 21 (Winter 1995): 27.

99. Brian Pace, "Syphilis," *JAMA, The Journal of the American Medical Association*, Vol. 284 (July 2000): 520.

100. *Journal of the American Medical Association*, "Primary and Secondary Syphilis–United States, 1998," Vol. 282 (10 November 1999): 1715.

101. Katherine Giscombe and Adrienne D. Sims, "Breaking the Color Barrier," *HR Focus*, Vol. 75 (July 1998): S9.

102. Ibid., S10.

103. Fernández-Kelly and Fallon, "How Is Globalization Affecting Inequalities," 267.

104. Lou Prato, "Women Move Up in TV Newsrooms," *American Journalism Review*, Vol. 18 (November 1996): 48.

105. T.L. Stanley, "Only One of 4 Behind Camera Is Female," *Media Week*, Vol. 6 (18 November 1996): 28.

106. U.S.Bureau of the Census. Education, *Statistical Abstract of the United States: 1999* (Washington, D.C.: U.S. Government Printing Office, 1999).

107. Jonathan Glater, "Women Are Close to Being Majority of Law Students," *The New York Times*, 26 March 2001, A1, A16.

108. Ibid.

109. *Annual Report*, 2000.

110. *PS: Political Science and Politics*, "Females Match or Exceed Males."

111. Taeuber, *Statistical Handbook*, 165.

112. Ortiz, "Women of Color," 26.

113. http://www.dol.gov/dol/wb/public/wb_pubs/asian97.htm

114. *WIN News*, "Commission on the Status of Women."

115. Taeuber, *Statistical Handbook*, 73.

116. Guy, "Three Steps Forward," 287.

117. http://www.bis.gov/opub/mir/1998/03/art5abs.htm

118. England and Browne, "Trends in Women's Economic Status."

119. Samar Farah, "Women Professors Still Face Hurdles," *Christian Science Monitor*, 6 February 2001, 12.

120. Reskin and Cassirer, "Occupational Segregation."

121. Cockcroft, "Gendered Class Analysis," 42.

5

Reproductive Technology and the Politics of Social Control

❖ ❖ ❖ ❖ ❖ ❖

A movement narrowly concerned with pregnancy and birth which does not ask questions and demand answers about the lives of children, the priorities of government; a movement in which individual families rely on consumerism and educational privilege to supply their own children with good nutrition, schooling, health care, while perceiving itself as progressive or alternative, exist only as a minor contradiction within a society most of whose children grow up in poverty and which places its highest priority on the technology of war.
Adrienne Rich

Reproductive technology may be defined as including "all forms of biomedical intervention and 'help' a woman may encounter when she considers having–or not having–a child."[1] This encompasses at least three general categories: first, alternative means to heterosexual reproduction (including artificial insemination, *in vitro* fertilization, and cloning); second, fetal monitoring (which entails all the attempts to safeguard, change, or even predetermine the fetus–prenatal screening, prenatal surgery, and sex determination); and third, technologies that aim to prevent or terminate pregnancies (such as condoms, diaphragms, intrauterine devices, and injectable contraceptives). This chapter will focus on selected technologies within each of these three broad categories.

Let me clarify my purposes. I am not offering an assessment of all the new reproductive technologies, but instead discussing a range of them to indicate some of the problems they entail and the necessity of a critical analysis. As we have seen in Chapter 3, the media often portray reproductive technologies in terms of their benefits: They reportedly help infertile women bear children, they improve women's lives and are administered for their own good and at their insistence, and they expand choice and give women increasing freedom and control. In fact reproductive technologies *have* brought benefits to the lives of many women. Ruth Cowan[2] notes that "the pill," for example, brought significant positive results. It enabled people to discuss contraception, it increased tolerance for an explicit discussion of sexuality, and it permitted premarital sexual activity without the risk of pregnancy. But the popularized image of reproductive technology in general as benefiting everyone ignores the larger social context, as well as the negative aspects of particular technologies. While acknowledging benefits associated with reproductive technologies, this chapter focuses on the more puzzling problems associated with them, particularly in light of gender, race, and class inequalities. To this end, we will look at a range of innovations (including artificial insemination, *in vitro* fertilization embryo transfer, sex selection techniques, and contraception) and discuss issues and concerns that have been raised about them (such as commercialization, potential health risks, coercive use, and deceptive practice regarding them). We will see that various forms of technology have problematic aspects for many women and differential impacts on various groups of women, all of which must be considered in any assessment of reproductive technology.

Reproductive rights have been fiercely contested in the United States for at least 150 years. As early as the 1840s, a vigorous anti-abortion campaign led by physicians succeeded in criminalizing abortion and restricting the power and influence of midwives and other so-called "non-professionals." The 1870s, on the other hand, saw the emergence of a feminist social movement that favored birth control. Although this movement attempted to give women more autonomy over sexual activity, it did so merely by insisting that a woman has a right to refuse sex within marriage. In the early twentieth century, a second birth control campaign advocated not only legal contraception but sexual freedom as well, asserting a woman's right to engage in sex, and thus suggesting a separation between reproduction and sexuality. The 1960s brought heightened interest, demand, and controversy regarding birth control and reproductive rights, which persists today.

Although pro–birth-control campaigns are usually depicted as liberal attempts to expand birth control rights for all women, they in fact often privileged white, heterosexual, middle-class women and also appealed to unexpectedly conservative political causes. For example, birth control was advocated by the Eugenics Movement with blatantly racist overtones as to who was fit or unfit to reproduce; by Population Control Movements, which had little interest in the rights of women in general let alone women of color; and Planned Parenthood, which was equally unconcerned about women's rights in the early nineteenth century and emphasized instead the strengthening of a very traditional nuclear family.[3] Thus significant complexities and apparent contradictions have marked the struggle for reproductive rights in the United States. While opinions have diverged passionately on birth control and abortion rights, more noteworthy is the fact that birth control has been integral to women's rights and part of their struggle for self-determination, while simultaneously a weapon of racism and profoundly conservative impulses. Current developments in reproductive technology similarly hold radical possibilities for enhancing women's lives, but also pose the threat of increasing divisiveness and control over women's choices. The negative aspects of these developments must be analyzed and understood. We begin by reviewing some alternative means to heterosexual reproduction, and problems associated with them.

ARTIFICIAL INSEMINATION

The simplest of the alternatives to reproduction through sexual intercourse is artificial insemination (AI). The process entails having a man ejaculate into a clean container, drawing the semen into a clean syringe, and injecting it into a woman's vagina. AI takes two forms: artificial insemination by one's husband (AIH) and by a donor (AID). The first successful attempt at AIH occurred as early as 1790 through the work of a Scottish doctor, John Hunter. Although AIH was practiced on a limited basis in Western Europe and the United States during the nineteenth century, the first reported instance of AID didn't occur until almost a hundred years later. As recently as the 1940s, AI was still relatively rare. It gained somewhat in popularity, however, and by the 1950s frozen sperm began to be used to produce a child. The first commercial sperm bank opened in the 1970s in Maryland. By the 1990s, approximately 60,000 to 80,000 women were undergoing artificial insemination each year in the United States and Canada.[4]

Given the technological simplicity of AI and public assertions as to the significance of personal choice, one might assume that it is available to all women in the United States. Since it does not involve sexual intercourse, it could, for example, be a great boon to single women and lesbians who are interested in conceiving children. AI, however, remains largely under medical control and is in fact highly restricted. Physicians choose who becomes a donor as well as a recipient.[5] Most U.S. clinics and physicians will not accept a client unless she is married or in a stable relationship with a man, although barriers for single women are diminishing, at least in larger metropolitan areas.[6] Deborah Steinberg's[7] survey of AID clinics in Great Britain demonstrated that services are limited to "heterosexual women and of these women, almost exclusively to married women or women in marriage-like domestic arrangements." She noted that most clinics were "decidedly hostile" to unmarried women and especially to lesbians. DeLair[8] discusses the significant barriers lesbians continue to face regarding access to artificial insemination in the United States, particularly physician discrimination. Disabled women are often denied access to this technology as well. Two infertility counselors wrote to *The Lancet* in 1991 expressing concern about giving a virgin access to AID. The 32-year-old woman had no plans for romantic involvement, and the counselors worried that her "resolutely single status" would jeopardize the psychosexual development of her future child. Their clinic agreed and demanded additional counseling for the woman.[9] Law professor Dorothy Roberts[10] observes that laws regulating AI "contemplate use by a married woman and recognition of her husband as the child's father." Significantly, "courts have been willing to grant parental rights to sperm donors against the mothers wishes 'when no other man is playing the role of father for the child,' such as when the mother is a lesbian or unmarried."[11]

A U.S. government report on artificial insemination confirms that many clinics routinely refuse to provide some women with the procedure. "The most common reason that physicians have rejected requests is that the patient is considered unsuitable for nonmedical reasons: She is unmarried (52 percent), psychologically immature (22 percent), homosexual (15 percent), or welfare dependent (15 percent)."[12] Half of physicians are likely to reject an unmarried woman even if she has a male partner. Without a male partner, her chances of rejection rise to 61 percent; if she is a lesbian, rejection increases to 63 percent.[13] Thus, AI is not available to all women, but restricted by physicians to the types of women deemed appropriate. This control is somewhat ironic since clinicians themselves are not required to have any special training or license to practice.[14] AI is generally safe, although seven women in the United States and twelve women worldwide have been infected with HIV through tainted donor's sperm.[15] The infections occurred before IVF testing became available, and now the Centers for Disease Control recommends that the donor be tested, the sperm frozen for six months, and the donor tested again. As Guinan[16] points out in *The Journal of the American Medical Association*, however, these recommendations are not mandatory and it is uncertain which clinics adhere to them.

Women's health groups have worked to make artificial insemination by a donor available to a wider range of women. The Oakland Feminist Women's Health Center, for example, established its own sperm bank and accepts any woman regardless of her marital status, sexual preference, or disability.[17] This health center aims to demedicalize the procedure and give women more control over their reproductive functions by accepting a variety of women and by encouraging them to inseminate themselves. Obviously, however, gender inequality as well as homophobia are evident in the more common implementation of this technology, with access only for those women who are in relationships with men. Thus it is not typically promoting alternative lifestyles for women nor revolutionizing gender roles.

IN VITRO FERTILIZATION (IVF)

It is technologically possible for a child to be conceived outside a woman's body, in a laboratory dish, and then implanted in her uterus. Research aiming to permit conception "*in vitro*" (in glass) rather than "*in vivo*" (in the body) began in 1879 in Vienna. One hundred years later two British doctors, Patrick Steptoe and Robert Edwards, successfully used the procedure to produce a human being. Louise Brown, born in Britain in 1978, was the world's first "test-tube baby": the first child born through a process known as *in vitro* fertilization. The event caused a worldwide media sensation; it seemed to many that a new era in reproduction had begun.

Initially used to treat women with blocked or damaged fallopian tubes, IVF now extends to a much wider range of fertility problems, including cases where the causes of infertility are unknown. Since the first "test-tube baby" was born in the United States in 1981, IVF has rapidly expanded in this country and throughout much of the industrialized world.[18] By 1984, there were over 200 IVF teams worldwide.[19] By 1987, 150 units in the United States alone had produced at least 4000 IVF babies.[20] By 1996, 26,000 IVF babies had been born in the United States.[21]

IVF is a complicated medical process. It involves making an incision in a woman's abdomen while she is under general anesthesia, and inserting an instrument called a laparoscope. This instrument is outfitted with a lens and a light to enable the doctor to find a mature egg and remove it through suction with a needle. Eggs may also be removed with a long, thin needle inserted through the vagina into the ovary when the woman is under light anesthesia. After removal the egg is placed in a special nutrient formula in a petri dish. About two days after it is fertilized with sperm, it is placed in a woman's uterus through the cervix and if it implants, a pregnancy is underway.

IVF raises startling possibilities and provides the basis for far more controversial technologies, including "the freezing of human embryos for research use, the donation of an embryo from one woman to another, surrogate motherhood, sex selection, gene therapy for inherited diseases, and ultimately, genetic engineering of basic human traits."[22] Once fertilization occurs outside the womb we can entertain the possibility of creating human/animal hybrids, fertilizing, as Dr. Edwards speculated in 1971, a human egg with gorilla sperm.[23] The National Institute of Health has specifically proscribed attempts to make such hybrids, as well as the process of interspecies uterine transfer.[24] However, fertilization outside the womb more readily permits experimentation with embryos, and genetic engineering to develop specific traits. It is possible to produce several embryos, identify the genetic traits of each, and implant the "best" embryo.

The Jones Institute for Reproductive Medicine, associated with the Eastern Virginia Medical School, has developed a procedure called implantation genetic diagnosis (IGD). It begins with IVF, but when the embryos have divided to four or eight cells, one or two of the cells are removed for genetic testing. When the test results are in, defective embryos are discarded and the healthy ones are implanted in a woman. As of 1996, about seventy-six babies had been born through IGD and it had only been used for patients with serious genetic conditions.[25] In 1999, the International Working Group on Preimplantation Genetics[26] reported that approximately 200 children had been born worldwide following IGD. It may ultimately be possible to modify genetic ability, building in preferred qualities, and then implanting the embryo. Scientists may, for example, be able to produce increasingly intelligent people. Or, if some people are genetically inclined toward sadness, perhaps they may be modified to be more cheerful.

Whatever the future holds, IVF is certainly more complicated, more controversial, and riskier than artificial insemination. It involves the risks of anesthesia and the possibility of trauma to the ovaries because of the egg removal. It also entails hormonal treatments to induce superovulation so more eggs can be removed at the same time. These hormones may result in ovarian cysts, and their long-term effects are unknown. Ectopic pregnancies (when gestation occurs outside the uterus in a fallopian tube) are also more common with IVF—5 percent to 10 percent of pregnancies, compared to .5 percent to 1 percent in the general population.[27] IVF pregnancies tend to be extensively monitored, so women are subjected to the risks of ultrasound and amniocentesis. Ultrasound is of particular concern since it is used repeatedly during IVF pregnancies, and its long-term effects on the fetus are uncertain. Ruth Hubbard[28] notes that it took twenty to thirty years for epidemiological studies to establish the connection between prenatal X-rays and leukemia and other cancers. She speculates that there is no reason to think that the effects of the irradiation associated with ultrasound will be evaluated any more quickly. Since more than one fertilized egg is usually implanted in a woman, multiple births are frequent with IVF (1 in 250 compared to the usual 1 in 10,000). They are associated with higher risks of death and disability including "increased rates of miscarriage and premature birth, perinatal mortality, long-term morbidity."[29] "For this reason, most clinics advise what they delicately call 'selective reduction' of higher order multiple pregnancies . . . aborting the 'excess' fetuses after about two months' gestation."[30] IVF babies are also typically delivered by Caesarian section.

Beyond the health risks associated with IVF, it is highly invasive, expensive, and remarkably unsuccessful.[31] In the United States as a whole, only about one in five couples trying IVF wind up with a baby.[32] The success rate per attempt is about 19 percent for women under 40, while older women have a success rate of approximately 7 percent. The overall success rate reaches 25 percent only because many couples make repeated attempts, with a cost of about $8,000 to $10,000 per attempt.[33] The *New England Journal of Medicine* reported that only 10 percent to 15 percent of attempts result in live births.[34] Similarly, a 1987 study of ninety-six U.S. clinics indicated 13.1 live births per 100 treatment cycles; data reported in *The Lancet* for 1991 through 1994 established a live birth rate of 13.6 per 100.[35] IVF clinicians have tried to cast their successes as favorably as possible, but progress is slow to say the least. According to a 1992 study, one's chances of success actually decrease with each attempt, to 7 percent success on the third try.[36]

Many clinics have *never* had a live birth, and mounting evidence indicates that some of them are deceptive when dealing with their clients about this. Some define "success" in terms of *pregnancies* per laparoscopy and then claim a success rate of up to 25 percent although they have had no live births.[37] Dr. Moon H. Kim, an IVF program director at Ohio State University Medical Center, claims that some clinics give clients a general success rate for IVF, not the actual success rate for their particular clinic. According to Dr. Moon: "If patients were told, 'We have been doing this business for two years and as of today, we have not gotten any pregnancies,' it's hard to believe that any sane-minded patient would go there to subject herself to such an expensive procedure. So the fact that they *are* going through indicates that something is not told to them."[38] The comments of one woman in an IVF program illustrates this deception:

During our first interview, we spoke to a doctor and the nurse coordinator. They were extremely nice and supportive and gave us detailed information about the procedure and what to expect. They told us that the success rate for this procedure was about 17 percent. At that time I didn't realize that they hadn't had any successes at all, and that they had been doing it for only six months.[39]

Major medical centers have been implicated in these deceptive practices. In 1994, Mount Sinai Medical Center in New York was required to pay $4 million to hundreds of former IVF clients after exaggerating their success rates. They claimed a success rate of 20 percent whereas the actual delivery rate was 13.7 percent or 10.9 percent, depending on how it was measured.[40] (The lower rate is the percentage of live deliveries per treatment cycle.) Even pregnancy rates are misleading since 18 percent of them ultimately result in miscarriage. The first public indications of deceptive practices came in 1988, when a congressional report revealed that many IVF clinics were signing up patients without telling them that they had never had a live birth. In 1992, Congress passed a law requiring fertility clinics to collect and report success rates. "But the lawmakers never appropriated any money for those tasks, and the law remains unenforced today."[41]

Unfortunately, these problems with deception are not isolated instances. The IVF program at the University of California, San Francisco, for example, claimed a 30 percent success rate yet its pregnancy rate in 1993 was only 14 percent for women under 40, and 20 percent of these women may be expected to miscarry. The University of California's clinic at Irvine was closed down when the physician in charge was found to be falsifying records "to cover up the fact that he was taking some couples' eggs and embryos to give to other patients."[42]

Ultimately, the great majority of embryos simply fail to implant when inserted in a woman, and no one knows why. "Even in natural conception, many embryos—perhaps as many as 75 percent—fail to implant. Dramatically improving the success rate may not be possible."[43] Many women, buoyed by optimistic media reports, have high hopes of success when they enter IVF programs. They tend to be unaware that even when an IVF child is produced, there are higher rates of birth complications and possibly birth defects.[44] Remarkably, the United States has no federal rules or guidelines regulating the estimated 300 fertility clinics that generate about $2 billion per year.[45]

Although women undergoing IVF treatments at U.S. clinics consider themselves patients, they are perhaps more aptly described as experimental subjects.[46] Consider the women involved in the early IVF attempts. From 1971 to 1977, Steptoe and Edwards implanted embryos in 80 women, all to no avail. By the end of 1980, 278 women were known to have been involved in these procedures; 3 had given birth—a "success" rate of .04 percent. Moreover, Steptoe and Edwards had taken an extraordinary departure from typical scientific procedures: "They (and subsequent researchers) had not verified the safety of *in vitro* fertilization in primates before attempting it in women."[47] Prior to the birth of Louise Brown, the only successful IVF births were 200 rabbits, 200 mice, and 50 rats. As recently as

1993, a Royal Canadian Commission reviewed IVF worldwide and concluded: "Unproven and quite possibly ineffective procedures are being offered as medical treatment, and women are undertaking the risks of these procedures without knowing whether they are more likely to have a child than if they received no treatment."[48]

EMBRYOS: TO SELL, TRANSFER, OR FREEZE

Given the low success rates of IVF, some clinics, like Columbia-Presbyterian Medical Center in Manhattan, are offering their clients frozen embryos for $2750.[49] There are long waiting lists for the "adoption" of these embryos, and the number of births in the last few years from their implantation is unknown. People may turn to this procedure once their financial resources have been depleted through more expensive fertility treatments. Some embryos are specifically created by doctors for clients, others are extras from the treatment of other infertile couples.[50]

Since eggs from younger women improve the chances of success with IVF for women over 40, many American IVF clinics are also pursuing "egg donation." This process requires the donor to inject herself with drugs for about a month to stimulate the ovaries and produce more eggs. Under anesthesia, the women's eggs are removed with a long needle inserted through her vagina. Arthur Caplan, director of the Center for Bioethics at the University of Pennsylvania, has bluntly asked, "Why are we calling it egg donation? It's egg sale. Would anyone be doing it if there was no payment involved?"[51] In fact, in the United States, compensation is the norm, which has led fertility specialists in Israel (which restricts egg donation) to buy donor eggs from abroad, primarily from the United States.

Physicians encourage couples to choose egg donors who are similar to them,[52] but recipients may choose a donor based on whatever they regard as important. Given a shortage of donors, infertility clinics and private individuals may advertise to find a donor and often do so in newspapers at elite colleges and universities.[53] To the dismay of many at Vassar College, such an ad appeared in its student newspaper, *The Miscellany News*, in the Spring of 1999. An "academic couple" from the Boston area was seeking an egg donor, 19 to 29 years old, for an East Coast clinic. The ad was remarkably specific: "Caucasian, dark-hair and complexion, over 5' 7," even-featured face, minimum SAT's 1300, lean/athletic build, excellent health/skin/eyesight. Describe background, education, and motivation, along with several photos." The "right candidate" was promised compensation of approximately $10,000, which is high since most egg donors are paid $1500 to $3000.[54] In 1994, almost 2000 IVF patients used donor eggs,[55] and currently the regulation of egg donation is "virtually nonexistent."[56]

It is also possible to wash an embryo from a pregnant woman and transfer it to another woman. With embryo transfer (ET), an infertile woman who cannot conceive may now carry and deliver her husband's genetically related fetus. The process again entails matching two women for appearance and menstrual cycle (done through hormonal treatments); the donor woman is then artificially insem-inated with the sperm of the infertile woman's husband. After five days, the embryo is flushed from her body with about two ounces of fluid that is injected into her uterus and removed with a catheter (a procedure called a uterine lavage). The embryo is then implanted in the infertile woman. In January of 1984, the first baby was born through this procedure. Conceived in one woman, the fetus was flushed from her body and reimplanted in another woman. The resulting baby boy was delivered at Harbor-UCLA Medical Center in Torrance, California through Caesarian section. Compared to IVF, this procedure is simpler and less invasive, and it has the advantage that the fetus has been conceived naturally. However, it still entails serious risks, particularly for the donor. The donor may remain pregnant if the embryo implants in her and cannot be flushed out. This has occurred on at least three occasions, and the donor was expected to have an abor-tion under these circumstances.[57] She also risks pelvic infection from the lavage, as well as the serious possibility of an ectopic pregnancy if the embryo gets washed up the oviduct during the lavage. The infertile woman also risks an ectopic preg-nancy from the transfer, and the unknown hazards of carrying a fetus that is genet-ically unrelated to her. Despite these risk factors, the cost, although less than IVF, is still approximately $3000 per cycle.

Embryo transfer permits an evaluation of the genetic makeup of embryos. Gena Corea[58] grimly warns that, "it may be possible to flush the embryos out of every single woman in the obstetrician's office as part of routine prenatal care, test it for every known genetic and metabolic defect and then if—and only if—the embryo is perfect, return that embryo to the woman's womb." The doctors who developed the procedure, Randolph Seed and Richard Seed, in fact support this idea and contend that ET could eliminate most birth defects.

As may be apparent from our discussion of frozen embryos, a woman may now conceive a fetus, have it washed from her body, frozen, and then reimplanted if and when she chooses. Alternatively, embryos created *in vitro* may be frozen rather than implanted. The technology to freeze human embryos began develop-ing in 1976, and Australian researchers produced the world's first "freeze-thaw" baby in 1984. By 1985 the Monash University IVF team in Australia, which pro-duced this baby, had approximately 200 frozen embryos; by 1992, almost 20,000 embryos were in storage in Australia alone.[59] Frozen in liquid nitrogen at −196 degrees Fahrenheit, the embryos could theoretically survive for hundreds of years, although the long-term effects of freezing are unknown. Robert Winston, one of the British pioneers of IVF, believes that embryo freezing requires more investiga-tion regarding its safety. According to Winston, "there is a potential risk which has never been properly evaluated and I think we need to do that urgently."[60]

Although IVF as well as embryo transfer and egg donation have been the subject of much media hype, it is clear that all these technologies entail significant health risks for women, a notable lack of success, and deceptive practices. This is problematic for all women who use them. But the expense of these procedures, their regulation, and the search for the "right candidate" for egg donation, for example, should begin to alert us to questions about the varying experiences of women with these technologies. As we will see, once race and class are considered explicitly, an entirely different set of concerns emerge.

SEX SELECTION

Sex determination methods can be divided into at least two groupings–those that detect sex after conception and those that predetermine the sex of a fetus before conception. Until recently, the only effective techniques were those that detected sex after conception, such as amniocentesis, and permitted the abortion of a fetus of the 'wrong' sex.[61] IVF and embryo transfer could be used for sex detection and selection if a fetus were tested for sex before being implanted. Use of medical technology and selective abortion of females is well documented in three societies: India, South Korea, and China.[62] Widespread abortions have resulted in approximately 1.7 million fewer infant girls in China,[63] while India has one of the highest levels of excess child mortality for girls: It exceeds that of boys by 43 percent.[64] Although abortions for sex selection are believed to be rare in the United States, the preference for boys, particularly the first born, remains strong. In fact in most societies, "boys are preferred and privileged over girls."[65]

In the United States, profit-making clinics advertised sex selection techniques for years, although efforts at predetermining or selecting sex (rather than detecting it) were largely unsuccessful until recently. The methods used at these clinics included sperm separation, an effort to separate sperm with X- or Y-bearing chromosomes and then, through AI, insert the former if a female is desired, the latter if a male is preferred. Operating on the premise that Y-bearing sperm are heavier and faster, separation techniques included

> Centrifugation and sedimentation (spinning sperm at high speeds so the heavier sperm will settle out); electrophoresis (using alleged differences in electrical charges of the two sperm types to separate them); racing (placing sperm in a test tube full of viscous liquid and letting the two sperm types "race" each other to the bottom); and ultrasound (snapping off the heads of 'wrong' sex sperm with sound waves).[66]

There was talk of a proposed vaccination against X- or Y-bearing sperm[67] and the possible production of a condom or diaphragm that can filter out X- or Y-bearing sperm.[68] Some speculated about the timing of intercourse or sexual position in terms of favoring the conception of a boy or a girl. Claims were also made that a mother's diet before conception influences the sex of her offspring: Sodium and potassium increase the chances for males, foods high in calcium and magnesium for females. These methods were all unreliable despite their availability to consumers through profit-making clinics.

More recently, the Genetics and IVF Institute in Fairfax, Virginia, developed a method that allows parents to select the sex of their children by separating sperm that carry X chromosomes to create females, from Y chromosomes to produce males. Through a process trademarked as Microsort, X and Y chromosomes are separated using a fluorescent dye that brightly illuminates the X chromosomes under a laser beam. The Institute has reported a 93 percent success rate. When reproductive biologist Edward Fugger and his colleagues published their findings in the science journal *Human Reproduction*, twelve women were pregnant, and nine had already delivered their babies.[69] No safety concerns were mentioned, although the researchers admit that much remains unknown. By May of 1999, 111 pregnancies and 46 births had resulted from the method, still a small sample for detecting problems.[70]

Like many forms of the new reproductive technologies, this purportedly began as an effort to help a very select group—carriers of genetic disorders like hemophilia that could be avoided if one's offspring were female. Now, however, the technology is taking aim at those who merely prefer a boy or girl. Fugger regards it as "dogmatic" to restrict the procedure.[71] So far, most U.S. clients are requesting girls. The success rate is lower for producing boys (73 percent), but Fugger believes this will improve with experience, since they have mainly been sorting for the X sperm.

Many concerns have been raised about the process of sex selection, including its consumerist approach to child-bearing, and the expectations engendered by preselecting a child. But some believe it enhances people's control in a positive way[72] and that restricting it may interfere with reproductive freedom.[73] Many countries, like France, Germany, Austria, and Sweden, prohibit sex selection, but this preceded the development of Fugger's technique.[74] Since Microsort is a procedure, not a drug, it requires no government approval. Fugger estimates that they will begin marketing the procedure either through their own clinics or by subcontracting it once they have achieved 300–500 births.[75]

COMMERCIALIZATION

Beyond the dangers and deception that characterize the use of particular reproductive technologies as just discussed, the commercialization of all of them introduces other difficulties. Reproductive technology supposedly gives infertile women therapeutic help and choice regarding their reproductive functions. While no one wants to argue against either therapy or choice, the validity of these claims is questionable. To begin, access to reproductive technology is far from simply a matter of "choice" but directly related to one's economic resources. As Barbara Wright[76] puts it, "If private happiness is the text, the subtext is economic gain." Approximately 1 million U.S. couples seek infertility treatments each year in what is now a multibillion dollar business.[77] Technologies like IVF and embryo transfer can be enormously expensive and they are often not covered by insurance. *The New York Times* reported in 1996 that the median costs for a single IVF procedure was $7800. Since many patients try three or more times, costs easily rise to $25,000 or more. About 85 percent of patients pay their own costs, so these treatments are largely for the affluent.[78] IVF also has a high incidence of multiple-gestation pregnancies, which dramatically increase hospital costs. In 1991, total charges for a singleton birth was approximately $10,000; for twins, costs rose to $38,000; and triplets were $110,000.[79] A survey of 54 (of 108) IVF clinics in the United States indicated that the vast majority of clients are white, middle to upper-middle class and well educated.[80] Since reproductive technology in the United States in fact tends to be commercialized and run for profit, its benefits are routinely denied to those who cannot pay, thus favoring the reproduction of a select portion of our population.

This skewed distribution of resources is ironic because infertility "and especially the infections that lead to tubal closure, are particular problems for black women and women on low incomes in Britain and the United States, but these are precisely the women who have least access to new conceptive technologies like in-vitro fertilization."[81] The infertility rate of black women is one and one-half times higher than that of white women in the United States,[82] but rather than treating all infertility, "state law makers have recently begun eliminating state subsidies for any fertility service in an effort to lower costs and keep poor women from having more children."[83] Thus, we treat only women whose infertility is defined as a problem, leaving the infertility of many minority women unaddressed. "In other words, the problem and its solution are out of joint, for reasons that have to do with economics, but even more with ideological judgements about who may or should reproduce."[84] Improved general health care, safer working conditions, and proper nutrition would go a long way toward improving the opportunities for women of color to bear healthy children, but these problems are not even acknowledged let alone addressed in most discussions of infertility. Infertility is also extremely high among women of color in Third World countries: "In some regions of Africa, the rate may be as high as 40 percent of the women of childbearing age."[85] Public health measures in the Third World do not focus on infertility, however, but on promoting contraception.

Commercialization also dramatically increases the likelihood that financial interests may outweigh more vital health concerns. When reproductive technologies are viewed as marketable commodities, there is a tendency to exaggerate their benefits and minimize their risks in order to expand the potential clientele. In the last ten years, IVF clinics have expanded from 30 to more than 300 in the United States alone. About half are associated with hospitals; the others are run by groups of physicians or a single practitioner. Embryo transfer is also expanding, though its risks have been minimized or overlooked. Richard Seed, a physicist and a consultant to the livestock industry, and his brother Randolph, a surgeon, developed this procedure and then formed a corporation, Fertility and Genetics Research (FGR), to apply embryo transfer, initially used on cattle, to women. FGR is financed by investors through the stock exchange and operates profit-making clinics in the United States and Europe. The Seed brothers present their technique as safe, despite its known risks. They see a large potential market for embryo transfer among those who suffer from infertility and also among women who carry undesirable genetic traits such as cystic fibrosis or sickle cell anemia.

CONTRACEPTIVE TECHNOLOGIES

The commercialization of medical technology has a particularly unsavory history in terms of contraceptives. Here, research indicates that profits have been made at the expense of the health and well being of women, particularly women of color. While birth control has helped many women, assisting them in planning the number and spacing of their children, it should also be pointed out that, "Far from being invented by doctors and scientists, effective forms of birth control were devised and administered by women in nearly all ancient societies."[86] Now, however, birth control is big business. "In the mid-1980s the U.S. retail contraceptive market alone was estimated to be almost $1 billion a year; worldwide sales were probably over twice this figure."[87] Pharmaceutical companies reap these profits, and growing evidence indicates that many of them have been more concerned with profit than the health of their clients. The birth control pill was first tested on poor women in Haiti and Puerto Rico who were administered doses of medication now known to be extremely hazardous. Researchers believed that any dangers to these women were outweighed by the need to control overpopulation. Controlling population (not personal choice or health care needs) was the initial purpose of the pill.[88] When combined with profit making, this spelled problems for both First and Third World women.

The IUD

The development and marketing of the intrauterine device (IUD) is an illuminating example of how the pharmaceutical industry often operates at the expense of women. An IUD is "a small coiled, looped, or T-shaped plastic or copper device inserted inside the uterus with a tail reaching down into the upper vagina."[89] This device apparently causes a slight infection of the uterus, which prevents fertilized eggs from implanting. IUDs are commonly associated with heavy bleeding and cramps; they may also perforate the uterus and cause pelvic inflammatory disease (PIC), which can result in infertility.

During the 1970s one particular IUD, the Dalkon Shield, had increased side effects, causing five times as many cases of PIC as other shields. For approximately ten years these side effects were ignored. Before it was finally banned, fifteen American women died from septic abortions associated with the Dalkon Shield, and eighteen died of PIC. The manufacturer, A. H. Robbins Company of Richmond, was aware of its dangers as early as 1971 but covered up and destroyed damaging evidence. Under FDA pressure, Robbins withdrew the Dalkon Shield from the American market in 1974. Subsequently, almost 10,000 women in the United States filed lawsuits against Robbins (which ultimately paid $520 million in damages). Honorable Miles Lord, the Chief U.S. District Court Judge of Minnesota, presided over the case and issued a stinging indictment of A. H. Robbins

> The only conceivable reasons you have not recalled this product are that it would hurt your balance sheet and alert women who already have been harmed that you

may be liable for their injuries. You have taken the bottom line as your guiding beacon and the low road as your route. This is corporate irresponsibility at its meanest.[90]

The damage done by the Dalkon Shield in the Third World, where approximately 440,000 women were using it, continued to escalate since a recall is ineffective in remote areas. In addition, Third World women are more at risk than
other women given their poverty and poor health. "The mortality rate from IUDs
in the Third World is roughly *double* that in the West because of increased risk
from infections, septic abortions, and untreated ectopic pregnancies."[91] Finally,
IUDs may cause increases in infertility, which already affects many Third World
women, and has disastrous consequences in any society where women are valued
in terms of their child-bearing. Nonetheless, IUDs (other than the Dalkon Shield)
continue to be promoted and used in the Third World, largely because of their
effectiveness and because a woman's lack of control over them is considered
advantageous: "Getting the IUD removed safely requires a visit to a health clinic,
which many women may find difficult to make, and once there, the doctor will not
necessarily take it out."[92]

Population control has been and remains the focus of developmental aid in
the Third World. "Today, the U.S. Agency for International Development (AID) is
the largest single funder of population control in the Third World, allocating over
a half billion dollars annually to population control activities."[93] Dr. R. T.
Ravenholt, former head of the Office of Population for AID, developed the "contraceptive inundation" approach and was responsible for the exportation of the
Dalkon Shield to the Third World. He defended his actions in terms of U.S. security and financial interests and bluntly explained that population control is essential
to maintain "the normal operation of U.S. commercial interests around the
world . . . Without our trying to help these countries with their economic and social
development, the world would rebel against the strong U.S. commercial presence."[94]

Norplant

Another high-tech contraceptive is Norplant. It consists of six capsules the
size of matchsticks that are inserted into and removed from a woman's upper arm
under local anesthesia, a process requiring sterile conditions and skilled personnel.
These capsules slowly release the hormone progestin into the bloodstream and
prevent pregnancy for up to five years. Norplant received FDA approval in
December, 1990 and is marketed by Wyeth-Ayerst in the United States. Although
hailed as the greatest development in contraception since the pill, many questioned
its safety since FDA documents indicate that the silicone capsules used in Norplant
were tested on only 402 women. Another 2000 women were tested but with a type
of silicone that differed from the final product.[95] Norplant's most common side
effect is "disruption of the menstrual cycle, resulting in prolonged bleeding, inter-
mittent spotting, or amenorrhea," as well as "headache, depression, loss of libido,
weight change, nausea, and acne."[96] In terms of the procedure itself, neither the

insertion nor the removal of Norplant is a simple matter. Difficulties with removal have occurred when the capsules were implanted too deep; the rods have also broken or moved to other parts of the body. This has led to lawsuits against the distributor: "Class action lawsuits consolidating hundreds of cases have been filed in Texas, Illinois, and Florida against Wyeth-Ayerst, claiming health problems connected with Norplant and difficulties in having the implants removed."[97] In addition, Norplant users have no control over it: "Women have been denied removals in Bangladesh and Egypt, and one can easily imagine how 'voluntary' Norplant use will be in China and India."[98] Removal has also proven difficult for poor women in the United States, not simply because doctors discourage it, but because it can cost as much as $150 to remove.[99]

As of 1994, fifty-five countries had Norplant, used by up to 2 million women. These countries are a remarkably diverse collection of developed and developing areas, but it is estimated that up to 80 percent of Norplant is used in Indonesia and the United States.[100] Within the United States, black women are more likely than white women to be Norplant users.[101] The technical procedure itself might raise doubts about its appropriateness in much of the Third World. Yet as Yanoshik and Norsigian[102] observe, women in the Third World have experienced a persistent pattern of abuse with regard to all these contraceptives, and Norplant may be no exception: "Health concerns are often shrugged off with references to high rates of maternal mortality, a shorter life expectancy, and the population crisis," all of which supposedly justify using problematic drugs.

The Population Council of New York reported on Norplant in Indonesia, focusing on whether it broadened choice, whether it was removed on demand, and if the five-year removal was assured. Its report concluded that Norplant was used by many women in Indonesia and improved their choices since it was offered free of charge. But this "choice" was circumscribed by the fact that the government encouraged use of "long-lasting and provider-dependent" methods, and women were often misinformed about the method. Moreover, the report noted that removal is not always fully available to women "because: 1) use of Norplant is encouraged for the full five years of effectiveness; 2) clients are given limited information about removal; and 3) because removal training is still limited."[103] Sonia Correa[104] observes that most reproductive rights activists find "the idea of enhancing 'choice' to be highly debatable, if the broader context of authoritarian government and gender inequalities is not challenged." In Indonesia, the dangers of contraception tend to be minimized by the government, given high rates of maternal mortality.

Norplant has also met with mixed reactions in the United States. Many argue that this is due, in part, to the U.S. history of sterilization: "As many as 45,000 people in the United States were sterilized between 1907 and 1945 and many of them were poor; compulsory sterilization was commonly practiced throughout the first half of this century."[105] Margot E. Young[106] reports that "women on welfare have a sterilization rate 49 percent higher than that of other women. Women of color are also disproportionately sterilized as the following sterilization rates indicate: 20 percent African-American women, 24 percent Native-American women, 37 percent Puerto Rican women, and 16 percent white women."

The National Black Women's Health Project sees dangers in Norplant beyond possible health risks. The group warns that "with the availability of Norplant, we are witnessing the aggressive imposition of punitive birth-control measures on poor women and women of color, just as sterilization and other so-called population control measures have been forced upon African-American women and new immigrants in this country historically, and continue to be imposed on women of color in developing or so-called Third World countries around the world."[107] Recent events substantiate these concerns. Only two days after FDA approval of Norplant, on December 12, 1990, the *Philadelphia Inquirer* published an editorial: "Poverty and Norplant: Can Contraception Reduce the Underclass?" The controversy it caused led the *Inquirer* to apologize within two weeks, but not before support was engendered for its proposal to use Norplant to solve inner-city poverty. Within a month of FDA approval, "a trial judge in California offered to release from prison a woman convicted of child abuse, if she would consent to use of Norplant."[108] Darlene Johnson, a 27-year-old African-American welfare recipient, was thus sentenced to three years on Norplant. The seriousness of her actions, or the need for a penalty, is not at issue here. What is of interest is how a new technology that may provide reliable contraception for women instead becomes a means of punishment and, more specifically, punishment directed at certain groups of women. Young[109] observes that coercive policies focus on those regarded as "bad mothers," including women of color, welfare recipients, and single mothers.[110]

In July of 1999, a privately funded initiative began in California and spread to numerous other states (such as Florida, Minnesota, Pennsylvania, New Hampshire, and Michigan). It offers drug-addicted women $200 in cash to be sterilized or to take a long-term contraceptive like Norplant. Billboards in Chicago announce: "If you are addicted to drugs, get birth control—get $200 cash." The group solicits private funds and has attracted the support of celebrities such as conservative radio talk show host Dr. Laura Schlessinger. It maintains a Web site: www.cracksterilization.com. Organizations like Planned Parenthood and the American Civil Liberties Union regard the program as highly coercive.[111]

It is noteworthy that Medicaid typically pays for the insertion of Norplant but often not its removal. For some, this is tantamount to forced sterilization. Explicit examples of the coercive use of Norplant come from Maryland where the governor proposed requiring mothers on welfare to get Norplant or lose their financial support. Similar bills were proposed in Mississippi and South Carolina.[112] In 1993, it was reported that a school for pregnant teens in a working-class neighborhood in Baltimore was offering its students Norplant without parental consent, and plans were being discussed to make the contraceptive available in schools throughout the city. A local black minister, Melvin Tuggle, strongly opposed the initiative, arguing that "in the Baltimore school system, a 12-year-old needs a letter from her parents to go to the zoo. She needs permission to get aspirin but she needs nothing to get Norplant."[113] Teen mothers account for approximately 7 percent of welfare recipients, but they have been a focus of attacks on welfare. Roberts[114] points out that Norplant is bound to be an ineffective solution to teen pregnancy because it does not address the roots of the problem: Teen pregnancy is, "in many cases, a problem of sexual abuse, of poverty, of racism, and of inadequate resources for teen mothers and their children." Moreover, as Roberts observes, most young teens have sex only sporadically, yet Norplant regularly doses young women with a powerful hormone and risks their health. In fact, Norplant's long-term side effects are unknown, particularly on teenage girls, who were not even included in the clinical trials.

Depo-Provera

Another form of contraception with a questionable history is Depo-Provera, an injectable contraceptive that delivers an intense concentration of progestin with one injection into the bloodstream that lasts from three to six months. Manufactured by Upjohn (now Pharmacia-Upjohn, the world's largest pharmaceutical multinational corporation), Depo-Provera is controversial because it has been associated with increased breast cancer in a test population of beagles. It has other side effects as well—increased bleeding and a lengthy delay in return to fertility once the drug is stopped (as long as two years). In fact, over two-thirds of women have no regular menstrual cycles during the first year of use; Depo-Provera is also associated with skin disorders, fatigue, headaches, nausea, hair loss, depression, and decrease in libido.[115] Upjohn is investigating the risk of bone loss and osteoporosis with long-term use.[116] The fact that it is long-lasting makes it convenient, but like Norplant it also gives the user much less control. If a woman suffers adverse effects from Depo, she is helpless until the injection wears off.

Since 1979, Depo-Provera's use in the Third World has been controversial. In the United States, it did not obtain FDA approval until 1992. International activists have condemned the double standard at work in its availability in many poorer nations, and the increased health risks for Third World women who have limited access to medical attention if side effects occur and for whom increased bleeding may spell serious health problems. Depo-Provera is often available without adequate medical supervision: "In Mexico it is sold over the counter in pharmacies and given by 'injectionists,' practitioners with little or no formal training."[117] There is also evidence of coercive use in the Third World: In South Africa, black and mixed-race women have been subjected to mass Depo-Provera campaigns, with no other medical care available, and sometimes they are forced to use the contraceptive in order to keep their jobs.[118]

Stung by charges of American imperialism and racism in the use of Depo-Provera, Dr. Malcolm Potts, executive director of the International Fertility Research Program (an AID-funded population control agency) proposed that the United States use Depo-Provera on certain "subgroups" within our own country. He specifically mentioned Mexican immigrants "who bring with them the same health problems, the same cultural assumptions, the same need for fertility regulation as they had in Mexico." Potts reasoned that if the FDA turned its attention to these groups in the United States, "we would not be faced with the situation in which we can be accused of having a dual standard of medical practice and drug regulation around the world. If you look hard enough in the States, I think you can find the same type of population–as I say, it may not be very large–as one finds in the North of Thailand."[119]

Despite Dr. Potts' schemes (some might say racist schemes), the evidence of a double standard in terms of health concerns for First and Third World people is overwhelming. Profit-seeking has obviously endangered the health and lives of Western women (as indicated by the Dalkon Shield scandal), but stricter drug regulations in the West have led unscrupulous corporations to shift their interests abroad where control is less rigorous and the market is large. Often the interests of government agencies and multinational corporations, not the needs of women, shape population policy, as well as the regulation, distribution, and even the design of birth control. For example, millions of dollars are spent developing and marketing oral contraceptives and injectables in part because they are most lucrative, despite the risks associated with them. "Research on improving or expanding the selection of safer and simpler barrier and natural methods is virtually ignored."[120]

A new and again controversial method of birth control is now being tested–contraceptive vaccines. They aim to cause infertility for six to twelve months by turning the immune system against elements essential for reproduction, such as hormones, eggs, sperm, or the early embryo. By 1995, "a coalition of over four hundred organizations from thirty-nine countries was demanding an immediate halt to the research."[121] Health activists are concerned about the potential abuses of this vaccine, given its very design: "prolonged duration of effectiveness, difficulty of voluntary reversibility by the user, and ease of administration–'vaccination' on a mass scale."[122] Massive amounts of money are being spent researching contraceptive vaccines.[123] Those opposed worry not only about women's lack of control over them, but the specter of tampering with the immune system.[124]

TECHNOLOGY AND SOCIAL CONTROL

Some conceptive technologies permit dramatic alternatives to child bearing, since they separate sex and reproduction. This is precisely why politically and religiously conservative groups and individuals often oppose them. Ironically, however, these technologies are designed as well as implemented in ways that do not threaten, but in fact support traditional notions of the nuclear family. They target women, for example, although infertility is as often a male as a female problem.[125] Access to these technologies is obviously limited in terms of class, but women are also restricted if their "choices" are unconventional. The U.S. government and virtually every European government has appointed commissions to examine the new reproductive technologies, and they have reached strikingly similar conclusions regarding the appropriate profile for clients. Britain's Warnock Committee, West Germany's Benda Committee and the Netherland's Gezondheidsraad Committee all emphasize that women should be legally married in order to use these technologies.[126] Claiming that children have more advantages in a two-parent family, the Warnock Committee recommended that "*in-vitro* fertilization, egg donation, embryo transfer, and artificial insemination were to be restricted to stable, cohabiting heterosexual couples. Moreover, the use by married women of these technologies was also ruled out unless the patient was able to obtain written consent from her husband."[127] Similarly, a report of the Ethics Advisory Board of the Department of Health, Education and Welfare in the United States recommended IVF for married couples only, and physicians in the United States typically adhere to this restriction. Robert Winston, one of the British pioneers of IVF created controversy when he helped lesbian couples conceive.[128]

In 1998 the New York Task Force on Life and Law, which consisted of doctors, lawyers, and ethicists, issued a report recommending legislation regarding reproductive technologies. Its suggestions are generally progressive, but the very nature of its recommendations indicate how problematic current practice is. The Task Force recommends, for example, that a birth mother be considered the legal mother, and that clinicians use methods that minimize multiple births (which pose serious medical risks for newborns). It also suggests licensing embryo labs, regulating the use of frozen embryos, and ending discrimination against unmarried couples and lesbians in the use of new technology. Finally, it suggests that New York require by law that patients be informed about the new reproductive technologies they may use, including the "low chance for success" and whether the technology is experimental.[129]

A Royal Commission established in Canada to study the new reproductive technologies also recommended regulation of infertility treatments and genetic testing, as well as the criminalization of surrogate motherhood, the commercial use of eggs and sperm, and the involuntary treatment of pregnant women. Valverde and Weir[130] argue that criminalization is unlikely to be effective since it ignores the more significant issue of the lack of knowledge about, and democratic control over, the scientists and corporations that are developing and selling these technologies, while focusing on the activities of the women who may use them.

Reproductive technologies are often viewed as expanding choice, and proponents argue that a woman should be allowed to make her own decision about using them. Barbara Menning, the founder and director of a U.S. counseling and referral service for infertile couples, defends IVF as a possible means of assisting infertile couples. She advocates rigorous screening of patients so that they are fully informed about the process and its low success rate, but she notes that without IVF some couples would have a 100 percent risk of being childless. As an infertile woman, she[131] resents the attempts of other feminists to make choices for her: "Let those of us who are infertile decide whether we are willing to subject ourselves to the instrumentation and intervention necessary . . . Let us make informed consent."

Unfortunately, the "informed consent" that Menning advocates can be difficult to come by. Moreover, the individual decision that she envisions is somewhat misleading. The concept of choice encourages us to think in private terms, but reproductive decisions are anything but private. Economic considerations surely limit choice, but so do prevailing beliefs and values. Spallone and Steinberg[132] capture this when critiquing IVF: "The alternatives of the pain and humiliation and danger of an *in vitro* fertilization program and the lowered self-esteem, devaluation, and loneliness of infertility, do not represent choices in any sense of the word that many feminists would want to uphold." The notion of choice must be examined in a wider political and economic context, since this context shapes our technologies and our choices. Barbara Katz Rothman[133] puts it very well: "The question then for feminism is not only to address the individual level of 'a woman's right to choose' but also to examine the social level, where her choices are structured." Framing the issue in terms of a personal decision conveniently masks profound differences in social power and resources and how we are constrained (sometimes unknowingly) by social and cultural conditions.

Many women, for example, are deeply influenced by the prevailing idea that they should bear and raise children. One woman in an IVF program at Royal North Shore Hospital in Australia dreaded having to tell people that she had no children: "They say: Gee, *you'll* have to get moving! Or are you one of those selfish ones who want to work and not have any children?"[134] Many felt guilty about their inability to bear children for their husbands and angry with themselves. As one woman put it,[135] "I felt my body was *cheating* me. It had let me down." Similarly, an infertile woman in an IVF program in the United States commented, "Intellectually, I know that this doesn't mean I'm a failure as a wife or a woman or that I'm not feminine. But, as many times as you go through this, your emotions take over and you do feel like a total failure. And new technologies make it harder to stop trying."[136] Reproductive technology has, in fact, intensified the social pressure to have a biologically related child. As Anne Donchin[137] points out, "The inability to produce a child at will, once deemed inevitable and accepted with resignation, is more likely to be regarded now as a surmountable impediment to personal self-fulfillment."

Lesley Brown, the mother of the first IVF baby, voiced the pressure on her to bear children. Given her fertility problems, she advised her husband to divorce her concluding that "I'm not a normal woman."[138] Mrs. Brown's story also powerfully illustrates the significance of class differences, and the centrality of bearing a child when class constraints limit other possibilities in life, including a fulfilling job or even adoption. As a working-class woman, she had a factory job that gave her little satisfaction. As she vividly puts it, "Years of just weighing and packing cheese and coming back to a quiet, empty flat stretched before me." In addition, adoption was not a choice for Lesley Brown. She and her husband went to an adoption agency, the Children's Committee, "But they didn't even bother to put down our names. There weren't enough babies to go round . . . and anyway, the committee preferred regular churchgoers to people like us."

The Browns endured enormous emotional and financial costs in their attempts to conceive a child. After Lesley's first laparoscopy, for example, they could not afford to stay in Oldham where the surgery was performed but had to change trains four times on their way back to Bristol. Lesley's incision opened and blood began to seep though her clothes. She describes changing trains at one station: "I was crying so much that John picked me up and carried me in his arms from one end of the platform to the next . . . John was so upset about the state I was in that he was crying too."

The good news is that Lesley and John Brown finally had a child, but their heart-wrenching experience and IVFs sobering failure rate provides a glimpse at the heartache many people endure with no happy ending. Virtually all the couples in one IVF program told stories of tremendous strain in their relationships as well as the pressure to persist. As one women stated, "If I see one more article or book that says, 'You *can* have a baby,' or 'New hope for childless couples,' I think I'll scream. Sure it's good for the public to know, but the message seems to be that if you just try hard enough or go to the right doctor you're sure to get pregnant. I wish it were so easy."[139]

Research conducted by Christine Crowe in the IVF program at the Royal North Shore Hospital in Sydney, Australia, indicates that for many women biological motherhood is *not* a major consideration. As one woman put it: "Just to have a child in the house. . . . as far as the biological—that passes."[140] They were much more deeply concerned about social motherhood, about nurturing and raising a child. Many of them were in an IVF program because of the long wait for an adopted child in Australia and because of the preferences of their *husbands'* for biological children. Several mentioned that their husbands would rather be childless than adopt: "My husband 'wasn't keen on it.' . . . It might put our marriage in jeopardy. He was worried he wouldn't be able to love an adopted child the way he loves his own children."[141]

Crowe surmises that parenthood has different meanings for men and women, with men more concerned about biological connections. She then assesses IVF, which emphasizes biological reproduction, as a male-centered technology, with male values implicit in its design. She argues that this focus on biological motherhood limits the potential for redefining our ideas about parenting and also contributes to the difficulties women experience when they are unable to reproduce. She concludes: "In a situation when women experience personal condemnation and social stigma because of their infertility and in which the social definition of motherhood necessitates a biological relationship, the question must be asked what *real* 'choices' do infertile women have?"[142]

Some women (I would argue that race and class are significant here) are thus constrained by an ideology that demands not just raising or caring for children, but biological motherhood. We hear this in the voices of infertile women interviewed by Lasker and Borg.[143] Gail, for example, tries to explain why adoption is a "last resort" for her: "Bill (her husband) thought he would feel more comfortable with a child that was ours biologically. He says he just couldn't accept an adopted child as his own." Reproductive technology reflects and reinforces this emphasis on having a biologically related child as though this constitutes "real" family. Consider all the media attention surrounding adopted children who search for their genetic parents. Stanworth[144] rightly claims that this "emphasizes the idea that genetic connection is an immutable and overriding element of identity." Families can obviously be defined and experienced in very different ways, including in terms of what individuals *do* for one another, not just who is related by blood to whom. This is apparent in the discussion about "other-motherng" in the black community, women who assist biological mothers in the care of children.[145] So why is there such concern about blood ties for some women, and why is it also apparently more important to men? Stanworth[146] argues that it may be because men are rarely involved in the daily care of children: "The fact that women care for children in most households—and the very success of the women's movement in emphasizing that this care is not an effortless outpouring of maternal sentiment, but real labor that forges a strong relationship between women and their children—means that men are more likely than women to be anxious about the basis of relationships with children they intend to father."

An absence of choice or informed consent is also evident in women's lack of knowledge about these procedures and their anticipated outcomes. As Anne Donchin[147] notes: "People seeking treatment seldom know whether any of the available medical interventions are likely to help them or whether a particular physician has the requisite expertise." Lesley Brown provides us with a startling example. Mrs. Brown did not realize until she was *six months pregnant* that her baby would be the first IVF baby in the world. She comments,

> I don't remember Mr. Steptoe saying his method of producing babies had ever worked, and I certainly didn't ask. I just imagined that hundreds of children had already been born through being conceived outside their mothers' wombs.[148]

Her husband, equally uninformed, commented disarmingly: "I didn't know we were to be the first test-tube parents—I wish we weren't." Judith Carr, the mother of the first IVF baby in North America, was equally unaware of the novelty of IVF until she too was pregnant. She remarked: "I never asked if they'd had any success . . . I was too polite to ask that question."[149]

Technology does not always increase personal control but often spells a loss of control to experts. Women increasingly experience their pregnancies in medical terms and learn to distrust their own bodies. Susan Squier[150] highlights this shift of control from women to medical professionals when she points out that, "Whereas once the interior space of the woman was unavailable to the scientific gaze, and pregnancy was marked by the woman's testimony that she had felt the fetus move," there has been a "shift from an emphasis on maternal testimony to a reliance on medical imaging and measurement." She is concerned about tendencies found in the new reproductive technologies that may operate against the interests of women: "1) the increasing subjectification of the fetus (that is, the increasing tendency to posit a fetal subject), 2) the increasing objectification of the gestating woman, leading to her representation as interchangeable object rather than unique subject, and 3) the increasing tendency to conceive of the fetus and the mother as social, medical, and legal antagonists." Squier relates the story of Kawana Ashley, a pregnant 19-year-old from Florida, who claimed she did not have enough money for an abortion and shot herself in the stomach. The fetus was delivered and died a week later. Ashley was then charged with third degree murder and manslaughter. Squier points to the irony of such forceful intervention on behalf of the fetus, "only to abandon that advocacy once the fetus becomes a person whose status is both racially and economically specific." Interestingly, she speculates that the fetus draws such attention precisely because it has an undefined race, class, or gender and does not have a voice. The same interest and attention was not given to the impoverished Kawana Ashley who was unable to afford an abortion or, apparently, a decent standard of living for a living child.

Several significant points are being made here. As is evident from our discussion of conceptive technology, when we speak about the pressures on women to reproduce and the role of reproductive technology in this regard, it cannot be assumed that this applies to all women. Although the design of new technologies may put women at risk by enhancing the status of the fetus, not all women will be equally at risk. As Dorothy Roberts[151] asserts: "Just as important to this controversy as the politics of fetal rights is the politics of race." And, in fact, the evidence indicates that pregnant women of color are increasingly the target of punitive actions on behalf of the fetus. Courts and the medical profession are inclined to impose legal penalties and restrictions on them for certain behaviors. The rationale is the protection of the fetus, although this demonstrates an alarming willingness to act against the wishes of a pregnant woman and creates a false dichotomy between her and her fetus. Hospitals in Colorado, Illinois, and Georgia have gotten court orders forcing women, primarily women of color, to have Cesarian sections against their wishes when their doctors believed their fetuses needed this surgery. A study of fifteen Cesarians ordered by the courts over and against the wishes of pregnant women, similarly found an overrepresentation of minorities: "81 percent involved black, Hispanic and Asian women; 24 percent were not native speakers."[152] Ikemoto[153] argues that pregnant women of color and poor women have a significantly greater risk of forced medical treatment due to stereotypes about being a "bad mother:" "It is the implicit assumption that women of color, particularly those who live in poverty, are not fit for motherhood."

Courts also have used laws against child abuse and neglect to arrest pregnant drug addicts despite the fact that incarceration may be unhealthy for the fetus given the stress and deprivations of prison life.[154] Prosecutions are increasing dramatically, and the defendants are overwhelmingly women of color.[155] "Even more common than criminal prosecution is court-ordered removal of the baby at birth, without trial or hearing, solely on the grounds that mother and/or infant have a positive drug test at the time of birth."[156] Research indicates that "although white women are more likely to be drug users than are black women, black women are ten times more likely than white women to be tested for drugs and reported to the authorities for drug abuse.[157] This disparity occurs in part because the drug testing of newborns is done almost exclusively at public hospitals, where minority women are overrepresented.[158] In addition, prosecutors have chosen to focus on the impact of crack addiction on the fetus despite the fact that it is not more widespread nor more harmful than, say, alcohol addiction. Targeting crack addicts (disproportionately black women) is far more socially acceptable than challenging white women who may be addicted to pills or alcohol. Dorothy Roberts makes this point convincingly when she discusses the 1994 movie *When A Man Loves A Woman*. Meg Ryan plays Alice, an alcoholic mother who neglects and misplaces her children, drives drunk with them, and even slaps her 8-year-old who catches her drinking. What interests Roberts[159] is that "the mother remains the sympathetic heroine throughout the movie, despite her atrocious care for her children. While audiences knew Alice desperately needed treatment for her drinking problem, it probably never occurred to them that she should be arrested or that her daughters should be taken away from her." Predictably, Alice gets all the help she needs by the end of the movie, help routinely unavailable to others. The lack of assistance for some women indicates that "fetal rights" may be more about punishing black women than protecting black fetuses.

The absence of prenatal care for poor women, combined with the fact that most drug treatment programs "either do not accept pregnant women or have waiting lists that extend long beyond due dates," makes these policies particularly cruel.[160] Many contend that punitive actions will not result in healthier pregnancies but instead will deter pregnant addicts from seeking help for fear of reprisals. "The number of pregnant women who are prosecuted or subjected to unwanted surgery for behavior which could harm their fetuses is likely to be relatively small in comparison with the number of women who would be induced by these regulatory incursions to avoid medical care."[161]

At this point, it might be worthwhile to explicitly acknowledge that women differ crucially in terms of access to all medical care depending not on their needs but on class and race inequalities. Given government cutbacks and the commercialization of many medical institutions, poor people in the United States find it increasingly difficult to get adequate medical care, let alone fertility treatments. Infant mortality rates are regarded as one of the best indicators of quality of life and, in the United States, the rates are higher than in at least twenty other major industrialized countries, as well as Costa Rica, Cuba, and Singapore.[162] Moreover, during the 1990s, the racial divide in the United States widened: "The rate was 16.8 for black infants, compared to 6.9 for whites."[163] Infant death is highest in America's big cities where "life can be, for some, the most privileged."[164] In New York City, infant mortality rates "exceeded 19 in the poor black communities of the South Bronx and Bedford-Stuyvesant and reached a staggering 27.6 in Central Harlem."[165] The same pattern is found in pregnancy-related deaths, which are four times higher for black women compared to white women.[166]

The Department of Health and Human Services in Washington, D.C. confirmed reports of differential infant mortality rates and cited one reason as the fact that fewer black women get prenatal care. Meanwhile, the Centers for Disease Control announced that low birth weight was more than twice as common among black infants as compared to whites and that this is a major cause of infant mortality and birth defects.[167] By 1995, the United States ranked twenty-second in the world in infant mortality, "losing thousands of babies each year to poverty, drugs, and lack of adequate health care,"[168] while only half of all black mothers received adequate prenatal care.[169] On virtually all health measures, blacks and other people of color continue to do less well than white Americans.[170]

This grim reality of infant death and disease is rooted in the crushing poverty that a disproportionate number of African Americans endure and the resulting inadequate access to health care, including health care for pregnant women. Cuts in maternal and infant health care programs play a role in this, and no social or health care initiatives are as yet underway to alleviate the situation. Margaret Boone,[171] who studied infant mortality in Washington, D.C., notes that "poverty and malnutrition are a root cause of poor infant health. But the mother is in poor health *first.*" It is fair to ask where the "therapy" or "choice" is for her in this age of technological miracles. Currently, "Black babies in the nation's capital die at a rate *triple* that of the country as a whole."[172]

Studies indicate that limited access to health care affects the experiences of women of color not only in terms of reproductive rights but also in health issues such as breast cancer, domestic violence, substance abuse, and AIDS.[173] Research by Bollini and Siem,[174] reviewing access to health care for migrant and ethnic minorities in industrialized countries including the United States, document that poor health outcomes are linked directly to lower entitlements.

COMMODIFICATION OF REPRODUCTION

Capitalism thrives on and expands consumerism and the impulse to turn everything into commodities—products to be bought or sold. Some of the new reproductive technologies, focusing on the production of a "quality" fetus, tend to reduce human beings themselves to commodities. An interest in creating "better" babies for some echoes the concerns of eugenics and an ideology that only the "fit" should reproduce. (Consider, for example, the well-publicized sperm bank in California that accepts only the sperm of so-called illustrious men.) Surrogate motherhood is often cited as an extreme example of the increasing commodification of human life and the emphasis on "quality" children. The technology it involves is simple: artificial insemination by a donor (AID). A woman agrees to be artificially inseminated with the sperm of an infertile woman's husband and to bear a child she will relinquish at birth, usually for a fee. This process permits the husband of an infertile woman to have a child that is *genetically* related to him and it also permits his infertile wife to adopt that baby. Surrogacy may be used not only by infertile couples, but single men and even fertile women who choose not to bear children.

Attorney Noel Keane has been closely associated with this practice since it began. Initially he brought couples together without any exchange of money. Once this worked successfully, he publicized it in the media and began charging for his services.[175] The practice costs an adoptive couple approximately $25,000: $10,000 for the woman who conceives, carries, and delivers the baby; the same amount for the lawyer making the arrangements; and about $5000 for insurance, medical bills, and maternity supplies. This is a lucrative business for the lawyers involved. Keane's surrogacy practice, for example, grossed $600,000 in 1986. As of 1986, twenty surrogacy programs were operating in the United States, and more than 500 babies were known to have been born to "surrogate mothers;"[176] ten years later, the number of births was estimated at nearly 5000.[177]

The story of Judy Stiver and Alexander Malahoff dramatically illuminates the commodification of birth entailed in surrogacy.[178] Mrs. Stiver had agreed to be a "surrogate mother" and to have a baby for Malahoff through artificial insemination. She also agreed not to smoke, drink, or take drugs during the pregnancy and to have amniocentesis and abort the fetus if it were disabled. Under the terms of her contract, if she had a miscarriage before the fifth month of pregnancy, she would receive no payment. If she miscarried after the fifth month or if the baby was born dead, she would be paid $1000. Otherwise, she would receive $10,000. Her baby boy was born in January, 1983 with microcephaly, a small head indicating that he might be mentally retarded. Neither Malahoff nor Stiver wanted the baby, and they proposed putting him up for adoption. The infant then developed a life-threatening strep infection, which had to be treated with antibiotics. Mrs. Stiver referred the doctor to Malahoff to get permission to treat the infant, and Malahoff refused. Ray Stiver, Judy's husband, claimed that Malahoff wanted the infant to die, and Judy to bear a new baby for him. According to Mr. Stiver: "It's just like buying a defective piece of merchandise."[179] The doctor took the issue to court where the Stivers were declared the parents, and they permitted treatment. Later medical evidence proved that Malahoff was not the father of the child. The Stivers had not been instructed to refrain from sexual intercourse the night before the artificial insemination, and they had conceived an unwanted child. Judy Stiver carried this fetus for nine months thinking Malahoff was the father, and the Stivers, already in a financially precarious position, took custody of the disabled baby. Legally, it remains difficult to determine who is responsible for an unwanted child produced in cases such as this.[180]

A similar example in terms of unexpected consequences occurred in the well publicized case of "Baby M." Mary Beth Whitehead had agreed, by contract, to bear a child for William and Elizabeth Stern for a fee of $10,000. She also agreed not to "form or attempt to form a parent-child relationship" with the baby. She was artificially inseminated with Mr. Stern's sperm and became pregnant, but then refused to accept the money or to give up the baby girl. Instead, Whitehead fled to Florida and hid from the Sterns and the law for eighty-seven days. When the baby was found and taken from her, a seven week trial ensued.

During the trial the Sterns argued for enforcing the contract Whitehead had signed, while Whitehead's defense lawyers claimed that New Jersey law forbids baby selling. Moreover, New Jersey adoption law gives birth mothers the opportunity to change their minds about the adoption. In the Bergen County Family Court, Judge Harvey Sorkow upheld the surrogacy contract, gave permanent custody to the Sterns, and terminated Whitehead's parental rights. One year later, in February of 1987, the New Jersey Supreme Court rendered a very different decision. They held the contract to be in violation of New Jersey law forbidding baby selling and restored Whitehead's parental rights to visit her child.

The New Jersey Supreme Court took a strong stand against the commodification they saw in surrogacy: "There are, in short, values that society deems more important than granting to wealth whatever it can buy, be it labor, love, or life."[181] The State Supreme Court observed how harshly Mary Beth Whitehead had been treated by the trial court and by some of the experts who testified about her behavior. They stated: "We do not know of, and cannot conceive of, any other case where a perfectly fit mother was expected to surrender her newly born infant, perhaps forever, and was then told she was a bad mother because she did not."[182] Although the court found the contract illegal, they gave custody of the baby to the Sterns, based largely on the financial instability of the Whitehead family, thus, a class-based decision.

The treatment of a surrogate's baby as a product to be bought and sold is vividly indicated by the fact that the surrogacy contract denies any payment to the natural mother if she has a miscarriage before her fifth month of pregnancy. Moreover, she is paid $1000, not $10,000 if the baby is born dead. Although payment is often defended in terms of money for services, it is reasonable to argue that it is payment for delivering a living child. Even Family Court Judge Sorkow, perhaps unwittingly, acknowledged this commodification when he stated in defense of William Stern: "Mr. Stern did take a risk, however, whether the child was normal or abnormal, whether accepted *or rejected*, he would have a lifetime obligation and responsibility to the child as its natural and biological father."[183] The child is thus a commodity that may be rejected if unsuitable; the obligation that remains is strictly financial.

Law professor Dorothy Roberts[184] offers that "our understanding of the evils inherent in marketing human beings stems in part from the reduction of enslaved blacks to their physical service to whites . . . The quintessential commodification of human beings was the sale of slaves on the auction block to the highest bidder." A consideration of reproductive technology in light of race quickly alerts us to the fact that as significant as the genetic tie is deemed to be, only the appropriate genetic tie will do: The eggs of black women are not valued as much as the eggs of white women. The class and race dimensions also become clear when cost savings is discussed by using poor women to carry an unrelated fetus to term, assuming that they would provide cheap labor. "Gestational surrogates" are those who carry and deliver fetuses completely unrelated to them. The process usually entails not embryo transfer, but IVF. A wife's eggs and her husband's sperm are fertilized *in vitro* and then implanted in a "gestational surrogate." The first birth in the United States through this method was reported in 1984. It is estimated that there were approximately eighty such births between 1987 and 1990.[185] Ralph Fagan, executive director of the Center for Surrogate Parenting in Beverly Hills, contends that it is easier to recruit women as gestational, rather than traditional surrogates, since "They feel they are not giving up their own genetic material, their own baby,"[186] indicating the power that biological connections assume in our society.

John Stehura, president of The Bionetics Foundation, Inc., a business that arranges surrogate pregnancies, is enthusiastic about gestational surrogates and has explicitly suggested Third World women, whose financial situation is precarious, might perform these services inexpensively.[187] Dorothy Roberts focuses on the racism that makes these scenarios possible. She[188] points to the court case, *Johnson v. Calvert*, which addressed a gestational surrogacy dispute. Anna Johnson, a black single mother, agreed to be a gestational surrogate for Crispina Calvert (a Filipina) and Mark Calvert (who is white). While pregnant, she changed her mind and both she and the Calverts filed lawsuits for custody. The courts in California, including the California Supreme Court, decided in favor of the Calverts based on the significance of the genetic tie. Roberts argues that the law need not place this emphasis on genetics: "There is little doubt, for example, that a court would not consider a woman who donated her eggs to an infertile couple to be the legal mother, despite her genetic connection to the child." Instead, she contends, the courts were preventing a black woman from being the "natural mother" of a white child.

In the United States, controversy continues to rage over the acceptability of paying surrogate mothers. Since 1980 about half the states have passed legislation regarding surrogacy, but they vary enormously.[189] Some states (such as New York) ban such arrangements; courts in other states (such as Nevada) have held that surrogacy does not violate state laws against baby selling.

PRENATAL SCREENING

Since we may now test an embryo and abort or reimplant only those that meet our specifications, concerns about the commodification of reproduction and quality control extend far beyond the comparatively few people involved in surrogate motherhood. Perhaps the best known procedure for prenatal screening is amniocentesis, which was developed in 1955. This test, performed in the second trimester, detects a range of birth defects, including Down's syndrome and spina bifida. The process itself is relatively simple and rapid. A long, hollow needle is inserted through a woman's abdomen into the amniotic sac, and a small sample of fluid is removed. Cells from this fluid are cultured and tested over a period of about two to four weeks. Although typically used to detect abnormalities, this test also reveals the sex of the fetus with virtual certainty. One of the great drawbacks of amniocentesis is that its results come late in a pregnancy, often after quickening, when a woman has felt the fetus move. If an abortion is elected, it must be performed within the next few weeks allowing little time for reflection or, in the case of reported disabilities, to learn something about those disabilities.

A newer method for detecting the condition of a fetus is chorionic villi sampling (CVS). For anyone considering the possibility of aborting a fetus depending on its sex or condition, this test offers the decided advantage of being performed as early as the ninth week of pregnancy, with results available overnight. It thus permits an early abortion, within the first three months. Given such early results, Ruth Hubbard speculates that CVS may increase pressure to screen, and abort, a so-called 'defective' fetus. This procedure, originally developed in China during the 1970s, entails inserting a syringe in a woman's uterus (monitored by ultrasound) and removing a few of the placenta's very fine projections, called chorionic villi. When tested, they reveal certain genetic defects. There have, however, been indications that CVS may not be as safe as originally assumed. Reports indicate that it may not only detect, but *cause* some rare defects: "missing or stubby fingers and toes, sometimes accompanied by a shortened tongue and an undersized jaw."[190] These reports led to a sharp decrease in the use of CVS.

Although these procedures have to be carefully analyzed in terms of the benefits they may provide women and society, the social pressure to control the terms of birth and to insure a "quality product" implies a devaluation of those who do not meet certain specifications. For the most part, the tests are intended to detect what we regard as a problem so that the fetus may be aborted. Several "Baby Doe" cases illustrate our devaluation of certain groups in our society. One particularly shocking example indicates our cultural fears of disability: In 1982, a baby boy was born with a blocked esophagus in a hospital in Bloomington, Indiana. Because he had Down's syndrome, his parents refused to permit him to have life-saving surgery, leaving him physically unable to eat. Although a surgeon was willing to perform the operation without cost, and Down's syndrome infants are adoptable, the parents were not moved. Child welfare workers went to court to get an injunction to force the surgery, but they were unsuccessful. As a result, he was allowed to lie in a crib, in an Indiana hospital, and literally starve to death.[191] He was sedated as necessary but given no food or water. He died in six days.

In this particular case, the obstetrician had advised that surgery would be difficult and painful (more so, one wonders, than starving . . . ?), and that the child's developmental disability would not allow a "minimally adequate quality of life" (it is unclear how this was determined). The parents had two other children whom they did not want to burden. Due to the notoriety of this case, a 1984 federal statute mandates treatment in similar cases, specifying that it may be withheld only in extreme situations.[192] No matter what a doctor now advises or prefers, courts would presumably not allow a similar course of action if the situation were called to their attention.

Many applaud the use of reproductive technologies for selective breeding. Dr. Robert Edwards, the man responsible for the first IVF baby, commented that donor eggs will be useful for women with genetic defects. He noted, "Many couples are responsible. They are to be commended that they don't want to bring an abnormal child into the world."[193] The appointment of ethicist Peter Singer in the Fall of 1999 as the DeCamp Professor of Bioethics at Princeton University's Center for Human Values caused controversy along these lines. It stems from Singer's advocacy of euthanasia for severely disabled newborns and those with Down's syndrome who "would need more care and attention than a normal child." Amy Gutmann, Director of Princeton's Center for Human Values, defended the appointment on the grounds of Singer's scholarly achievements and in terms of the University's commitment to "honest, creative, and open intellectual engagement with the most important issues concerning the human condition, no matter how controversial those issues may be."[194]

Given these technological developments, a discussion has evolved regarding disability rights and how the reproductive rights movement has preyed upon fears of disability. Anne Finger[195] defends abortion rights but is disturbed by technology that enables us to abort *particular* fetuses (selective abortion). She advocates amniocentesis counseling when it permits a woman to know more about a possible disability, but she contends that this counseling is not always informed. The choices surrounding amniocentesis are literally life and death decisions, but often they are made with little time and equally little information. Finger wonders if pregnant women are told that 95 percent of Down's syndrome children have moderate to mild retardation, that they are adoptable, and that, as adults, many manage their own apartments and jobs.

According to disability rights activists, the prevailing assumption that a disabled fetus should automatically be aborted merits serious discussion. Marsha Saxton, for example, sees the decision to abort as revolving around the resources parents and communities have to welcome a child, but she rejects the notion that life is not worth living if one is disabled. A woman has a right to have a child with disabilities and to resist the fear our society instills regarding disability. Saxton contends that most of the suffering people with disabilities face is rooted in social attitudes, not in the disabilities themselves. She recommends more knowledgeable counseling with amniocentesis, so that parents may adequately assess their ability to care for a disabled child. The issue is more than access to accurate information: We need to ensure that new technologies will not conflict with the necessity of creating a better society for the people with disabilities among us.

Currently, there are no therapies for most of the conditions diagnosed by prenatal screening. It is generally assumed that detecting an abnormality will result in an abortion, despite the fact that these tests do not inform us of the severity of any particular disability.[196]

GENDER, RACE, AND CLASS INEQUALITIES

Reproductive technology is typically regarded as a powerful agent of change for women. It has been seen as freeing them from biological destiny and as giving them more options as to when and how to reproduce. It has also been praised for assisting infertile women in their quest for biological children. And indeed it has been extraordinarily helpful in many respects. Consider, for example, the value of safe and affordable contraceptive technology and its potential benefits for women and men. But the evidence compiled in this chapter should indicate that not all reproductive technology is beneficial nor does it assist all groups of women. It might be noted that there is no one feminist stand regarding the new reproductive technologies: Donchin[197] observes that while feminists are in agreement about certain problems regarding procreation—such as the growing view of the fetus as independent of the pregnant woman, the marketing of fertility treatments, and the connections between medical authorities and commercial interests—there are also areas of significant disagreement. Some feminists are decidedly opposed to the new reproductive technologies and call for a ban on them. Others argue that such a rejection is inadequate "because many of them offer women indispensable resources with which to fulfill their maternal instincts. These new technologies have the potential to empower as well as to disempower women."[198]

We need not, however, make a judgement on reproductive technology in general as good or bad. When we stand back from this material and consider it within a framework of gender, race, and class, we begin to see that technology is not a deterministic force for the good of all but is shaped by a particular social context and its varying forms of inequality. For this reason, it distributes its benefits differentially.

The technology that we have developed and the ways in which it has been implemented bears the earmarks of gender inequality, for example, and the power differentials between women and men. Restricted access to technologies such as artificial insemination and IVF bolsters a traditional gendered social order in significant ways since often only married women, or women in a stable relationship with a man, are permitted to utilize conceptive technologies. In addition, virtually all birth control technology is *designed* for women, not men, implying that birth control and indeed children are the responsibility of women, a very traditional notion. Condoms seem to be the obvious exception, but they were developed not to prevent pregnancy but as protection from venereal disease.[199] Designating birth control as women's responsibility is particularly vexing given that it is often far from safe or completely reliable. We might also reflect on the extent to which reproductive technology has actually "freed" women from biological destiny. Women may delay childbearing, but in a society such as ours, which views women, particularly white women, as wives and mothers, few finally "choose" to be childless.

The public discussion surrounding IVF casts infertility as an *individual* woman's problem not, for example, as a social problem of delayed childbearing due to the lack of options most women (including professional women) have regarding work or as a social problem of inadequate primary health care (which significantly affects poorer women). Infertility is also steadfastly treated as a *woman's* problem "even though significant numbers of couples who become involved in IVF programs do so because of low male fertility."[200] Thus IVF addresses infertility in a way that is rooted in gendered and individualistic under-standings and expectations regarding reproduction.

Certainly, the new conceptive technologies provide significant options regarding reproduction, and they have assisted some infertile women. But we must be mindful of their high failure rates, the lack of knowledge many women have about them, and the pressure they exert on some women to continue pursuing the possibility of biologically conceiving a child despite the limited chances of success. This pressure to pursue technological solutions is often rooted in expectations regarding a woman's proper role as wife and biological mother and impinges on a woman's freedom to choose to *stop* using them. These technologies have also fos-tered an escalating medicalization of women's reproductive processes and, rather than increasing women's control, have shifted control to medical experts who tend to be white males. Women are rarely involved in developing these technologies or in running the businesses that market them.[201]

For many women racial inequality intersects with gender inequality and sig-nificantly affects their experiences with reproductive technology. For example, far from being the recipients of high technology to help conceive children, many women of color have instead been subjected to racist understandings of who may or should reproduce. The "fit" mother is not only stereotyped by gender but race and class. The problems regarding Norplant—including its safety, its use in the Third World, and rising concerns about its punitive use on women of color in the United States—reflect race as well as gender inequality. Differences in the imple-mentation of Norplant (as with all technologies) depend on the social and political context. Sonia Correa[202] argues, for example, that Norplant was made safer in the United States than in Indonesia because of an active U.S. reproductive rights movement and close scrutiny of Wyeth, the company that markets Norplant. She acknowledges, however, the abuse of Norplant within the United States despite its special circumstances when she observes that safety nets may not be effective "in those settings most directly affected by racial, ethnic, and class inequality."[203]

We have seen that white women in the United States are more likely to be drug abusers than are black women, but pregnant drug addicts, who are the tar-get of punitive action (rather than high-tech medical assistance), are overwhelm-ingly women of color. Prosecutors have chosen to focus on the dangers of crack addiction rather than alcohol, thus aiming at impoverished black women. The clearest indication of the racism (and classism) involved in these policies is the lack of prenatal care for poor women and the fact that many drug treatment pro-grams refuse to accept pregnant women. Punitive policies conveniently shift atten-tion from the larger social issue of inadequate and biased reproductive health care policies to individual black women's actions as primarily responsible for the ill-ness and death of their infants. Such criminalization is much easier, as Roberts[204] notes, than creating an equitable health care system in the United States. Ultimately, the message underlying "fetal rights" has little to do with healthy babies or healthy women but, instead, the imagery of fetal rights is used to condemn and punish stigmatized groups, while diverting attention from the need for basic reproductive health care.

Although reproductive technologies herald the possibility of controlling reproduction and ensuring healthy infants, they do not address the basic causes of our health problems, and they may even increase unequal access to needed reproductive health care: "To the extent that proposed 'high-tech' solutions divert attention and funding away from prevention of infertility or infant mortality, they exacerbate rather than solve, these major public health problems."[205] As Henifin rightly notes,

> What is needed is not more emphasis on court-ordered interventions or new technological 'fixes' but the basics—prenatal care, quality housing, nutrition, and medical care. The issues are ones of access and equity, not technological wizardry or draconian court orders.

Thus racial inequality has channelled the benefits of reproductive technology to some women as opposed to others, and it characterizes the context in which technology may be used punitively. In the process, it is not an agent of progress but instead serves to reinforce racial stereotypes and racial inequality.

Class also plays a significant role in the development and implementation of reproductive technology. It affects access to high technology, which can be extremely expensive and thus available to some women and not to others. But the class (and race) differentials regarding reproductive technology go far beyond issues of access, as the research of Patricia Hill Collins[206] demonstrates. She argues that white women of different social classes are encouraged to conceive and carry children, but in terms of rearing these children, working class white women receive much less support. If they are young and unmarried, they may even encounter pressures to relinquish their babies for adoption. Black women, given the long-standing notion of them as "unfit" mothers, are subjected to coercive population policies. Collins also discusses the exploitation of undocumented Latinas who care for the children of more affluent women. She summarizes:

> Middle-class white women are encouraged to reproduce and are provided with infertility services and top-notch prenatal care. Working-class white women are encouraged to reproduce only if they absorb the costs of child rearing or relinquish their children to another home. Working-class African-American women, especially those living in poverty, are discouraged from reproducing at all. Finally, as employable mothers, undocumented Latinas remain virtually invisible.[207]

The commercialization entailed in selling products at a profit also has a decided impact on reproductive technology. It determines *what* will be produced—only products that sell at a profit. The concern for profit making has led to deceptive practices on the part of the medical establishment, including major hospitals, in order to ensure that these products are sold. This includes exaggerating the benefits and minimizing the risks of many procedures such as IVF, embryo transfer, and sex selection. The overriding concern with profit puts many women in the First and Third Worlds at risk as illustrated, for example, by the marketing and sale of the Dalkon Shield.

Surrogacy offers a particularly blatant example of the connection between class privilege and reproductive technology, although some have steadfastly denied these implications. Lori Andrews,[208] for example, is a liberal feminist who defends surrogate motherhood as a woman's right to do as she wishes with her body. She denied the existence of any class bias in the Baby M case in which surrogate mother Mary Beth Whitehead refused to relinquish her baby to William Stern who had contracted for the child. Andrews argues that Stern was not from a privileged family since his father was a short-order cook, while Mary Beth Whitehead's father was a teacher with a Master's degree. Andrews continues, "Yet the Baby M case is generally described as a battle between the classes. Rather than acknowledging that a woman might become a surrogate willingly, enthusiastically, it is necessary to construct a fable about a desperate women needing money."

Some women may indeed be enthusiastic candidates for surrogacy, but arguing in terms of individual "choice" and denying the implications of class in the Baby M case, or in surrogacy in general, ignores major structural constraints that individuals must negotiate. Despite what anyone's father may have done or achieved (a remarkably traditional way of assessing a *woman's* social status), the income differential between the Sterns and the Whiteheads was a hefty $92,000 a year.[209] This alone put Mary Beth Whitehead at a decided disadvantage. Moreover, custody of the baby was ultimately awarded to the Sterns, based in large measure on social class.

Those directly involved in surrogacy have been more forthcoming about its financial implications. Psychologist Howard Adelman, for example, who screens women for a surrogacy organization in Philadelphia put the matter bluntly: "I believe candidates with an element of financial need are the safest. If a woman is on unemployment and has children to care for she is not likely to change her mind and want to keep the baby she is being paid to have for someone else."[210] This captures the class inequality evident in surrogacy, which necessarily shapes women's "choices." Unfortunately, class inequality is not simply limited to one's choices regarding the use of high technology but, as we have seen, extends to the very availability of prenatal care and indeed the death rate of American infants.

CONCLUSION

In sum, a consideration of gender, race, and class inequalities provides a deeper understanding of the development and implementation of reproductive technologies and helps us make sense of their varied implications in the lives of diverse women. Far from revolutionizing the status of women, reproductive technology operates within the constraints of gender, race, and class inequalities. We will now turn to a consideration of the electronic office, where we will see many of the same patterns at work.

NOTES

1. Rita Arditti et al., *Test-Tube Women: What Future for Motherhood?* (London: Pandora Press, 1984), 1.

2. Ruth Schwartz Cowan, *Social History of American Technology* (New York: Oxford University Press, 1997).

3. Linda Gordon, "Women's Freedom, Women's Power: Notes for Reproductive Rights Activists," *Radical America*, Vol. 19 (November–December 1985): 34.

4. Marjorie Rosen, "Betrayal of Hope," *People Weekly*, Vol. 42 (5 September 1994): 5.

5. Cheryl Meyer, *The Wandering Uterus: Politics and the Reproductive Rights of Women* (New York: New York University Press, 1997), 21.

6. Judith M. Siegel, "Pathways to Single Motherhood: Sexual Intercourse, Adoption, and Donor Insemination," *Families in Society: Journal of Contemporary Human Services*, Vol. 79 (January–February 1998): 75.

7. Deborah Lynn Steinberg, "Selective Breeding and Social Engineering: Discriminatory Policies of Access to Artificial Insemination by Donor in Great Britain." In *Made to Order: The Myth of Reproductive and Genetic Progress* (New York: Pergamon, 1987), 185–186.

8. Catherine DeLair, "Ethical, Moral, Economic, and Legal Barriers to Assisted Reproductive Technologies Employed by Gay Men and Lesbian Women," *DePaul Journal of Health Care Law*, Vol. 4 (Fall 2000): 147.

9. Hilde L. Nelson, "Held to a Higher Standard," *The Hastings Center Report*, Vol. 21 (May–June 1991): 2–3.

10. Dorothy Roberts, *Killing the Black Body: Race, Reproduction, and the Meaning of Liberty* (New York: Random House, 1997), 248.

11. Ibid., 248.

12. U.S. Congress, Office of Technology Assessment, *Artificial Insemination: Practice in the United States: A Summary of a 1987 Survey* (Washington, D.C.: U. S. Government Printing Office, 1988), 9.

13. Ibid., 9.

14. Mary E. Guinan, "Artificial Insemination by Donor: Safety and Secrecy," *The Journal of the American Medical Association*, Vol. 273 (15 March 1995): 890–891.

15. Ibid.

16. Ibid.

17. Francie Hornstein, "Children by Donor Insemination: A New Choice for Lesbians." In *Test-Tube Women: What Future for Motherhood?* (London: Pandora Press, 1984), 373–381.

18. There are a number of variations on the basic process of IVF. With gamete intrafallopian transfer (GIFT), egg and sperm are combined and inserted in a woman's body within an hour. Through a laparoscopy, the mixture is placed at the entrance to the fallopian tubes so that the egg is fertilized *in vivo*. Although a woman must have at least one unblocked fallopian tube for this process to work, it may be more successful than IVF simply because fertilization occurs within a woman's body, thus in its normal site (Lasker and Borg, *In Search of Parenthood*). Another process, pronuclear stage tubal transfer (PROST), involves fertilizing an egg in the glass petri dish, but transferring it at the pronuclear stage, not at the four- or eight-cell stage as is typical with IVF. "Tubal embryo transfer" (TET) takes an embryo that has already undergone some divisions and places it in the fallopian tube. Finally, zygote intrafallopian transfer (ZIFT) involves fertilizing the egg *in vitro*, like PROST, and placing it in the fallopian tube before any cell division. All these variations are very similar to IVF, which remains the most popular method.

19. Gena Corea, *The Mother Machine: Reproductive Technologies from Artificial Insemination to Artificial Wombs* (New York: Harper and Row, 1985).

20. James Gleick, "Reproductive Help: Widespread and Unregulated," *The New York Times*, 11 March 1987, A16.

21. Denise Grady, "How to Coax Life," *Time*, Fall 1996, 36–39.

22. Peter Singer, "Technology and Procreation: How Far Should We Go?" *Technology Review*, Vol. 88 (February/March 1985): 22, 24.

23. Corea, *The Mother Machine*, 123.

24. Squier, "Fetal Subjects and Maternal Objects: Reproductive Technology and the New Fetal/Maternal Relation," *The Journal of Medicine and Philosophy*, Vol. 21 (1996): 516.

25. Grady, "How to Coax Life."

26. International Working Group on Preimplantation Genetics, "Preimplantation Diagnosis: An Alternative to Prenatal Diagnosis of Genetic and Chromosomal Disorders," *Journal of Assisted Reproductive Genetics*, Vol. 16 (1999): 161–164.

27. Corea, *The Mother Machine.*

28. Ruth Hubbard, "Personal Courage Is Not Enough: Some Hazards of Childbearing in the 1980's." In *Test-Tube Women: What Future for Motherhood?* (London: Pandora Press, 1984), 331–355.

29. Tamara Callahan et al., "The Economic Impact of Multiple-Gestation Pregnancies and the Contribution of Assisted-Reproduction Techniques to Their Incidence," *The New England Journal of Medicine*, Vol. 331 (28 July 1994): 270.

30. *Consumer Reports*, "Fertility Clinics: What Are the Odds?" February 1996, 53.

31. Trip Gabriel, "High-Tech Pregnancies Test Hope's Limit," *The New York Times*, 7 Janaury 1996, 1, 18–19.

32. Ibid., 1.

33. *Consumer Reports*, "Fertility Clinics."

34. Peter Neumann, Soheyla Gharib, and Milton Weinstein, "The Cost of a Successful Delivery with In Vitro Fertilization," *The New England Journal of Medicine*, Vol. 331 (28 July 1994): 240.

35. Marsden Wagner, "IVF: Out-of-Date Evidence, or Not?" *The Lancet*, Vol. 348 (23 November 1996): 1394.

36. Geoffrey Cowley, "The Future of Birth," *Newsweek*, 25 September 1995, 42.

37. Gena Corea and Susan Ince, "Report of a Survey of IVF Clinics in the U.S." In *Made to Order: The Myth of Reproductive and Genetic Progress* (New York: Pergamon, 1987), 133–145.

38. Ibid., 139,

39. Judith Lasker and Susan Borg, *In Search of Parenthood: Coping with Infertility and High-Tech Conception* (Boston: Beacon Press, 1987), 55.

40. Gabriel, "High-Tech Pregnancies," 19.

41. *Consumer Reports*, "Fertility Clinics," 52.

42. *Consumer Reports*, "Fertility Clinics," 52.

43. Singer, "Technology and Procreation," 24.

44. Susan Sherwin, *No Longer Patient: Feminist Ethics and Health Care* (Philadelphia: Temple University Press, 1992), 125.

45. *Newsweek,* "The Infertility Trap," 4 April 1994, 30–31.

46. Corea, *The Mother Machine.*

47. Ibid., 112.

48. Gabriel, "High-Tech Pregnancies," 19.

49. Gina Kolata, "Clinics Selling Embryos Made for 'Adoption,' " *The New York Times,* 23 November 1997, 1.

50. Ibid., 1, 34.

51. Lisa Belkin, "Pregnant with Complications," *The New York Times Magazine*, 26 October 1997, 38.

52. Meyer, *The Wandering Uterus,* 33.

53. Kolata, "Clinics Selling Embryos," 34.

54. Belkin, "Pregnant with Complications," 36.

55. Ibid., 38.

56. Meyer, *The Wandering Uterus,* 39. A clinic in Atlanta reported the birth of twins using a frozen egg (Kolata, "Successful Births Reported"). Fertility clinics have frozen sperm and embryos, but never eggs. Researchers hope this will make donor eggs less expensive since fertility drugs produce as many as thirty eggs at a time, which might be stored. It is instructive to learn that the researchers in Atlanta had difficulty finding a woman willing to use a frozen egg, given the uncertainty of the procedure's safety. It took over two years to find someone who agreed. This particular woman had run out of money due to the high cost of IVF with donor eggs, so she was offered free IVF if she would accept frozen eggs. She consented.

57. Lasker and Borg, *In Search of Parenthood.*

58. Corea, *The Mother Machine*, 90.

59. Meyer, *The Wandering Uterus,* 60.

60. Caroline Daniel, "His Colleagues Call Him 'God'," *New Statesman,* Vol. 127 (19 June 1998): 29.

61. See Faust, "Baby Girl or Baby Boy," for details on the history of sex selection techniques.

62. Alison Renteln, "Sex Selection and Reproductive Freedom," *Women's Studies International Forum*, Vol. 15 (May/June 1992): 405–426.

63. Nora Frenkiel, " 'Family Planning,': Baby Boy or Girl?" *The New York Times,* 11 November 1993, C6.

64. Fred Arnold et al., "Son Preference, the Family Building Process and Child Mortality in India," *Population Studies*, Vol. 52 (November 1998): 301–315.

65. Joni Seager, *The State of Women in the World Atlas* (London: Penguin Books, 1997), 34.

66. Corea, *The Mother Machine*, 199.

67. Betty B. Hoskins and Helen B. Holmes, "Technology and Prenatal Femicide." In *Test-Tube Women: What Future for Motherhood?* (London: Pandora Press, 1984), 237–255.

68. Corea, *The Mother Machine.*

69. Kathleen Fackelmann, "It's a Girl!" *Science News*, Vol. 154 (28 November 1998): 350–351.

70. Lisa Belkin, "Getting the Girl," *The New York Times Magazine*, 25 July 1999, 26.

71. Ibid., 29.

72. Ibid.

73. Daniel Goodkind, "Should Prenatal Sex Selection Be Restricted? Ethical Questions and Their Implications for Research and Policy," *Population Studies*, Vol. 53 (March 1999): 49–61.

74. Belkin, "Getting the Girl," 38.

75. Ibid.

76. Barbara Drygulski Wright, "Introduction," In *Healing Technology: Feminist Perspectives* (Ann Arbor: University of Michigan Press, 1989), 21.

77. *The Ecologist,* "Fertility for Sale," Vol. 25, No. 4 (July/August 1995), 137.

78. Gabriel, "High-Tech Pregnancies," 8.

79. Callahan et al., "The Economic Impact."

80. Corea and Ince, "Report of a Survey of IVF."

81. Michelle Stanworth, ed., *Reproductive Technologies: Gender, Motherhood, and Medicine* (Minneapolis: University of Minnesota Press, 1987), 14–15.

82. Roberts, *Killing the Black Body*, 252.

83. Ibid., 254.

84. Wright, "Introduction," 18.

85. Virginia Walther and Alma Young, "Costs and Benefits of Reproductive Technologies," *Affilia*, Vol. 17 (Summer 1992): 112.

86. Judy Wajcman, "Delivered into Men's Hands? The Social Construction of Reproductive Technology." In *Power and Decision: The Social Control of Reproduction* (Cambridge: Harvard University Press, 1994), 168–169.

87. Betsy Hartmann, *Reproductive Rights and Wrongs: The Global Politics of Population Control* (Boston: South End Press, 1995), 176.

88. Kim Yanoshik and Judy Norsigian, "Contraception, Control, and Choice: International Perspectives." In *Healing Technology: Feminist Perspectives* (Ann Arbor: University of Michigan Press, 1989), 67; Hartmann, *Reproductive Rights and Wrongs*, 190.

89. Hartmann, *Reproductive Rights and Wrongs*, 213.

90. Ibid., 217.

91. Ibid., 218.

92. Ibid., 219.

93. Ibid., 106.

94. Barbara Ehrenreich et al., "The Charge: Genocide; The Accused: The U.S. Government," *Mother Jones*, November 1979, 31.

95. *The Nation*, "Norplant and the Social Cleansers, Part II," July 25/August 1, 1994, 116.

96. Hartmann, *Reproductive Rights and Wrongs*, 208.

97. Roberts, *Killing the Black Body*, 127.

98. Hartmann, *Reproductive Rights and Wrongs*, 211.

99. Ibid., 212.

100. Sonia Correa, "Norplant in the Nineties: Realities, Dilemmas, Missing Pieces." In *Power and Decision: The Social Control of Reproduction* (Harvard University Press, 1994), 290.

101. Jennifer Malat, "Racial Differences in Norplant Use in the United States," *Social Science and Medicine*, Vol. 50 (May 2000): 1297.

102. Kim Yanoshik and Judy Norsigian, "Contraception, Control, and Choice: International Perspectives." In *Healing Technology: Feminist Perspectives* (Ann Arbor: University of Michigan Press, 1989), 84.

103. Sheila Ward et al., "Service Delivery Systems and Quality of Care in the Implementation of Norplant in Indonesia." Report prepared for The Population Council, New York (February 1990): 74.

104. Correa, "Norplant in the Nineties," 291.

105. Ibid., 294.

106. Margot E. Young, "Reproductive Technologies and the Law: Norplant and the Bad Mother." In *Families and Law* (Binghamton, NY: The Haworth Press, 1995), 264.

107. Ethel Long-Scott and Judy Southworth, "Norplant: Birth Control or Control of Poor Women?" *Extra!*, Special Issue 1992, 17.

108. John A. Robertson, *Children of Choice: Freedom and the New Reproductive Technologies* (Princeton, NJ: Princeton University Press, 1994). 71.

109. Young, "Reproductive Technologies," 269.

110. In her study of how race contributed to attitudes toward single mothers before *Row* v. *Wade*, Solinger (*Wake Up Little Susie*, 58) observes that attitudes toward black unwed mothers, "constructed of race, gender, and class prejudices, shaped by fear of high welfare costs and supported by convictions about the biological bases of black behavior, led to a harsh conclusion: If black women had babies without the sanction of legal or religious institutions, that strongly suggested that these women were normless and immoral."

111. Pam Belluck, "Cash-for-Sterilization Plan Draws Addicts and Critics," *The New York Times*, 24 July 1999, A8.

112. Roberts, *Killing the Black Body*, 110.

113. Barbara Kantrowitz and Pat Wingert, "The Norplant Debate," *Newsweek*, 15 February 1993, 37.

114. Roberts, *Killing the Black Body*, 121.

115. Hartmann, *Reproductive Rights and Wrongs*, 202.

116. Roberts, *Killing the Black Body*, 144.

117. Hartmann, *Reproductive Rights and Wrongs*, 205.

118. Ibid., 206.

119. Ehrenreich et al., "The Charge," 36.

120. Yanoshik and Norsigian, "Contraception, Control, and Choice," 70.

121. Roberts, *Killing the Black Body*, 148.

122. Soheir Morsy, "Biotechnology and the Taming of Women's Bodies." In *Processed Lives: Gender and Technology in Everyday Life* (New York: Rutledge, 1997): 169.

123. Roberts, *Killing the Black Body*, 146.

124. Morsy, "Biotechnology," 170.

125. *The Ecologist*, "Fertility for Sale."

126. Stanworth, *Reproductive Technologies*.

127. Stanworth, *Reproductive Technologies*, 25.

128. Daniel, "His Colleagues Call Him 'God.' "

129. Julie Brienza, "Assisted Reproductive Technology Studies by New York Task Force," *Trial*, Vol. 34 (July 1998): 109.

130. Mariana Valverde and Lorna Weir, "Regulating New Reproductive and Genetic Technologies: A Feminist View of Recent Canadian Government Initiatives," *Feminist Studies*, Vol. 23 (Summer 1997): 419–431.

131. Barbara E. Menning, "In Defense of IVF." In *The Custom-Made Child?: Women-Centered Perspectives* (Clifton, NJ: Humana Press, 1981), 264.

132. Patricia Spallone and Deborah Lynn Steinberg, eds., *Made to Order: The Myth of Reproductive and Genetic Progress* (New York: Pergamon, 1987), 7.

133. Barbara Katz Rothman, "The Meanings of Choice in Reproductive Technology." In *Test-Tube Women: What Future for Motherhood?* (London: Pandora Press, 1984), 32.

134. Christine Crowe, "Women Want It: *In Vitro* Fertilization and Women's Motivations for Participation." In *Made to Order: The Myth of Reproductive and Genetic Progress* (New York: Pergamon, 1987), 89.

135. Ibid., 90.

136. Lasker and Borg, *In Search of Parenthood*, 25.

137. Anne Donchin, "Feminist Critiques of New Fertility Technologies: Implications for Social Policy," *The Journal of Medicine and Philosophy*, Vol. 21 (1996): 476.

138. Brown, *Our Miracle Called Louise, A Parents' Story* (London: Paddington Press, 1979), 83, 88, 108.

139. Lasker and Borg, *In Search of Parenthood*, 17.

140. Crowe, "Women Want It," 87.

141. Ibid., 88.

142. Ibid., 93.

143. Lasker and Borg, *In Search of Parenthood*, 16.

144. Stanworth, *Reproductive Technologies*, 20–21.

145. Stanlie M. James, "Mothering: A Possible Black Feminist Link to Social Transformation?" In *Theorizing Black Feminism: The Visionary Pragmatism of Black Women* (New York: Rutledge, 1993), 44–54.

146. Stanworth, *Reproductive Technologies*, 22.

147. Donchin, "Feminist Critiques," 492.

148. Brown, *Our Miracle Called Louise*, 106, 168.

149. Corea, *The Mother Machine*, 168.

150. Squier, "Fetal Subjects," 516, 519, 533.

151. Roberts, *Killing the Black Body*, 154.

152. Dorothy Roberts, "The Future of Reproductive Choice for Poor Women and Women of Color," *Women's Rights Law Reporter*, Vol. 14 (Spring/Fall 1992): 312–313.

153. Lisa C. Ikemoto, "Furthering the Inquiry: Race, Class, and Culture in the Forced Medical Treatment of Pregnant Women." In *Critical Race Feminism: A Reader* (New York: New York University Press, 1997), 140.

154. Meyer, *The Wandering Uterus,* 102.

155. Young, "Reproductive Technologies," 110.

156. Ibid., 110–111.

157. Judy Scales-Trent, "Women of Color and Health: Issues of Gender, Community, and Power," *Stanford Law Review*, Vol. 43 (July 1991): 1366.

158. In March 2001, the Supreme Court ruled 6–3 that public hospitals in South Carolina cannot test a pregnant woman for drugs and give results to police without the woman's consent. The majority of the Justices found that this is a violation of the Constitution's protection against unreasonable searches (L. Greenhouse, "High Court Bars Some Drug Tests").

159. Roberts, *Killing the Black Body*, 179.

160. Young, "Reproductive Technologies," 113.

161. Deborah Krauss, "Regulating Women's Bodies: The Adverse Effect of Fetal Rights Theory on Childbirth Decisions and Women of Color," *Harvard Civil Rights–Civil Liberties Law Review*, Vol. 26 (Summer 1991): 548.

162. Roberts, *Killing the Black Body*, 183–184.

163. Ibid., 183.

164. Margaret S. Boone, *Capital Crime: Black Infant Mortality in America* (Newbury Park, CA: Sage Publications, 1989), 27.

165. Roberts, *Killing the Black Body*, 184.

166. *U.S. Newswire,* "Black Women's Health Project: Why Is Motherhood So Unsafe for Women of Color?" 18 June 1999.

167. *American Health,* "Forgotten Americans: Special Report," November 1990, 41–42.

168. *The Ecologist,* "Fertility for Sale," 137.

169. Roberts, *Killing the Black Body*, 184.

170. Sharon M. Keigher, "Reflecting on Progress, Health, and Racism: 1900 to 2000," *Health and Social Work,* Vol. 24 (November 1999): 243.

171. Boone, *Capital Crime,* 193.

172. Roberts, *Killing the Black Body*, 184.

173. Barbara Blair and Susan E. Cayleff, eds., *Wings of Gauze: Women of Color and the Experience of Health and Illness* (Detroit: Wayne State University Press, 1993).

174. Paola Bollini and Harald Siem, "No Real Progress Toward Equity: Health of Migrants and Ethnic Minorities on the Eve of the Year 2000," *Social Science and Medicine,* Vol. 41 (1995): 819–828.

175. Lori Andrews, *Between Strangers: Surrogate Mothers, Expectant Fathers and Brave New Babies* (New York: Harper and Row, 1989). 28.

176. Lasker and Borg, *In Search of Parenthood.*

177. Meyer, *The Wandering Uterus,* 71.

178. Andrews, *Between Strangers,* 40–45.

179. Corea, *The Mother Machine,* 219.

180. Meyer, *The Wandering Uterus,* 79.

181. Phyllis Chesler, *Sacred Bond: The Legacy of Baby M* (New York: Random House, 1988), 152.

182. Ibid., 154.

183. Katha Pollitt, "The Strange Case of Baby M," *The Nation,* 23 May 1987, 667.

184. Roberts, *Killing the Black Body*, 278.

185. Carol Lawson, "New Birth Surrogates Carry Couples' Babies," *The New York Times,* 12 August 1990, 24.

186. Ibid.

187. Corea, *The Mother Machine,* 274.

188. Roberts, *Killing the Black Body*, 280–281.

189. Meyer, *The Wandering Uterus,* 75.

190. Gina Kolata, "Amid Fears About a Fetal Test, Many Are Advising Against It," *The New York Times,* 15 July 1992, C3.

191. Anne Finger, "Claiming All of Our Bodies: Reproductive Rights and Disabilities." In *Test-Tube Women: What Future for Motherhood?* (London: Pandora Press, 1984), 281–297.

192. Martha Pott, "Selective Nontreatment of Handicapped Newborns." In *More than Kissing Babies?: Current Child and Family Policy in the United States* (Westport, CT: Auburn House, 1994): 179–206.

193. Corea, *The Mother Machine,* 128.

194. *National Catholic Reporter,* "Appointment of Ethicist at Princeton Criticized," 23 October 1998, 9.

195. Finger, "Claiming All of Our Bodies."

196. Mary S. Henifin, "New Reproductive Technologies: Equity and Access to Reproductive Health Care," *Journal of Social Issues,* Vol. 49 (1993): 69.

197. Donchin, "Feminist Critiques," 477.

198. Wajcman, "Delivered Into Men's Hands?" 158.

199. Brody, *Jane Brody's The New York Times Guide to Personal Health* (New York: Times Book, 1982), 199.

200. Young, "Reproductive Technologies," 263.

201. Walther and Young, "Costs and Benefits," 116–117.

202. Correa, "Norplant in the Nineties," 306.

203. Correa, "Norplant in the Nineties," 303. Costa Rica offers an illustration of the significance of social context. Although it is relatively poor compared to the United States, its infant mortality rates are lower (Roberts, *Killing the Black Body*, 183–184). Life expectancy rates for women are only slightly lower, and for men they are higher than in the United States. Longman ("The Slowing Pace") explains that most Costa Ricans have access to basic health care, as well as enough money to feed and house themselves and their children at least adequately. Their lack of high tech medical procedures is not a fundamental issue.

204. Dorothy Roberts, "The Bias in Drug Arrests of Pregnant Women," *The New York Times*, 11 August 1990, 25.

205. Henifin, "New Reproductive Technologies," 62, 72.

206. Patricia Hill Collins, "Producing the Mothers of the Nation: Race, Class, and Contemporary U.S. Population Policies." In *Women, Citizenship, and Difference* (London: Zed Books, 1999), 118–129.

207. Collins, "Producing the Mothers," 127.

208. Andrews, *Between Strangers*, 259–260.

209. Anne Taylor Fleming, "Our Fascination with Baby M," *The New York Times Magazine*, 24 March 1987, 33–38, 87.

210. Corea, *The Mother Machine*, 229.

6

The Electronic Office
A Counterfeit Revolution

❖ ❖ ❖ ❖ ❖ ❖

In what does this alienation of labour consist? First, that the work is external to the worker, that it is not part of his nature, that consequently he does not fulfill himself in his work but denies himself, has a feeling of misery, not of well-being, does not develop freely a physical and mental energy, but is physically and mentally debased . . . his work is not voluntary but imposed, forced labour . . . Finally, the alien character of the work for the worker appears in the fact that it is not his work but work for someone else, that in work he does not belong to himself but to another person.
Karl Marx

We now turn our focus to technological developments in the office, which have been praised for either eliminating or reducing boring and routine office jobs while providing not only more interesting but far more skilled employment. For many women workers, however, developing technologies have yet to deliver as promised. Countless studies document both positive and negative changes in the electronic office, but the most significant social fact is that technology has done little to improve the overall status of women in the workplace: Women are still overrepresented at the bottom of the office hierarchy in all respects, including pay, prestige, and control over working conditions. We will review some of the technological changes that have occurred and examine five specific concerns regarding the electronic office: the threat it poses regarding job loss, the reduction (rather than enhancement) of work skills, computer monitoring, health risks in the automated office, and the negative implications of the increasing flexibility of office location. We will see that each of these issues are of particular concern for women, given their location in the work force.

116

THE ELECTRONIC REVOLUTION

The first electronic computers, developed during World War II, were cumbersome, expensive, and very delicate. They had to be housed in spacious rooms, with carefully regulated temperatures. Rapidly improved, computers became smaller, more powerful, and more dependable. By the early 1960s microelectronics developed: Electronic components could now be integrated on a single chip of silicon, smaller than a thumb nail. Computers have become increasingly powerful, more reliable, and less expensive, and improvements are likely to continue.

Office technology has been lavishly praised as being capable of upgrading jobs and skills, producing better quality work, and facilitating decision making. Since it also allows flexibility in terms of the location of work, some have envisioned a future of "electronic cottages," where families work and play together in the home. In addition, computers permit ready and reliable feedback on worker performance through computer monitoring. Finally, electronic offices may also provide cost savings: Teleconferences, for example, occur on television screens, eliminating the need and expense of traveling to distant locales.

These developments have been viewed as permitting more challenging jobs in an environment that is increasingly efficient and productive. As we have seen, the media foster positive notions of computerization. For example, when *Time* magazine chose the computer as the "Machine of the Year," reporter Otto Friedrich[1] jubilantly announced that the information revolution

> has arrived, bringing with it the promise of dramatic changes in the way people live and work, perhaps even in the way they think. Americans will never be the same.

Friedrich assured readers that the computer is even powerful enough to alter Third World development:

> While robot factories could fill the need for manufactured goods, the microprocessor would create miriad new industries, and an international computer network could bring important agricultural and medical information to even the most remote villages.

In fact, a growing reliance on computer-based technology has marked a significant change in the workplace, and the impact of technology on clerical work has been particularly dramatic. Clerical employment includes the work of secretaries, stenographers, typists, file clerks, bookkeepers, accounting and financial clerks, and general office clerks. As we have seen, women are segregated in "female-dominated" fields such as these, as well as occupations like receptionist, telephone operator, bank teller, and postal clerks. In 1999, according to the U.S. Department of Labor, ten (of more than 500) occupational categories accounted for almost one-third of all women workers, and seven of these ten were at least 75 percent female. In particular, the category of secretary is 98.6 percent female, receptionists are 98.6 percent female; bookkeepers and accounting and auditing clerks are 91.4 percent female.[2] The gender division of labor continues to confine the majority of women to relatively few occupations, which tend to be less skilled and underpaid. At the upper end of the scale, less than one-third of the nation's 1.3 million programmers and systems analysts are women.[3] Currently, women attain fewer than 28 percent of U.S. bachelor's degrees in computer science and that number has been dropping. Women represent only 9 percent of engineering degrees, and they are only 20 percent of the work force in information technology.[4] Given their location in the job market, women thus find themselves at the bottom of the office hierarchy, and subsequently on the front lines of some of the major changes in the office, particularly automation.

Race is a significant factor as well. Historically, men and women of color have been associated with labor-intensive, low-technology work. Since World War II, minority women have entered clerical and sales occupations as well as professional technical fields. However, they remain concentrated in routine, largely manual jobs—particularly those that have been negatively affected by new technology, such as filing and keypunching. The clerical jobs in which black women dominate, such as telephone operators, key punchers, and duplicating machine operators, are special targets of office automation. A study of computer use in various work settings noted that in the hierarchy of U.S. jobs, "black women are found most frequently in the lowest paid and most tedious jobs crammed into back rooms where they work with and among outdated and health-threatening VDTs, inappropriate furniture, and poor lighting conditions."[5] "What this means is that even though racial ethnic women have moved into white collar work, they are nonetheless ghettoized within it. In effect there is now a racial stratification of jobs within the office."[6]

Greater occupational segregation exists in high-tech fields compared to other industries.[7] Top positions of computer scientist and programmer tend to be held by white males, while the lower-level categories of computer operator and data entry occupations are largely held by minority women. Clerical and sales jobs were open to minority women through affirmative action, but with technological change many of these jobs have been eliminated or reduced.[8] Downsizing is often particularly harmful to minority women, who have only recently attained these jobs or who have been chosen for work such as public relations, which is targeted for elimination because it is not profit-making.[9] The restructuring of the corporation has also meant the elimination of jobs that were previously routes to upward mobility in the workplace. As a result, higher education becomes necessary to secure desirable jobs. Minority women, however, with fewer resources to go to college, are likely to be disadvantaged by this.[10]

This pattern of gender and racial segregation is the context for a consideration of the electronic office and its implications. We will begin by discussing the issue of job loss.

JOB LOSS

Perhaps the central issue regarding the electronic office is whether it creates new jobs and enhances existing ones, or whether it results in job loss and the degradation of those jobs that remain. Certainly the technology is, *by design*, labor-saving. Cash machines replace bank tellers, file clerks are unnecessary when there is little paper, and the skills of calculating machine operators simply become obsolete. Ide and Cordell[11] illustrate how automation decreases the need for workers in a range of industries. They note, for example, that computerizing operator services will enable AT&T to eliminate approximately 6000 operators by replacing them with "voice recognition" technology that responds to the caller. A computer, not an operator, asks, "Will you accept this collect call?" and then recognizes a " yes" or "no" response. Between 1983 and 1993, banks eliminated 179,000 tellers and replaced them with automatic teller machines.[12] The electronic office similarly threatens the jobs of millions of clerical workers. Secretaries may be particularly hard hit since some predict that "the conversion from a paper-handling to an electronic–processing office will save 45 percent of all secretarial time."[13]

Several aspects of the wider economic picture indicate that the situation for women is even more precarious than it may initially seem. On the one hand, their traditional, low-skilled occupations have been expanding with the shift in our economy from the manufacturing sector toward service and clerical jobs. But as these stereotypical "women's jobs" have expanded, opportunities for both women and men outside this sector have shrunk. Job loss for women has been offset by the expansion of the service sector, but this does not necessarily mean genuine improvement since these jobs are the least desirable. Moreover, there is no guarantee against future unemployment as a result of automation.

Computers have also created jobs, many of them skilled jobs, but these new positions are often filled by men. A telling example comes from AT&T where the introduction of automated equipment resulted in the loss of 22,000 jobs by women. Almost 14,000 new skilled positions were created by technology, but these were virtually all filled by men.[14] Promises of retraining women at higher levels have generally been unmet at AT&T and elsewhere.

A study of the insurance industry documented the loss of low-skill clerical jobs as well as the creation of some *more* skilled clerical positions. Significantly, however, the automation of lower-level professional jobs removed rungs from the occupational ladder, and led to fewer opportunities for upward mobility and thus increased polarization of the labor force in terms of skilled and unskilled labor.[15] As Albin and Appelbaum[16] note: "The gap between the skills of clerical workers and those of professionals has widened despite the reduction in less-skilled clerical work. Skill requirements for clerical workers have increased at the same time that jobs have become overwhelmingly dead-end." Beverly Burris[17] concurs that there are observable trends in the workplace, including an increasingly bifurcated workforce between expert workers like programmers and engineers, and the nonexpert such as clerical workers. This has negative implications not only for upward mobility, it has also been associated with reinforcing race and sex segregation in some firms.[18]

Since investment in technology aims at saving labor, Aronowitz and DiFazio[19] make the point that professionals and managers, who in the past held secure jobs, are also experiencing difficulties. For example, not only operators are being replaced at AT&T, but with easy access to financial information, firms can cut large financial departments and with them middle managers.[20] AT&T is closing thirty-one offices in eleven states and cutting 400 management jobs.[21] With new technology, many companies have introduced the virtual office, providing their employees with electronic equipment but no regular office space. For example, "Dun and Bradstreet Software cut its real estate costs by 30 percent by implementing a telecommuting plan."[22] Aronowitz and DiFazio[23] worry about and anticipate a grim future where technology increasingly replaces both intellectual and manual labor, a future that lacks jobs for all who seek them, and ultimately a future of economic stagnation. Current economic shifts may thus be accompanied by automation and the displacement of millions of workers.

Although government statistics indicate that unemployment is down, Jeremy Rifkin[24] argues that this conceals the fact that millions of workers now find themselves in low-wage employment or in temporary jobs: "The reality is that the world is polarizing into two potentially irreconcilable forces: on one side, an information elite that controls and manages the high-tech global economy and, on the other, a growing number of permanently displaced workers who have few prospects and little hope of meaningful employment in an increasingly automated world."

Optimistic predictions that women will avoid large-scale job loss are based on the assumption that the U.S. economy will grow at an average rate. But if economic performance deteriorates, economic pressures on employers may incline them to use technology to cut costs, resulting in substantial technological displacement. Thus dramatically increasing unemployment for women may only await a serious economic downturn.

Recall that the gender division of labor remains intact with computerization: Women are still concentrated in lower level jobs, while white men dominate the more prestigious positions. As mentioned earlier, the situation of minority women is even more precarious. However, the desire of corporations to control costs may have ironic implications where women, particularly minority women, are concerned. Since women are consistently paid less than men, they may forestall the introduction of more technology since it may be cheaper to keep them than to bear the costs of innovation. In research conducted in Silicon Valley, employers indicated that they preferred hiring immigrant women as opposed to men because the women worked for less. According to one engineer:

> We already have the technology to fully automate everything we do here—it's just more expensive. We could definitely automate every step of the process if it ever becomes cheaper to do that than to use human labor. Because of the large supply of unskilled immigrants in the area, labor is still cheaper for doing certain jobs than machines are.[25]

Thus, women have yet to experience drastic job loss in clerical work, but they remain at risk. Gender and racial segregation persists, and the jobs filled by women and minorities are more likely to be subject to technological displacement.[26] Women have less influence than men over the use of technology in the workplace given their position in office hierarchies, as well as their relative lack of technical expertise and unionization. Black women, in particular, are most at risk in the electronic workplace since they are in the very jobs most likely to be eliminated.

DESKILLING VS. JOB ENHANCEMENT

The debate about office automation also centers on the quality of the jobs that remain once technology is in place. The possibility of eliminating boring, repetitious tasks through technology, and thus allowing workers to concentrate on more creative enterprises, is captured in an IBM slogan: "Machines should work, people should think." It is perhaps difficult to defend the position that human beings should continue doing tasks that machines are capable of performing, but the situation is not as simple as this suggests. Technology does not simply replace a person with a machine for a particular task: Instead, it reorganizes the work process itself so that jobs are divided into increasingly specialized and less challenging units. Increasing mechanization can thus mean "a reduction in the variety of work activities, reduction in actual physical mobility, and judgement concerning one's work."[27] This "deskilling"–or reduction in required expertise–can result in diminishing job satisfaction as tasks become fragmented and boring, and the office begins to resemble an assembly line in a factory, with a decline in the range of skills previously needed to accomplish tasks. Empirical studies provide increasing evidence of deskilling among clerical workers. Steven Vallas, for example, found significant deskilling in his study of the communications industry, and he also documented "a substantial trend toward greater alienation from work" among clerical workers.[28] Suzanne Damarin's[29] analysis of computer implementation in various settings reached a similar conclusion: "In all cases, the functions of the majority of workers are changed to accommodate the efficiency of computer operations; work becomes increasingly fragmented, meaningless, and repetitive, and a large number of jobs become nothing more than the preparation and entry of data for computer manipulation." This automation reflects, in part, the failure to develop or implement technology from the perspective of those who actually use it, as well as management's goal of cutting costs.[30]

Beverly Burris[31] contends that both deskilling and upgrading can exist in the workplace, and we need "more complex and nuanced theory, multidimensional and multilevel theory" to understand the variety. In *Technocracy at Work*, Burris[32] observes that "women have long been segregated into clerical and secretarial jobs with restricted mobility prospects, but in technocratic organizations this process is extended and structurally legitimated: the wider structural gap between expert and nonexpert sectors creates new types of credential barriers for nonexpert-sector women." Elsewhere she[33] notes that the least skilled jobs are disproportionately eliminated and that computerization is also consistent with an increase in monitoring and managerial control.

Harry Braverman[34] pioneered an analysis of the ways in which the division of tasks and the increasing split between thinking and doing enhances management's control over labor:

> Knowledge of the machine becomes a specialized and segregated trait, while among the mass of the working population there grows only ignorance, incapacity, and thus a fitness for machine servitude. In this way the remarkable development of machinery becomes for most of the working population, the source not of freedom but of enslavement, not of mastery but of helplessness, and not of the broadening of the horizon of labor but of the confinement of the worker within a blind round of servile duties.

A comprehensive study of office automation by the National Research Council[35] contains support for Braverman's class-based analysis. Although this report minimizes the impact of automation regarding job loss and deskilling, it acknowledges that the implementation of technology depends on factors such as competition and labor force availability, as well as the distribution of knowledge and authority in a given organization. Ultimately, the introduction of technology is management's decision, and within a capitalist economy, management is necessarily concerned with reducing costs and increasing profits. The report concludes: "The limited evidence available suggests that the decision to introduce new technology is typically dominated by economic considerations." Thus the attitudes of workers or the effects on them within the organization are seldom considered crucial. This echoes a point made by Albury and Schwartz[36] that the perspective of users and the needs of people tend to be overlooked in favor of the point of view of the management: "The problems that are set for science and technology are the problems of the owners and controllers of industry and allied institutions." Management's interest in control also affects the introduction of technology since computerization increases such control in numerous ways: One is by blatant monitoring, another is by changing the work process, transferring—as Braverman points out—the skills, knowledge, and independence of action from workers to management.

It is important to focus on the fact that much of the work that has been rationalized and deskilled is women's work.[37] Some have utilized and significantly extended Braverman's insights regarding deskilling and managerial control by including an emphasis on gender. Linda Valli[38] for example, agrees that automation is designed to increase productivity and not to improve the condition of workers. Significantly, however, she contends that capitalist relations do not fully explain the difficulties. The gender division of labor is constructed and reproduced in order to confine women to certain occupations (at home and at work), and Valli argues that office automation must be understood not only in terms of a profit-oriented economy, but also in terms of the status of women in society. While acknowledging automation's potential to rigorously control workers, she also argues that deskilling theorists "are mistaken when they posit the intrinsic unity of automation's capabilities (controlling, fragmenting, and deskilling) and when they overlook workers' struggles to upgrade their position through automation."

Judy Wajcman[39] agrees with the need to consider gender as well as class, observing that the gender stereotyping of jobs has remained remarkably stable, "even when the nature of the work and the skills required to perform it have been radically transformed." The movement of women into a previously male-dominated profession typically means the lowering of skill and wages for that work. In the face of widely divergent visions of the future, Wajcman claims that "the overall tendency is for technology-led changes to operate within and reinforce preexisting differences in the patterns of work." Consider, for example, that automation might have stabilized production in certain sectors and permitted a shorter work week. The trend, however, is going in the opposite direction.[40] As David Noble[41] explains,

> Instead of seeing the number of working hours reduced in the wake of so-called labor-saving automation, workers have seen the average work week either remain constant at 40 hours or actually increase due to compulsory overtime and shiftwork imposed by a management intent upon getting the fullest utilization of their expensive new equipment . . . In short, labor-saving technologies have not been used to save workers' labor (meaning physical and mental effort) but rather to save capital labor (meaning workers, and wages).[42]

In a study of five computerization movements, Kling and Iacono[43] document evidence of *both* deskilling and upskilling in regard to office automation, but they also pointedly refer to what I regard as an essential issue in this debate: Despite any and all the changes, "the clerical work force is likely to retain jobs near the bottom of the American occupational structure in terms of pay, prestige, and control of working conditions." As we have seen, these jobs are typically occupied by women, and the most precarious positions by minority women.

Technology may be capable of producing skilled, high-paying jobs but in reality most new jobs "have been contingent, part-time, benefit-free and frequently temporary."[44] Jeremy Rifkin[45] notes that, "In February 1993 alone, 90 percent of the 365,000 jobs created in the United States were part-time, and most of them went to people in search of full-time employment." He forcefully makes his point by referring to a former sheetmetal worker, Craig Miller, who lost his job at TWA making $15.65 an hour. Craig and his wife now manage four jobs between them and make less than what he previously made. "When Miller hears the Clinton administration boast of creating new jobs, he responds with a forced chuckle, 'Sure—we've got four of them. So what?'"[46] Our increasingly two-tiered labor force is evident in the fact that the percentage of Americans working full-time but still poor increased by 50 percent between 1979 and 1992, while in roughly the same period, the salaries of top executives rose by 220 percent.[47]

The implications of this have been illuminated by Jackie Rogers'[48] analysis of the increases in temporary clerical work in the United States. Temporary clerical workers are part of the contingent economy, which includes "part-time employment, temporary employment, job sharing, and domestic day work." By 1989, contingent workers represented 25 percent to 30 percent of the workforce. This work is characterized by low pay, few benefits, lack of unionization, and little security; and many of these workers would prefer regular employment. This part of the work force is also dominated by women (more than 64 percent) and African Americans (more than 20 percent). "Thus, the problems associated with temporary employment are disproportionately the problems of women and African Americans. And the number of Americans being introduced to these working arrangements is increasing every year."[49]

Braverman[50] illustrated how clerical work is becoming deskilled, but as Rogers[51] notes, clerical temps are even more deskilled and at times completely uninformed about the work they are required to do. Here is one worker describing her job assignment to Rogers:

> For some reason they were redoing all their files because they changed something, they changed the districts or something like that. Whatever, I don't really know.

Most of the those interviewed by Rogers described their work as boring, even robotic, but they also resisted the strains of their work by taking longer-term assignments, reminding themselves that it was only temporary, or even leaving an assignment. Rogers cites one particularly creative woman, Sarah, who found a memorable way to avoid the label of "the temp," which frequently substitutes for a woman's name:

> All you do is introduce yourself as 'Jill, as in Jack and . . .' and people never forget. So that's the name I use when I'm temping.

Rogers appreciates these examples of resistance, but recognizes that these workers operate within a context of tremendous constraint and that these tactics will not change the larger situation.

COMPUTER MONITORING

Computer monitoring is an extreme form of the managerial control that Braverman discusses, and it has become increasingly controversial. With new technology, the amount of information managers are able to gather on their workers sharply escalates. In effect, this advanced technology has introduced nineteenth-century labor discipline to the office.[52] Managers vary in terms of whether or not they choose to monitor their employees, but computer surveillance is rapidly developing in many industries and affecting both women and men at work. Attached to trucks, a computer can, for example, report any incident of speeding, as well as the number of stops the vehicle made. Iacono and Kling[53] point to some reasons for the negative effects of monitoring on telephone operators: "Surreptitious monitoring—both of the number of calls taken and the rate at which they are handled and of the operator's demeanor—increases the tension." Kristen Nelson[54] vividly illustrates this when discussing the work of telephone operators in an oil firm:

> for each operator the computer measures the number of calls taken, the length of each call, the number of callers who 'abandoned' before being answered, and the amount of time spent off the telephone or away from the work situation. In order to monitor performance, supervisors listen in on 10% of each operator's daily call volume (approximately 16 calls) each month, using a telephone pickup that cannot be heard by the operator.

Computers can monitor how many pages a typist produces per day or per hour. "Keystrokes and pages typed have become measures of productivity and serve as criteria for employee evaluation."[55] By the late 1980s, 4 million to 6 million American office workers were already subjected to such forms of surveillance.[56]

Many managers see positive results from this technology. They claim it motivates employees, makes them more productive, and provides an objective means of rating performance when determining raises or promotion. However, concern about this practice is growing among unions, government officials, and labor experts. Monitoring is regarded not only as stress-producing but dehumanizing. Many argue that "surveillance can create a hostile environment in which workers feel pressured, paranoid, and prone to stress-related illness. Surveillance also can be used punitively, to intimidate workers or to justify their firing."[57] Some unions have adopted official positions against it.

Systematic information about surveillance is lacking, but James Rule's and Peter Brantley's[58] study of a representative sample of 186 computerized firms in New York added significantly to the literature. They defined workplace survelliance as "any systematic monitoring by management of individual employees' job performance, where carried out with an eye to ensuring compliance with management expectations," and then documented such practices at a wide range of firms including factories, banks, insurance companies, restaurants, and veterinary clinics. They found that surveillance is widespread in all kinds of jobs to control and rationalize work. Significantly, it evolved as a *"by-product of computerization for other purposes."* Although technology may have liberating possibilities, Rule and Brantley find no evidence that it is being used to this effect in the real work world. Instead, it increases the ability of managers to control the fine details of the work of their employees. Rule and Brantley see no natural limits to increasing surveillance and suggest that we reflect on how to protect workers from its intrusions: "For it should be clear that recourse to systems like these is an increasingly basic feature of today's work life."

Traditionally, supervision measures a final project, but computer monitoring does far more: It scrutinizes *how* you work. According to Harley Shaiken, former labor analyst at MIT, this purpose is profoundly different. Shaiken compares it to knowing that your phone is tapped: "You tend to act differently, which is exactly what computer monitoring is supposed to make you do."[59] Although computer monitoring provides substantial advantages for employers by allowing closer supervision and control of their workers, surveillance may ultimately be ineffective if it leads to increased stress, illness, and job turnover. According to Shaiken, "In the overwhelming majority of cases, monitoring degrades the quality of the job and, ironically, can actually impair productivity."[60]

Computer monitoring is increasing in many settings (offices, airlines, super-markets, trucking, and so forth), and the implications of being watched all the time worries workers. As Langdon Winner[61] points out, "Now workers can be ubiquitously monitored in units calculable to the nearest microsecond." And failure to meet speed requirements or quotas can result in sanctions. Oxford Industries Incorporated has a slacks factory in Monticello, Georgia, that provides a stunning illustration of this. The factory has a system that tracks workers' pace to the thousandth of a minute. The workers, mostly women, are paid according to how their speed compares with the factory standard for their job. If a women produces 10 percent more than the standard, she gets a 10 percent increase in wages; a 10 percent lower production rate means that 10 percent is deducted from her salary. Each worker has a terminal at her work station that provides a running account throughout the day of her pace and her wages.[62]

Electronic monitoring is a vivid example of workers' loss of control in the workplace, and it has been associated with both stress and health problems in clerical VDT operators. Let's look further at the connections between health issues and the electronic office.

HEALTH CONCERNS

Office automation is increasingly associated with health hazards. Not only the new equipment, but the changing work process—the division of tasks, the isolation of workers, the pace, and the monitoring—is faulted. Those who use computers report numerous physical and psychological problems including vision problems, musculoskeletal disorders, and concerns about the effects of radiation on pregnancy.[63] Khalil and Melcher[64] specifically address the vision impairments:

> Eye discomfort, strain, burning, itching, irritation, and aching are among the most frequently reported problems experienced by VDT users. Workers even complain of blurred vision, double vision, color fringes, deterioration of visual acuity, and headaches.

Stress-related diseases stem from low-paid, fast-paced, repetitive jobs over which workers have little or no control. As Rifkin[65] puts it, "The new computer-based technologies have so quickened the volume, flow, and pace of information that millions of workers are experiencing mental 'overload' and 'burnout.'" Clerical workers who use computers suffer high levels of stress, which often leads to problems such as ulcers, high blood pressure, and strokes.[66] An employee at a Midwestern bank explains the stress associated with some of these jobs:

> Put yourself in my shoes. Imagine yourself viewing a jet-black screen displaying hordes of small, difficult-to-read, bright green numbers, keeping in mind that you must get these numbers absolutely accurate. You sit in front of this screen for six or seven hours on the night shift without any break, and handle an average of six critical deadlines each night, with your boss at your back.[67]

Work related health problems are caused by improperly designed work stations. Although companies could invest in ergonomic furniture and train workers in anti-stress techniques, they are not inclined to do so. Significantly, IBM filed and won a lawsuit against San Francisco when the city attempted to require employers to provide ergonomic furniture; a similar law was thrown out in court in Suffolk county in 1992.[68] Thus, computer work is designed in a way that causes injury and stress, but business fights efforts to change this.

Concerns have been expressed about the radiation associated with the use of video display terminals (VDTs). More specifically, some fear an increase in miscarriages and birth defects among women who use them. Khalil and Melcher[69] point out that this is a serious issue "in view of the greater proportion of women in the data entry and clerical professions." Over 20 million women use VDTs in the workplace. If emissions are a problem, those at greatest risk are probably these women, "for example, telephone operators, mail order clerks, and airline reservation clerks—who are exposed to massive emissions from numerous terminals lined up in small, poorly ventilated areas."[70] Many computer manufacturers are designing lower-emission products but, fearful of implying that earlier products were unsafe, they are saying nothing about it publicly.[71]

The National Research Council recommends that the federal government explore the possibility of epidemiological research to study the health concerns of VDT operators in the United States. However, as Meyer[72] notes, even though everyone agrees that we need more research, nothing has been forthcoming fifteen years after clusters of miscarriages were first reported. The problems of VDT injuries are typically insidious since they may take years to develop.

Repetitive strain injury (RSI) is the major occupational illness of our time since many jobs (typing is only one of them) require constantly repetitive motions.[73] According to the Bureau of Labor Statistics, RSI's accounted for 62 percent of all occupational illnesses in 1992. Carpal tunnel syndrome is perhaps the most well known of the RSIs, and it is a debilitating disease. While doctors and the medical establishment tend to be uninformed about this syndrome, it could be prevented simply through ergonomics, the science of safe workplace design. Creating safe and healthy workplaces may be expensive but observers have pointed out that the alternative is serious health problems.[74] Meyer[75] observes that "VDT-related injuries already affect at least 5 million people in the United States, costing corporations millions in health care claims, loss of productivity, and compensation premiums." Health problems are also found among U.S. clericals who work at home. The testimony of women before a government subcommittee indicated that the problems of homework include physical injuries: back, neck, and shoulder problems.[76]

Richardson[77] pointedly summarizes the problem within the United States: "New technologies have been used to create workplaces where people are continuously monitored, where processes are increasingly lean, where repetitive strain injuries (RSIs) are commonplace, where stress is increasing, where new chemical hazards are introduced daily, and where dull and dead-end occupations reign." As a result of automation, offices may be less safe than they used to be when office workers did a variety of tasks that permitted them to move around; now they may work at a keyboard all day. Khalil and Melcher[78] suggest ergonomically designed equipment, training in using the equipment safely, and frequent breaks. Richardson[79] contends, however, that the most significant impact of new technology is not RSI's, stress or even job loss: "These are merely symptoms of an overwhelming loss of power on the part of the vast majority." He reasons that with power, workers could demand the kinds of conditions that would make better, more secure jobs. On the contrary, however, he sees an increasing imbalance of power with new technology.

The electronics industry that produces this computer technology is also noted for creating complicated health hazards for workers, including headaches and nausea, as a result of the chemical fumes. Steve Fox[80] expands on the specifics:

> Scores of the chemicals used in electronics are known to cause, when inhaled or absorbed to excess, drunkenness, nerve damage, hormonal disruption, heart rhythm problems, kidney, lung, or thyroid damage, cancers, mental dysfunction, and emotional disturbance.

Supporting the research findings of numerous local studies, a massive U.S. study into the electronics industry found that pregnant women in production plants have an increased risk of miscarriage.[81] In Third World countries, long days and long work weeks in electronics assembly plants result in serious health problems. One survey reported that 95 percent of South Korean electronics workers "develop eyestrain, astigmatism, or chronic conjunctivitis within their first year of employment;" this is directly related "to the strain of working under pressure for long hours through microscopes."[82] Devon Pena[83] observes that the electronics industry, while hazardous, appears to be less threatening to women workers on the global assembly line than the chemical and furniture sectors. Nonetheless, "many problems associated with the use of toxic solvents and other chemicals in electronics assembly have longitudinal aspects not easily detected by a methodology relying on one-time, fixed counts." When used in unsafe conditions, these chemicals "can expose workers to synergistic mixtures of so many different chemical fumes that pinpointing causes of symptoms is impossible. Effects on workers may be acute and sudden, or cumulative and latent."[84]

WORK LOCATION

The combination of telecommunications and microprocessing technology now makes it possible for office work to be decentralized and geographically dispersed. Indeed, work can be done at home, in nonunionized parts of the country, or overseas. Potentially, this offers workers tremendous flexibility and encourages visions of work being done leisurely in one's home, to the distinct advantage of the worker. Consider how helpful homework might be to handicapped workers, residents of rural areas, or those without ready transportation. A report from the Clinton administration specifically cites the benefits of this: "reduced automobile pollution and traffic congestion, improved quality of work, smoother integration of work and family life."[85]

Many, however, contend that this optimistic image of telecommuting is more fantasy than reality: "It confused the freedom of the skilled computer professional, usually a man, with the necessities that made home-based labor attractive to female clerical workers in a society without adequate dependent care."[86] Although the popular media cast homeworking as the solution to women's responsibilities regarding work and family, for most clericals, homework has meant reduced wages and stress. It is simply part of the contingent labor force: "As part of a corporate search for flexibility, downsizing, and general cost cutting, employers began to replace full-time 'regular' employees with involuntary part-time, home, and contracted-out or temporary workers."[87] By 1988, about 350 companies had some telecommuting; by 1992, there were an estimated 6.6 million telecommuters, an increase of 20 percent from the previous year.[88] Women comprise more than half of all telecommuters; men who work at home tend to be self-employed.

As we have noted, women tend to work at the low end of high tech industry, few are managers, and fewer still are key decision makers. Homeworking is now being promoted as a solution to job loss in this industry.[89] Significantly, however, clerical home-based work can be quite varied. Kathleen Christensen[90] distinguishes three types of home-based workers: "company employees who retain all the rights and privileges of being employees; genuinely self-employed business owners, and those self-employed independent contractors who work for only one company and whose employment status is highly questionable." As U.S. corporations attempt to remain competitive, they frequently turn to this third category of workers, a secondary labor force that is primarily female. These workers provide huge savings for corporations since they are paid by piece rates, require no overhead, and typically receive no fringe benefits.

Although electronic technology may enable women to work at home, and thus reconcile their unpaid housework and paid homework, this prospect raises a host of concerns. Theoretically new technology allows both men and women more flexibility and shared involvement in housework and child care, but the fear of what it will mean in reality is captured in Alvin Toffler's cheerful observation that computers will allow "married secretaries caring for small children at home to continue to work."[91] Note the assumptions about women's paid and unpaid labor packed into this brief comment: Women are understood to be the primary caretakers of children and relegated to occupations limited in pay and prestige.

Many have challenged the ideas espoused by Toffler and other optimistic experts. Christensen, for example, denies that a woman can do computer work and child care simultaneously. Her research shows instead that the vast majority of women do not even try to work when their children are awake. They either make other child care arrangements, or they work after the children go to sleep. "By rising well before the children awake and by working deep into the night, they obtain the quiet and concentration they need to work . . . This type of work pattern affects the family: Our in-person interviews reveal that it takes a toll on the woman's relationships with her husband *and* the children."[92] Boris[93] cites a Wisconsin mother describing her homework: "When I get the claims at night, I try to put in an hour while the kids are watching TV. Then I get up at 4:30 a.m. to work before the kids get up. It all depends on what the kids are doing . . . During the day, I turn on the TV and tell my preschooler to watch . . . Then, when she takes a nap, I can work."

Ann Blackwell, a homeworker from Elgin, South Carolina, also illuminates these issues. She worked at home for five years for Blue Cross-Blue Shield as a "cottage keyer." She averaged fifty hours of work a week, mainly when her children were at school, but late at night if necessary. She was paid $.16 per claim, and by completing about 2,000 claims, she earned approximately $100 a week: "That is for a fifty-hour week, with no paid vacation time, no paid sick leave and no fringe benefits." Blackwell, however, wasn't complaining: She liked the flexibility and convenience of working at home, although she admitted that the work is lonely and boring.[94]

The absence of a national family policy on child care or paid parental leave severely constrains women's choices. Lacking this, technology may actually increase control over women and function to keep them in their traditional place in terms of both paid and unpaid labor. Boris[95] asserts that for most clerical homeworkers, "the choice was not between outside work and homework; the choice was between home or no work. In that context, homework appeared better than no income at all." Boris[96] observes that the economic changes that brought U.S. women to homework are part of a global pattern of growth in the informal sector: "An international gender division of labor made global the production of a wide range of goods and services, from data entry to garments." Christensen's research also challenges the assumption that women *like* working at home: They may prefer it to not working, but "of women who have primary responsibility for child care, most report the combination as stressful and isolating."[97] Homework is an option for women, but one that is chosen in a society that provides working mothers very few alternatives. It may, in fact, mean deteriorating work conditions since their isolation makes it difficult for them to share grievances with other women and organize collectively. Homework may provide flexibility for women, but it typically lacks essential features of worker protection such as unemployment insurance, medical benefits, or pensions. Not only is the pay substantially lower than in the corporation, there is no economic security when workers are old or disabled. In addition, "The simple fact that workers are isolated from one another can make homework a form of disempowerment, depriving women of the measure of social status that working with others provides."[98] The New Right has advocated home work for women. Conservative Republican Newt Gingrich, for example, echoed Alvin Toffler's enthusiasm and gender bias when he argued that homework would "strengthen neighborhoods and allow working mothers with preschool children to earn a living while staying at home."[99]

Hilary Silver's[100] analysis of a national sample of homeworkers largely supports the perspective that they suffer from overload rather than liberation. Working-class women in particular perform more homework and child care. Significantly, Silver found no evidence of any breakdown of gender roles as a result of homework. Even when men worked at home, this had little effect on their contributions to the household: "Men working at home, whatever their occupations, spend no more time in housework or child care than men working elsewhere." Silver concludes that gender determines who does the unpaid work of the household.

Given the different types of home work, some have suggested that only those who do genuinely self-employed homework—as opposed to company employment in the home—are truly liberated. Nancy Jurik[101] studied self-employed homework (SEH) by interviewing predominantly female, white collar, professional workers to examine this liberatory image. She added significantly to the literature by also comparing women in different social locations. Self-employment tends to be low among black and Hispanic women, approximately 5 percent for blacks, and 1 percent for Hispanics, but they are the most marginalized of homeworkers. In distinct contrast to a lucrative image of SEH, Jurik found that, "With some exceptions, respondent earnings tended to be low as is the case for much SEH. Women's earnings tended to be lower than men's earnings." Attempts to make one's business profitable often undermined the initial goals of working at home, such as personal fulfillment or family care. As one respondent put it: "The worst thing about this (SEH) is the insecurity. I often don't know where my next work is coming from. When things get really bad, I pick up part-time work . . . When things are bad I think . . . if a good (outside) job comes along, I would take it." The more necessary the income, the more self-exploitative the job became, which ultimately reduced its flexibility. As one respondent put it, "Yes, I have flexibility. I have the flexibility to work all night, and weekends . . . if I want to keep eating."

Women enter SEH ventures for a variety of reasons, many because of their responsibilities as wives and mothers, inadequate leave policies at work, as well as for autonomy and fulfillment. "Married women respondents of all racial/ethnic groups were more likely than men to mention care responsibilities (for example, for children or older relatives) as a motivating factor for SEH."[102] Although homework is supposed to benefit women with young children, Jurik found that SEH does little to change the traditional division of household work, and many women wind up with the familiar double workdays. "Low-income respondents combined SEH with full- or part-time jobs. This meant double and even triple workdays when unpaid domestic labor was also included."[103]

Jurik concludes that these workers are not typically exploited piece workers but neither are they liberated. They still do the majority of the unpaid labor in the home, and they face economic insecurity. "These findings suggest that policy makers' hopes for SEH and other small businesses as solutions to the economic devastation of corporate downsizing ad family-work conflicts are misplaced. SEH works best for highly skilled individuals or for those with additional income sources."[104]

Working at home for pay is not new, and a brief consideration of its history is instructive. Since the 1880s, reformers have fought homework. The 1938 Fair Labor Standards Act prohibited it in several industries, where wage and hour regulations were flagrantly violated. At best, an occupation such as sewing at home enabled women in the early decades of the twentieth century to supplement their husbands' income while providing home and child care. Done for a few hours a day, this may be helpful and convenient. But for many women in the early twentieth century, this homework became a desperate effort to earn as much as possible despite low piece rates and long hours:

> Some working class women spent every waking moment sewing and required the labor of as many family members as were available. It was common for children to be kept home from school so that more garments could be sewn. The sewing machine transformed such households into miniature sweatshops.[105]

Prohibitions resulted from the belief that homework simply could not be effectively regulated. Unions remain steadfastly opposed to it, but legislative efforts have moved in the direction of deregulating homework, despite the assumption of organized labor that it is intrinsically exploitative.

Although technology offered bright promises regarding homework, Boris[106] argues that it is exploitative, "not because the location of labor necessarily oppresses, but rather because the labor contract reflects the overall social positions of working women, some of whom earn more precisely because other earn less." She contends that most homeworkers, "lack control over their labor, having chosen homework as the best of a bad set of options as they attempt to earn wages and care for dependents." The upsurge of interest in home-based work in the 1990s was a response not only to the technological changes that allowed homework to be effective, but also to international economic changes including the decentralization of production around the globe that was negatively affecting women's economic position.[107] Wage labor at home and housework have both been invisible, and both have been part of the larger gender division of labor. "Employers have structured work to take advantage of sexual divisions and gender ideology. They pay women less because women belong in the home, and this self-perpetuating prophecy intensifies the structural barriers that women often face in seeking waged labor."[108]

Boris[109] agrees with the International Ladies Garment Workers Union that unionized shops should replace homework, which has undermined labor standards and organizing activities. She observes, however, that "solutions to homework have failed to confront the underlying reasons why women are homeworkers. Focusing more on 'home' than on 'work,' policymakers often forgot that homeworkers were working mothers who needed social support and sought empowerment."

Richardson's[110] discussion of Fleet Bank pointedly illustrates why unions are concerned:

> In 1994, Fleet Bank in Boston moved back-office jobs from Boston to Utica, New York, where wage rates (and rents) were lower. The bargaining power of the Boston workforce was completely undercut by the ability of the bank to use information and telecommunications technology to move the work at will. The bargaining power of the remaining workers at the bank was also diminished by this effective demonstration of their distensibility.

Richardson contends that workers have been convinced "that they have neither the right nor the ability to effectively comment on technology issues." Just saying no has been seen as a backward response to technology, even when it eliminates one's livelihood.

Kristen Nelson's[111] analysis of the suburbanization of office work in U.S. metropolitan areas is useful in illuminating the centrality of race and gender in terms of the location of office work. Her research indicates that low paid clerical work is moving from the central cities (where it was often performed by low-income minority women) to white, middle-class suburban areas. Nelson investigated back offices in the San Francisco–Oakland area where highly automated, low paying clerical work was performed. She attempted to understand why these offices are now located in white, middle-class suburbs. She found that technological considerations could not explain the shift: High minority areas such as Oakland met all the requirements of low rentals, good highway access, and so forth. The explanation, rather, was found in the labor force itself. Managers are seeking "an educated but tractable labor supply: one that will remain not only productive but resistant to militacy at the usual low job rewards."[112] Nelson argues that minority women, often responsible for supporting families, are viewed as less compliant, as well as less educated. White suburban women, on the other hand, are "high quality" in terms of class and education, and controlled by their lack of power in the market and at home. Nelson quotes a male manager who vividly articulates this desirable combination of class and gender control:

> We get a lot of women who get married, and then work here because of the opportunity to work close to home. Most of them have worked before and most of them have some college experience. They have families and own homes, so they tend to be more stable workers, with a stronger work ethic . . . When we moved out here, we tapped the beautiful source of suburban womanhood!

Nelson recognizes that this trend has serious consequences for female minority workers whose families often depend on their income.

Homework is definitely attractive to women since they *are* responsible for the care of children, the elderly, and the ill.[113] They are also often relegated to poorly paid occupations so their choices are more limited. Homework, however, does nothing to challenge this discrimination against women, to challenge the gendered division of labor, or the vast amount of unpaid work women perform. Instead, it provides an individualistic solution: It enables some women to cope with an oppressive situation by combining paid work and child care in the home; and, in effect, it bolsters traditional arrangements. The literature on women in development has alerted us to the double edge of women's home-based work: "On the one hand, women stretch their working day to combine paid work and household tasks, often suffering from exploitation by employers, family, and themselves; on the other hand, they earn much-needed income, gain self-confidence, and sometimes improve their social status."[114]

Albin and Appelbaum[115] focus on another dimension of work location when they discuss the large clerical processing centers that are increasingly common in suburban areas and economically depressed small cities, and the routine work performed there. They draw interesting connections between the fragmentation of work and its geographical dispersion, observing that workers in the suburbs have little or no opportunities for advancement, since they are geographically removed from higher level jobs and from opportunities to train for them. They contend that:

> Labor cost savings are achieved not through making the most productive use of the technology, but by the use of low-wage and/or part-time or temporary workers who are denied fringe benefits and by closely monitoring clerical workers and setting standards such as those for keystrokes per minute.

The use of low-paid labor and the fragmentation of work is extended to extremes in jobs offshore, that is, work done outside the United States—usually in developing countries. The cheap and even dangerous assembly line work that makes much office technology possible is frequently done by women in electronics factories in the Third World. Susan Tiano[116] has pointed out that capitalist expansion, both nationally and globally, affects women by "replicating on a global scale the gender-based divisions within and between domestic and capitalist modes of production." This expansion of gender-based divisions provides a framework for understanding the targeting of women for work on the global assembly line and the terms of their employment. The women who work in the electronic office are likely to be using technology assembled by Latin American or Asian women but, moreover, inequalities of gender, race, and class are embodied in all their labor. The "electronic revolution" and the problems it entails are thus not bound by national borders but part of an intricate global picture.

INTERNATIONAL DIVISION OF LABOR

Since the mid-1960s, the electronics industry in the United States has relied heavily on assembly line work done in developing countries. This has created what is referred to as a "new international division of labor." Electronic components are so inexpensive, in part, because of this underpaid work force around the globe where electrical and electronic goods are assembled. In an industry shaken by constant innovation, the limited benefits and low wages of these workers allow major corporations to save considerable costs and to remain competitive.

Electronics firms generally prefer to hire young, unmarried women, although by the 1990s firms differed in their ability to be this selective. In Mexico, electronics assembly plants are able to be more selective than apparel firms, since electronics work is preferred by women.[117] By the 1990s, managers were expressing an interest in women employees with children, claiming that "children are an asset to women's successful job performance because the responsibilities of caring for children make women more reliable in all aspects of their lives, including their job performance." Tiano[118] suggests that this, as well as managers' preference for women with partners, reflects their adaptation to the constraints of labor availability and high turnover rates.

What remains constant, however, is the targeting of female employees who, because of their subordinate position in their households and larger society, constitute a highly vulnerable work force. Colclough and Tolbert[119] observe that: "As U.S. electronics production jobs have moved offshore, the proportion of women and minorities in domestic high-tech production work has increased." Both nationally and internationally, managers use gender stereotypes to justify their labor choices: the patience, dexterity, and willingness of women to do boring work. Managers are also looking for a flexible labor force: "Women and minorities accept these low-wage jobs, can be trained fairly quickly, are replaced if they leave, and are more easily laid off if warranted by a drop in production demand."[120] Although the percentage of males employed in the industry has been increasing since 1983, women still account for almost 75 percent of electronics jobs, and men are "disproportionately present in technical, repair, maintenance, group-chief, and supervisory positions."[121] Temporary agencies also began to emerge to supply employers with workers during the mid-1980s. The short-term nature of this employment works to disrupt labor organization and prevents solidarity among workers.[122]

Although many researchers have documented the exploitation of Third World women by multinational corporations, it must be acknowledged that the employment opportunities these companies provide also improve conditions for women by giving them some measure of independence and increased opportunities. For example, in researching high-tech industries in California, Fernández-Kelly and Garcia[123] spoke with a young Mexican woman who had worked in an electronics assembly plant in Tijuana. She used a microscope to solder tiny gold filaments onto circuits; she liked the gadgets around her and felt like she was working in a laboratory. In the early 1980s, she earned $.65 an hour for a 48-hour week. She commented that it was a better job than most in Tijuana, but she decided to go to the United States, live with her aunt, and earn more. As an illegal, she got a job with an electronics firm in California where where she earned $5 an hour for a 40-hour work week. She gave $200 a month to her aunt's household and sent another $350 per month to her family in Tijuana. Fernández-Kelly[124] observes that many women have to work to support themselves and their children, but these jobs "do not provide channels for occupational mobility, increased earnings over time, or improvements in status."

The essential point is that many women in both the First and Third Worlds are employed at the lowest levels of the job hierarchy whether they "choose" these occupations or not. Moreover, the source of the difficulty is not just the attitudes or employment policies of their immediate employers, but also the discrimination and lack of opportunity in other spheres. Indeed, new forms of control may be exerted on women through paid labor. Aihwa Ong's[125] study of women electronics workers in Malaysia, for example, portrays a situation of profound cultural change, and the women she encountered were enduring as well as resisting the shift to industrial production. Employment in a multinational company may temporarily provide Third World women with some measure of autonomy and independence, but they are not freed from control—instead they endure a changing form of patriarchy and exploitation.[126] Simply put, hiring women for short periods of time does not benefit them or their families in any permanent way.

Tiano[127] found that most of the women she studied in Mexican *maquiladoras*—assembly plants located in developing countries by corporations of the developed world to take advantage of lower wages and less restrictive labor laws—enjoy some of the benefits of working and would choose to remain in the work force. Nonetheless, they are ambivalent about their role as wage earners. She proposes that "This ambivalence might also help explain why *maquiladoras* prefer female labor, in that it makes women more likely than men to serve as a transitory and flexible labor source."

During the 1960s, electronics assembly plants began being established in various Third World countries as a means for industrialized nations to reduce labor costs. By 1980, 120 "Export Processing Zones" (EPZs) existed in developing countries and their ramifications have been mixed. In Singapore, Hong Kong, and Taiwan, they provide thousands of jobs and an appearance of prosperity; in Sri Lanka and the Philippines, they have heightened rural-urban migration and resulting cultural tensions.[128] EPZs grew in number because they offered U.S. companies what they could not easily find at home: large numbers of single, young women willing to do semi-skilled or unskilled work in non-union factories for wages that are often less than U.S. $5 a day.[129] The average wages in these multinational factories as recently as 1987 are illuminating: In Hong Kong, it was $1.18 per hour; Taiwan was $.57; South Korea was $.63; and in the People's Republic of China, wages were $.16 an hour.[130] In electronics factories, this low-paid work can entail looking through a microscope all day long, bonding gold wires as thin as hairs to silicon chips. A report by The North American Congress on Latin America [131] provides a good description of the work:

> The workers begin with a tiny piece of silicon or germanium, often no larger than a millimeter square. An incredibly complex pattern of circuitry has already been engraved on the chip before it reaches the offshore plane. Once here, the work involves attaching a variety of miniscule wire leads to their proper connection in the larger component. The work usually requires some visual aid, either a microscope or a high-powered magnifying lens. With a typically complex circuit, workers are expected to produce between 60 and 100 assemblies an hour.

Some countries, such as Mexico, have supported EPZs as a means of creating and upgrading skills and jobs for unemployed male agricultural workers. By 1989, Mexico had more than 1,000 *maquiladoras,* 60 percent manufacturing electronic products. These plants employed nearly 400,000 workers.[132] "Since NAFTA's implementation in 1994, *maquiladora* employment has risen by 20 percent. Electronics and garment *maquiladoras* are the largest employers of female workers in Northern Mexico."[133] Women typically remain on the job for less than three years performing "numbing manual labor" with high production quotas and low wages.[134] Guendelman et al.[135] studied two electronics plants, one Japanese and one American, and also found a very high turnover rate for women: "Almost 17 percent of the women quit in the first 30 days. By the end of the 24-month study, 54 percent of the workers had quit." This research documented the fact that family responsibilities played a role in these decisions, but health problems also contributed to women's decisions to leave their jobs. The researchers noted the difficulty in assessing the health effects of these plants given the high turnover rates.

In Mexico, *maquiladoras* currently constitute the most significant economic activity in cities such as Ciudad Juarez. A report was issued by the Diocese of Ciudad Juarez in order to address pressing problems associated with them. It observed that the *maquiladoras* offer the possibility of expanded job opportunities, particularly for young women. They also cause migration into the city: 65.7 percent of the maquila workers in Juarez are migrants.[136] Despite the boon in industry, they also bring a host of social and economic troubles: The most acute are "the low salaries, the long working hours, health risks, and the disintegration of the family."[137]

Given high unemployment in Mexico, multinational companies know that they can be selective about their employees. They consistently hire working class women.[138] The majority of workers earn about 150 to 180 pesos ($20 to $24) per week.[139] They typically work 45 hours, but are often required to do overtime. Moreover, many commute three to four hours a day. Susan Tiano's research[140] suggests that "women need to generate household income not because their menfolk are unemployed but because these men's wages are insufficient to cover family expenses or because there are no men in their households." Given their low salaries, the children of these workers are often required to leave school and work. In sum, "While it is true that the *maquiladoras* have been a source of work for many and have brought foreign currency to Mexico, we must not ignore the fact that they have also brought poverty, marginalization, and disintegration of the family."[141]

Global factories are negatively impinging on some workers in the United States as well. "The microelectronics industry is, in fact, at the forefront of corporate capital's trend to relocate manufacturing production in peripheral and semi-peripheral areas where cheap, often state-controlled, women's labor is plentiful, particularly in Southeast Asia but also in Mexico, Puerto Rico, and other locations in Asia, Central America, South America, and Europe."[142] U.S. employers often argue that women and/or people of color are more content with this type of labor and are unqualified for other work. This global pattern is replicated in the United States as employers in the electronics industry in California's Silicon Valley, for example, hire primarily Asian and Latina women for operative jobs. Hossfeld (1994)[143] interviewed immigrant women workers in Silicon Valley as well as their employers and managers. She views employers' explanations for targeting women of color as sexist and racist ideologies, which permit them to maximize their profits. The microelectronics industry sharply stratifies labor according to class, race, gender, and nationality: "The high-profile, high-paid engineers, executives, and investors are overwhelmingly white, male U.S. citizens. On the opposite end of the occupational spectrum, the majority of low-paid manufacturing workers are Third World women." More specifically, women account for at least 68 percent and by some accounts 90 percent of the operative jobs in Silicon Valley, but only 18 percent of managers and 17 percent of professional employees. Similarly, only 12 percent of managers and 16 percent of professionals are minorities, as opposed to a minority total among operative jobs as high as 50 to 75 percent.

Employers indicated to Hossfeld that they preferred hiring immigrant women as opposed to men because the women worked for less. They also see immigrant women as a malleable labor force. As one particularly blunt manager told Hossfeld:[144]

> One month I may have to let a third of my production people go, and the next month I may need to double my work force. Let's face it, when you have to expand and contract all the time, you need people who are expendable. When I lay off immigrant housewives, people don't get as upset as if you were laying off regular (sic) workers.

Asian immigrant women are the preferred employees; most managers regard African Americans as the least desirable and most undependable. Hossfeld contends that employers' use of racial- , gender- , and class-based discrimination reproduces these forms of discrimination. They are also effective tools for dividing and controlling workers.

Fernández-Kelly and Garcia[145] studied an electronics firm in California, Nova-Tech, which had a policy of hiring Hispanics. The researchers called the firm, spoke in English about a job vacancy, and were told all the jobs were filled. Moments later they called, spoke Spanish, and were asked to come and file an application. The general manager, Mr. Carmichael, explained:

> We have a good product but we can only stay alive by producing efficiently and selling at a competitive price . . . American workers are spoiled by wealth and prosperity; unions have priced them out of the market. Foreign workers, whether Vietnamese or Mexican, are driven by the same forces that led our ancestors to succeed. They are reliable, they work hard, they don't make trouble, they are what a pioneering industry like ours needs.

Fernández-Kelly and Garcia note that Nova-Tech reported sales of $75.2 million and its profits reached $12.9 million. Workers were paid $5 an hour.

Off-shore factories, as well as U.S. immigrant labor, have thus been used to weaken unions and union benefits for workers in industrialized countries such as the United States. Only 5 percent of U.S. electronics workers are unionized, and it is unlikely that they will be unionized in the near future:

> Work climates in these firms are very bureaucratic, rule-oriented, and punishment-centered with dismissal used frequently as a control strategy. Frequent evaluations and close supervision are common in these plants, and levels of insecurity among workers are high.[146]

Colclough and Tolbert note that inequality among workers in high-tech industries is great and shows no indication of lessening.

GENDER, RACE, AND CLASS IN THE OFFICE

Although the implications of the electronic office have been interpreted in various ways, the most optimistic hopes of progress or emancipation for women simply cannot be supported by the evidence. The bleakest predictions may be overstated (such as massive job loss), but office technology is neither neutral nor necessarily progressive. There is, for example, nothing neutral about a machine that monitors workers by the minute. Researchers are acutely aware of the differential effects of technology in the office, and they often suggest that the electronic office not be seen as a unitary phenomenon. Types of equipment, the processes being automated, levels of automation, and the larger picture must be considered. The importance of the conditions under which technology is introduced and the size of the office are also important.

Increasing sophistication about the varied outcomes of office automation is welcome: It adds richness of detail and clarity to our understanding of both the problems and the opportunities of this phenomenon. But as we attend to all this specificity (office size, skill levels, organization of workers, methods of introducing technology, and so forth), we must avoid getting so mired in details that we obscure the larger picture: specifically the fact that despite any and all of these varying effects, women's work on the whole remains gender-typed and subordinate, and technology is doing little to alter gender inequality. As Randy Albeda[147] notes, most women still work in low-wage jobs without prospects for promotion and with few benefits. Moreover, minority women are concentrated in the very jobs most negatively affected by automation. Both racist and sexist ideologies are used to maintain these power divisions on a global scale. The pervasive myth that the electronic office reduces routine and monotonous jobs and provides more interesting and highly skilled work must yield instead to the reality that it frequently maintains and increases managerial control over women who predominate in positions of limited power, prestige, and income. Women, particularly women of color, are seldom retrained for more prestigious positions, while the alleged benefits of homework typically come at the price of lower wages and fewer job benefits.

Telecommuting is a good example of an aspect of the electronic revolution that held a great deal of potential. Here was an opportunity for women and men to do paid labor at home under flexible circumstances. Unfortunately, the jobs that telecommuting provides for most women have been low-paying, with few benefits. Telecommuting admittedly gives some women the degree of flexibility that they often seek, but it also keeps them at the lowest economic levels and it keeps them at home where they remain responsible for the household and the children. Homework has been ineffective in challenging traditional gender roles. Even when men do paid work at home, their household responsibilities remain minimal. Homework may provide some women with a choice, but it is a "choice" they make within a larger social context characterized by gender discrimination, by an absence of adequate and affordable child care, as well as an absence of lucrative jobs for women in the larger work force, or even household support from men. Technology is thus implemented in a way that locks some women more securely into traditional positions in the family and the secondary labor force, rather than dramatically improving their situation or status.

Telecommuting also reflects the polarization of the American work force into expert and nonexpert sectors, which in turn parallels and reinforces gender segregation. It permits some typically male professionals and managers to work at home or in the office and gives them increasing control over their labor, but the situation of the majority of women clerical workers is strikingly different. As Applebaum observes:

> They are more likely to be paid piece rates, less likely to receive fringe benefits, and are sometimes required to pay rent for the equipment they need to do the work . . . Supervision of off-site clerical workers is viewed as a problem by management.

Companies deal with this problem by giving clerical telecommuters discrete tasks that have a definite beginning and ending points and that can easily be measured and by paying piece rates.[148]

Thus the form that telecommuting takes is not simply neutral or technical in nature but reflects and even reinforces gender inequalities.

Sally Hacker's study of automation at AT&T illustrates how gender inequality affects women in terms of both their paid and unpaid labor. As we saw earlier, Hacker documented the loss of thousands of women's jobs at AT&T when automation was implemented. This in itself is one form of discrimination, which occurs when women are relegated to certain jobs, the very jobs targeted for automation. But Hacker's[149] analysis moves beyond this significant point. She helps us understand that gender inequality functions against women in a far more pervasive manner. It certainly restricts women's options in terms of paid employment, but it also saddles women with home responsibilities that, in turn, restrict their options at work. At AT&T, for example, women found not only male co-workers and unions unresponsive to their efforts to organize, but husbands were also opposed to the time and energy such organizing takes. The combination of these forms of discrimination inhibited women's ability to protect their interests at AT&T, as gender inequality pervaded both paid and unpaid labor. Women's inequality at home and at work thus interact and increase the obstacles they face in order to have technology serve their interests rather than the interests of elites.

The absence of improvement for women in the electronic office must also be explicitly understood in terms of a racially divided society. Women of color are the special targets of automation because they remain located in less skilled occupations. Indeed racial segregation is even greater in the computer industry than in other fields, and women of color are among the most marginalized of those who do computer work at home. Racism is evident in the rationalizations used for hiring minority women in electronics assembly plants in the First and Third Worlds, and racist conceptions of Hispanic women, black women, and Asian women are used to justify and maintain their place as cheap, even "expendable," labor. Racial inequality and discrimination affect the use of technology, rather than technology acting as a pure agent of change. Occupations remain racially segregated, and the labor force divided.

Kristen Nelson's[150] analysis of the suburbanization of office work in U.S. metropolitan areas illuminates the centrality of both race and gender in terms of the location of office work. Her research documents the movement of clerical work from the central cities to the suburbs where managers have found a preferred labor force of middle-class white women. This trend has serious consequences for female minority workers and indicates structural differences among women—obviously privileged white, middle-class women.

In the Third World, racial inequality vis-à-vis technology is particularly apparent since these societies often lack the constraints of a neo-liberal state, and thus illuminate the ways in which technology serves the interests of the more powerful segments of society, rather than simply being a force for progressive social change. Multinational firms target women in the Third World for employment: Given their subordination in the home and in the work force, they are the workers with the weakest bargaining power. Health hazards are particularly extreme in Third World electronics assembly plants, while the growth of temporary jobs in this industry threatens to further marginalize women of color. The absence of legal protections regarding homework also exacerbates health risks for Third World women.

Third World women are hired in electronics assembly plants within the United States for many of the same reasons evident in the Third World: They provide comparatively cheap labor and can be hired and fired as needed. Various studies have demonstrated a clear preference on the part of managers for Asian women and Spanish-speaking women. Racial inequality thus serves big business and affects the implementation of technology. Rather than providing gains for women of color, technology has often functioned to maintain their position in the lowest echelons of the labor force.

The electronic revolution might have brought more satisfying jobs, and perhaps even shorter work weeks for employees. But these promises never materialized. Instead working hours have expanded, job quality has often deteriorated, and workers have been threatened with unemployment. The gender division of labor remains intact and the gap between clerical workers and professionals is growing.

The limited improvement women have experienced in the labor force, despite the electronic office, also has to be understood in terms of the creation and implementation of this technology within an economic system that is divided by class and oriented toward profit. Class divisions in the office mean, quite simply, that management has the decision-making power, not workers. The very purpose of automation is to increase productivity, reduce costs, and increase profits—which reflects the interests of elite male power as well as capitalist control. It is claimed that by enhancing productivity and keeping the United States competitive, workers' jobs will be protected. But management does not aim to enhance the quality and quantity of jobs for the working class, women, or minorities. If this were to happen as a result of the electronic office, it would be mere happenstance. If, on the other hand, new technology adversely affects women or other workers, management could not be expected to be their allies. Even if the initial intent is not to eliminate or deskill jobs, a deteriorating economic situation could encourage this. Office technology is designed to save labor. And, as we have seen, the office jobs of women and minorities are most at risk precisely because of their location in the job market.

The electronic "revolution" has increased management's control over the work force through the fragmentation of work, which decreases the skill and significance of each part of the labor process. This, in turn, makes workers more easily replaceable, with fewer opportunities for advancement. Computer monitoring is the most blatant example of increasing control through the use of technology and, as we have seen, research indicates that it is widespread among telephone operators and computer operators. The geographical dispersion of work to nonunionized areas of the United States or to foreign markets has further enhanced the power of management. Workers' demands can now be countered with the threat to move the corporation to a more congenial area. Some cite the loss of power on the part of workers as the central difficulty regarding the automation of the workplace: "New workplace technologies emerge from a system that is generally unresponsive to the needs of the broad populace and over which the broad populace exerts little or no control."[151] The electronic office might have benefited working women, but its creation in a society divided by class has instead meant that in crucial respects it supports the interests of management in profit maximization and labor control.

CONCLUSION

In sum, we have witnessed the development of numerous forms of electronic technology that have the potential to greatly enhance the lives of women and men. This technology, however, has been developed in a context flawed by inequality. Rather than undermining that inequality, it has been implemented in a way that serves the interests of a few. It has not challenged but instead replicated much of the gender, race, and class inequality experienced by women. Thus, there is relatively little to cheer about regarding the electronic office: It is deeply implicated in maintaining women's traditional and inferior position in the labor market.

NOTES

1. Otto Friedrich, "The Computer Moves In," *Time*, 3 January 1983, 14.

2. http://www.dol.gov/dol/wb/public/wb_pubs/20lead99.htm

3. Rob Kling, "Computerization at Work." In *Computerization and Controversy: Value Conflicts and Social Choices* (New York: Academic Press, 1996), 283.

4. Elisabeth Goodridge, "Untapped Pool of Talent," *Information Week*, April 2000, 17.

5. Suzanne K. Damarin, "Women and Information Technology: Framing Some Issues for Education," *Feminist Teacher*, Vol. 6 (1992): 17.

6. Evelyn Nakano Glenn and Charles M. Tolbert II, "Technology and Emerging Patterns of Stratification for Women of Color: Race and Gender Segregation in Computer Operations." In *Women, Work, and Technology: Transformations* (Ann Arbor: University of Michigan Press, 1987), 320.

7. Melanie Stewart Millar, *Cracking the Gender Code: Who Rules the Wired World?* (Toronto: Second Story Press, 1998), 42.

8. *Institute for Women's Policy Research*, "Impact of the Glass Ceiling and Structural Change on Minorities and Women." December 1993.

9. Ibid.

10. Ibid.

11. Thomas R. Ide and Arthur J. Cordell, "Automating Work," *Society*, Vol. 31 (September–October 1994): 65–72.

12. Jeremy Rifkin, *The End of Work: The Decline of the Global Labor Force and the Dawn of the Post-Market Era* (New York: G. P. Putnam's Sons, 1995), 144.

13. Ibid., 148.

14. Sally Hacker, "Sex Stratification, Technology, and Organizational Change: A Longitudinal Case Study of AT&T," *Social Problems*, Vol. 26 (1979): 539–557.

15. Eileen Appelbaum, "Technology and the Redesign of Work in the Insurance Industry." In *Women, Work, and Technology: Transformations* (Ann Arbor: University of Michigan Press, 1987), 182–201.

16. Peter Albin and Eileen Appelbaum, "The Computer-Rationalization of Work: Implications for Women Workers." In *Feminization of the Labor Force: Paradoxes and Promises* (New York: Oxford University Press, 1988), 147.

17. Beverly H. Burris, "Computerization of the Workplace," *Annual Review of Sociology*, Vol. 24 (1998): 141–157.

18. Ibid., 144.

19. Stanley Aronowitz and William DiFazio, "High Technology and Work Tomorrow," *Annals of the American Association of Political and Social Sciences*, Vol. 544 (March 1996): 52–67.

20. Ide and Cordell, "Automating Work."

21. Rifkin, *The End of Work*, 141.

22. Ibid., 150.

23. Aronowitz and DiFazio, "High Technology and Work Tomorrow."

24. Jeremy Rifkin, "A New Social Contract," *Annals of the American Association of Political and Social Science*, Vol. 544 (March 1996): 19.

25. Karen J. Hossfeld, "Hiring Immigrant Women: Silicon Valley's 'Simple Formula.'" In *Women of Color in U.S. Society* (Philadelphia: Temple University Press, 1994), 74–75.

26. Beverly H. Burris, *Technocracy at Work* (New York: State University of New York Press, 1993).

27. Margaret Lowe Benston, "For Women, The Chips Are Down." In *The Technological Women* (New York: Praeger, 1983), 47.

28. Steven Peter Vallas, "New Technology, Job Content, and Worker Alienation: A Test of Two Rival Perspectives," *Work and Occupations*, Vol. 15 (May 1988): 170.

29. Damarin, "Women and Information Technology," 17.

30. Joan Greenbaum, *Windows on the Workplace: Computers, Jobs, and the Organization of Office Work in the Late Twentieth Century* (New York: Monthly Review Press, 1995).

31. Burris, "Computerization of the Workplace," 154.

32. Burris, *Technocracy at Work*, 98.

33. Burris, "Computerization of the Workplace," 149, 152.

34. Braverman, *Labor and Monopoly Capital: The Degradation of Work in the Twentieth Century* (New York: Monthly Review Press, 1974), 194–195.

35. National Research Council, *Computer Chips and Paper Clips: Technology and Women's Employment*, Vol. 1 (Washington D.C.: National Academy Press, 1986), 151.

36. Dave Albury and Joseph Schwartz, *Partial Progress: The Politics of Science and Technology* (London: Pluto Press, 1982), 63.

37. Barbara S. Burnell, "Book Reviews: Windows on the Workplace," *Feminist Economics*, Vol. 3 (Fall 199): 110–113.

38. Linda Valli, *Becoming Clerical Workers* (Boston: Routledge and Kegan Paul, 1986), 115.

39. Judy Wajcman, *Feminism Confronts Technology* (University Park, PA: Pennsylvania State University Press, 1991), 33, 31.

40. Charley Richardson, "Computers Don't Kill Jobs, People Do: Technology and Power in the Workplace," *The Annals of the American Academy of Political and Social Science*, Vol. 544 (March 1996): 178.

41. David Noble, "Automation Madness, or the Unautomatic History of Automation." In *Science, Technology, and Social Progress* (London: Associated University Presses, 1989), 87.

42. In 1969, workers averaged 53.5 hours a week on the job or doing chores at home. By 1999, this had increased to 57.5 hours working (Lipke, "Truth Be Told").

43. Rob Kling and Suzanne Iacono, "The Mobilization of Support for Computerization: The Role of Computerization Movements," *Social Problems*, Vol. 35 (June 1998): 233.

44. Aronowitz and DiFazio, "High Technology and Work Tomorrow," 52.

45. Rifkin, *The End of Work*, 167.

46. Ibid., 167.

47. Ibid., 169.

48. Jackie Krasas Rogers, "Just a Temp: Experience and Structure of Alienation in Temporary Clerical Employment," *Work and Occupations*, Vol. 22 (May 1995): 138.

49. Ibid., 141.

50. Braverman, *Labor and Monopoly Capital.*

51. Rogers, "Just a Temp," 146, 155.

52. Barbara Garson, "Manager Inside the Machine: Electronic Monitoring Is the Scourge of Today's Knowledge Workers, Who Still Consider Themselves White-Collar," *Information Week*, 18 July 1994, 36.

53. Suzanne Iacono and Rob Kling, "Computerization, Office Routines, and Changes in Clerical Work." In *Computerization and Controversy: Value Conflicts and Social Choices* (New York: Academic Press, 1996), 310.

54. Kristen Nelson, "Labor Demand, Labor Supply, and the Suburbanization of Low-Wage Office Work." In *Production, Work, Territory* (Boston: Allen and Unwin, 1986), 154.

55. Glenna Colclough and Charles Tolbert II, *Work in the Fast Lane: Flexibility, Divisions of Labor, and Inequality in High-Tech Industries* (New York: State University of New York Press, 1992), 141.

56. Langdon Winner, "Electronic Office: Playpen or Prison." In *Computerization and Controversy: Value Conflicts and Social Choices* (New York: Academic Press, 1996), 83–84.

57. Tony Horowitz, "Mr. Edens Profits from Watching His Workers' Every Move." In *Computerization and Controversy: Value Conflicts and Social Choices* (New York: Academic Press, 1996), 324.

58. James Rule and Peter Brantley, "Computerized Surveillance in the Workplace: Forms and Distributions," *Sociological Forum*, Vol. 7 (1992): 410, 422.

59. Carey W. English, "Is Your Friendly Computer Rating You on the Job?" *U.S. News and World Report*, 18 February 1986, 66.

60. Michael W. Miller, "Productivity Spies: Computers Keep Eye on Workers and See if They Perform Well," *Wall Street Journal*, 3 June 1985, 1.

61. Winner, "Electronic Office," 83.

62. Miller, "Productivity Spies," 15.

63. Carol Clark, "VDT Health Hazards: A Guide for End Users and Managers," *Journal of End User Computing*, Vol. 13 (Jan–March 2001): 13.

64. E.M. Omar Khahil and Jessie E. Melcher, "Office Automation's Threat to Health and Productivity: A New Management Concern," In *Computerization and Controversy: Value Conflicts and Social Choices* (New York: Academic Press, 1996). 834.

65. Rifkin, *The End of Work*, 188.

66. Ibid., 189.

67. Ellen Cassedy and Karen Nussbaum, *9 to 5: The Working Women's Guide to Office Survival* (New York: Penguin; 1983), 89.

68. J.A. Savage, "Are Computer Terminals Zapping Workers' Health?" *Business and Society Review*, Winter 1993, 41–43.

69. Khalil and Melcher, "Office Automation's Threat," 833.

70. Cheryl Meyer, *The Wandering Uterus: Politics and the Reproductive Rights of Women* (New York: New York University Press, 1997), 129.

71. Savage, "Are Computer Terminals," 42.

72. Meyer, *The Wandering Uterus.*

73. Laura McClure, "Thinking Ergonomics," *The Progressive*, Vol. 58 (August 1991): 40–41.

74. McClure, "Thinking Ergonomics."

75. Meyer, *The Wandering Uterus*, 127.

76. Eileen Boris, *Home to Work: Motherhood and the Politics of Industrial Homework in the United States* (New York: Cambridge University Press, 1994), 334.

77. Richardson, "Computers Don't Kill Jobs," 170-171.

78. Khalil and Melcher, "Office Automation's Threat."

79. Richardson, "Computers Don't Kill Jobs," 172.

80. Steve Fox, *Toxic Work: Women Workers at GTE Lenkur* (Philadelphia: Temple University Press, 1991), 12.

81. Savage, "Are Computer Terminals."

82. Ursula Huws, *Your Job in the Eighties: A Women's Guide to New Technology* (London: Pluto Press, 1982), 41.

83. Devon Pena, *The Terror of the Machine: Technology, Work, Gender, and Ecology on the U.S.–Mexico Border* (Austin, TX: Center for Mexican-American Studies, 1997), 299.

84. Fox, *Toxic Work*, 12.

85. Burris, "Computerization of the Workplace," 145.

86. Boris, *Home to Work*, 305.

87. Ibid., 325–326.

88. Ibid., 327, 329.

89. Sara Diamond, "Taylor's Way: Women, Cultures, and Technology." In *Processed Lives: Gender and Technology in Everyday Life* (New York: Routledge, 1997), 85.

90. Kathleen Christensen, "Home-based Clerical Work: No Simple Truth, No Single Reality." In *Homework: Historical and Contemporary Perspectives on Paid Labor in the Home* (Chicago: University of Illinois Press, 1989), 187.

91. Jan Zimmerman, "Technology and the Future of Women: Haven't We Met Somewhere Before?" In *Women, Technology, and Innovation* (New York: Pergamon Press, 1982), 358.

92. Christensen, "Home-based Clerical Work," 193.

93. Boris, *Home to Work*, 331.

94. Philip Mattera, "High-Tech Cottage Industry: Home Computer Sweatshops," *The Nation*, 2 April 1983, 390.

95. Boris, *Home to Work*, 334.

96. Ibid., 361.

97. Christensen, "Home-based Clerical Work," 193.

98. Mattera, "High-Tech Cottage Industry," 392.

99. Ibid., 392.

100. Hilary Silver, "Homework, and Domestic Work," *Sociological Forum*, Vol. 8 (1993): 201.

101. Nancy K. Jurik, "Getting Away and Getting By: The Experiences of Self-Employed Home-workers," *Work and Occupations*, Vol. 25 (1998): 12, 22, 24.

102. Ibid., 19.

103. Ibid., 24.

104. Ibid., 32.

105. Joan W. Scott, "The Mechanization of Women's Work," *Scientific American*, Vol. 247 (September 1982): 178.

106. Boris, *Home to Work*, 17.

107. Eileen Boris and Elisabeth Prugl, "Introduction." In *Homeworkers in Global Perspective: Invisible No More* (New York: Routledge, 1996), 5.

108. Ibid., 7.

109. Boris, *Home to Work,* 17.

110. Richardson, "Computers Don't Kill Jobs," 175, 176.

111. Nelson, "Labor Demand, Labor Supply."

112. Ibid., 153, 154.

113. Eileen Boris, "A Woman's Place?," *The Nation*, 18 October 1986, 365–366.

114. Boris and Prugl, "Introduction," 7–8.

115. Albin and Appelbaum, "The Computer-Rationalization of Work," 144.

116. Susan Tiano, *Patriarchy on the Line: Labor, Gender, and Ideology in the Mexican Maquila Industry* (Philadelphia: Temple University Press, 1994), 37.

117. Tiano, Ibid., 74.

118. Ibid., 92.

119. Colclough and Tolbert, *Work in the Fast Lane,* 21.

120. Ibid., 22.

121. Pena, *The Terror of the Machine,* 258.

122. Ibid.

123. Maria Patricia Fernández-Kelly and Anna M. Garcia, "Invisible Amidst the Glitter: Hispanic Women in the Southern California Electronics Industry." In *The Worth of Women's Work: A Qualitative Synthesis* (Albany: State University of New York Press, 1988), 277.

124. Maria Patricia Fernández-Kelly, "Broadening the Scope: Gender and International Economic Development," *Sociological Forum,* Vol. 4 (1989): 627.

125. Aihwa Ong, *Spirits of Resistance and Capitalist Discipline: Factory Women in Malaysia* (Albany: State University of New York Press, 1987).

126. Lourdes Benaria, ed., *Women and Development: The Sexual Division of Labor in Rural Societies* (New York: Praeger, 1982).

127. Susan Tiano, "Maquiladora Women: A New Category of Workers?" In *Women Workers and Global Restructuring* (New York: Cornell University Press, 1990), 222.

128. Maria Patricia Fernández-Kelly, "Gender and Industry on Mexico's New Frontier." In *The Technological Woman* (New York: Praeger, 1983), 18–29.

129. Fernández-Kelly and Kathleen M. Fallon, "How Is Globalization Affecting Inequalities Between Women and Men?" In *Sociology for a New Century* (Boston: Pine Forge Press, 2001), 239–260.

130. Ellen I. Rosen, *Bitter Choices: Blue Collar Women In and Out of Work* (Chicago: University of Chicago, 1987), 22.

131. North American Congress on Latin America (NACLA), "Electronics: The Global Industry," *NACLA's Latin America and Empire Report,* Vol. 11 (April 1977): 14.

132. Fernández-Kelly, "Broadening the Scope," 625.

133. Sylvia Guendelman et al., "Women Who Quit Maquiladora Work on the U.S.–Mexico Border: Assessing Health, Occupation, and Social Dimensions in Two Transnational Electronics Plants," *American Journal of Industrial Medicine,* Vol. 33 (1998): 501.

134. Fernández-Kelly, "Gender and Industry."

135. Guendelman et al., "Women Who Quit Maquiladora," 506.

136. West Cosgrove, trans. "Maquiladoras, Foreign Investment and Poverty," *News Notes,* Vol. 21 (May/June 1991): 10.

137. Ibid.

138. Fernández-Kelly and Fallon, "How Is Globalization Affecting Inequalities," 253.

139. Cosgrove, "Maquiladoras," 10.

140. Tiano, "Maquiladora Women," 223.

141. Cosgrove, "Maquiladoras," 10.

142. Hossfeld, "Hiring Immigrant Women," 67.

143. Ibid., 71–72.

144. Ibid., 78.

145. Fernández-Kelly and Garcia, "Invisible Amidst the Glitter," 278.

146. Colclough and Tolbert, *Work in the Fast Lane,* 25.

147. Randy Albeda, "Improving Women's Employment in the U.S.A." *Industrial Relations Journal,* Vol. 28 (December 1997): 275–282.

148. Beverly Burris, "Technocracy and Gender in the Workplace," *Social Problems,* Vol. 36 (April 1989):170.

149. Sally Hacker, "The Culture of Engineering: Women, Workplace and Machine." In *Women, Technology and Innovation* (New York: Pergamon Press, 1982), 342.

150. Nelson, "Labor Demand, Labor Supply."

151. Richardson, "Computers Don't Kill Jobs," 169.

7

Household Labor
and Technology
in a Consumer Culture

❖ ❖ ❖ ❖ ❖ ❖

The real liberators of American women were not the feminist noise-makers, they were the automobile, the supermarket, the shopping center, the dishwasher, the washer-dryer, the freezer.
Pat Buchanan

One of the most appealing images of household technology is that it single-handedly liberates women by automating the burdens of housework right out of existence. Many are convinced that technology makes housework easier, less time consuming, and perhaps even more equitably distributed in the home. These ideas hold so much power that traditional social research took them for granted instead of proving or disproving them empirically. Now, however, we know that the effects of washers, dryers, and microwaves on women have not been uniformly beneficial—and housework is far from a thing of the past. Any fair assessment of household technology indicates mixed blessings, striking patterns of both change and non-change. Many of the changes have been welcome, and the drudgery that has been left behind is all to the good. But there is another side to this story. Empirical research continues to document that American housewives spend about 33 hours a week on household chores, excluding child care. Women working full time outside the home do about 72 percent of the unpaid labor in the house.[1] How could this be, given all the advantages of technology and the supposed changes in gender roles? Several factors explain the apparent paradox, but first and foremost—and despite any new technology—housework is still largely designated as women's work.[2]

THE MORE THINGS CHANGE . . .

Households are significant sites of technological knowledge and artifacts in terms of food preparation, cleaning, caring for others, and even entertainment.[3] Crucial developments have included the transition from kitchen heating to central heating, outdoor to indoor plumbing, and the shift from homemade to store bought clothes and food. Before industrialization, most housework entailed producing the goods and services that were then used within one's household. Housewives worked hard, but husbands and children also helped. With industrialization, however, women began to bear the burden of housework themselves while, for husbands and children, the home slowly became a place of leisure.[4] As increasing numbers of men and single women entered factory work, housewives began to assume the work of the household, and they began consuming as well as producing the bounty of American industrialization. By 1920, for example, most clothes were no longer made by women in the home, thus eliminating the tasks of sewing, knitting, and so forth; but the new tasks of shopping for and cleaning the clothing were done solely by women.

Ruth Cowan[5] argues that the commonplace notion that the household simply shifted from a unit of production to consumption is misleading. It not only fails to consider new tasks but it ignores other factors, such as the loss of servants and rising expectations, as well as the fact that mechanization took place in an isolated, private home. In a comprehensive fashion, Cowan analyzes household technology in terms of eight interlocking systems: food, clothing, health care, transportation, water, gas, electricity, petroleum. Food, clothing, and health care fit the model of production to consumption but transportation, for example, indicates a very different pattern of *increasing* work as delivery services disappeared and shopping tasks increased. Judy Wajcman[6] observes that "To argue that domestic labor time has been reduced is only meaningful if it means that leisure or discretionary free time has increased. If, however, mechanization results in less physical work but more 'personal services' work in the sense of increased time and quality of child care, then surely this does not mean a real decrease in work."

As men's share in domestic activity began to disappear, housework truly became "women's work." Some of the physical labor associated with housework was reduced, but the considerable work that remained shifted onto the individual housewife. Consider, for example, gas stoves. They are labor-saving devices, but the labor they eliminated was chopping and gathering of wood to fuel the stove (tasks men performed), not cooking the food or cleaning the stove (work designated for women). Similarly, washing machines made it far easier to clean clothes, but women remained largely responsible for performing this work. Machines thus reorganized the process of work, rather than saving the labor of women. "Industrialization, at least in these its earliest phases, had in fact created the material conditions under which the doctrine of separate spheres could take root and flourish."[7] Men learned the skills to work for wages, while relinquishing the tasks done at home.

There has been a great deal of optimism that household appliances would somehow free women. Yet technology has not been the liberator it is portrayed as being nor has it been the solution to gender inequality in the home. The advanced electronic home systems and smart houses that we discussed earlier have been viewed as extraordinarily "progressive," particularly by futurists, but these optimistic observers give no concrete reasons why such developments will bring beneficial changes in domestic labor.[8] In fact, the households they describe are remarkably traditional. Contemporary research continues to demonstrate that women—even when employed outside the home—do at least twice as much household labor as men. Wives spend an average of 33 hours in household labor per week, while their husbands average about 14 hours.[9] Husbands consistently make only modest contributions to housework;[10] on average, women are responsible for 75 percent of the work.[11] Since the 1960s much less work is being done in American homes, and more reliance is being placed on the service economy (such as fast food) and family standards of cleanliness are simply declining.[12] Nonetheless, the person doing the housework is still usually female. An adult son who lives at home increases the housework of the women, while an adult daughter reduces the labor of both the other women and men.[13]

Women and men also do quite different household chores: Wives do the daily chores, husbands assume responsibility for the less frequent repairs and the labor that comes up outside and around the house.[14] Even the tasks done by children are segregated by gender: "While differences in individual resources within the family influence the allocation of housework, gender influences it more; women from outside the household are hired, daughters are given more housework than sons, and employed women reduce their own housework more easily than they seek or obtain increases in their husbands' contributions."[15]

Arlie Hochschild[16] interviewed fifty women who were lawyers, corporate executives, word processors, and day-care workers, as well as many of their husbands. She found that although increasing numbers of women are working outside the home, they still work about 15 hours per week more than men on housework and child care: That is an extra month a year. Women do the daily jobs like cooking and cleaning, while men change the oil and take trips with the kids. She speaks of a "stalled revolution": Women have moved into the first shift work, but they are still responsible for the second shift. Cynthia Cockburn[17] documented similar patterns in her research on the relationship between household technologies and changing gender roles in eight European countries. She found what she describes as a mutually shaping process: unequal relations influenced emerging technologies, and the technologies themselves affirmed or reformulated this inequality. Even when women believe that household labor should be shared, designers and engineers don't believe this is happening. As one advertiser commented: "It would be folly to present a commercial . . . where, if the woman was present, she was not the one doing the work in the kitchen . . . It just wouldn't be credible because, you know, it's an area of excellence which they are meant to understand."[18] Cockburn's research also indicates that household technologies are regarded by the men who typically design and sell them as relatively insignificant. She contrasts the low regard for refrigerators, freezers, and so forth with what is considered "state of the art" technology, such as television and video equipment.

In sum, increasing work for women *outside* the home has not resulted in a more equitable distribution of labor *inside* the home, despite the belief that this is the case. Social changes that have begun with paid labor for women need to be completed by men doing more of the unpaid labor. Chafetz and Hagan[19] pointedly summarize the pattern of change as "a major shift in the gender division of labor by which women have come increasingly to resemble men in their rates of labor force participation, within a context where men have not come to resemble women in their domestic/familial work." In fact, married women with children spend more hours at housework than do single mothers with the same number of children. Such factors led economist Heidi Hartmann[20] to speculate that "husbands may require more housework than they contribute," and indeed, when couples marry, women's housework hours increase while men's decline.[21] Women who work part-time, or part of the year, and those who do shift work frequently spend more time doing housework[22], but these forms of paid labor are also more insecure, provide fewer benefits, and are often poorly paid. Women seem to be at a crucial transition point: They recognize the unfairness of the current situation but have yet to see change.[23]

Orbuch and Eyster[24] note that discussions of gender inequality in terms of housework frequently refer only to the dominant white culture. Household roles vary, however, in many respects. Their research documents, for example, that "black couples are more egalitarian than white couples in their attitudes toward women's work and the division of household labor" and, moreover, that "blacks are more likely than whites to criticize gender inequality and traditional views of masculinity and femininity." Their analysis of newly married black and white couples in Michigan supports earlier studies and indicates that "black wives report greater participation from their husbands in female-type tasks than do white wives." Hispanic women and men are more inclined to accept a traditional division of household labor and less likely to see it as unfair to women.[25] Nonetheless, Stohs reports that almost two-thirds of all multicultural women in her study (including African-American, Asian, Hispanic, and Middle Eastern women) reported some conflict with their partners during the week regarding housework, specifically when they feel they are doing too much of the housework relative to others.

The gender gap in housework is greatest among married couples, as compared to cohabitants or those who have never married.[26] The distribution of household labor appears to be more equitable among remarried couples, in large measure because of the woman's prior experiences with housework and her demands for change.[27]

Housework remains extremely time consuming, in part because even as technology began to ease some arduous tasks, new ones were defined that transformed housework rather than eliminating it. For example, hot and cold running water ended pumping, hauling, and heating water, while washing machines eliminated scrubbing clothes. But women still do the bulk of the laundry and cooking, in addition to much of the shopping, chauffeuring, hostessing, and child care. Household tasks may be less taxing, but in some respects they have proliferated.

To elaborate on this, drudgery may have disappeared but the laundry has not. By the 1980s and with the help of technology, the American housewife "was processing roughly ten times (by weight) the amount of laundry that her mother had been accustomed to . . . The average time spent on this chore in 1925 had been 5.8 hours per week; in 1964 it was 6.2."[28] Appliances have also had mixed results: Storing, cleaning, and repairing them means new forms of labor. It makes sense to assume that industrialization made life easier for the average American woman, but empirical research tells a very different and unexpected story. As Ruth Cowan[29] puts it: "What a strange paradox that in the face of so many labor-saving devices, little labor appears to have been saved."

The "double day" of paid and unpaid labor takes a significant toll on U.S. women: It is virtually a guarantee of being exhausted.[30] For employed mothers, "child care and housework constitute the lion's share of their personal life."[31] This pattern seems particularly resistant to change. Some researchers suggest that change will only come through collective action, including public policy initiatives regarding the gender division of household labor.[32]

Two additional factors figure prominently in terms of understanding the continuing burden of housework despite technological developments. One is the disappearance of servants for economically privileged women, the other, rising expectations of women's work in the home. After World War I, technological developments, as well as public health measures such as safe water, diphtheria inoculations, and garbage collection, meant a higher standard of living for everyone. This was accompanied by the diffusion of helpful household appliances, but also by the disappearance of domestic servants. Women in higher social classes were increasingly expected to do housework single-handedly, as servants were drawn into industrial work. On the other hand, these appliances made working-class women better able to provide their families with basic needs. Cowan[33] summarizes: "The spread of affluence and the diffusion of amenities was accomplished not, as earlier commentators guessed, by an increase in leisure for housewives of both classes, but, rather, by increases in the amount of work that some housewives had to do, and in the level of productivity that others were able to achieve." Some women were working harder than their mothers because of the lack of servants, others were working just as hard, but achieving greater results.

Housework also remains time consuming because of increasing expectations; women use technology to pursue ever-rising standards. Late nineteenth-century germ theory played a part in encouraging increasing cleanliness and more frequent changing and washing of clothes. Standards of nutrition have also risen, giving women more work in terms of providing quality meals. Rugs were previously beaten once a year as part of ritual spring cleaning (a task assigned to children); vacuuming, however, became a weekly chore typically done by women. In addition, higher expectations regarding child care (in terms of time, energy, and results) came to be widely accepted and made further demands on women's time in the home.

Thus, monumental technological changes took place that permitted many families to live "at a level of health and comfort that not so long ago was reserved only for those who were very rich,"[34] but these innovations did not serve to shorten a woman's work day. Rather, they raised American living standards while keeping homemakers isolated and relatively inefficient. Technology allowed individual labor to substitute for the loss of servants and other female helpers and raised the standards of living, but women have not been released from expectations regarding their role in the household. While some hail the machine age as causing a "household revolution" that freed women from toil, technology did more to *change* labor than to *save* it.

CONSUMERISM

The increasing standards of household labor associated with new technology and the drive for more household appliances did not develop by happenstance. Instead, the centrality of consumerism and a consumer economy must be acknowledged. Women were educated to new standards through advertising, media, and domestic science classes, which played a significant role in defining housework at the beginning of this century. The role of the housewife and mother was idealized, and women were assured that their work was important and emotionally rewarding. The vision of women as guardians of the family was used to promote increasing standards of cleanliness and nutrition, but it also promoted the growing consumption of commodities for the household. Women were taught to be good managers and consumers, and buying household appliances was part of this.[35] The early twentieth century marked the shift to a new kind of consumer and a new form of advertising. Susan Strasser[36] illuminates the scope of the changes:

> Advertisers came to see women as their audience; home economists taught women how to shop and how to plan for shopping; new, interrelated products like washing machines and soap powders appeared on the market, each encouraging the use of another; mail-order houses, department stores, supermarkets, and chain stores, emphasizing impersonal relationships between buyer and seller and dominated by large corporations, replaced small shops, country stores, and public markets.

With new technology, the home was envisioned as a well-run machine and the homemaker as not only a moral guardian but, more in tune with modern industrial society, as "a lab assistant and efficiency expert who knew how to manage modern technology."[37] Assumptions about the role of women reflected and reinforced the design and marketing of household machines.[38] Manufacturers and public utilities also used domestic science classes to assist them in marketing since the interests of appliance manufacturers and the ideology of domestic science coincided: Both maintained that women belonged in the home, with appliances designed for their individual use—not communally shared. Collectivist movements of the late nineteenth century, which advocated more communal solutions to the work of the household—including communal child care, laundry, and food preparation—had been defeated,[39] and household products began to be actively marketed by the 1920s and 1930s. Culture industries "mobilized female desire for commodity goods and have constructed notions of femininity which are complicit with consumption.[40] Automatic laundry equipment, for example, was used in commercial establishments in the nineteenth century, but then transferred to the home in the 1920s. "Rather than selling a few large machines to centralized businesses, manufacturers sought to sell many smaller units to private households. The return of laundry to the home affirmed women's roles as consumers of individual products instead of shared central services.[41] Cynthia Cockburn notes that the focus of the industry remains on "stand-alone" appliances that bring the most profit and reflect the absence of any overall planning regarding the development and marketing of household technologies. "Competition produces an appearance of great choice in the market economies; there are scores of models of each item available . . . But they are not always designed to answer user needs."[42] Lupton[43] is even more forthright: "In a consumer economy, objects are manufactured primarily to be sold, and only secondarily to satisfy a human need." Wajcman[44] provides an illustration: "The drive to motorize all household tasks—including brushing teeth, squeezing lemons, and carving meat—is less a response to need than a reflection of the economic and technical capacity for making motors."

Both advertising and the corporations producing household products encouraged the view of housework as women's work that expressed family love and devotion. "Housework became conceptualized as a personal task made easier by the purchase of an ever-increasing array of products which women bought because they wished to care for their families in the best, most modern way possible."[45] Researchers vary in their interpretations of the precise relationship between advertising messages regarding household technology and their impact on women, but there is general agreement that advertisers aimed "to fashion the housewife into the ultimate consumer in order to sell their products."[46] In an analysis of advertisements in *The Ladies' Home Journal* from 1910 to 1980, Bonnie J. Fox[47] found that ads consistently advocated housework as women's work and as private work. This reflected and reinforced the association of women with household labor, despite the fact that this labor continues to be unpaid or low-paid and devalued.

Although advertisers are interested in anyone who might buy the products they promote, their decision to focus their efforts on women reinforced women's role as the primary consumers. Time spent on consumption only added to women's responsibilities in the home: "Advertisements used guilt and fear to promote dependence on products, creating artificial burdens to substitute for the disappearing real ones. (Women, it seems, were meant to be burdened)."[48]

Many argue that advertising campaigns, rather than being relatively straightforward, are manipulative. Marketing strategies create needs, rather than meet them, and intentionally encourage the purchase of more and more unnecessary products. In the advertisements of the 1920s, for example, appliances became equated with freedom: Toasters and washing machines meant liberation for women. According to Ewen,[49] this illustrates "how the feminist demand for equality and freedom for women was appropriated into the jargon of consumerism." New "corporate diseases" began to emerge: underarm offense, sneaker smell, ashtray breath.[50] These developments were designed to increase the profits of business and advertising—more "time-saving" devices, more specialized products, and more products to enhance self-esteem. Technologies were developed and marketed to individual housewives, who were targeted as the ones buying and using these items. "The very activity of buying came to represent happiness, and perhaps indeed to produce it, if only temporarily . . . The expandable task of consumption, like the other new task of motherhood, capable of taking up whatever time the new products released, became ever more necessary as families adapted their daily lives to manufactured existence."[51] Appliances were also explicitly portrayed as relieving women of work. A 1946 Bendix advertisement for automatic washing machines, for example, shows a smiling woman seated on a stool next to her washer claiming, "It's Wonderful! -how my BENDIX does all the work of washing."[52]

Wajcman[53] makes the point that the relationship between technology and change is fundamentally indeterminate and cannot be completely predicted. She provides the example of the telephone, which was initially designed as a business machine, but telephone executives resisted its use for what they termed "trivial gossip." As Lupton[54] puts it, they "dismissed women's talk as 'idle chatter' that tied up the lines." By the late 1920s, however, AT&T began to see the financial advantages of encouraging women to use the telephone, and during the depression, Bell began targeting women in their advertising.

Advertising is a powerful U.S. industry, with domestic ad spending reaching $200 billion in 1998.[55] It continues to portray housework as easy and fulfilling, creating the impression that homes require relatively little care, given available technology. Likewise, it still implies that buying more products makes people happier.[56] But, to the extent that domestic technologies are "designed to support the home system, and thereby keep women economically marginal to the larger society, they may actually increase dissatisfaction with housework."[57] In addition, the privacy, freedom, and individualism symbolized in the single family home and its extensive technology is paradoxical in modern society. As Spigel[58] points out: "Consumer products promised people the everyday experience of liberation in return for their increasing dependence on corporate production." Freedom, it seems, is a microwave oven, which in turn presupposes a consumer society . . . which may be anything but freeing.

Some have also questioned the safety of these household products. Harriet Rosenberg, for example, sees the home not as a haven but as a dumpsite for unsafe and unnecessary products. She contends that not only is the Third World a place where unsafe products are dumped: "The household in North America is also intimately linked to this global process of commodification and danger."[59] She contends that in the household, thousands of "untested or under-tested chemical products . . . endanger the health and safety of its members."[60] She notes, for example, that automatic dishwashing detergent is a major cause of poisoning in children and that the residue they leave on dishes may have long-term effects. She also cites the dangers of drain cleaners, oven cleaners, and chlorine bleach and points to readily available (and safe) alternatives to them.

Observers disagree about various aspects of the relationship between gender and household technology. Ruth Cowan[61] acknowledges that technology is developed by men, but contends that "for reasons which may have been alternatively economic, ideological, and structural, there was very little chance that American homes would become part of the industrial order in the same sense that American businesses have, because very few Americans, powerful or not, have wished it so— and the ones who have wished it so have not been numerous enough or powerful enough to make a difference."[62] Wajcman[63] believes that this gives too much primacy to values and minimizes the material conditions of women's lives. She argues that women negotiated the ideology of motherhood and housework given their circumstances, and she insists that we acknowledge the extent to which choice is constrained by structural forces. "The available alternatives to single-family houses were extremely limited, especially for the working class. In fact, state policy in the area of housing and town planning played a key role in promoting privatism. Without the extensive provision of different options, it is not clear to what extent people freely chose private domestic arrangements."[64]

Likewise, Cynthia Cockburn[65] notes that women have generally lacked agency in terms of the development of technologies supposedly designed for their benefit, and she observes that even in scholarly accounts of technology, the domestic sphere tends to receive short shrift. She argues that "technological development is driven by the thrust for profit and/or for political and military control. At the same time, the technologies we know we most need, the ones that support domestic functions in both public and private spheres—nourishment, health, shelter, care—get a fraction of the investment received by those others."[66]

Given the search for profits, class interests as well as gender relations have figured prominently in the development and marketing of household technologies. Racist ideas have also been mobilized when useful. As Lupton[67] points out: "Playing on racism and xenophobia, large commercial establishments promoted their technologically advanced (cleaning) services as superior to the unschooled labors of the 'ignorant washer-women' (commonly black) or the suspect practices of the 'hand laundry' (often run by Chinese-American families)." We now turn to a consideration of paid domestic labor and a more explicit consideration of race and class as well as gender.

PAID DOMESTIC LABOR

Many studies identify gender as the central factor in the distribution of work in households. Skeptical of biological explanations and strictly psychological perspectives, social scientists have proposed structural and cultural explanations for this and have analyzed the links between family life and the wider society. Feminist researchers, in particular, recognize that the ideology and practice of housework rests on and reinforces a gender division of labor that leaves women responsible for the daily work of the family, no matter what technology is available. But contemporary feminist literature has also begun to attend to the ways in which class and racial divisions among women impinge upon housework and directly shape women's experiences. Race and class divisions among women tend to be eclipsed when we focus solely on gender and, more specifically, on *unpaid* housework. But if we broaden our analysis to a consideration of *paid* household labor, structural divisions connected to and beyond gender quickly emerge. Ideologies of gender, race, and ethnic superiority shape household labor, which in turn perpetuates these ideologies, as is evident in the experiences of African-American and Mexican-American women.[68] This is significant in light of the fact that domestic labor is increasing in U.S. homes, with approximately 9.4 million households employing domestics in 1996.[69]

Ruth Cowan[70] observed that the relationship between women and technology is bound to be different for different social classes. Vanek[71] points out that in the early twentieth century, appliances were only affordable by the rich, who had these devices as well as servants at their disposal. Susan Kleinberg's study of working-class women at the turn of the century in Pittsburgh demonstrated that changes in domestic and municipal technology reached the middle and upper classes decades before they reached the working classes, thus making class distinctions crucial in understanding women's work. Indeed, as Kleinberg[72] points out: "The long term effect of the government and private enterprise pay-as-you-go philosophy was to heighten class and sex role differentiations."

But the implications of class divisions regarding household work extend beyond the basic issue of who has access to technology. An analysis of paid domestic service vividly illustrates the consequences of class privilege and race and ethnic inequality and sheds a very different light on the discussion of household technology "freeing" women. Since the 1980s, increasing attention has been given to paid domestic work and how the oppression it reflects is structured by race and class relations as well as by gender. Roger Sanjek and Shellee Colen[73] argue that the structure of household labor in the home reinforces inequality within various societies. Domestic work entails significant and often multiple power differentials between employer and employee, including gender, race, class, and migration status. Household labor itself is regarded as "low status, even stigmatized work, or not *real* work at all,"[74] and thus serves to reproduce the low status of those who perform it. Domestic service is a form of women's employment often evident in a transitional stage of industrialization, when a growing urban middle class needs household help to maintain its lifestyle.[75] Many women have been drawn into industry, but community services for the household (such as child care) remain insufficient.

Throughout much of the twentieth century, a labor shortage has existed in terms of domestic service, and the ratio of servants to households has been steadily declining. The reasons for this, according to some observers, are relatively clear:

The work is sheer drudgery, done under abysmal conditions, live-ins are always on call and have little time off, they are denied their own family life, and the work itself is considered demeaning. Once women could escape this work by moving into factory work, they did so. Job work (domestic work in several homes and paid by the job) is regarded as an advance over live-in work (and pay by the hour) because a woman is able to live with her own family, and has more control over the job than when she is paid by the hour. Nonetheless, it is still extremely privatized and isolating.[76] The ranks of domestics have thus been filled by women with few other options, traditionally immigrant women. A European immigrant typically "entered service upon leaving school in early adolescence and worked until her early or mid-twenties. After marriage she left service and usually did not return."[77] This worker seldom experienced upward mobility but often her daughter did.

Paid household work has always been a significant occupation for women of color, including African Americans, Native Americans, Hispanic women, and some groups of Asian women. Until World War I, domestic service was the largest paid occupation for women in most U.S. cities. This remained the case for African-American women until World War II. Gradually, white immigrant women left domestic work and the number of African-American and Latina women grew.[78] However, the experience of racially distinct groups in this occupation has been strikingly different: For black women, upward mobility across generations was often absent. Instead, domestic service was a lifetime occupation and discrimination prevented improvement for the next generation. The experiences of Mexican-American women follow a pattern similar to that of black women. "Women of color were locked into the occupation over generations because of the deliberate exclusion of these women from other kinds of jobs, because of the wage hierarchy within the occupation based on race, and because of obstacles to men of color in obtaining a family wage."[79] Evelyn Nakano Glenn[80] notes that in the first half of the twentieth century, the lowest forms of labor were performed by European immigrant women in the Northeast, Mexicans in the Southwest, African Americans in the South, and Japanese women in Northern California. Significantly, "White-skin privilege transcended class lines, and it was not uncommon for working-class whites to hire black women for housework." Racist beliefs confirmed the suitability of particular women for domestic work:

> These justifications ranged from the argument that Black and Mexican women were incapable of governing their own lives and thus were dependent on whites—making white employment of them an act of benevolence—to the argument that Asian servants were naturally quiet, subordinate, and accustomed to a lower standard of living. Whatever the specific content of the racial characterizations, it defined the proper place of these groups as in service: they belonged there, just as it was the dominant group's place to be served.[81]

Domestic service remains a crucial occupation for recent immigrants, particularly women from Latin America and the Caribbean because they are cheap labor and willing to work long and hard hours. Increasingly, Latina women have been entering domestic service.[82] Denied equal access to education and jobs, they have relatively few other choices. Domestic labor is still ranked among the lowest of occupations, and Glenn[83] believes that this is due in part to the worker's personal subordination: "Even machine tending is accorded higher status than domestic service."

Domestic service, however, offers workers the possibility of flexible hours and also pays more than some other forms of labor available to working-class women. In addition, some women regard this work as a route to becoming independent and increasingly autonomous.[84] Nonetheless, empirical evidence of the problematic aspects of this work is powerful. Vicki Ruiz,[85] for example, documented the struggles of Mexican-American women in domestic service. In Ciudad Juarez, Mexico, many women do factory work, which provides needed social benefits, but it pays as little as $3.50 per day. This sends many women across the border to El Paso in search of better working conditions. Thousands of women do domestic labor in households in El Paso where they average $15 a day; live-ins earn from $30 to $60 per week.[86] In El Paso, Anglos as well as Mexican-Americans employ these household workers. Economic necessity obviously drives these women: Their own children, whom they visit on weekends, are usually cared for by relatives.

Kathy Dobie[87] notes that much has been written about the difficulties middle-class white women face trying to balance careers and families. She cites an article in *The New York Times* entitled, "How to Nurture and Maintain a Family Culture When You Work All Day, Your Mother Lives in Omaha and Your Housekeeper Comes From Ethiopia." "Omaha" represents the distance among the generations, while "Ethiopia" is clearly "a metaphor for blackness and foreignness." Through poignant interviews with black nannies in New York City (mainly immigrant women from Jamaica, Haiti, and the Caribbean Islands), Dobie illustrates the significant point that not only do these women serve to keep white families intact, but they are simultaneously "striving mightily against the pressures of poverty, single parenthood, and institutionalized racism to hold their own families together." Some immigrant women are forced to leave their children behind in order to find work and support them. Mirta Ojito offers the image of a Honduran woman pushing another woman's child on a swing in an Upper East Side playground, while her own 10-year-old daughter celebrates her birthday without her mother in the northern mountains of Honduras.[88]

Much empirical research, including the testimony of domestic workers, provides evidence of the problems associated with live-in jobs including the isolation from family and friends, denial of basic wages and benefits, and sexual harassment.[89] Sanjek and Colen[90] note that "in most if not all places studied, sexual advances from males, harassment, and rape, occur in some household workplaces, and this threat or danger is widely appreciated by women household workers." Human Rights Watch recently released a report on domestic workers, almost all young women, who received special visas to work for diplomats in Washington,

D.C., and New York City.[91] The report details cases of physical and sexual assault and also notes that these workers' median work day was 14 hours, at $2.14 an hour including room and board.

A theme found in the stories of many domestics is the disrespect with which they are treated by employers. Mary Romero[92] interviewed Mexican-American domestic workers living in Denver who spoke about employers treating them as unskilled and giving them detailed instructions about the simplest tasks, carefully monitoring everything they do. The workers were required to regularly perform chores their employers would never do routinely, such as moving and cleaning behind the refrigerator. West Indian women interviewed by Colen[93] commented on being expected to wear uniforms, to set them apart. Employers left food for their children but not the domestic, although she might have an eight-or-twelve hour shift. The women contended that notions of "family" were used to manipulate them:

> whenever they want you to give it your all in their favor, or anyway to feel comfortable to do what they want you to do, they use the words 'we are family.' That's the one I hate. 'You are one of the family.' That's not true. That's a password as sorry . . . if you're one of the family, don't let me eat after you. . . . They say it to make you feel O.K., but at the same time, they're not doing the right thing.[94]

Romero[95] also noted that emotional labor is often part of the job— "being there" for your employer and his or her children, although this is seldom reciprocal. In a similar vein, Rollins[96] who interviewed workers and employers in Boston and also worked as a household worker, noted that the relationships between workers and employers varies considerably, but certain themes emerged that led her to conclude that "the relationship is essentially one of psychological as well as material exploitation." Domestics not only do the housework but also enhance the employer's ego and validate certain forms of privilege. According to Rollins, this is evident in the demands for deference, such as using the workers' first name while employers are addressed formally. Employers assume the right to ask personal questions; eating arrangements confirm the status differentials. Maternalism is also evident and a means of affirming the superiority of the employer. Rollins cites many forms of this: "treating workers as children, loaning money, explaining bills, demanding to meet friends, replacing the household worker's last name with that of the employer . . . and, most common, giving gifts." The gifts are typically old items, such as old clothes, used furniture, and leftover food. Rollins notes that it takes the place of higher wages. She also argues that employers demand evidence of the worker's inferiority to enhance their own psyches and comments: "During my work as a household worker I was frequently spoken to as if I were close to retarded. It was impossible for me to discern how many of these assumptions about my intellect were racism and how many were class prejudices."

Despite the hard work involved in household labor, many employers are unwilling to pay domestics a market value for their work. In the United States, domestics typically work below the minimum wage, and, although social security benefits are attached to household employment, they are often unpaid by employers with the consent of the worker.[97] Although many states have minimum wages that are higher than the federal minimum wage, some specifically exempt domestic workers from these laws.[98] Finally, domestic workers typically remain responsible for the housework in their own homes. Husbands "help out," particularly with child care when the wife is working, and children have chores, but the woman is responsible for the overall operation of the home.

Domestic service highlights the contradictions in any feminist analysis that argues for women's entitlement to work outside the home, but fails to make men more responsible for household labor.[99] As we have seen, the traditionally male sphere of paid labor has increasingly been opening to women, but this has not led to a significant reallocation of tasks within the home. Prevailing social expectations demand that individual women (with an emphasis on both privacy and gender) provide the services and comforts needed to run a household. This has clear race and class implications, as Colen[100] points out in her study of West-Indian women doing household work in New York City: "Shunned by men, this work becomes multiply devalued as it is passed from one woman to another along class, racial, ethnic, and migration lines, within the cash nexus." Similarly, Romero[101] incisively observes: "Employed middle- and upper-middle-class-women escaped the double day syndrome by hiring poor women of color to perform household and child care, and this was characterized as progress." Hiring paid domestic workers is apparently far more appealing (and certainly easier) for most middle and upper middle class Americans than any radical alternatives, since it does little to disrupt the traditional social arrangements in the family. Romero casts a glaring light on what some may prefer to ignore when she boldly contends that "Instead of challenging the sexual division of labor, white middle-class homemakers sought refuge in strategies that reduced the negative aspects of sexism by exploiting women of color." Like Romero, Rollins notes that hiring household workers relieves privileged women from the burdens of such labor while leaving patriarchal ideas intact and thus helping perpetuate gender inequality. Interestingly, she also reflects on the effects of this on the employer's children: "The children learn that it is appropriate that they be served, that such dirtywork is appropriate for the lower classes and darker people, that housework and child care are women's work."[102] She concludes that this relationship is not only based on inequality, "but also *reinforces* and *reproduces* class, racial, and gender stratification."

Shellee Colen's[103] interviews with ten West-Indian women about their experiences as domestic workers illuminates the negative aspects of this work as well as the stark contrasts in the status of various groups of women. She observes that the pain of leaving their own children is central to the experiences of West-Indian women, particularly those who leave children behind in a distant land. She adds:

> Being torn between affluent and poor material worlds is cause for more emotional balancing. The West Indian woman may work in a world of relative wealth in which she witnesses waste 'that makes your heart bleed' and go home to another with her

low wages where she confronts demands from a 'third world' to send goods which she cannot afford.

The inequality is even more vividly evident in the comparison of one woman's employers, a couple who own a chain of clothing stores, with her situation:

> The wife worked part-time in the business and devoted the rest of her time to shopping for antiques, decorating, attending cooking classes, entertaining, traveling, and participating in her children's school. Joyce worked sixteen hours or more a day, was on call twenty-four hours a day, seven days a week, caring for the large house and three children for $90 a week ($110 at the time she quit).

Bonnie Thornton Dill's[104] research among African-American domestics indicated that they were keenly aware of the different resources they and their employers had regarding their children. As one woman remarked:

> There was alot of things they (employers) did that I wanted to do for mine, but I just couldn't afford it . . . Like sending them to school. Then they could be somebody; child slow, they could hire a tutor for the child. I wish I could have been able to do what they done. And then too, they sent them to camps, nice camps, not any camp but one they'd pick out. . . . So that's what I wished I could have done for him (her son) . . . See, whether it was right or wrong, I couldn't do it because I didn't have the money to do it. I wasn't able to do it. So that's the way it was. I did what I could and that was better than nothing.

A final example of contrast comes from the work of Sanjek and Colen[105] on household workers. They cite a press release from *The New York Times* on September 10, 1987, which captures the global relations of inequality regarding household labor. From this column by Crystal Nix, entitled, "Americans Find the Good Life in Guatemala," I quote at length:

> ANTIGUA, Guatemala–The attractions are obvious in the picturesque colonial town. Spanish-style mansions, with two acres of gardens and pools, can go for the equivalent of $20,000. Live-in servants are paid about $40 a month.
>
> The lure of life is so strong, that many Americans have foregone suburbia, big-city living or retirement in California and Florida to settle in what has become one of Latin America's strongest American communities.
>
> "One of the benefits you can't deny is the servant help. What we pay in a month here you would pay in one day or a week in the States." . . .
>
> The contrast between the lives of the Americans and the Guatemalans is striking.
>
> Many Guatemalans live in wooden huts in the mountains without running water or enough food. Many Americans live in mansions that used to house five or six Guatemalan families . . .
>
> Many Guatemalans say that while they appreciate the jobs Americans provide, they resent their control of local industries and their comfortable style of life that is beyond what Guatemalans can afford . . .

"Most Americans live here because they want slaves," said one foreigner who has lived in Antigua for several years. "You thought slavery ended? It hasn't" . . .

As this example vividly indicates, the varying forms of inequality evident in domestic service within the United States are equally apparent in a global context. Increasing employment outside the home among women in industrialized countries has created a need for quality child care. Some women seek to hire live-in workers, but given the conditions of this work (long hours, low pay, and little control over one's situation), few people are willing to engage in it. Thus, it is often Third World women, subject to unequal global relations and few options, who have stepped in to fill this specific need.

Bakan and Stasiulis[106] provide a recent case study of live-in workers in Canada, which illustrates and analyzes these issues. In Canada, foreign workers are granted temporary residence for two years and then become eligible for permanent residence. Bakan and Stasiulis focus on the Canadian Live-in Caregiver Program, which brings women, mainly from the Philippines and the Caribbean, to Canada to work as live-in domestics for two years, and thus gain access to Canadian residency.[107] The relationship between domestics and their employers is rooted in wider structural and international inequalities: Poverty and underdevelopment compel many women to seek work abroad and to accept harsh conditions of employment. "In Canada, many Third World domestic workers endure a minimum of two years of virtual bonded servitude, institutionalized through the federal government's foreign domestic worker program. The program continues to attract applicants only because of the promise of gaining permanent residence status."[108] Bakan and Stasiulis contend that agencies that supply these workers accept and perpetuate racial-ethnic and gender stereotypes—stereotypes that continue to restrict the employment opportunities of these workers even after citizenship is gained. "Migration and paid domestic service are thus elements of a global set of linkages in which gendered and racialized ideologies play a significant part."

In sum, "the legacy of imperialism has combined with modern conditions of indebtedness to generate large pools of female migrant labor in some Third World states that can be tapped to fill the demands in the domestic care industry of industrially advanced states."[109] Bakan and Stasiulis note that underdevelopment in the Philippines and the Caribbean have made these areas major sources of domestic workers for Canada. A recent editorial forcefully makes a similar point about the debt crisis providing more privileged women with domestic servants from other countries:

> When a woman from Mexico, Jamaica, or the Philippines decides to emigrate in order to make money as a domestic servant she is designing her own international debt politics. She is trying to cope with the loss of earning power and the rise in the cost of living at home by cleaning bathrooms in the country of the bankers.[110]

According to this editorial, each foreign worker is estimated to be supporting about five family members at home. Significantly, this is not simply a First

World–Third World split: Many women from Third World countries are doing domestic labor in the homes of more affluent racial-ethnic women. "In Latin America, 'domestic worker' is the single largest job category for women."[111]

Third World women in the United States and migrant women are usually portrayed as benefiting from, rather than enduring, paid domestic labor. While there may be some truth to this, an emphasis on the positive aspects of the situation for women masks vivid global inequalities and the privileges of the few who benefit from these divisions. Unfortunately, it is only by confronting the very uncomfortable fact of how implicated many of us are in structural and global inequalities that we can begin to challenge the roots of multiple forms of oppression.

Milkman, et al.[112] focus on class divisions and the increasing inequality among women in the United States. They argue that paid domestic labor reflects this inequality, as women at the lower end of the economic scale, frequently women of color, perform the household tasks of professional women. They ask what accounts for the size of the paid domestic labor force and its variations (for example, it is widespread in Kuwait, rare in Sweden, and mixed in U.S. cities). They argue that one crucial factor is the degree of economic inequality: the more inequality, the easier it is for rich households to employ the poor. This helps explain the higher proportion of domestics in Los Angeles, and their near absence in Sweden. Milkman, et al. speculate that given the growing inequality in the United States, this occupation may prove to be increasingly resilient.

Domestic workers often face their harsh circumstances with courage and a determination to survive despite these conditions. Resistance comes in the form of great determination, religious beliefs, and support networks of family and friends, although none of these change the structural problems.[113] Informal networks among domestics play a critical role in enabling them to confront the challenges of their employment. They "teach one another how to negotiate pay, how to placate employers, and how to get the job done in the most expedient manner."[114] Through interviews, Dill[115] explored the strategies of African-American mothers who work as domestics and found that one of the driving factors in the lives of these women was the goal of giving their children a better chance than they had. As one worker commented:

> I tell you I feel really proud and I really feel that with all the struggling that I went through. I feel happy and proud that I was able to keep helping my children, that they listened and that they all went to high school. So when I look back, I feel really proud, even though at times the work was very hard and I came home very tired. But now, I feel proud about it, they all got their education.[116]

Romero[117] advocates treating domestic workers as professionals, with respect, decent pay, and benefits. She realizes that this does not address the class and race divisions among women, but she believes that current social conditions make any other immediate solution unrealistic. Her analysis illuminates two issues still confronting feminism: the failure "to make men take equal responsibility for the household and children" and the lack of success "in establishing collective solutions to the problem of household labor." The lack of collective solutions is, for Romero, strikingly evident in the absence of government policies for such programs as day care, maternity leave, or family leave. Household technology has done little to resolve the most significant social issues surrounding equity in the home, and it must be kept in mind that a crucial feature of domestic work is not only the gender division of labor but its class and racial division as well.

GENDER, RACE, AND CLASS INEQUALITIES

Household technology has eased some of the most physically demanding forms of household labor, and it has raised the standards of living for many people. In the United States, the living conditions of most people have improved significantly in the past fifty years. Ruth Cowan[118] argues that we tend to forget just how well off we have become: As recently as 1940, one-third of Americans were still carrying water in buckets, two-thirds had no central heating, and only 53 percent had built-in bathroom equipment. These amenities are now regarded as basic standards in the United States. Nonetheless, when we use a lens of gender, race, and class to examine household technology, we see that once again the larger (non-egalitarian) social context has constrained the development and use of technology even within our households. Gender inequality, for example, has been crucial in shaping household technology and its use. Although this technology has become increasingly sophisticated and powerful, it has not reduced the time spent in household labor: Women have assumed new tasks, new expectations, new standards of cleanliness, which effectively eroded any extra time technology may have permitted. Many improvements in the twentieth century have been accomplished largely through the increased productivity of individual women. According to Cowan,[119] "Modern technology enabled the American housewife of 1950 to produce single-handedly what her counterpart of 1850 needed a staff of three or four to produce: a middle-class standard of health and cleanliness for herself, her spouse, and her children." Despite technology, households remain places of intensive domestic labor.

Moreover, technology has been unable to change the allocation of labor by gender. The work of women and men remain sharply segregated: Most women still do the bulk of the housework and child care, men contribute modest amounts. Far from being "revolutionary," the development and marketing of household technology reflects and reinforces a specific middle-class ideal of a single-family household, with a wife responsible for the household labor. Thus gender inequality has, in significant ways, dictated who will use household technology. In many ways, technology has been used to reinforce the gender division of labor, not to undermine it. It may even have made it increasingly difficult to dislodge some household tasks from the home. Bose, Bereano, and Malloy[120] give three reasons for this:

> First, the small scale of household work and technologies are labor intensive. Second, the work has become so laden with emotion that attaining a more communalized form may be impossible. Finally, since women's labor at home is unpaid and this is seen as "cheap," it could be indefinitely used for these tasks, retaining the specialization of labor within the home and keeping housework structurally separated from the paid labor market.

Increasing numbers of women are employed outside the home, but the inequitable distribution of housework remains. Empirical studies consistently demonstrate that even women employed full-time outside the home continue to bear responsibility for most of the housework, daughters do more housework than sons, and when someone outside the family is paid to do the work, the employee is typically a woman. Even specific tasks are influenced by gender. And technology has been unable to alter any of this.

Our social understanding that women are primarily responsible for household labor has had important design consequences. Washing machines, vacuum cleaners, and refrigerators have all been designed and marketed for use by individual women, in individual homes. Household labor, and certainly large appliances, could have been shared, but given the isolated and gendered understanding of housework, such alternatives failed. Women remain the targets of advertising and consumerism for all manner of household items. Their responsibilities in the home are glorified, and traditional gender roles are bolstered in the process. When men are found in advertisements for household technology, they are often portrayed as incompetent. Only a woman *really* knows how to vacuum a living room rug. Put differently, housework is women's work. Household technology may have modified, but it did not fundamentally alter, the gender division of household labor.

Not only gender inequality, but racism has penetrated the organization of our households and household labor. At the most basic level, some have access to household technology that is unavailable to others. This includes home computers which have been hailed as revolutionizing households. But Julianne Malveaux[121] points out that given existing social and racial inequalities, certain groups simply lack the money to get computers and communication tools for the home. Technology cannot enhance or alter the lives of those who cannot afford it, and recent discussions of the "digital divide" have barely begun to address this issue.

In her groundbreaking work on household technology, Ruth Cowan[122] wisely suggests that we revise some of the unwritten rules about housework, including our high standards and our notions of who is responsible for this work. She aims to neutralize the association of gender and housework, as well as neurotic ideas of cleanliness, and enable us to exert control over household technology instead of it controlling us. Her argument is compelling regarding middle-class, white women, but if we think of household technology and household labor in broader, less individualistic terms, this type of privatized solution is inadequate. Women do an unequal share of the unpaid labor in the home as a result of gender inequality, but some women are able to shift the burden of housework onto paid domestic workers, typically lower-class minority women. When we consider paid domestic labor, the liberatory vision of household technology becomes increasingly suspect. It is misguided, at best, to revel in the liberating effects of household technology with a tense and exhausted professional woman shouldering a double day, but for a weary domestic worker earning $15 a day and then trudging home to more housework, it may be absurd. Moreover, social inequalities both connected with and beyond gender inequality become vividly apparent.

Widening our analysis of domestic labor and including paid as well as unpaid work in the home, raises a considerably different set of concerns. It becomes evident that household labor is structured in our society in terms of class and race as well as gender inequality. All women lack economic rewards as well as security or prestige for the household labor they perform. As paid employment, domestic work is extremely low-paid and devalued, and working conditions tend to be unacceptable to anyone with decent alternatives. Thus the ranks of domestic workers are filled by impoverished women of color, those with the fewest options. This includes U.S. citizens as well as a global trade in live-in minority women workers.

Evelyn Nakano Glenn[123] observes that the activities and relationships involved in maintaining people, such as cooking, cleaning, and caring for children and other adults, are typically defined as women's work. But she argues that the *racial* division of this labor "is key to the distinct exploitation of women of color and is a source of both hierarchy and interdependence among white women and women of color." Racist beliefs confirm the suitability of certain women for paid domestic work, although the particularities of the stereotypes conveniently shift depending on the racial group—we are told that Asians are quiet and thus suited to work in the home whereas African Americans are dependent and thus need such employment.[124] Researchers have implicated racism in the way household workers are treated including poor pay, demands for deference, and the manipulation of them as "one of the family."

The current division of household labor not only reinforces gender, class, and racial divisions within the United States, but highlights global inequalities as well. Heart-rending stories of immigrant women from Mexico, Jamaica, the Philippines, and the Caribbean demonstrate the gendered and racist nature of household labor, and technology has apparently been powerless to undermine the status quo in this regard.

Glenn[125] argues that sexist notions of women's place in the home are in fact bolstered by racialized ideas that permit women of color to be used to do the most degrading work, thus protecting the gendered division of labor: "By providing them an acceptable self-image, racial constructs gave the white housewives a stake in the system that ultimately oppressed them." The racial division of labor also protects the position of white men because opposition between white women and men can be redirected to clashes among women. Thus with domestic workers, race and class divisions pit groups of women against one another and, as Glenn astutely observes, maintain gender inequality in the process since what is uncontested is the assumption that, paid or unpaid, housework is *women's* work.

Class divisions are also crucial. They affect what technology individuals can afford to purchase for the home, but more significantly, the apparent advantages of household technology conceal the ways in which they serve capitalist production far more than they serve the traditional housewife. Household technology is a profit-making enterprise, and consumers only get to choose between profitable alternatives. Our corporate economy develops technology not simply to meet household needs but to foster consumerism. With the help of advertising, the public is educated to new standards of consumption and new products to buy for the household. Large appliances are designed for use in individual households, again assuring the purchase of as many items as possible. Thus the centrality of consumerism and profit-making fuels the development of many household technologies, not an effort to free women from labor nor any genuine human need. The consumerism and proliferation of household gadgets is also jarring in a context of global hunger and increasing homelessness among U.S. women.

The targeting of women as the primary consumers of household technology plays a significant role in relegating women to the home and maintaining their place in the gender division of unpaid labor. This also keeps them economically marginal, given that the heavy responsibilities they assume for the care of the home and its dependents hinders their ability to assume certain positions in the paid labor force. Advertising glorifies and mystifies the role of the housewife as guardian of the home and premier consumer, thus binding women ideologically to the home.

Paid household labor illustrates class divisions even more vividly, given the profound economic disadvantages confronting domestic workers. When a household becomes a site of paid employment, class divisions necessarily separate the interests of employers and employees.[126] But whether household labor is paid or unpaid, the technology in the home has not simply freed women, but operates instead within class constraints and illustrates both hierarchy and interdependence among women.

None of this is intended to idealize a less industrialized past. Some women may have lost the satisfactions of their labor and the intimacy of work with others in the home, but as Susan Strasser[127] reminds us, "Craft satisfaction, intimacy, and community went along with grueling amounts of heavy labor, a lack of privacy that most modern Americans would find intolerable, and the oppression of women on both individual and social levels." Technological changes in the twentieth century have benefited many women. Judy Wajcman[128] criticizes the emphasis some feminists put on the negative effects of domestic technology and the assumption that women are worse off now because of technology. She believes this has led to the view that women have simply been duped. She argues instead that, "Once we recognize that the mechanization of the home did bring substantial improvements to women's domestic working conditions, even while it introduced new pressures, women seem less irrational." Wajcman notes that women blame themselves for the failure of technology to ease the work of the home, rather than recognizing the design of the technologies and the social relations in the home. Her point is well taken, but while we acknowledge the considerable benefits of technology, let's not ignore the lack of change and the persistent inequalities of race, class, and gender that remains a significant and unacceptable part of the picture.

CONCLUSION

What we have seen from our discussion not only of household technology but reproductive and office technology as well, is that none of these technologies have functioned in a truly revolutionary way to dislodge the inequality of women or to challenge the traditional divisions of paid and unpaid labor. None of them have been "progressive" in the sense of undermining the structural inequality that impinges on the lives of so many.

Instead, gender, race, and class inequalities shape the conditions of women's lives and their experiences with technology. Thus, technology is not the independent or neutral instrument it may appear to be, but is instead deeply affected by the larger social and political context. Certainly it can be co-opted or used for more progressive purposes, as will be discussed in our final chapter, but more significant social change will not come without directly addressing the very purpose of technology and the way in which it currently supports rather than undermines hierarchy.

We will first turn to a discussion of the myth of progress, which helps explain in part why we have not been more aware of the connections between technology and social inequality.

NOTES

1. Theodore N. Greenstein, "Gender Ideology and Preception of the Fairness of the Division of Household Labor: Effects on Marital Quality," *Social Forces*, Vol. 74, (March 1996): 1029.

2. Suzanne Bianchi et al., "Is Anyone Doing the Housework? Trends in the Gender Division of Household Labor," *Social Forces*, Vol. 79 (September 2000): 191.

3. Cynthia Cockburn, "Domestic Technologies: Cinderella and the Engineers," *Women's Studies International Forum*, Vol. 20 (1997): 361–371.

4. Ruth Schwartz Cowan, *More Work for Mother: The Ironies of Household Technology from the Open Hearth to the Microwave*, (New York: Basic Books, 1983), 47.

5. Ibid.

6. Judy Wajcman, *Feminism Confronts Technology* (University Park, PA: The Pennsylvania State University Press, 1991), 93–94.

7. Cowan, *More Work for Mother*, 66–67.

8 Wajcman, *Feminism Confronts Technology*.

9. Greenstein, "Gender Ideology."

10. Richard A. Feinberg, "'Man May Work From Sun to Sun But Woman's Work Is Never Done': A Short Note on Why the Issue of Household Work Is Important Socially, Economically, and Politically," *Family and Consumer Sciences Research Journal*, Vol 24 (June 1996): 355.

11. Toni Calasanti and Carol Bailey, "Gender Inequality and the Division of Household Labor in the United States and Sweden: A Socialist-Feminist Approach," *Social Problems*, Vol. 38 (February 1991): 35.

12. Bianchi et al., "Is Anyone Doing the Housework?"

13. Scott J. South and Glenn Spitze, "Housework in Marital and Nonmarital Households," *American Sociological Review*, Vol. 59 (June 1994): 327.

14. Sampson Blair and Michael Johnson, "Wives' Perceptions of the Fairness of the Household Division of Labor: The Intersection of Housework and Ideology," *Journal of Marriage and the Family*, Vol. 54 (August 1992): 570; John P. Robinson and Geoffrey Godbey, *Time for Life* (University Park, PA: Pennsylvania State University Press, 1997).

15. Myra Marx Ferree, "Beyond Separate Spheres: Feminism and Family Research," *Journal of Marriage and the Family*, Vol. 52 (November 1990): 877.

16. Arlie Hochschild, *The Second Shift: Working Parents and the Revolution at Home* (New York: Viking, 1989).

17. Cockburn, "Domestic Technologies."

18. Ibid., 364.

19. Janet Saltzman Chafetz and Jacqueline Hagan, "The Gender Division of Labor and Family Change in Industrial Societies: A Theoretical Accounting." *Journal of Comparative Family Studies*, Vol. 29 (Summer 1996): 187–188.

20. Heidi Hartmann, "The Family as the Locus of Gender, Class and Political Struggle: The Example of Housework," *Signs*, Vol. 6 (Spring 1981): 383.

21. Sanjiv Gupta, "The Effects of Transitions in Marital Status on Men's Performance of Housework," *Journal of Marriage and the Family* Vol. 61 (1999): 700–711.

22. Hilary Silver and Frances Goldscheider, "Flexible Work and Housework: Work and Family Constraints on Women's Domestic Labor." *Social Forces*, Vol. 72 (June 1994): 1103–1119.

23. Joanne Hoven Stohs, "Predictions of Conflict Over the Household Division of Labor Among Women Employed Full Time," *Sex Roles*, Vol. 33 (1995): 257–275.

24. Terri L. Orbuch and Sandra Eyster, "Division of Household Labor Among Black Couples and White Couples," *Social Forces*, Vol. 76 (September 1997): 301–332.

25. Joanne Hoven Stohs, "Multicultural Women's Experience of Household Labor, Conflicts, and Equity," *Sex Roles: A Journal of Research,* March 2000, 339.

26. South and Spitze, "Housework."

27. Oriel Sullivan, "The Division of Housework Among 'Remarried' Couples," *Journal of Family Issues*, Vol. 18 (March 1997): 205.

28. Ruth Schwartz Cowan, "Less Work for Mother?" Invention and Technology, Spring 1987, 61.

29. Cowan, *More Work for Mother*, 44.

30. Hochschild, *The Second Shift*.

31. Silver and Goldscheider, "Flexible Work," 104.

32. Chris Kynaston, "The Everyday Exploitation of Women: Housework and the Patriarchal Mode of Production," *Women's Studies International Forum*, Vol. 19 (May–June 1996): 221.

33. Cowan, *More Work for Mother*, 192.

34. Cowan, "Less Work for Mother?" 63.

35. Joann Vanek, "Household Technology and Social Status: Rising Living Standards and Status and Residence Differences in Housework," *Technology and Culture*, Vol. 19 (July 1978): 367–368.

36. Susan Strasser, *Never Done: A History of American Housework* (New York: Pantheon Books, 1982), 243.

37. Lynn Spigel, *Make Room for TV: Television and the Family Ideal in Postwar America* (Chicago: University of Chicago Press, 1992), 22.

38. Ellen Lupton, *Mechanical Brides: Women and Machines from Home to Office* (New York: Cooper-Hewitt National Museum of Design Smithsonian Institute and Princeton Architectural Press, 1993), 4.

39. Harriet Rosenberg, "The Kitchen and the Multinational Corporation: An Analysis of the Links Between the Household and Global Corporations," *Journal of Business Ethics*, Vol. 6 (1987): 179–194.

40. Lynn Spigel and Denise Mann, "Women and Consumer Culture: A Selective Bibliography," *Quarterly Renew of Film and Video*, Vol. 11 (1989): 85.

41. Lupton, *Mechanical Brides*, 15.

42. Cockburn, "Domestic Technologies," 366.

43. Lupton, *Mechanical Brides*, 10.

44. Wajcman, *Feminism Confronts Technology*, 100.

45. Rosenberg, "The Kitchen," 184.

46. Bonnie J. Fox, "Selling the Mechanized Household: 70 Years of Ads in *Ladies Home Journal*," *Gender and Society*, Vol. 4 (March 1990): 26–27.

47. Ibid.

48. Strasser, *Never Done*, 8.

49. Stuart Ewen, *Captains of Consciousness: Advertising and the Social Roots of the Consumer Culture* (New York: McGraw-Hill Book Company, 1976), 160.

50. Strasser, *Never Done*, 253.

51. Ibid., 262.

52. Lupton, *Mechanical Brides*, 19.

53. Wajcman, *Feminism Confronts Technology*, 104.

54. Lupton, *Mechanical Brides*, 38.

55. Gary Ruskin and Robert Weissman, "The Cost of Commercialism," *Multinational Monitor*, Vol. 20 (January–Feburary 1999): 9.

56. Ibid.

57. Christine Bose, Philip Bereano, and Mary Malloy, "Household Technology and the Social Construction of Housework," *Technology and Culture*, Vol. 25 (January 1984): 64.

58. Spigel, *Make Room for TV*, 21.

59. Rosenberg, "The Kitchen," 179.

60. Ibid.

61. Ruth Schwartz Cowan, "From Virginia Dare to Virginia Slims: Women and Technology in American Life," *Technology and Culture*, Vol. 20 (January 1979): 51–63.

62. Ibid., 61.

63. Wajcman, *Feminism Confronts Technology*.

64. Ibid., 98.

65. Cockburn, "Domestic Technologies."

66. Ibid., 370.

67. Lupton, *Mechanical Brides*, 16.

68. Judith Rollins, "Ideology and Servitude." In *At Work in Homes: Household Workers in World Perspective* (American Ethnological Society Monograph Series, No. 3, 1990), 74–88; Mary Romero, *Maid in the U.S.A.* (New York: Routledge, 1992).

69. Shannon Dortch, "Maids Clean Up," *American Demographics*, Vol. 18 (November 1996): 4.

70. Ruth Schwartz Cowan, "A Case Study of Technology and Social Change: The Washing Machine and the Working Wife." In *Clio's Consciousness Raised* (New York: Octagon Books, 1976), 245–252.

71. Vanek, "Household Technology."

72. Susan Kleinberg, "Technology and Women's Work: The Lives of Working Class Women in Pittsburgh, 1870–1900." In *Dynamos and Virgins Revisited: Women and Technological Change in History* (Metuchen, NJ: Scarecrow Press, 1979), 200.

73. Roger Sanjek and Shellee Colen, "Introduction." In *At Work in Homes: Household Workers in World Perspective* (American Ethnological Society Monograph Series, November 3, 1990), 1–13.

74. Ibid., 4.

75. Evelyn Nakano Glenn, *Issei, Nisei, War Bride: Three Generations of Japanese-American Women in Domestic Service* (Philadelphia: Temple University Press, 1986).

76. Pierrette Hondagneu-Sotelo, "Regulating the Unregulated?: Domestic Workers' Social Network," *Social Problems*, Vol. 41 (February 1984): 50–64.

77. Glenn, *Issei, Nisei, War Bride*, 103.

78. Dorothea Schneider, "The Work That Never Ends: New Literature on Paid Domestic Work and Women of Color," *Journal of American Ethnic History*, Vol. 17 (Winter 1998): 61.

79. Rollins, "Ideology and Servitude," 75.

80. Evelyn Nakano Glenn, "From Servitude to Service Work: Historical Continuities in the Racial Division of Paid Reproductive Labor," *Signs*, Vol. 18 (Autumn 1992): 10.

81. Ibid., 14.

82. Schneider, "The Work That Never Ends."

83. Glenn, *Issei, Nisei, War Bride*, 167.

84. Schneider, "The Work That Never Ends."

85. Vicki Ruiz, "By the Day or the Week: Mexicana Domestic Workers in El Paso." In *Women on the U.S.-Mexico Border: Responses to Change* (Boston: Allen and Unwin, 1987): 61–76.

86. Ibid., 63.

87. Kathy Dobie, "Black Women, White Kids: Tale of Two Worlds," *The Village Voice*, 12 January 1988, 20.

88. Ojito, "Nannies," B1. Pierrette Hondagneu-Sotelo and Ernestine Avila ("I'm Here, but I'm There") use the term "transnational motherhood" to discuss immigrant Latina women who live and work in the United States while their children remain in their country of origin. Their research focuses on paid domestic workers in Los Angeles. These women contradict the dominant U.S., white, middle-class models of motherhood as well as most Latina notions. Their children are cared for by grandmothers, other female kin, fathers, and paid caregivers.

89. National Organization of Women (NOW) Legal Defense and Education Fund, Inc., "Out of the Shadows—Strategies for Expanding State Labor and Civil Rights Protections for Domestic Workers," Part I, 1997.

90. Sanjek and Colen, "Introduction," 181.

91. Steven Greenhouse, "Report Outlines the Abuse of Foreign Domestic Workers," *The New York Times*, 14 July 2001, A20.

92. Romero, *Maid in the U.S.A.*

93. Shellee Colen, " 'With Respect and Feelings': Voices of West Indian Child Care and Domestic Workers in New York City." In *All American Women: Lines That Divide, Ties That Bind* (New York: The Free Press, 1986), 46–70.

94. Ibid., 60.

95. Romero, *Maid in the U.S.A.*

96. Rollins, "Ideology and Servitude," 78, 81, 83.

97. Sanjek and Colen, "Introduction."

98. NOW Legal Defense and Education Fund, Inc., "Out of the Shadows."

99. Romero, *Maid in the U.S.A.*

100. Colen, " 'With Respect and Feelings,' " 47.

101. Romero, *Maid in the U.S.A.*, 95, 98.

102. Rollins, "Ideology and Servitude," 85, 86.

103. Colen, " 'With Respect and Feelings,' " 50, 64.

104. Bonnie Thornton Dill, " 'The Means to Put My Children Through': Child Rearing Goals and Strategies among Black Female Domestic Servants." In *The Black Woman* (Beverly Hills: Sage Publications, 1980), 114.

105. Roger Sanjek and Shellee Colen, "Conclusion." In *At Work in Homes: Household Workers in World Perspective* (American Ethnological Society Monograph Series, No. 3, 1990), 186.

106. Abigail B. Bakan and Daiva K. Stasiulis, "Making the Match: Domestic Placement Agencies and the Racialization of Women's Household Work," *Signs*, Vol. 20 (Winter 1995): 303–335.

107. See Rhacel Salazar Parrenas, "Migrant Filipina Domestic Workers and the International Division of Reproductive Labor." *Gender and Society*. Vol. 14, August 2000: 560, for a discussion of the role of Filipina domestics not only in Canada, but globally.

108. Bakan and Stasiulis, "Making the Match," 306, 315.

109. Ibid., 315.

110. *New Statesman & Society*, "Maids for Export," 1 December 1989, 29.

111. Ibid., 31.

112. Ruth Milkman et al., "The Macrosociology of Paid Domestic Labor," *Work and Occupations*, Vol. 25 (November 1998): 483.

113. Colen, " 'With Respect and Feelings.' "

114. Hondagneu-Sotelo, "Regulating the Unregulated?" 60.

115. Dill, " 'The Means to Put My Children Through.' "

116. Ibid., 113.

117. Romero, *Maid in the U.S.A.*

118. Cowan, *More Work for Mother.*

119. Ibid., 100.

120. Bose, Bereano, and Malloy, "Household Technology," 77.

121. Julianne Malveaux, "Will Technology Bridge the Gap Between Black and White?" *Black Issues in Higher Education*, Vol. 13 (22 August 1996): 48.

122. Cowan, *More Work for Mother.*

123. Glenn, "From Servitude to Service Work," 3.

124. Ibid.

125. Ibid., 34.

126. Bakan and Stasiulis, "Making the Match."

127. Strasser, *Never Done*, 8.

128. Wajcman, *Feminism Confronts Technology*, 82.

8

The Myth of Progress

❖ ❖ ❖ ❖ ❖ ❖

The fate of our times is characterized by rationalization and intellectualization and,
above all, by the "disenchantement of the world."
Max Weber

The opposite of love is not hate but the persistent use of the rational mind.
Dostoevski

The great enemy of the truth is often not the lie, deliberate, contrived, and dishonest,
but the myth, persistent, persuasive, and unrealistic.
John F. Kennedy

In previous chapters we have seen how the development and implementation of technology is affected by structural inequalities of gender, race, and class. A focus on inequality illuminates the variety, extent, and seriousness of the problems associated with reproductive, office, and household technologies and helps explain why technology has not been a more powerful agent of social change regarding women. What remains perplexing, however, is why many of us are so poorly informed about these issues, why our impressions of technology are so favorable and so difficult to dislodge and why the inequality associated with technology has not been remedied.

On reflection, it should be abundantly clear that our assumptions about technology are not in the least accidental or haphazard. Instead we are carefully taught a very specific cultural understanding of technology and repeatedly reminded of it through the media. This chapter concentrates on our cultural notion of progress in an effort to understand how this celebrated belief prevents a critical analysis of technology and simultaneously serves to preserve the status quo. The myth of progress implies that technology is beneficent or neutral and, as Dickson[1] observes, it "disguises the exploitative and alienating role technology plays within industrialized capitalist societies, and leads us to accept a particular mode of technological development as being a unique, inevitable, and politically neutral process." A crucial part of the notion of progress is the idea that technological developments operate independently of their social contexts.[2] This conveniently masks questions of power and who makes the decisions. The evidence from previous chapters does not support the claim that technological knowledge or designs are value-free. Rather, they reflect and amplify the inequalities we observed.

Social symbols and beliefs permit and maintain inequalities either by justifying them or by disguising the problems in the first place. Our difficulties with technology are hidden from us, disguised, and ignored by a belief system that casts technology as progressive and eschews any evidence to the contrary. This belief in progress through technology has deep roots in Western culture and, in its contemporary form, is fundamentally misguided.

HISTORICAL PERSPECTIVES REGARDING PROGRESS

Since at least the eighteenth century, Western civilization and American society in particular has espoused the inevitability of progress. Although many cultures associate progress with individual improvement, it is characteristically Western to think of progress primarily as a feature of society as a whole.[3] This rather peculiar conception is captured in J. B. Bury's classic definition of progress as the belief "that civilization has moved, is moving, and will move in a desirable direction."[4] Initially, science and technology were viewed as particularly progressive, but ultimately all realms, including material and cultural development, were invested with this belief.[5] Hannah Arendt[6] summarizes nicely: "The notion that there is such a thing as Progress of mankind as a whole was unknown prior to the eighteenth century and became an almost universally accepted dogma in the nineteenth century."

Some scholars contend that the idea of progress existed in the classical world as well as in medieval times. Robert Nisbet,[7] for example, attests to its power and centrality by stating that "no single idea has been more important than . . . the idea of progress in Western civilization for nearly three thousand years." Nisbet believes that it has also been more beneficial than any other idea. He includes among its premises a conviction of the superiority of Western civilization, an acceptance of economic and technological growth, and a faith in reason, science, and scholarly knowledge. In sum, a belief in progress has been a hallmark of Western civilization, and more specifically for our purposes, technology is "the dominant symbol of progress, at the least its most visible external measure."[8] Technology is accepted as powerful and thrilling and, initially, it was regarded as the way to achieve democratic goals of political and social equality by making conveniences accessible to all.

The fusion of technology and progress is particularly pronounced in the United States where proof of inevitable progress was shaped by the particularities of America's settlement and the frontier. Thomas Berger[9] reminds us what a remarkable feat this settlement was:

transportation systems were evolved, cities founded, commerce expanded, and an industrial way of life established. The superabundance of the land, forest, and minerals gave rise to a conviction that the continent's resources were inexhaustible.

Progress is America's destiny, and technology is the method and the evidence. Leo Marx[10] claims that to call progress merely "an idea" among many is to belittle it. Instead, by the 1840s "it had become the fulcrum of an all-encompassing secular world view, and, in a sense, modernity's nearest secular equivalent of the creation myths that embody the belief systems of premodern cultures."

Significantly, this cultural worldview claims not only that technology assures continuous improvement in the West, but that it also allows "the rest of the world to advance quickly to Western economic and technical standards."[11] Thus, a Western definition and standard of progress through technology is viewed as a universal standard, not culture bound,[12] implying (as Nisbet bluntly asserts) the superiority of Western civilization. Melanie Stewart Millar[13] makes the point clearly: "Science and technology became the hallmarks of Western cultural superiority, important not only for the institutionalization of a male-dominated culture but also for the construction of Western identity as superior to that of non-Western peoples." Societies are still judged as "advanced" or "backward" depending on their level of technological development with little effort to consider other ways of measuring the quality of life.

PUBLIC ATTITUDES TOWARD TECHNOLOGY

Opinion polls regularly indicate that Americans are firm believers in the characteristically Western notion of progress through technology. The idea that science and technology are widely criticized is belied by polls that consistently show Americans to be "remarkably steady and optimistic supporters of technological enterprise."[14] Susan Mitchell[15] analyzed American attitudes as indicated by National Opinion Research Center (NORC) polls and commented that, "Americans don't just love new technologies, they believe the future depends on them." In 1998, fully three-fourths of Americans approved government support to develop technology, an increase from two-thirds in 1985; only 6 percent are opposed to this.[16] Since 1974, yearly polls conducted by Yankelovich, Skelly, and White have included the statement: "Science and advanced technology have brought us more benefits, through better products and an easier, healthier life, than the problems they may have created." Eighty-one to 84 percent of Americans consistently agree. Polls conducted for the National Science Foundation (NSF) indicate that even the Challenger disaster and the Chernobyl accident do "not seem to have harmed the generally high level of public support for science and technology."[17]

The Harvard University Program in Science and Technology surveyed popular attitudes toward technology by polling people in the larger Boston area in 1970. Their findings supported previous national studies: "whatever their discontents with what might be called 'the quality of life,' most people do not hold technology responsible. On the contrary, the sample views technology as being generally more beneficial than harmful."[18] Of the people surveyed, 83 percent thought technology did more good than harm; only 7 percent believed it to be more harmful. 94 percent of respondents agreed that "machines have made life easier." Similarly, in 1996, a national Roper Center poll found that 90 percent of respondents agreed (strongly or somewhat) that "Science and technology are making our lives healthier, easier, and more comfortable." The Harvard survey found that those with higher education and incomes were most likely to feel this way: "skilled workers were most negative, and the professional-managerial, most positive in evaluating technology."[19] Again, a 1996 national poll conducted by Roper found that 37 percent of people earning $15,000–19,000 felt technology would have a negative effect on their opportunities; only 12 percent of those earning $75,000 or higher thought this was so.

Polls have also documented general satisfaction with "experts" and their authority. In a preliminary interview for the Harvard survey, a young working-class woman supported the need for expert control of technology as she disarmingly explained why citizens cannot have decision-making power: "They're only everyday people, that deal with everyday life, and if they're not deeply involved or know all the statistics about everything, they need a representative."[20]

Research on specific types of technology reveal similar optimism and the same willingness to associate technology with progress. In a survey regarding computer technology, 67 percent of the respondents agreed that "the computer revolution will ultimately raise production and therefore living standards."[21] Seventy-three percent of those surveyed believe that the computer would allow more people to work at home, and 80 percent expect computers to be commonplace in American homes. A 1998 Roper poll reported that 61 percent of respondents "like" computers and technology; only 6 percent reported "disliking" them. A study of public attitudes toward communication technologies confirm the persistence of these themes: The public is optimistic about this technology, and those with higher incomes and more education tend to be the most favorable.[22]

Public opinion is also supportive of reproductive technology. Two polls conducted by Harris and Gallup in 1985 revealed majority approval of *in vitro* fertilization (IVF) as a means of helping infertile couples.[23] Harris found agreement as high as 85 percent when the procedure was intended to help married couples who could not otherwise have children. (But note: Only 22 percent believed IVF should be available to single women, and a mere 11 percent found it acceptable for lesbians or gay men.) As of 1987, there were no comparable national surveys on IVF, "but smaller studies of selected groups show continued support for IVF."[24] A 1998 Roper poll noted that 75 percent of respondents believe that it is ethical to use medical technology to identify and treat birth defects in a fetus. However, the same percentage (75 percent) labeled unethical the use of technology to select the sex of a child. According to 1998 National Opinion Research Center (NORC) polls, 50 percent of Americans believe genetic screening will do more good than harm; only 25 percent believe the reverse. Whites are more confident about this than black respondents: 54 percent of whites agree as compared to 42 percent of blacks.[25] NORC polls in 1998 also found that 60 percent of Americans agree that hiring surrogate mothers should be permitted.[26]

After examining two decades of research on public opinion of science and technology, Pion and Lipsey[27] reached the familiar conclusion that the public has a very favorable attitude toward both: "Overall, there seems to be a faith in the 'technological fix,' even for problems which stem from technology itself, and the same applies to the public's faith in science." A 1996 Roper Center poll again offers support for this: 78 percent of respondents feel that science and technology will solve some or most problems faced by our society. Thus, a significant amount of social research indicates that Americans consistently support technology and remain convinced of its benefits.

A striking finding of the 1987 survey is that public confidence in science and technology is based on very little concrete information.[28] This absence of public knowledge was also noted in 1969 when Louis Harris and Associates sampled a cross section of 1,600 adults regarding the new reproductive technologies. Their conclusion is instructive:

> Although most people are almost totally unfamiliar with the elements of the biological revolution which is in the offing, there is a remarkable willingness—especially among the young and better-educated—to accept it, provided it strengthens and not weakens the bonds of love and family.[29]

Similarly, polls conducted by the National Science Foundation (NSF) in the mid-1980s indicated that only 31 percent of those surveyed had a clear understanding of what radiation is, and only 24 percent knew what computer software is. Also in the mid-1980s, and again for NSF, Jon Miller found that two in five people polled believe that rocket launchings affect the weather and that vehicles from outer space have visited earth. Miller concludes that we have "a large number of people who believe in science, who have unrestrained faith in it, but who haven't the foggiest notion of why it happens."[30]

Public faith in technology, despite a lack of knowledge about it, is compelling evidence of the existence of a powerful cultural belief system that portrays technology as progressive and which minimizes, if not ignores, evidence to the contrary. Some are sanguine about this absence of information and argue that the public is not capable of making decisions about technology—this is best left to the "experts." But it is difficult to imagine a more undemocratic recipe for technological development than this mix of myth, ignorance, and abdication of public control.

CRACKS IN THE ARMOR

Let me qualify some of my earlier statements. No culture is reducible to total acceptance of some beliefs and rigid rejection of others: Values shift at different points in time and sometimes even contradict one another at the same time. There has never been a single, persistent American attitude toward technology.[31] Confidence in technology is surely part of an American heritage: It is echoed repeatedly in standard versions of American history, it has been validated in many of our own lives, and it is regularly featured in favorable media reports on new technological developments. But concerns about the dangers of technology have been articulated by many Americans of varying social backgrounds. Even by the mid-nineteenth century, doubts were being registered, and, after World War I, ambivalence grew and many worried that machines might be out of control and enslave workers in mindless routines. World War II brought deepening concerns specifically about technologies of destruction. In the 1960s, these concerns resurfaced and hostility toward technology marked many discussions, especially in terms of threats to the environment. Even the polls cited earlier provide intriguing evidence of ambivalence: concern, for example, that people may have become too dependent upon machines, or even dehumanized. Roper Center polls noted in 1999 that 54 percent of Americans worried that computers invade privacy, and in 1996 that 63 percent agreed that science and technology make our lives change too fast.

But the overriding association of technology with progress, documented by social research, continues to hamper a critical and comprehensive understanding of technology. In a 1996 Roper Center poll, 83 percent of the respondents described their reaction to science and technology in terms of "satisfaction or hope (47 percent), "excitement or wonder" (36 percent). A mere 6 percent cited "fear or alarm." This view of technology blinds us to its problematic aspects and resists an analysis of these problems even when we sense them. A compelling finding of the Harvard study cited earlier is that a significant number of people (50 percent) believe that *other* people are critical of technology. But when they were asked why, they were confounded: Most (47 percent) claimed that it was ignorance, 17 percent cited fear, only 18 percent pointed to the harms of technology, and 12 percent cited ecological dangers. Thus, "only a little over one-third of the sample could find legitimate reasons for a critical view of technology."[32] Why is this?

The belief that technology spells progress makes critique difficult and resisting technological development almost impossible, for this is tantamount to opposing progress which is, by definition, desirable. As Pollard[33] notes, "The idea of progress is, in the modern age, one of the most important ideas by which men live, not least because most hold it unconsciously and therefore unquestioningly." Thomas Berger[34] refers to it as "the secular faith of our time." Critics of technology thus appear cranky, odd, perhaps even foolish. They are regarded as modern Luddites who would halt the inevitable—indeed halt our movement toward a brighter future. But let's look closely at our notions of technology and progress and reconsider the conventional wisdom, not with an eye toward condemning technology but to gain a deeper understanding of our cultural view of it.

ON CRITICIZING "PROGRESS"

Let's admit that the very word progress is loaded: Who could be against it? Like a cool drink on a hot day, it seems inherently good. In fact, "progress" is assumed to be desirable by people who have profoundly different notions of it or who have never even given it much thought. Often progress is simply defined as continuous technological development, with the assumption that this is good for most if not all people. But surely it is now apparent that recent advances in technique have not been uniformly beneficial for all, but have had mixed results. The evidence amassed in the previous chapters should demonstrate at the very least the inability of technology to undermine inequality, and significant problems with many particular technologies such as IVF or computer monitoring. Certainly many basic conveniences such as electricity and indoor plumbing have brought great improvements, but beyond the basics things are questionable. Paul Goodman[35] remarks, for example, that "Cars are designed to go faster than it is safe to drive; food is processed to take out the nourishment; housing is expertly engineered to destroy neighborhoods; weapons are stockpiled that only a maniac would use."

The Industrial Revolution brought prosperity and material benefits and fostered the idea that constant growth is good by definition. But American culture is now driven by excessive patterns of consumption, to the point of depleting global resources. It is appropriate to question such "progress" and its national and international implications and to challenge the belief that technology cannot and should not "be impeded or diverted."[36]

A significant body of literature articulates the need for a profound analysis of our basic ideas and optimism regarding progress and technology. Critics like Langdon Winner,[37] for example, challenge the assumption "that the progress of mankind is inextricably linked to new technological apparatus." John Staudenmaier[38] helps us understand that our belief in progress is dangerous since it fosters passivity by portraying technology as determinist, and men and women as passive adaptors to it. This concedes far too much power to technology and studiously ignores the inequalities of gender, race, or class inherent in its development. Staudenmaier argues that the ideology of progress encourages violent aggression by justifying colonialism through claims that Western civilization is the epitome of all that is desirable. Thus he takes what Nisbet[39] regards as a beneficial premise of progress (a belief in the superiority of Western civilization) and casts a clear and critical eye on its damaging consequences.

What Staudenmaier, Winner, and others are suggesting is that we stop and rethink our basic working assumptions regarding progress and technology. Most significant among these is the belief that progress is inevitable and that it is measured by technological change. This implies an unquestioning acceptance of technological development since it is, by definition, progressive. But it is imperative to challenge this assumption and examine the *purpose* and *direction* of technological development. We need to be more concerned about a just distribution of its benefits. Efforts at improving the human condition have to be separated from mere technological innovation and our fascination with technique. As Braun[40] puts it,

> The challenge to society is not how to innovate faster, but how to safeguard the environment and how to find the financial means to develop public transport, health services, educational facilities, and so forth. What people need most is these things, not

high definition television, digital tape recording, broadband communications, or more television channels dispensing the same trash as the existing ones.

THE DISENCHANTMENT OF THE WORLD

One of the most insightful critiques of our ideas of technology and progress is found in the work of German sociologist Max Weber. For Weber, Western civilization, and the United States in particular, is becoming increasingly ordered and mechanical. Cultural values such as efficiency and control are emphasized while the nonrational aspects of life, such as emotion, spontaneity, and even religious beliefs, tend to be mistrusted or disparaged. This process, which Weber termed rationalization—making a more mechanical, less magical world—has vast and profound repercussions. Signaled by increasing efficiency, an emphasis on what can be calculated, and a reliance on experts, Weber sees rationalization as dehumanizing and not necessarily progressive. Rationalization is intimately connected with the growth and development of technology since technology plays a key role in facilitating efficiency and control.

Weber pinpointed a driving force in the Western world as the continuous and accelerating transformation of all aspects of life along rational lines, and he argued that in the process reason had lost its grounding in values and was instead purely instrumental. Rationality, more specifically instrumental rationality, characterizes modernity and ironically implies increased individual autonomy alongside increased impersonal domination, as rationalization spreads to every aspect of existence, and rational calculation dominates. In other words, all behavior and development is now in the service of *means* (quicker, more efficient, more readily measured), not valued *ends*. (What are we moving toward? What is the purpose of all this efficiency?) For Weber, this meant that rationality was ultimately and ironically in service to irrationality. Numerous contemporary examples illustrate his point. Fast-food may indeed be faster, but does anyone think it is more nutritious or tastes better? Mistakes on the computer keyboard may now be calculated precisely, but how does this affect workers, and does it really improve performance? What could we be thinking when what we refer to as "defense" weapons could ultimately destroy the planet or at least all human life?

Weber fears that science and technology have taken the magic and mystery from the world, leaving instead rational-empirical approaches to everything. Modernity in fact came into being through increased rationalization. According to Weber, rationalization is significant as a structure (bureaucracy) and as a process, because it comes close to defining the total social system of our age. For him, bureaucracy and modernity are virtually synonymous. Weber was the first modern social thinker to look beyond the debate surrounding the benefits of capitalism or socialism and recognize that the independent dynamic of technology and bureaucracy would pervade modern life.[41] In fact, the inevitable and accelerating rationalization of modern life led Weber to eschew the hope that a better world would be found in the demise of capitalism. He knew that whether capitalism or socialism triumphs, bureaucracy and rationalization will be there to insure the continuing (and even intensified) domination of humanity. This belief accounts for Weber's[42] merciless assessment of modernity:

> Specialists without spirit, sensualists without heart; this nullity imagines that it has attained a level of civilization never before achieved.

Ambivalent (at best) about the bureaucratization and secularization of society, Weber observed that we may have wonderful machines and, to cite his example, be able to ride streetcars, but what do we really know about our machines? We know next to nothing about how they operate, unlike the so-called "savage" who knew "incomparably more about his tools." In the modern world, technical knowledge of most accomplishments is in the hands of very few. Consider, as an example Weber might appreciate, my mother-in-law, riveted by the television images of Neil Armstrong walking on the moon: "My God," she muttered, "there are men on the moon, and I don't know how my doorbell works."

Increasing rationalization not only separates us from the machinery we use each day, it also encourages us to define problems as technological and requiring experts for solutions. This implies that ordinary citizens do not have enough knowledge to make valid judgements and thus cedes authority as well as political power to the "experts." (The young woman in the Harvard study, who feels "everyday people" can't make decisions about technology, comes to mind.) The dangerous implications of allowing control of technology to reside in the hands of a few are unrecognized since we are convinced that the process of developing and implementing technology is objective and thus independent of political or economic interests. Burris[43] makes the point that given such assumptions of objectivity, any challenge to technology may be construed "as irrational or as incompetent."

It is reasonable, however, to question the extent to which the public can exert informed control over technology, given the scientific and technological complexity of many contemporary issues. Are the matters we have been discussing too complicated for democratic decision making? Are they best left to the "experts?" Many studies dispute this. In an article appropriately entitled "You Don't Have To Be a Rocket Scientist . . ." John Doble and Amy Richardson, for example, report the results of a study by the Public Agenda Foundation, which indicates that people can quickly learn the essentials of various issues (in this particular study, global warming and solid waste disposal) and make reasonable policy decisions. "By and large, participants in the study made the same choices as a group of scientists. Moreover, the participants' positions made sense even when they differed from those of the scientists."[44] Extensive and detailed scientific knowledge is not necessarily required for competent decision making and arguing to the contrary insures that major public issues will be kept in the hands of a few. David Dickson[45] observes that: "By dressing up political issues as complex technical ones, the technocracy removes responsibility from the individual and by doing so, appears to isolate him from the political process."

Doble and Richardson[46] make an intriguing comparison between public decisions on scientific matters and our jury system. Juries, comprised of "non-expert" citizens, are relied upon to make significant legal decisions. This insures that the legal system is open to the participation of the pubic, which is regarded as crucial in a democratic society. It is arguable that the public can and must be informed participants in technological decisions as well and that this is equally critical in a modern democracy. The general public may be awed and mystified by technology and feel incompetent compared to the "experts," but this is a socially created fear and respect. One need not be Bill Gates to understand the possibility of unemployment associated with electronic offices nor does it take a medical degree to grasp the high failure rate of IVF. But given powerful cultural assumptions about science, rationality, and technology, control is relinquished to the "experts."

For Weber, rationalization ultimately spells the growing domination of nature and humanity and the thorough "disenchantment" of the world. This means the end of belief in magic, spirits, and indeed, the sacred. Reality has become bland and empty—filled only with frantic, useless activity. Old moral values and ideals are being pushed aside, as all of society strains toward nothing but production for its own sake. As Weber puts it, growth becomes an end in itself, an irresistible force pushing modern society "until the last ton of fossilized coal is burnt." Since we are encouraged to think about the world in mechanical and secular terms, a moral framework often must be one's own creation. We tend unwittingly to emphasize order and control in our lives and decisions, demanding that, like machines, we become more efficient, more productive, and more rational.

Each of the technologies we have explored illustrates the growth and pervasiveness of rationalization. Household technology focuses on efficiency, speed, and increasing consumerism, not an assessment of end results or the necessity of such scrupulous standards of cleanliness. The office is fixated on efficiency, despite the fact that its more mechanized atmosphere often works to the detriment of workers' health as well as jobs. We have seen how electronic technology enables managers to exert powerful control over women workers in the First and Third Worlds through the extreme subdivision of tasks. Management also attempts to control the women's self-perception by citing, for example, the "natural" ability of "Oriental" women's fingers, eyes, and passivity to withstand the low-skilled, mind-deadening work. "The reduction of the social person to technological instrumentality is no mere mystification. It constitutes everyday reality for the perception and treatment of workers."[47] In a similar vein, in Latin American and California, Hispanic and African-American women doing data entry in back offices "are defined in computer jargon as "wetware," that is, biological material essential for the operation of the machines."[48] Finally, reproductive technology offers the production of "high-tech" babies and focuses on the compulsion to be able to calculate that a child will be "normal." Let's consider the last example in more detail.

Much discussion regarding reproductive technology and disability can be understood in Weberian terms by considering our cultural preoccupation with predictability and control, which, in turn, is reflected in and reinforced by the medical profession. Dr. Henry Klapholz,[49] for example, claims that anti-technology feelings interfere with an "objective" assessment of the benefits of fetal monitoring. He acknowledges that 98 out of 100 pregnancies have favorable outcomes, but nonetheless stresses the importance of monitoring *every* fetus. His language[50] is instructive:

> If one is interested in gambling and taking that 2 percent chance, then fetal monitoring is unnecessary. If one is interested in optimizing the chances for every fetus, fetal monitoring is essential.

Dr. Klapholz[51] presents his information as value-free, as simply factual: "Here I will try to present to you information and not opinions. I will deal neither with feelings nor emotions, but simply with information that has been accumulated." Notice how "feelings" and "emotions" are devalued here. But we are not simply provided information, we are instead given a mandate to use fetal monitoring unless we are willing to "gamble" with the fate of our children. Ironically, clinical trials have now demonstrated that fetal monitoring does not reduce fetal mortality, morbidity, or cerebral palsy, but instead has very high false positive rates and also correlates strongly with a rise in cesarean sections.[52] But pervasive rationality nonetheless enhances the power of experts. When problems increasingly come to be viewed as technological, the vast majority of us are suddenly regarded as lacking the expertise to hold opinions, let alone make decisions.

Ruth Hubbard[53] observes that despite prenatal diagnosis, most disabled babies will be born; this is not simply a personal problem nor one that "science" can resolve. She notes that given the social context, most women will probably welcome any and all technological intervention aimed at avoiding disability, but we cannot pretend that this is simply a matter of personal choice:

> For, as long as childbearing is privatized as women's individual responsibility and as long as bearing a disabled child is viewed as a personal failure for which parents (and especially mothers) feel shame and guilt, pregnant women are virtually forced to hail medical 'advances' that promise to lessen the social and financial burdens of bearing a disabled child (however rare and unlikely it may be that any particular one of us may do so).

Attempts to avoid disability may easily shift from a sincere (if perhaps misguided) interest in preventing suffering to an interest in simply avoiding the responsibility of caring for the disabled. Stanworth,[54] for example, is concerned that "research which might reduce the number of genetic defects will replace research to improve the prospects of people with disease or disability; that attempts to reduce genetic variability will be substituted for efforts to create an environment in which the range of human variability can flourish."

The very development of certain types of reproductive technology (such as prenatal diagnosis) reflects a rational society that aims to control the creation and terms of life itself. When technology then presents us with the possibility of detecting and aborting a "defective" fetus, we are forced to choose whether or not to take advantage of it. Our choices are subtly shaped by its very availability and the tendency to view the issue in technological, not ethical, terms. Concerns about "quality control" are vividly evident in a paper by Dr. M. Neil Macintyre[55] presented at a conference on antenatal diagnosis. Macintyre asks us to try to imagine looking forward to having our first child, a beautiful, perfect child. "Then," he says, "this emerges!" He refers the audience to a picture of the face of a severely deformed newborn and continues: "This is what you are presenting to society as representing the very best in you and your spouse. This thing with no eyes and with a mess for a face represents the focus of your dreams and aspirations." Dr. Macintyre contends that concern for the child is not the issue, but instead, "What are people going to think of me for having produced that." He concludes:

> In this situation, you and your spouse are in desperate need of help from someone who will understand; someone who is an expert in such matters and can make you understand that it really wasn't your fault . . . someone who can help you do the one thing which will really help to heal your wounds; that is, to produce a beautiful, normal, and healthy child. That someone . . . is the genetic counselor.

Macintyre graphically, if unwittingly, illustrates many of the values we are taught to espouse in American society: a dread fear of disability; the idea that bearing a disabled child is somehow a personal failure; the notion that the problem is a deformed face, rather than deformed social structures that demand pleasing faces, working limbs, and normal IQs. These attitudes encourage us to seize any means to avoid the disability we have been so carefully taught to fear. And the "experts" are available to assist. How "progressive" are such developments?[56]

A recent article in the *Journal of Medicine and Philosophy* in my mind connects the growth of rationalization with the larger social context of inequality: Laura Purdy[57] takes issues with the "negativism" regarding prenatal screening for defects and the subsequent abortion of the fetus that this implies. She asserts that disabled children may require enormous amounts of care and the chances are great that the mother will bear the burden of this care. She points out that childrearing is already difficult for many women:

> Despite twenty years of feminist argument and activism, daycare is still a luxury, not a right—even though most women must work. There is still no guaranteed health care. There is still significant discrimination against women in both education and workplaces. Women still earn, on average, far less than men. Divorce is still common, and so is unemployment.

As she sees it, given this wider context, if a woman chooses abortion instead of raising a disabled child, it is inappropriate to label her choice immoral or selfish.

She points to the lack of resources for many people including those with health problems, and the fact that our national priorities in terms of spending (defense budgets vs. welfare spending) is not likely to shift any time soon. She[58] concludes, "Other things being equal, I believe that existing persons should have first call on resources. Therefore, if programs to prevent the birth of children who are likely to have serious health problems cost less than the alternatives, there is a moral argument in their favor."

Here we have the epitome of a technological solution to a social problem: We are encouraged to decide on the lives of special-needs children in terms of how much they cost and in terms of the inequality women shoulder. Purdy raises issues that need to be addressed and she is probably right when she says we should be wary of harshly judging a woman who decides to abort a disabled fetus. But let's not spare any wrath at the social conditions and social values that have brought us to this moment.

The elevation of values such as rationality and control, fueled by notions of progress, and the disparagement of emotion or spontaneity that Weber observed, finds its way into our assessment of all types of technology. Lori Andrews[59] illustrates this in her defense of "surrogate motherhood." She acknowledges that surrogacy violates a number of "taboos," which she equates with "deeply held emotional beliefs" about the proper relationship between a mother and her child. But she counsels us to avoid such emotional thinking and stick to reason and rationality. Andrew's argument shuts the door on the possibility that "rationality" itself may be a problem (which Weber as well as Dostoevski understood), and thus she neglects any consideration of viable alternatives to it beyond a sloppy emotionalism that rejects intellectual assessment.

Weber mentioned ways in which the process of rationalization might be halted or derailed (such as the rise of a charismatic figure), but he finally despairs of the possibility of preventing it in the West or the rest of the world. He believed that this unique cultural development with all its inherent flaws would eventually permeate the entire planet. We may struggle against the degradation of all that is personal in life but, in Weber's mind, it is fanciful to imagine a genuine escape from this "iron cage." His deep pessimism is apparent in the following statement, cited in Mayer[60] and quoted in its entirety:

> Imagine the consequences of that comprehensive bureaucratization and rationalization which already today we see approaching. Already now . . . in all economic enterprises run on modern lines, rational calculation is manifest at every stage. By it, the performance of each individual worker is mathematically measured, each man becomes a little cog in a machine and, aware of this, his one preoccupation is whether he can become a bigger cog . . . It is apparent that today we are proceeding towards an evolution which resembles the ancient kingdom of Egypt in every detail, except that it is built on other foundations, on technically more perfect, more rationalized, and therefore much more mechanized foundations. The problem which besets us now is not: how can this evolution be changed?–for that is impossible, but: what will come of it?

TOWARD A RECONSIDERATION OF PROGRESS

Max Weber's scathing critique of Western civilization's blind faith in technology linked to progress is compelling, in large measure because it vividly illuminates some of the most profound problems and pervasive experiences confronting modernity. His analysis also offers a blunt and incisive vision of the vanity and misguided direction of Western culture. But he offers no solution. He vehemently denied that his sociology depicted a deterministic direction for global civilization, but what else are we to think? His deep pessimism eschews any genuine alternative. But Weber's pessimism can and must be rejected and rejected in the name of (and on the strength of) the very values he saw in retreat in modern society.

Critics of instrumentalism, more hopeful than Weber, have recommended that we subordinate our emphasis on technical means and reflect upon the ends we want to pursue. Many of the global problems we confront, including poverty, nuclear threat, and environmental problems, have been created by the instrumental thinking Weber illuminated. And, as Jansen[61] points out, instrumental thinking will be needed to solve these problems "but, unless instrumentalism is resituated within grammars of human motives, relationships, values, concepts of community, and social responsibility, we are all imperiled by the emerging global structures of information-capitalism." Thus, the values marginalized by industrialism and instrumental rationality have to be reclaimed. Perhaps Weber, in many ways the epitome of the "rational man," the architect of value-freedom, and self-described as "religiously unmusical," is the least likely to be able to propose an alternative vision of the future. But others have.

Feminists, in particular, have been skeptical of universal and universalizing claims about progressive technology. They are acutely aware that technology has frequently worked against the interests of women, racial and ethnic minorities, sexual minorities, and members of non-Western cultures, and they have taken, as we shall see in the next chapter, concrete steps toward social change. But let's return to Merritt Roe Smith[62] and Leo Marx,[63] whose insights into our cultural idea of progress, and suggestions for change were raised in the Introduction.

Smith and Marx asserted that in early American history progress was closely associated with human betterment and with the search for a more democratic, less hierarchical society. Technology was the *means* to those larger social goals, as both Thomas Jefferson and Benjamin Franklin understood it. But Smith and Marx, along with Weber, recognize the shift that has taken place, with technology *itself* coming to be viewed as progressive and the emphasis placed on innovation, profit, efficiency, and rationality as ends in themselves. As Marx astutely notes, we have witnessed the appropriation of the belief in progress for the defense of an anti-egalitarian status quo. This shift in our cultural understanding of progress points to the absence of social goals in our society and to our narrow vision of civic responsibility.

The challenge before us is to begin to reassess the purpose of technological development, to keep focused on what the myth of technology and progress obscures, to keep focused, as Weber understood, on valued ends, such as equality and democracy, which are the genuine measures of progress. This points to the significance of an analysis of technology centered on gender, race, and class that puts the emphasis on social goals and re-envisions technology as a means to those ends.

Albury and Schwartz[64] point out that the "myth of technology as the driving force behind progress prevents us from rethinking the role that it could play in restructuring the economy and improving our lives, prevents us from seeing that the wider interests of the mass of the people have been systematically ignored in favour of profit, power, and privilege for the few." We need to consider the common good and ways to improve the quality of American life generally. For, "if we recognize that 'technology evaluation' really means spelling out what we feel a technological society ought to be and setting out to make it that way, then we have reason to expect that we have a chance to succeed in putting technology to work to serve the values we believe in."[65]

Louis Mumford is among those who have advocated a more humane and personalized society. He proposed, for example, less reliance on technology and less consumption. His view of the good life was one of simplicity, self-sufficiency, and community. Although some argue that these ideals are no longer part of the American dream, they are as American as Emerson, Thoreau, and Whitman—in whose writings Mumford found his intellectual and moral roots. The current unease in America about the "success" of our technological society may signal a readiness to reassert these beliefs and values; it may signal a willingness to shift toward a less instrumental understanding of progress.

Part of what is required is wresting control of technology from the "experts." We need democratic debate and democratic control of the development and implementation of technology, with public policy aimed at problems of major social concern such as the quality of life, public health, and public safety. The nineteenth-century idea of progress assumed that what is good for the industrialist is good for everyone else, but this studiously ignores the systematic exclusion of Americans who are unable to afford market prices. As Braun[66] asserts, "Technology has become too important to be left to technologists or, worse still, to the market." Put differently, technology is too important to be regulated only by business values and not humanistic or social concerns.

CONCLUSION

Constant technological development, no matter how breathtaking, is never a guarantee of social improvement. But our cultural myth of technology and progress encourages precisely this association and bolsters our popular understanding of technology itself as ultimately beneficent and apolitical. Consider how the media discussion of technology focuses on technique and technical capabilities, not social values. Attention is directed toward how this, that, or the other amazing technology works, not whether we need it, whom it affects, how to regulate it, or its purpose. Many of the problems with technology discussed in previous chapters get ignored or minimized. The idea of progress can, however, be reconnected to notions of a just society and human betterment. We need to challenge the assumption that technological development equals progress, and interrogate our very notion of progress: Progress for whom? According to what?

NOTES

1. David Dickson, *The Politics of Alternative Technology* (New York: Universe Books, 1974), 183.

2. John M. Staudenmaier, "Perils of Progress Talk: Some Historical Considerations." In *Science, Technology, and Social Progress* (London: Associated University Presses, 1989), 268–298.

3. Hans Jonas, "Reflections on Technology, Progress, and Utopia," *Social Research*, Vol. 48 (Autumn 1981): 411.

4. Warren W. Wagar, *Good Tidings: The Belief in Progress from Darwin to Marcuse* (Bloomington, IL: Indiana University Press, 1972), 4.

5. Sidney Pollard, *The Idea of Progress: History and Society* (Baltimore: Penguin Books, 1968), 31.

6. Hannah Arendt, *On Violence* (New York: Harcourt, Brace and World, 1969), 25.

7. Robert Nisbet, *History of the Idea of Progress* (New York: Basic Books, 1980), 4.

8. Jonas, "Reflections on Technology," 412.

9. Thomas R. Berger, "Conservation, Technology, and The Idea of Progress," *Canadian Literature*, Vol. 96 (Spring 1983): 61.

10. Leo Marx, "Technology: The Emergence of a Hazardous Concept," *Social Research*, Vol. 64 (Fall 1997): 969.

11. Pollard, *The Idea of Progress*, 10.

12. Dona Richards, "European Mythology: The Ideology of 'Progress.' " In *Contemporary Black Thought: Alternative Analyses in Social and Behavioral Science* (Beverly Hills: Sage Publications, 1980), 59–79.

13. Melanie Stewart Millar, *Cracking the Gender Code: Who Rules the Wired World?* (Toronto: Second Story Press, 1998), 31.

14. Eliot Marshall, "Public Attitudes toward Technological Progress," *Science*, Vol. 205 (July 1979): 284.

15. Susan Mitchell, *American Attitudes: Who Thinks What About the Issues That Shape Our Lives.* (Ithaca, NY: New Strategist Publications, Inc., 1998), 174.

16. Ibid.

17. Constance Holden, "Japanese Views on Science Compared to U.S. Attitudes," *Science*, Vol. 240 (April 1988): 277–278.

18. Irene Taviss, "Notes and Queries: A Survey of Popular Attitudes Toward Technology," *Technology and Culture*, Vol. 13 (1972): 611.

19. Ibid., 611.

20. Ibid., 619.

21. *Time*, "Machine of the Year: The Computer Moves In," 3 January 1983, 13–39.

22. Stephen D. Reese, Pamela J. Shoemaker, and Wayne A Danielson, "Social Correlates of Public Attitudes Toward Communication Technologies," *Journalism Quarterly*, Winter 1987, 675–682.

23. Peter Singer and Deane Wells, *Making Babies: The New Science and Ethics of Conception* (New York: Charles Scribner's Sons, 1985).

24. Judith Lasker and Susan Borg, *In Search of Parenthood: Coping with Infertility and High-Tech Conception* (Boston: Beacon Press, 1987), 173.

25. Mitchell, *American Attitudes*, 83.

26. Ibid., 85.

27. Georgine M. Pion and Mark Lipsey, "Public Attitudes Toward Science and Technology: What Have the Surveys Told Us?" *Public Opinion Quarterly*, Vol. 45 (1981): 311.

28. Ibid.

29. Louis Harris, "The LIFE Poll," *Life Magazine*, 13 June 1969, 54.

30. I. Peterson, "Knowing Little About How Things Work," *Science News*, Vol. 129, 22 February 1986, 118.

31. See, for example, Howard Segal, "The Cultural Contradictions of High Tech: Or the Many Ironies of Contemporary Technological Optimism" in Ezarahi et al., 1994: 175–216. Segal also examines four ways in which high tech promotes itself–prophecies, advertising, world's fairs/theme parks, and technological literacy campaigns.

32. Taviss, "Notes and Queries," 610.

33. Pollard, *The Idea of Progress*, 13.

34. Berger, "Conservation, Technology," 60.

35. Paul Goodman, "The Morality of Scientific Technology," *Dissent*, January-February 1967, 49.

36. Berger, "Conservation, Technology," 64.

37. Langdon Winner, "On Criticizing Technology," *Public Policy*, 1972, 50–51.

38. Staudenmaier, *Technology's Storytellers*.

39. Nisbet, *History of the Idea*.

40. Ernest Braun, "Can Technological Innovation Lead Us to Utopia?" *Futures*, Vol. 26 (1994): 860.

41. Hermann Strasser and Gunther Schlegl, "Gemeinschaft or Gessellschaft? Two Competing Visions of Society in Werner Stark's and Max Weber's Sociology of Religion," Presented at the meetings of the American Sociological Association, August 1988.

42. Max Weber, *The Protestant Ethic and the Spirit of Capitalism* (New York: Charles Scribner's Son, 1958), 182.

43. Beverly Burris, "Technocracy and Gender in the Workplace," *Social Problems*, Vol. 36 (April 1989): 174.

44. John Doble and Amy Richardson, "You Don't Have to Be a Rocket Scientist . . .," *Technology Review*, January 1992, 52.

45. David Dickson, *The Politics of Alternative Technology*, (New York: Universe Books, 1974), 29.

46. Doble and Richardson, "You Don't Have to Be a Rocket Scientist."

47. Aihwa Ong, "Disassembling Gender in the Electronic Age," *Feminist Studies*, Vol. 13 (Fall 1987): 622–623.

48. Suzanne K. Damarin, "Women and Information Technology: Framing Some Issues for Education," *Feminist Teacher*, Vol. 6 (1992): 17.

49. Henry Klapholz, "The Electronic Fetal Monitor in Perinatology." In *Birth Control and Controlling Birth* (Clifton, NJ: The Humana Press, Inc., 1980), 167–173.

50. Ibid., 173.

51. Ibid.

52. Margaret Lent, "The Medical and Legal Risks of the Electronic Fetal Monitor," *Stanford Law Review*, Vol. 51 (April 1999): 807–837.

53. Ruth Hubbard, "Personal Courage Is Not Enough: Some Hazards of Childbearing in the 1980's." In *Test-Tube Women: What Future for Motherhood?* (London: Pandora Press, 1984), 350.

54. Michelle Stanworth, ed., *Reproductive Technologies: Gender, Motherhood, and Medicine* (Minneapolis: University of Minnesota Press, 1987), 32.

55. M. Neil Macintyre, "Counseling in Cases Involving Antenatal Diagnosis." In *Antenatal Diagnosis* (Chicago: University of Chicago Press, 1972), 63–67.

56. What *is* progressive is the disability rights movement that has enhanced the lives of people with disabilities through inclusion and access to the resources of larger society.

57. Laura M. Purdy, "What Can Progress in Reproductive Technology Mean for Women?" *The Journal of Medicine and Philosophy*, Vol. 21 (1996): 506–507.

58. Ibid., 509.

59. Lori Andrews, *Between Strangers: Surrogate Mothers, Expectant Fathers, and Brave New Babies* (New York: Harper and Row, 1989), 253.

60. Jacob Peter Mayer, *Max Weber and German Politics: A Study in Political Sociology* (London: Faber and Faber, 1956),126–127.

61. Sue Curry Jansen, "Gender and the Information Society: A Socially Structured Silence," *Journal of Communication*, Vol. 39 (Summer 1989): 210.

62. Merritt Roe Smith, "Technology, Industrialization, and the Idea of Progress in America," in *Responsible Science: The Impact of Technology on Society* (New York: Harper and Row, 1986): 1–30.

63. Leo Marx, "Does Improved Technology Mean Progress?" *Technology Review*, Vol. 90 (January 1987): 32–46, 71.

64. Dave Albury and Joseph Schwartz, *Partial Progress: The Politics of Science and Technology* (London: Pluto Press, 1982), 8.

65. Paul T. Durbin, "Technology and Values: A Philosopher's Perspective," *Technology and Culture*, Vol. 134 (1972): 575.

66. Braun, "Can Technological Innovation," 859.

9

Demands and Promises
Implications for Social Change

❖ ❖ ❖ ❖ ❖ ❖

No matter how completely technics relies upon the objective procedures of the sciences, it does not form an independent system, like the universe: it exists as an element in human culture and it promises well or ill as the social groups that exploit it promise well or ill. The machine itself makes no demands and holds out no promises: it is the human spirit that makes demands and keeps promises.
Louis Mumford

The evidence before us demonstrates that the promise of technology has yet to be fulfilled for many women. Although there have been great improvements in many respects, women remain far from equal politically, economically, or socially. The work force is highly segregated by gender, and women of color occupy its lowest ranks; positions of prestige in both the business world and government are still largely the reserve of privileged white men. Improved levels of education among women have not translated into substantial economic or political power. Despite inroads made into traditionally male-dominated fields, women have not been successful in shifting a fair share of their traditional responsibilities to men, and this is one of the keys to genuine social equality. Women are still responsible for the overwhelming bulk of unpaid work—the housework, child care, and care of the sick and the elderly. In addition, racism is still pervasive and class differences are intensifying. Many of the benefits technology could confer on women remain the privilege of those who can afford it.

My objectives in this chapter on social change are modest: I want to clarify the implications for social change when one makes a sociological argument as I have regarding technology, I want to offer my optimistic conviction that beneficial change is possible, and I want to provide examples of how the process of change may proceed.

THE IMPLICATIONS OF SOCIAL THEORY

In dealing with any social issue, the first step toward change is to assess accurately the root causes of the problems confronting us. In the absence of such understanding, it is easy to misinterpret not only the causes of a problem but, by implication, its solutions. Given our fiercely individualistic culture and the media's enthusiastic portrayal of technology, it is understandable that people may misinterpret any difficulties they confront regarding technology and reduce these problems to self-blame. The implied remedy is then personal change (or endurance). I have argued, on the contrary, that many of our problems with technology are ultimately based in social inequality and the blinding myth of progress. Inequality allows and even necessitates a grossly unfair distribution of technology's benefits and burdens as well as unequal control of technology, while a staunch belief in progress through technology obscures this inequality and its effects. If many of our difficulties with technological development and implementation are rooted in existing inequalities and social values, then it logically follows that structural and cultural change is ultimately needed to remedy these problems. In other words, what is required is not simply personal or individual change, but deliberate and significant social and institutional change.

Attempts to halt completely the growth and development of technology are futile and also beside the point. At issue is not whether to have technology, but how to insure that what we do create is able to serve the common good. Since technology itself is implicated in the problems of our society, existing technology or even new techniques will not offer the solution. The concerns we discussed regarding reproductive rights, for example, will not be altered by new medical discoveries, but rather by challenging the inequality that restricts quality medical care to some groups and not others, dictates the terms of its availability, and restricts knowledge and control over it. If we want healthy infants, for example, we don't need more high tech solutions but basic prenatal care available to all women.

Let's be clear. The change that is required entails nothing less than confronting existing economic, political, and cultural processes that limit resources and control to small groups of people. We must look beyond technology and shake the very structures of oppression, including varying forms of inequality and the cultural values and beliefs that support them. As Judith Lorber[1] notes, "If we want to eliminate the exploitation of any social group by any other social group, a society has to be structured for equality." Technology will not determine the future, and focusing on mere technological development prevents a serious reconsideration of social goals and how technology might serve those goals. Julianne Malveaux[2] puts it very well:

> Our future is not a function of technology, but of the principles that dictate the division of resources in this country. Right now, the principles dictate that the rich get richer, the poor get poorer, and that issues concerning African-Americans should be ignored, not addressed. Technology won't change those trends.

The task before us is immense, but concrete steps can be taken, even as we aim toward more substantial change. As community organizer Gale Cinotta observed, "People are always saying you can't do it. But maybe you can. You can do a piece of it. At least you can build a base for someone else to build on."[3]

NEEDS AND POSSIBILITIES

Women are confronted by diverse sources of oppression, which require diverse solutions. Gita Sen and Caren Grown[4] point out: "There is and must be a diversity of feminisms, responsive to the different needs and concerns of different women, and defined by them for themselves." This diversity should be applauded not feared, since in many ways it adds to the power of feminism as a political movement. It broadens the struggle to one that attends to all forms of oppression and strengthens connections among women. Neither gender inequality nor other forms of inequality can be relegated to second place; they are linked. One type of subordination (such as gender subordination) will not necessarily wither as other forms of oppression (like class oppression) are challenged.

Feminism has moved far beyond attempts to improve the status of a few white women, to an inclusive understanding of solidarity against multiple forms of oppression, an acknowledgement of difference, and an honoring of diversity. It increasingly recognizes that women's issues include class and race inequality, as well as significant global dimensions. This necessitates organization at local, national, and international levels. Let's briefly review some of the fundamental needs that must be met.

Worldwide, women need equal employment opportunities, accessible family planning, and education. More simply, they need the possibility of a decent standard of living for themselves and for the children they frequently support. For women in poverty or on the brink of poverty, this means access to essentials that no human being should be denied: food, clean water, medical care. Globally, feminists advocate increased education for women, improved family planning and health care, the elimination of legal discrimination, and increased access to science and technology. Some of these goals have been attained for many in the United States, where women have made significant advances in terms of formal legal equality and increased educational opportunities. But even these changes are incomplete, particularly for minority women, and an urgent problem facing most American women is the difficulty of combining paid employment and child care. Efforts to eliminate job discrimination will not suffice if women have no relief from the double responsibilities they face from the combination of paid and unpaid labor. Compared to most of the world's industrially developed or rich countries, the United States has one of the worst records in terms of national policies and legislation for working women during and after childbirth, and for working women with small children. Ultimately everyone needs "better and greater access to health care; safer and healthier workplaces and communities; recognition of the value of women's work, including mothering, and more and better paying jobs for all people; comprehensive parental leave policies; high-quality and affordable day care; and fundamental reforms in the welfare system."[5]

The list of required changes is long and daunting, particularly when challenges must be leveled not only against gender discrimination but class and race discrimination as well. But existing social conditions and technology are amenable to change. We must, as David Noble[6] argues, "transcend the ideology of technological determinism by demystifying technology and recognizing that human choice, not technology, moves history." Through concerted action for change, technology can be redesigned and redirected toward goals that serve the vast majority.

It is instructive to compare the United States and Sweden in terms of existing social conditions and social policies, with an eye toward possibilities for social change. The similarities they share as advanced Western, capitalist, and democratic societies indicate that Swedish policies are within the realm of possibility in the United States, although currently Sweden provides a striking contrast in terms of its social achievements. In the 1994 Swedish elections, for example, "women attained the highest legislative profile in the world, capturing 41 percent of the seats in the Riksdag."[7] In contrast, as of 2000, women accounted for only 13 percent of the seats in the U.S. House Representatives and 9 percent in the Senate. Swedish women can boast of the smallest gender gap in the world in wages, earning 89 percent of men's wages in 1995. In the same year, U.S. women earned 75 percent of men's wages. Although the United States is one of the wealthiest nations in the world, it is also "the only developed country in the world without a national policy on medical care, child care, or maternity leave."[8] Sweden, on the other hand, has been vigorous in using social policy to assist women and families. Its policies include universal health care as well as extensive public works and job training programs. Paid maternity leave began in Sweden in the 1940s and was extended to fathers in the 1970s. Parents are now able to share a twelve–month leave, compensated at 75 percent of their salary. An additional three months is available at a flat rate of compensation.[9] Women are also entitled to fifty days of paid pregnancy leave, and parents receive up to ninety days paid leave to care for sick children.

Compare these policies to the U.S. Family and Medical Leave Act passed in 1993, which permits employees in firms of more than fifty to take up to twelve weeks *unpaid* leave to care for a child or other needy family member.[10] This legislation passed after fifteen years of controversy and two presidential vetoes by George Bush.

Like the United States, Sweden has high rates of divorce and a similar proportion of its mothers are single. Significantly, however, Swedish mothers and children do not face the kinds of economic disadvantage endured by U.S. women. When women in the United States are required to support themselves and their children without a male provider, their economic inequality becomes vividly apparent since they are frequently plunged into poverty. The Swedish example demonstrates, however, that "family composition need not be associated with female poverty."[11]

Sweden's Child Care Act of 1985 guaranteed a place in day care for every child age one to age six. The United States still does relatively little in the way of public policy regarding child care. As of 1986, the United States had child care facilities for approximately 2.1 million children, although more than 10 million children under age six were living in families where the single parent or both parents were employed.[12] Working women in the United States still do the bulk of the housework, but American society does not provide outside support to ease the double burden for working women. Despite the economic problems Sweden experienced in the 1990s and the fact that the situation of Swedish women is still far from equal to that of men, the strategies they have adopted ease the responsibilities of home and paid work for women. As Durrant and Olsen[13] correctly observe, "a priority has been placed upon the reduction of parental stress produced by work-family conflicts and upon the well-being and nurturance of children." The point is women's problems are not insoluble: Maternity leave, subsidized child care, decent wages, and flexibility in paid labor go a long way toward improving the situation of women once this—rather than mere technological development—becomes a focused goal.

Given our previous discussion of the problems surrounding the care of children with disabilities, it is instructive to note that in Sweden not only is national health care available for all children, but a full range of special services is available for children with disabilities and their families, including additional parental leave, a car allowance, appliances, and free rehabilitation services.[14] Families are also entitled to respite care and special programs for non-disabled siblings. As disability rights activists Asch and Fine[15] observe regarding Sweden, "A supportive context diminishes the alleged negative impact—which we contend is massively overestimated—of having a child with a disability."

Perhaps it is useful to think of short- and long-term strategies for change, particularly at a time when the United States is in full retreat from federal involvement or responsibility for families or the poor. The profound change required to eradicate inequality will not occur overnight. Nonetheless, specific reforms can be targeted and accomplished in the short term, even as we work toward greater change. Donchin,[16] for example, suggests specific strategies to enhance reproductive choices, such as making adoption processes more accessible, since many turn to the new reproductive technologies after being turned away from adoption agencies or baffled by complicated procedures. Programs could be developed to address certain causes of infertility, such as untreated pelvic infections and delayed child bearing. More specifically, work place strategies could be devised "to reduce barriers that make it so costly for women to combine childbearing and work during their peak years of fertility."[17]

CO-OPTING TECHNOLOGY

Technology itself often has a contradictory nature, and although it may be designed to serve the needs of a small minority, it can have unanticipated consequences. Thus it is not only a threat but also an opportunity, since moments of transition are often opportunities for change.[18] Van Zoonen[19] provides a useful illustration with a revealing discussion of the introduction of the telephone in the United States. Initially, the telephone was intended strictly for business as a rational, efficient machine; women were accused of misunderstanding the telephone by using it for personal reasons. Although developed and marketed for a particular male audience, many of its actual users (women) "resisted and overruled these prescriptions and turned the telephone from a rational, business medium into an instrument for maintaining friendship and kinship. Therefore in the long run not only the social meaning of the telephone changed, but production, distribution, and marketing were affected as well."

Another useful example is the automobile. Virginia Scharff's[20] intriguing history of this machine, *Taking the Wheel: Women and the Coming of the Motor Age*, tells a story of struggle over its gendered meanings. As with the telephone, women were initially segregated from the masculine imagery of the car, but finally succeeded in finding a place for themselves in terms of this technology. Scharff deduces that there is nothing inevitable about the masculinity of technology. She offers an interactive approach to technology and culture, demonstrating how constructs of gender were affected by—and affected—the cultural construction of the car. Although technology typically reflects and reinforces the values of dominant and powerful groups in society, there is room for the transformation of existing power relationships. Illustrations such as these encourage a more imaginative response to certain types of technology and a consideration of how particular technologies might serve feminist politics.

Related to our specific concerns, Judy Wajcman[21] acknowledges that gender relations and economic forces have shaped contraceptive technology, but she still contends that the effects of technology are indeterminant. For example, "the Pill's inventors thought they were solving the 'population explosion' of the underclass. As it turned out, the Pill was mainly taken up by Western women who saw in it a means to free their sexuality from the constraints of reproduction." Wajcman believes it is crucial not to underestimate the possibilities of using technology to women's advantage.

GRASS-ROOTS ORGANIZING

The idea that technology frees women, even if it has to be co-opted to do so, is appealing since the notion of a technological fix seems so quick, painless, and relatively easy. But history ultimately teaches us that the actions of women themselves, not technology, have been most responsible for beneficial social change. As Margaret Mead pointedly advised: "Never doubt that a small group of thoughtful committed citizens can change the world; indeed, it's the only thing that ever has." Grass-roots organizations have recreated America in significant and unexpected ways. The women's movement offers a sterling example of a grass-roots movement that produced dramatic change, reasserting values often ignored in a highly rationalized society, and debating the very goals of science and technology.

Nationally and internationally, strategies that involve the self-organization of women, particularly poor women, have been crucial to successful change.

Ella Baker provides an inspiring example of grass-roots organizing and its basic philosophy. As a major political leader from the 1940s through the 1960s in the National Association for the Advancement of Colored People (NAACP), the Southern Christian Leadership Conference (SCLC), and the Student Non-Violent Coordinating Committee (SNCC), she believed that the membership of organizations should be directly involved in programming. She urged organizing low-income people with such tactics as "sending organizers into pool rooms and taverns; her experience had been that some people would join up out of sheer surprise."[22] For Baker, local (not national) offices had to be the focal points. She emphasized recruiting women and young people–the very constituencies that would become so significant in the 1960s.

A central premise in Baker's approach to activism is "the idea of group-centered leadership, rather than leader-centered groups."[23] For her, leadership entailed teaching others to rule themselves. As she once put it,

> My basic sense of it has always been to get people to understand that in the long run they themselves are the only protection they have against violence or injustice . . . People have to be made to understand that they cannot look for salvation anywhere but to themselves.

Like many contemporary feminists, Baker was concerned about how to deal with difference and bring people together. She believed that the best structures for change were small organizations of people working hard among themselves, but connecting with other small groups so that larger group action would be possible when necessary.

For Baker, social change is all about organizing people through slow, mundane work. She contrasts this with "mobilizing," which involves large numbers of people for relatively dramatic events. Both are necessary, but as Baker puts it:

> I just don't see anything to be substituted for having people understand their position and understand their potential power and how to use it. This can only be done, as I see it, through the long route, almost, of actually organizing people in small groups and parlaying those into larger groups.[24]

This type of organizing is arduous and may take longer than other forms of social change, but the results are more secure since people have been educated in terms of understanding both problems and solutions.

COALITION BUILDING

Just as Ella Baker recognized the need for groups to connect with one another in the interests of larger social change, coalition building is a central theme among contemporary feminists. The agenda for many feminists now includes the struggle against various forms of oppression, not just a narrowly defined (read: white, middle class) gender oppression. Coalition building is admittedly difficult, not just because of the different priorities of various groups, but also because it entails challenging the privileges of some groups in order to insure the rights of others. This is clearly illustrated in Mary Romero's[25] study of paid domestic workers. Romero challenges the idea that all women share the same situation and vividly demonstrates the clashing interests of private household workers and their women employers. Many domestic workers are struggling to gain control over the work process and to create a more businesslike relationship. This requires that tasks be more clearly delineated and that workers be paid a market wage with vacations and raises. By gaining such control, household workers may avoid the demeaning aspects of domestic labor. But the interests of middle class women for cheap household help could work to maintain and support the unjust conditions of domestic workers. Bonnie Thornton Dill[26] tries to resolve this dilemma by arguing that what is required is "an examination of the exploitation inherent in household labor as it is currently organized for both the paid and unpaid worker. The question is, "What can we do to upgrade the status of domestic labor for ALL women?" She envisions a point "where the differences between us ENRICH our political and social action rather than divide it." But coalition and genuine community among women is necessarily difficult to attain given the profound structural differences in women's lives. Evelyn Nakano Glenn[27] astutely advises, however, that

> This does not mean that we give up the goal of concerted struggle. It means we give up trying falsely to harmonize women's interests. Appreciating the ways race and gender division of labor creates both hierarchy and interdependence may be a better way to reach an understanding of the interconnectedness of women's lives.

ORGANIZING FOR SOCIAL CHANGE

It is wise to remind ourselves periodically of what has been accomplished when people organize for social change. Although social problems often seem monumental, they have been confronted and altered. Numerous anthologies document this: Some describe successful social justice organizing at the grass roots level in the United States,[28] others provide specific examples from the thousands of feminist organizations that have developed over the last thirty years,[29] still others offer compelling stories of women organizing in their communities around a variety of issues.[30] Claire Reinelt's research[31] reminds us that the battered women's movement created shelters for women across the United States, redefined the way we think about domestic violence, and provided dramatic changes in the lives of women confronting violence at home. Powerful testimony is also available regarding the resistance women have offered in global assembly plants.[32] Sara Mosle[33] documents the successful organizing activities of hotel maids in Las Vegas, while Gary Delgado[34] tells the story of the Asian American Women Advocates' (AIWA) battle to secure back wages and fair treatment for Asian women in the garment industry: Confronted by a widespread grass-roots campaign, Jessica McClintock,

Inc. finally agreed to AIWA's demands to pay each of twelve workers $10,000 in back pay and to contract only with fully bonded factories.[35]

In *Toxic Work*, Steve Fox[36] discusses the legal battle of unskilled workers, mostly Hispanic women, doing assembly work of electronic components at the Lenkurt division of GTE, one of the world's largest communications organizations. With the help of a dedicated local lawyer, Josephine DeLeon Rohr, 250 workers filed claims of occupational disease and disablement against Lenkurt. They cited unusual forms of cancer, "frequent miscarriages, excessive menstrual bleeding and hysterectomies, odd neurological problems, and a strange array of other conditions."[37] Fox provides a compelling story of an effective legal action for compensation, and the commitment of these workers and their lawyer to justice and change.

These case studies are useful in documenting the possibilities for change when citizens decide to take action. The feminist movement itself offers yet another powerful illustration. Largely through grass-roots organizing, it has successfully initiated a struggle for freedom of choice, identified discrimination and opposed the laws that sustain it, portrayed women not merely as victims but survivors and agents of change, and challenged the given division of labor and the very definition of women.[38] Inspired by the women's movement, the UN Decade for Women (1977–1987) resulted in an emerging global consensus on the centrality of certain issues including legal and economic equality, violence against women, and international peace. As Tinker and Jaquette[39] note, "The most conspicuous change over the Decade is the exponential increase in the number and types of women's groups in every country of the world, and the complex of networks and organizations which unite them." Through these remarkably varied groups, women are learning a great deal about each other and striving to maintain international networks. The full effects of the Decade are difficult to estimate, but "there is no doubt that the Decade solidified and enhanced the international women's movement; women will continue to work together to effect change."[40] The Fourth World Conference on Women, held in Beijing in 1995, inspired a platform for action that calls for a coherent approach to women's health care needs, implemented at national and international levels, and specifically incorporating gender concerns into health care decision making.[41] It may be useful to look in more depth at one example of people organizing for change: the women's health movement.

WOMEN'S HEALTH MOVEMENT

The women's health movement is a superb example of what grass-roots organizing and coalition building can accomplish, and it prefigures a vastly different sort of science and technology. The movement began in the late 1960s with small groups of women meeting to discuss and confront their problems with the medical care system. It initially focused on abortion rights, reproductive freedom, and affordable health care, and illuminated fundamental problems with American medicine through the consciousness raising that it sparked. It taught women to be responsible for their health needs and to seek reliable information rather than leaving it to the "experts." The movement also challenged traditional approaches to childbirth and promoted a healthy skepticism regarding the medical profession.[42] As Sandra Morgen[43] notes, "The movement articulated a radical critique of the U.S. health care system, including a condemnation of medicine as an institution of social control, of racism and sexism in health care institutions and policies, and of the failure of the system to meet the most basic health needs of many, most particularly the poor." The women's health movement ultimately improved the quality of health services available to many women, created a more humane approach to medical care and has been part of a larger project to transform science and society. Hundreds of feminist health clinics currently exist. From the beginning they emphasized "self-help; lay involvement in all phases of patient care; and accessible, affordable, and woman-centered services."[44] Activists in the women's health movement monitored and publicized developments in women's health care with bestselling books like *Our Bodies, Ourselves*, written by The Boston Women's Health Care Collective.

Our Bodies, Ourselves started unassumingly as notes written by women in feminist discussion groups and serves as an illustration of the power of women organizing within the larger movement. The first edition was written in 1970 by twelve young, white, American feminists. It reflected the view that "the personal is political," and it used women's experiences to critique the health care establishment. It also emphatically aimed for social change. Since 1970, more than 3 million copies of *Our Bodies, Ourselves* have been printed in six editions and twelve different languages. "Over 100,000 copies of the 1992 edition were sold in the first three months it was released for sale."[45] Currently, the book addresses various communities of women, and different authors are used to focus on far more diverse populations. The aim is to inform and empower women, and most observers agree that whatever its limitations, it has profoundly affected the way many women think about their bodies and medical care including the new reproductive technologies

The women's health movement now includes an impressive array of organizations working toward change. During the 1980s, women of color organized several national and local women's health organizations, "even as they continued to challenge oppressive social relations within white-dominated feminist groups."[46] Byllye Avery founded the National Black Women's Health Project after her problems with pulmonary disease alerted her to the difficulties black women confront with the medical establishment.[47] The National Women's Health Network (NWHN) is a prominent health care advocacy group: With over 16,000 members and 500 local organizations, NWHN has successfully instigated the first large, long-term, controlled study of estrogen replacement therapy and won Congressional approval for a 300 percent increase in the funding for breast cancer research. In other groups, such as an organization called "Jane," women have organized quietly yet just as effectively for change. Developed in Chicago in 1969,

Jane was an abortion counseling and referral service. Women in the group learned to perform abortions themselves, thereby making the costs more affordable and thus serving impoverished women of color who had no other recourse.[48] Counseling was sometimes done individually, sometimes in small groups, and all was accomplished without the benefit of high technology or traditional medical expertise.

Today health activists form a worldwide network that has launched impressive struggles. Since 1987, for example, The Women's Health Movement in Latin America has waged a "Campaign Against Maternal Mortality and Morbidity."[49] It attracted the attention and efforts of women's health groups throughout Latin America and has resulted in significant advances. Perhaps most important among these is the public attention it brought to the issue of preventable maternal deaths, inadequate health care, and the deteriorating economic situation of women. The activities sponsored by this organization have been as varied as the countries in which women have organized. In Brazil, pamphlets were distributed listing women's demands for social change including safe abortion, improved general health care, and stable employment. In Chile, women participated in workshops organized around what it means to be healthy, women's reproductive health, and public health service. In Peru, a theater contest was held on the issue of maternal mortality and morbidity. A series of dramas were presented to explore the lives of women in the family, social services, and the reasons women seek abortions. Personal testimonies accompanied each of these as women articulated the relationship between maternal mortality and morbidity and larger social conditions. Significantly, the women in Peru "did not view this issue as a medical problem to be solved through technological magic, but as an element inherent in their inferior social status."[50]

In sum, locally, nationally, and globally, the women's health movement has made profound improvements in the lives of many women and children not through technological development but through grass-roots organizing, steadfastly focused on social goals.

CONCLUSION

The point of this chapter has been to cite some examples of people organizing for social change as one way to indicate that beneficial change is possible. Admittedly, problems of the scope we have examined do not lend themselves to easy solution. The inequality is profound, but not inevitable. We cannot, however, rely on technology—no matter how dazzling—to resolve social issues. It is not value-free but introduced within the existing social order that shapes its very form and its outcomes and, as a result, often reproduces and amplifies inequality.

Instead, the social order itself and its myths must be confronted and changed. Given the evidence before us, there can be no defending the formula that technology equals progress. I would offer that genuine progress entails the movement toward a society in which all people have access to basic human needs of food, shelter, clothing, and quality medical care. A society in which work is satisfying and secure. A society in which differences among people are valued and respected and in which a wide distribution of power ensures the inclusion of many groups, much debate, and genuine choices about issues that matter. A society that nurtures all its citizens and protects the needy. A society, in short, which is democratic, egalitarian, and just.

These principles deserve our energy and our commitment and a sustained consideration of the ways in which our technology might enhance them. It is possible to envision and aim to create a more democratic, non-hierarchal social order, and to use our idealism and deep convictions to develop the most practical and effective social programs. Technology could then be in service to these ends, in service to the commonweal, and not in service to the powerful few or the interests of profit. It is quite realistic to think of people having control over the design and implementation of advanced technology if we think in terms of immediate concerns. Workers are fully capable of learning about office technology just as women with fertility problems can understand reproductive technology. Citizen groups can collect and disseminate information, as the women's health movement has demonstrated.

The solution to our problems with technology will ultimately be found in a more democratic and egalitarian society and world. This presupposes a shift in priorities from a societal emphasis on technological *means,* to a situation in which clearly articulated *ends* determine the appropriate means toward a more humane society. The challenge before us is thus a political one: the struggle for social and economic justice to ensure that technology serves the common good, rather than the few, the interests of profit, or mindless efficiency. Social theorist Werner Stark[51] captures the faith and modesty that both intellectual and political struggle entail:

> In this enterprise, as in all others in mortal life, it is not given us to know the issue: we must be satisfied, and more than that, if we may hope that we are travelling in the right direction.

NOTES

1. Judith Lorber, *Gender Inequality: Feminist Theories and Politics* (Los Angeles: Roxbury Publishing Company, 1998), 197.

2. Julianne Malveaux, "Will Technology Bridge the Gap Between Black and White?" *Black Issues in Higher Education,* Vol. 13 (22 August 1996): 48.

3. Anne Witte Garland, *Women Activists: Challenging the Abuse of Power* (New York: The Feminist Press, 1988), 55.

4. Gita Sen and Caren Grown, *Development, Crises, and Alternative Visions: Third World Women's Perspectives* (New York: Monthly Review Press, 1987), 18–19.

5. Kim Blankenship et al., "Reproductive Technologies and the U.S. Courts," *Gender and Society,* Vol. 7 (March 1993): 9.

6. David Noble, "Social Choice in Machine Design: The Case of Automatically Controlled Machine Tools, and a Challenge for Labor," *Politics and Society,* Vol. 8 (1978): 313–347.

7. Naomi Neft and Ann D. Levine, *Where Women Stand: An International Report on the Status of Women in 140 Countries 1997–1998* (New York: Random House, 1997), 415.

8. Doris Anderson, *The Unfinished Revolution: The Status of Women in Twelve Countries* (Toronto: Doubleday Canada Limited, 1991), 178.

9. Joan E. Durrant and Gregg M. Olsen, "Parenting and Public Policy: Contextualizing the Swedish Corporal Punishment Ban," *Journal of Social Welfare and Family Law*, Vol. 19 (1997): 452.

10. Neft and Levine, *Where Women Stand*.

11. Gertrude Goldberg and Eleanor Kremen, "The Feminization of Poverty: Only in America?" *Social Policy*, Vol. 17 (Spring 1987): 10.

12. Eschel Rhoodie, *Discrimination Against Women: A Global Survey of the Economic, Educational, Social and Political Status of Women* (London: McFarland & Company, Inc., 1989), 453.

13. Durrant and Olsen, *Parenting and Public Policy*, 453.

14. Ibid.

15. Adrienne Asch and Michelle Fine, "Shared Dreams: A Left Perspective on Disability Rights and Reproductive Rights." In *Women with Disabilities: Essays in Psychology, Culture, and Politics* (Philadelphia: Temple University Press, 1988), 300.

16. Anne Donchin, "Feminist Critiques of New Fertility Technologies: Implications for Social Policy," *The Journal of Medicine and Philosophy*, Vol. 21: 493.

17. Ibid.

18. Donna Haraway, "A Cyborg Manifesto: Science, Technology, and Socialist–Feminism in the Late Twentieth Century," *Simians, Cyborgs and Women: The Reinvention of Nature* (New York: Routledge, 1990).

19. Liesbet Van Zoonen, "Feminist Theory and Information Technology," *Media, Culture, and Society*, Vol. 14 (1992): 24.

20. Virginia Scharff, *Taking the Wheel: Women and the Coming of the Motor Age* (New York: Free Press, 1991).

21. Judy Wajcman, "Delivered Into Men's Hands? The Social Construction of Reproductive Technology." In *Power and Decision: The Social Control of Reproduction* (Cambridge: Harvard University Press, 1994), 172.

22. Charles Payne, "Ella Baker and Models of Social Change," *Signs*, Vol. 14 (1989): 888.

23. Ibid., 892, 893.

24. Ibid., 898.

25. Mary Romero, *Maid in the U.S.A.* (New York: Routledge, 1992).

26. Bonnie Thornton Dill, "Race, Class, and Gender: Prospects for an All-Inclusive Sisterhood," *Feminist Studies*, Spring 1983, 147.

27. Evelyn Nakano Glenn, "From Servitude to Service Work: Historical Continuities in the Racial Division of Paid Reproductive Labor," *Signs*, Vol. 18 (Autumn 1992): 37.

28. John Anner, ed., *Beyond Identity Politics: Emerging Social Justice Movements in Communities of Color* (Boston: South End Press, 1996).

29. Myra Marx Ferree and Patricia Yancey Martin, eds., *Feminist Organizations: Harvest of the New Women's Movement* (Philadelphia: Temple University Press, 1995).

30. Garland, *Women Activists*; Nancy A. Naples, ed., *Community Activism and Feminist Politics: Organizing Across Race, Class, and Gender* (New York: Routledge, 1998).

31. Claire Reinelt, "Moving onto the Terrain of the State: The Battered Women's Movement and the Politics of Engagement." In *Feminist Organizations: Harvest of the New Women's Movement* (Philadelphia: Temple University Press, 1995), 84–104.

32. Devon Pena, *The Terror of the Machine: Technology, Work, Gender, and Ecology on the U.S.–Mexico Border* (Austin, TX: Center for Mexican-American Studies, 1997); Kathleen Staudt, "Programming Women's Empowerment: A Case from Northern Mexico." In *Women on the U.S.–Mexico Border: Responses to Change* (Boston: Allen and Unwin, 1987); Susan Tiano, *Patriarchy on the Line: Labor, Gender, and Ideology in the Mexican Maquila Industry* (Philadelphia: Temple University Press, 1994); Gay Young, "Gender Identification and Working Class-Solidarity among Maquila Workers in Ciudad Juarez: Stereotypes and Realities." In *Women on the U.S.–Mexico Border: Responses to Change* (Boston: Allen and Unwin, 1987), 105–128.

33. Sarah Mosle, "Letter from Vegas: How the Maids Fought Back," *The New Yorker*, 26 February and 4 March 1996, 148–156.

34. Gary Delgado, "How the Empress Gets Her Clothes: Asian American Immigrant Women Fight Fashion Designer Jessica McClintock." In *Beyond Identity Politics: Emerging Social Justice Movements in Communities of Color* (Boston: South End Press, 1996), 81–94.

35. Ibid., 94.

36. Steve Fox, *Toxic Work: Women Workers at GTE Lenkur* (Philadelphia: Temple University Press, 1991).

37. Ibid., 8.

38. Sen and Grown, *Development, Crises, and Alternative Visions.*

39. Irene Tinker and Jane Jaquette, "UN Decade for Women: Its Impact and Legacy," *World Development*, Vol. 15 (1987): 426.

40. Ibid., 426.

41. *Women and Health: Mainstreaming the Gender Perspective into the Health Sector* (New York: United Nations Publication, 1999).

42. Andrea B. Eagan, "The Women's Health Movement and Its Lasting Impact." In *An Unfinished Revolution: Women and Health Care in America* (New York: United Hospital Fund of New York, 1994), 15–27.

43. Sandra Morgen, " 'It Was the Best of Times, It Was the Worst of Times': Emotional Discourse in the Work Cultures of Feminist Health Clinics." In *Feminist Organizations: Harvest of the New Women's Movement* (Philadelphia: Temple University Press, 1995), 236.

44. Ibid., 237.

45. Susan E. Bell, "Translating Science to the People: Updating The New Our Bodies, Ourselves," *Women's Studies International Forum*, Vol. 17 (1994): 10.

46. Morgen, "It Was the Best of Times," 214.

47. Stephen Simurda, "Shooting Star: A Crusader for Black Women's Health," *American Health*, Vol. 12 (March 1993): 28–31.

48. "Jane," "Just Call Jane," The Fight for Reproductive Freedom: A Newsletter from Student Activists, Vol. 4 (Winter 1990): 1–4.

49. Regina Rodriguez, "Maternal Morality and Morbidity: From Tragedy to Prevention: *Women's Health Journal*, Vol. 35 (1990): 36–50.

50. Ibid., 45.

51. Werner Stark, *The Sociology of Knowledge: An Essay in Aid of a Deeper Understanding of the History of Ideas* (London: Routledge and Kegan Paul, 1958), 346.

Bibliography

❖ ❖ ❖ ❖ ❖ ❖

ACKER, JOAN. "Rewriting Class, Race, and Gender: Problems in Feminist Rethinking." In *Revisioning Gender*. Edited by Myra Marx Ferree, Judith Lorber, and Beth Hess. Thousand Oaks, California: Sage Publications, 1999: 44–69.

AKTAR, FARIDA. "Wheat for Statistics: A Case Study of Relief Wheat for Attaining Sterilization Target in Bangladesh." In *Made to Order: The Myth of Reproductive and Genetic Progress*. Edited by Patricia Spallone and Deborah Lynn Steinberg. New York: Pergamon, 1987: 154–160.

ALBURY, DAVE and JOSEPH SCHWARTZ. *Partial Progress: The Politics of Science and Technology.* London: Pluto Press, 1982.

ALBEDA, RANDY. "Improving Women's Employment in the U.S.A." *Industrial Relations Journal. Vol. 28*, December, 1997: 275–282.

ALBIN, PETER and EILEEN APPELBAUM. "The Computer-Rationalization of Work: Implications for Women Workers." In *Feminization of the Labor Force: Paradoxes and Promises.* Edited by Jane Jenson, Elisabeth Hagen, and Ceallaigh Reddy. New York: Oxford University Press, 1988: 137–152.

ALEXANDER, JEFFREY C. and PIOTR SZTOMPKA, eds. *Rethinking Progress: Movements, Forces, and Ideas at the End of the 20th Century.* Boston: Unwin Hyman, 1990.

AMERICAN CIVIL LIBERTIES UNION. *Background Briefing: The Civil Liberties Issues of Welfare Reform.* New York: Reproductive Freedom Project, 1995.

American Health. "Forgotten Americans: Special Report." November, 1990: 41–42.

AMOTT, TERESA and JULIE MATTHAEI. *Race, Gender, and Work: A Multicultural Economic History of Women in the United States.* Revised Edition. Boston: South End Press, 1996.

ANDERSON, DORIS. *The Unfinished Revolution: The Status of Women in Twelve Countries.* Toronto: Doubleday Canada Limited, 1991.

ANDREWS, LORI. *Between Strangers: Surrogate Mothers, Expectant Fathers, and Brave New Babies.* New York: Harper and Row, 1989.

ANNER, JOHN, ed. *Beyond Identity Politics: Emerging Social Justice Movements in Communities of Color.* Boston: South End Press, 1996.

Annual Report on the Economic Status of the Profession 1999–2000. American Association of University Professors Survey Database, 2000.

ANTROBUS, PEGGY, ADRIENNE GERMAINE, and SIA NOWROJEE. "Challenging the Culture of Silence: Building Alliances to End Reproductive Tract Infections." *WIN News*. Vol. 21, Winter 1995: 27.

APPELBAUM, EILEEN. "Technology and the Redesign of Work in the Insurance Industry." In *Women, Work, and Technology: Transformations*. Edited by Barbara Drygulski Wright. Ann Arbor: University of Michigan Press, 1987: 182–201.

ARDITTI, RITA, RENATE DUELLI KLEIN, and SHELLEY MINDEN, eds. *Test-Tube Women: What Future for Motherhood?* London: Pandora Press, 1984.

ARENDT, HANNAH. *On Violence*. New York: Harcourt, Brace and World, 1969.

ARMBRUSTER, KARLA. "Ecofeminist Natures: Race, Gender, Feminist Theory and Political Action." (Review). *NWSA Journal*. Vol. 12, Spring 2000: 210.

ARNOLD, ERIK. "The Appliance of Science: Technology and Housework." *New Scientist*. Vol. 106, April 18, 1985: 12–15.

ARNOLD, ERIK, LYNDA BIRKE, and WENDY FAULKNER. "Women and Microelectronics: The Case of of Word Processors." In *Women, Technology and Innovation*. Edited by Joan Rothschild. New York: Pergamon, 1982: 321–340.

ARNOLD, FRED, MINJA KIM CHOE, and T. K. ROY. "Son Preference, the Family Building Process and Child Mortality in India." *Population Studies*. Vol. 52, November 1998: 301–315.

ARONOWITZ, STANLEY and WILLIAM DiFAZIO. "High Technology and Work Tomorrow." *Annals of the American Association of Political and Social Sciences*. Vol. 544, March 1996: 52–67.

ASCH, ADRIENNE and MICHELLE FINE. "Shared Dreams: A Left Perspective on Disability Rights and Reproductive Rights." In *Women with Disabilities: Essays in Psychology, Culture, and Politics*. Edited by Michelle Fine and Adrienne Asch. Philadelphia: Temple University Press, 1988: 297–305.

BAKAN, ABIGAIL B. and DAIVA K. STASIULIS. "Making the Match: Domestic Placement Agencies and the Racialization of Women's Household Work." *Signs*. Vol. 20, Winter 1995: 303–335.

BAKER, MAUREEN. "Parental Benefit Policies and the Gendered Division of Labor." *Social Service Review*. Vol. 71, March 1997: 5.

BANDARAGE, ASOKA. "Victims of Development." *The Women's Review of Books*. Vol. 5, October 1987: 1, 3–4.

BARAN, BARBARA. "Technological Transformation of White-Collar Work: A Case Study of the Insurance Industry." In *Computer Chips and Paper Clips*. Vol. 2: *Case Studies and Policy Perspectives*. Edited by Heidi Hartmann. Washington, D.C.: National Academy Press, 1987: 25–62.

BARAN, BARBARA and SUZANNE TEEGARDEN. "Women's Labor in the Office of the Future: A Case Study of the Insurance Industry." In *Women, Households and the Economy*. Edited by Lourdes Benería and Catharine Stimpson. New Brunswick, NJ: Rutgers University Press, 1987: 201–224.

BARON, AVA. "Contested Terrain Revisited: Technology and Gender Definitions of Work in the Printing Industry, 1850–1920." In *Women, Work, and Technology: Transformations*. Edited by Barbara Drygulski Wright. Ann Arbor: University of Michigan Press, 1987: 58–83.

BAXANDALL, ROSALYN, ELIZABETH EWEN, and LINDA GORDON. "The Working Class Has Two Sexes." *Monthly Review*. Vol. 28, 1976: 1–9.

BEGLEY, SHARON. "The Baby Myth." *Newsweek*. September 4, 1995: 38–40, 43–46.

BELKIN, LISA. "Getting the Girl." *The New York Times Magazine*. July 25, 1999: 26–31, 38, 54–55.

BELKIN, LISA. "Pregnant with Complications." *The New York Times Magazine.* October 26, 1997: 34–39, 48–49, 67–68.

BELL, DANIEL. *The Coming of Post-Industrial Society.* New York: Basic Books, 1973.

BELL, SUSAN E. "Translating Science to the People: Updating The New Our Bodies, Ourselves." *Women's Studies International Forum.* Vol. 17, 1994: 9–18.

BELLUCK, PAM. "Cash-for-Sterilization Plan Draws Addicts and Critics." *The New York Times.* July 24, 1999: A8.

BENENSON, HAROLD. "Women's Occupational and Family Achievement in the U.S. Class System." *The British Journal of Sociology.* Vol. 35, March 1984: 19–40.

BENARÍA, LOURDES, ed. *Women and Development: The Sexual Division of Labor in Rural Societies.* New York: Praeger, 1982.

BENSTON, MARGARET LOWE. "For Women, The Chips Are Down." In *The Technological Women.* Edited by Jan Zimmerman. New York: Praeger, 1983: 44–54.

BERGER, LESLIE. "A Racial Gap in Infants Deaths, and a Search for Reasons." *The New York Times.* June 25, 2000: 13.

BERGER, THOMAS R. "Conservation, Technology, and The Idea of Progress." *Canadian Literature.* Vol. 96, Spring 1983: 60–68.

BERK, SARAH FENSTERMAKER. "Women's Unpaid Labor: Home and Community." In *Women Working: Theories and Facts in Perspective.* Edited by Ann Helton Stromberg and Shirley Harkess. Mount View, CA: Mayfield Publishing Co., 1988: 287–302.

BIANCHI, SUZANNE, MELISSA MILKIE, LIANA SAYER, and PAUL ROBINSON. "Is Anyone Doing the Housework? Trends in the Gender Division of Household Labor." *Social Forces.* Vol. 79, September 2000: 191.

BLAIR, BARBARA and SUSAN E. CAYLEFF, eds. *Wings of Gauze: Women of Color and the Experience of Health and Illness.* Detroit: Wayne State University Press, 1993.

BLAIR, SAMPSON and MICHAEL JOHNSON. "Wives' Perceptions of the Fairness of the Household Division of Labor: The Intersection of Housework and Ideology." *Journal of Marriage and the Family.* Vol. 54, August 1992: 570–581.

BLANKENSHIP, KIM, BETH RUSHING, SUZANNE ONORATO, and RENEE WHITE. "Reproductive Technologies and the U.S. Courts." *Gender and Society.* Vol. 7, March 1993: 8–31.

BLAU, FRANCINE D. *Trends in the Well-Being of American Women, 1970–1995.* Cambridge, MA: National Bureau of Economic Research, 1997.

BLEIER, RUTH. *Science and Gender: A Critique of Biology and Its Theories On Women.* New York: Pergamon Press, 1984.

BLOCK, JEFF. "The Computer Chip as Cook." *Forbes.* Vol. 137, March 1986: 158–162.

BLUM, LINDA and VICKI SMITH. "Women's Mobility in the Corporation: A Critique of the Politics of Optimism." *Signs.* Vol. 13, 1988: 528–545.

BODENHEIMER, THOMAS S. "The Transnational Pharmaceutical Industry and the Health of the World's People." In *Issues in the Political Economy.* Edited by John B McKinlay. New York: Tavistock, 1984: 143–186.

BOGRAD, MICHELE. "Strengthening Domestic Violence Theories: Intersections of Race, Class, Sexual Orientation, and Gender." *Journal of Marital and Family Therapy.* Vol. 25, July 1999: 275–289.

BOLLINI, PAOLA and HARALD SIEM. "No Real Progress Toward Equity: Health of Migrants and Ethnic Minorities on the Eve of the Year 2000." *Social Science and Medicine.* Vol. 41, 1995: 819–828.

BOONE, MARGARET S. *Capital Crime: Black Infant Mortality in America.* Newbury Park, CA: Sage Publications, 1989.

BORGMANN, ALBERT. *Technology and the Character of Contemporary Life: A Philosophical Inquiry.* Chicago: University of Chicago Press, 1984.

BORIS, EILEEN. *Home to Work: Motherhood and the Politics of Industrial Homework in the United States.* New York: Cambridge University Press, 1994.

BORIS, EILEEN. "A Woman's Place?" *The Nation.* October 18, 1986: 365–366.

BORIS, EILEEN and ELISABETH PRUGL. "Introduction." In *Homeworkers in Global Perspective: Invisible No More.* Edited by Eileen Boris and Elisabeth Prugl. New York: Routledge, 1996: 3–17.

BOSE, CHRISTINE and PHILIP BEREANO. "Household Technologies: Burden or Blessing?" In *The Technological Woman: Interfacing with Tomorrow.* Edited by Jan Zimmerman. New York: Praeger, 1983: 83–93.

BOSE, CHRISTINE, PHILIP BEREANO, and MARY MALLOY. "Household Technology and the Social Construction of Housework." *Technology and Culture.* Vol. 25, January, 1984: 53–82.

BOSE, CHRISTINE and GLENNA SPITZE. *Ingredients for Women's Employment Policy.* Albany: State University of New York Press, 1987.

BRADSHAW, YORK W. "How Can Sociology Help Us Understand Global Trends?" In *Sociology for a New Century.* Edited by York W. Bradshaw, Joseph F. Healey, and Rebecca Smith. Boston: Pine Forge Press, 2001: 1–31.

BRADSHER, KEITH. "Gap in Wealth In U.S. Called Widest in West." *The New York Times.* April 17, 1995: A1, D4.

BRAUN, ERNEST. "Can Technological Innovation Lead Us to Utopia?" *Futures.* Vol. 26, 1994: 852–861.

BRAVERMAN, HARRY. *Labor and Monopoly Capital: The Degradation of Work in the Twentieth Century.* New York: Monthly Review Press, 1974.

BREWER, ROSE M. "Theorizing Race, Class, and Gender: The New Scholarship of Black Feminist Intellectuals and Black Women's Labor." In *Theorizing Black Feminisms: The Visionary Pragmatism of Black Women.* Edited by Stanlie M. James and Abena P.A. Busia. New York: Routledge, 1993: 13–30.

BRIENZA, JULIE. "Assisted Reproductive Technology Studies by New York Task Force." *Trial.* Vol. 34, July 1998: 109.

BRODY, JANE. *Jane Brody's The New York Times Guide to Personal Health.* New York: Times Book, 1982.

BROWN, LESLEY and JOHN BROWN, with SUE FREEMAN. *Our Miracle Called Louise, A Parents' Story.* London: Paddington Press, 1979.

BROWN, WENDY. "Challenging Bureaucracy." *Women's Review of Books.* Vol. 2, 1984: 16–17.

BUNCH, CHARLOTTE. "Not for Lesbians Only." *Quest.* Vol. 2, Fall 1975: 50–56.

BUNKLE, PHILLIDA. "Calling the Shots: The International Politics of Depo-Provera." In *Test-Tube Women: What Future for Motherhood?* Edited by Rita Arditti, Renate Duelli Klein, and Shelley Minden. London: Pandora Press, 1984: 165–187.

BURNELL, BARBARA S. "Book Reviews: Windows on the Workplace." *Feminist Economics.* Vol. 3, Fall 1997: 110–113.

BURRIS, BEVERLY H. "Computerization of the Workplace." *Annual Review of Sociology.* Vol. 24, 1998: 141–157.

BURRIS, BEVERLY H. *Technocracy at Work.* New York: State University of New York Press, 1993.

BURRIS, BEVERLY H. "Technocracy and Gender in the Workplace." *Social Problems.* Vol. 36, April 1989: 165–180.

BUSH, CORLANN GEE. "Women and the Assessment of Technology: To Think, To Be, To Free." In *Women, Technology and Innovation.* Edited by Joan Rothschild. New York: Pergamon, 1982.

Business Week. "Home Computers: Sales Explode as New Uses Turn PCs into All-Purpose Information Appliances." November 28, 1994c: 89–94.

Business Week. "In the Digital Derby, There's No Inside Lane." Special Bonus Issue 1994: 21st Century Capitalism. November 18, 1994a: 146–154.

Business Week. "The Information Revolution: How Digital Technology Is Changing the Way We Work and Live." Special Bonus Issue 1994: 21st Century Capitalism. November 18, 1994b: 21–47.

Business Week. "The New Face of Business." Special Bonus Issue 1994: 21st Century Capitalism. November 18, 1994c: 98–120.

Business Week. "Laptops Take Off." March 18, 1991: 118–124.

CACOULLOS, ANN R. "American Feminist Theory." *American Studies International.* Vol. 39, February 2001: 72.

CALASANTI, TONI and CAROL BAILEY. "Gender Inequality and the Division of Household Labor in the United States and Sweden: A Socialist-Feminist Approach." *Social Problems.* Vol. 38, February 1991: 34–53.

CALLAHAN, DANIEL. "The Primacy of Caring: Choosing Health-Care Priorities." *Commonweal.* February 23, 1990: 107–112.

CALLAHAN, TAMARA, JANET E. HALL, SUSAN L. ETTNER, CINDY L. CHRISTIANSEN, MICHAEL F. GREENE, and WILLIAM F. CROWLEY. "The Economic Impact of Multiple-Gestation Pregnancies and the Contribution of Assisted-Reproduction Techniques to Their Incidence." *The New England Journal of Medicine.* Vol. 331, July 28, 1994: 244–249.

CARTER, VALERIE. "Office Technology and Relations of Control in Clerical Work Organization." In *Women, Work, and Technology: Transformations.* Edited by Barbara Drygulski Wright. Ann Arbor: University of Michigan Press, 1987: 202–219.

CASSEDY, ELLEN and KAREN NUSSBAUM. *9 to 5: The Working Woman's Guide to Office Survival.* New York: Penguin, 1983.

CHAFETZ, JANET SALTZMAN. *Feminist Sociology: An Overview of Contemporary Theories.* Itasca, IL: F.E. Peacock Publishers, 1988.

CHAFETZ, JANET SALTZMAN and JACQUELINE HAGAN. "The Gender Division of Labor and Family Change in Industrial Societies: A Theoretical Accounting." *Journal of Comparative Family Studies.* Vol. 27, Summer 1996: 187–219.

CHAVKIN, WENDY, ed. *Double Exposure: Women's Health on the Job and at Home.* New York: Monthly Review, 1984.

CHERRY, RONA. "Chronicle of a Scandal." *The New York Times Book Review.* September 22, 1985: 37.

CHESLER, PHYLLIS. *Sacred Bond: The Legacy of Baby M.* New York: Random House, 1988.

CHILDREN'S DEFENSE FUND. *CDF Reports: Births to Teens.* December 1994a: 7–11.

CHILDREN'S DEFENSE FUND. *CDF Reports: Child Poverty Highest in Three Decades.* November, 1994b: 1–12.

CHILDREN'S DEFENSE FUND. *CDF Reports: Priority Agenda for Children.* July 1994c: 6–7.

CHILDREN'S DEFENSE FUND. *CDF Reports: Latino Child Poverty.* October 1993: 10.

CHRISTENSEN, KATHLEEN. "Home-based Clerical Work: No Simple Truth, No Single Reality." In *Homework: Historical and Contemporary Perspectives on Paid Labor in the Home.* Edited by Eileen Boris and Cynthia R. Daniels. Chicago: University of Illinois Press, 1989: 183–187.

CHRISTENSEN, KATHLEEN. *Women and Home-based Work: The Unspoken Contract.* New York: Henry Holt and Company, 1988.

CHRISTIAN, BARBARA. "The Race for Theory." *Cultural Critique.* Vol. 6, Spring 1987: 335–345.

CLANCY, CAROLYN and CHARLEA MASSION. "American Women's Health Care." *Journal of the American Medical Association.* Vol. 268, October 1992: 1918–1920.

CLARK, ADELE. "Subtle Forms of Sterilization Abuse: A Reproductive Rights Analysis." In *Test-Tube Women: What Future for Motherhood?* Edited by Rita Arditti, Renate Duelli Klein, and Shelley Minden. London: Pandora Press, 1984: 188–212.

CLARK, CAROL. "VDT Health Hazards: A Guide for End Users and Managers." *Journal of End User Computing.* Vol. 13, Jan-March 2001: 13.

COCKBURN, CYNTHIA. "Domestic Technologies: Cinderella and the Engineers." *Women's Studies International Forum.* Vol. 20, 1997: 361–371.

COCKBURN, CYNTHIA. *Machinery of Domination: Women, Men and Technical Know-How.* London: Pluto Press, 1985.

COCKBURN, CYNTHIA. *Brothers: Male Dominance and the New Technology.* London: Pluto Press, 1983.

COCKCROFT, JAMES D. "Gendered Class Analysis: Internationalizing, Feminizing, and Latinizing Labor's Class Struggle in the Americas." *Latin American Perspectives.* Vol. 25, November 1998: 42–74.

COLCLOUGH, GLENNA and CHARLES TOLBERT II. *Work in the Fast Lane: Flexibility, Divisions of Labor, and Inequality in High-Tech Industries.* New York: State University of New York Press, 1992.

COLEN, SHELLEE. " 'With Respect and Feelings': Voices of West Indian Child Care and Domestic Workers in New York City." In *All American Women: Lines That Divide, Ties That Bind.* Edited by Johnetta B. Cole. New York: The Free Press, 1986: 46–70.

COLLINS, JOHN. "Reproductive Technology–The Price of Progress." *The New England Journal of Medicine.* Vol. 331, July 28, 1994: 270–271.

COLLINS, PATRICIA HILL. *Black Feminist Thought: Knowledge, Consciousness and the Politics of Empowerment.* Second edition. New York: Routlegde, 2000a.

COLLINS, PATRICIA HILL. "It's All in the Family: Intersections of Gender, Race, and Nation." In *Decentering the Center: Philosophy for a Multicultural, Postcolonial, and Feminist World.* Edited by Uma Narayan and Sandra Harding. Bloomington: Indiana University Press, 2000b: 156–176.

COLLINS, PATRICIA HILL. "Producing the Mothers of the Nation: Race, Class, and Contemporary U.S. Population Policies." In *Women, Citizenship, and Difference.* Edited by Nira Yuval-Davis and Pnina Werbner. London: Zed Books, 1999: 118–129.

COLLINS, PATRICIA HILL. *Black Feminist Thought: Knowledge, Consciousness, and the Politics of Empowerment.* Boston: Unwin Hyman, 1990.

COLLINS, PATRICIA HILL. "Toward a New Vision: Race, Class, and Gender as Categories of Analysis and Connection." Keynote Address: May 24, 1989 at *Integrating Race and Gender into the College Curriculum: A Workshop.* Memphis State University, Memphis, TN, 1989: 1–28.

COLLINS, PATRICIA HILL. "Learning From the Outsider Within: The Sociological Significance of Black Feminist Thought." *Social Problems.* Vol. 33, December 1986: 14–32.

COLTRANE, SCOTT and MASAKO ISHII-KUNTZ. "Men's Housework: A Life Course Perspective." *Journal of Marriage and the Family.* Vol. 54, February 1992: 43–57.

COMBAHEE RIVER COLLECTIVE. "A Black Feminist Statement." In *But Some of Us Are Brave.* Edited by Gloria T. Hull, Patricia Bell Scott, and Barbara Smith. Old Westbury, NY: Feminist Press, 1982.

CONDIT, CELESTE MICHELLE. "Hegemony in a Mass-Mediated Society: Concordance About Reproductive Technologies." *Critical Studies in Mass Communication.*" Vol. 11, 1994: 205–230.

Consumer Reports. "Fertility Clinics: What Are the Odds?" February 1996: 51–54.

COOL, LISA COLLIER. "Forgotten Women: How Minorities Are Underserved by Our Health Care System." *American Health For Women.* May 1997: 37–40.

CORE, FRANCOISE. "The Continuing Saga of Labour Market Segregation." *OECD Observer.* March 1999: 42–43.

COREA, GENA. *The Mother Machine: Reproductive Technologies from Artificial Insemination to Artificial Wombs.* New York: Harper and Row, 1985.

COREA, GENA and SUSAN INCE. "Report of a Survey of IVF Clinics in the U.S." In *Made to Order: The Myth of Reproductive and Genetic Progress.* Edited by Patricia Spallone and Deborah Lynn Steinberg. New York: Pergamon, 1987: 133–145.

CORREA, SONIA. "Norplant in the Nineties: Realities, Dilemmas, Missing Pieces." In *Power and Decision: The Social Control of Reproduction.* Edited by Gita Sen and Rachel C. Snow. Cambridge: Harvard University Press, 1994: 287–309.

COSGROVE, WEST, trans. "Maquiladoras, Foreign Investment and Poverty." *News Notes.* Vol. 21, May/June, Washington, D.C.: Maryknoll Peace and Justice Office, 1996: 9–10.

COWAN, RUTH SCHWARTZ. *Social History of American Technology.* New York: Oxford University Cowley Press, 1997.

COWAN, RUTH SCHWARTZ. "Less Work For Mother?" *Invention and Technology.* Spring 1987: 57–63.

COWAN, RUTH SCHWARTZ. *More Work For Mother: The Ironies of Household Technology from the Open Hearth to the Microwave.* New York: Basic Books, 1983.

COWAN, RUTH SCHWARTZ. "From Virginia Dare to Virginia Slims: Women and Technology in American Life." *Technology and Culture.* Vol. 20, January 1979: 51–63.

COWAN, RUTH SCHWARTZ. "A Case Study of Technology and Social Change: The Washing Machine and the Working Wife." In *Clio's Consciousness Raised.* Edited by Mary Hartman and Lois Banner. New York: Octagon Books, 1976a: 245–252.

COWAN, RUTH SCHWARTZ. "The 'Industrial Revolution' in the Home: Household Technology and Social Change in the 20th Century." *Technology and Culture.* Vol. 17, January 1976b: 1–23.

COWLEY, GEOFFREY. "The Future of Birth." *Newsweek.* September 25, 1995: 42–44.

CRENSHAW, KIMBERLE WILLIAMS. "Demarginalizing the Intersection of Race and Sex: A Black Feminist Critique of Antidiscrimination Doctrine, Feminist Theory, and Antiracist Politics." In *Feminism and Politics.* Edited by Anne Phillips. New York: Oxford University Press, 1998: 314–343.

CRENSHAW, KIMBERLE WILLIAMS. "Beyond Racism and Misogyny: Black Feminism and 2 Live Crew." In *Feminist Social Thought.* Edited by Diana Tiejens Meyers. New York: Routledge, 1997: 246–263.

CRENSHAW, KIMBERLE WILLIAMS. "Mapping the Margins: Intersectionality, Identity Politics, and Violence against Women of Color." In *Critical Race Theory: The Key Writings That Formed the Movement.* Edited by Kimberle Crenshaw, Neil Gotanda, Gary Peller, and Kendall Thomas. New York: The New Press, 1995: 357–383.

CROTEAU, DAVID and WILLIAM HOYNES. *Media Society.* Second edition. Thousand Oaks, CA: Pine Forge Press, 2000.

CROWE, CHRISTINE. "Women Want It: *In Vitro* Fertilization and Women's Motivations for Participation." In *Made to Order: The Myth of Reproductive and Genetic Progress.* Edited by Patricia Spallone and Deborah Lynn Steinberg. New York: Pergamon, 1987: 84–93.

CYERT, RICHARD M. and DAVID C. MOWERY, eds. *Technology and Employment: Innovation and Growth in the U.S. Economy.* Washington, D.C.: National Academy Press, 1987.

DALY, KATHLEEN. "Class-Race-Gender: Sloganeering in Search of Meaning." *Social Justice.* Vol. 20, 1993: 57–72.

DAMARIN, SUZANNE K. "Women and Information Technology: Framing Some Issues for Education." *Feminist Teacher*. Vol. 6, 1992: 16–20.

DANIEL, CAROLINE. "His Colleagues Call Him 'God.'" *New Statesman*. Vol. 127, June 19, 1998: 28–29.

DASILVA, JOSELINA. "Anti-Sterilization Campaign of Brazil." *Newsletter of the Third World Women's Project*. February, 1991: 5.

DAVIES, MARGERY. *Woman's Place Is at the Typewriter: Office Work and Office Workers 1870–1930*. Philadelphia: Temple University Press, 1982.

DAVIS, ANGELA. *Women, Race, and Class*. New York: Random House, 1981.

DELAIR, CATHERINE. "Ethical, Moral, Economic, and Legal Barriers to Assisted Reproductive Technologies Employed by Gay Men and Lesbian Women." *DePaul Journal of Health Care Law*. Vol. 4, Fall 2000: 147.

DELGADO, GARY. "How the Empress Gets Her Clothes: Asian American Immigrant Women Fight Fashion Designer Jessica McClintock." In *Beyond Identity Politics: Emerging Social Justice Movements in Communities of Color*. Edited by John Anner. Boston: South End Press, 1996: 81–94.

DERBER, CHARLES. *The Pursuit of Attention: Power and Individualism in Everyday Life*. New York: Oxford University Press, 1979.

DEVITT, TIFFANY. "Abortion Coverage Leaves Women Out of the Picture." *Extra!* Special Issue, 1992a: 18–19.

DEVITT, TIFFANY. "Silicone Breast Implants: Women's Health Disaster or 'P.R. Nightmare'?" *Extra!* Special Issue, 1992b: 25–26.

DIAMOND, SARA. "Taylor's Way: Women, Cultures, and Technology." In *Processed Lives: Gender and Technology in Everyday Life*. Edited by Jennifer Terry and Melodie Calvert, New York: Routledge, 1997: 82–92.

DICHRISTINA, MARIETTE. "Home Newsfront." *Popular Science*. May 1992: 48–50.

DICKSON, DAVID. *The Politics of Alternative Technology*. New York: Universe Books, 1974.

DIDIO, LAURA. "Look Out for Techno-hazing." *Computerworld*. Vol. 31, September 1997: 72–73.

DILL, BONNIE THORNTON. "Race, Class, and Gender: Prospects for an All-Inclusive Sisterhood." *Feminist Studies*. Spring 1983: 131–150.

DILL, BONNIE THORNTON. "'The Means to Put My Children Through': Child-Rearing Goals and Strategies among Black Female Domestic Servants." in *The Black Woman*. Edited by La Frances Rodger-Rose. Beverly Hills: Sage Publications, 1980: 107–124.

DOBASH, R. EMERSON and RUSSELL DOBASH. *Violence Against Wives: A Case against Patriarchy*. New York: The Free Press, 1979.

Dobie, Kathy. "Black Women, White Kids: A Tale of Two Worlds." *The Village Voice*. January 12, 1988: 20–27.

DOBLE, JOHN and AMY RICHARDSON. "You Don't Have to Be a Rocket Scientist . . ." *Technology Review*. January 1992: 51–54.

DODOO, F. NII-AMOO and PATRICIA KASARI. "Race and Occupational Location in America." *Journal of Black Studies*. Vol. 25, March 1995: 465–474.

DONCHIN, ANNE. "Feminist Critiques of New Fertility Technologies: Implications for Social Policy." *The Journal of Medicine and Philosophy*. Vol. 21, 1996: 475–498.

DORTCH, SHANNON. "Maids Clean Up." *American Demographics*. Vol. 18, November 1996: 4.

DOUGLAS, SUSAN J. "Missing Voices: Women and the U.S. News Media." *Extra!* Special Issue, 1992: 4–5.

DOWLING, CLAUDIA GLENN. "Miraculous Babies." *Life*. December 1993: 75–84.

DURBIN, PAUL T. "Technology and Values: A Philosopher's Perspective." *Technology and Culture*. Vol. 134, 1972: 556–576.

DURRANT, JOAN E. and GREGG M. OLSEN. "Parenting and Public Policy: Contextualizing the Swedish Corporal Punishment Ban." *Journal of Social Welfare and Family Law*. Vol. 19, 1997: 443–461.

EAGAN, ANDREA B. "The Women's Health Movement and Its Lasting Impact." In *An Unfinished Revolution: Women and Health Care in America*. Edited by Emily Friedman. New York: United Hospital Fund of New York, 1994: 15–27.

The Ecologist. "Fertility for Sale." Vol. 25, No. 4, July/August, 1995: 137–138.

EHRENREICH, BARBARA, MARK DOWIE, and STEPHEN MINKIN. "The Charge: Genocide, The Accused: The U.S. Government." *Mother Jones*. November 1979: 26–37.

EHRENREICH, BARBARA and FRANCES FOX PIVEN. "The Feminization of Poverty: When the Family-Wage System Breaks Down." *Dissent*. Spring 1984: 162–170.

ELLUL, JACQUES. *The Technological Society*. New York: Knopf, 1964.

ELMER-DEWITT, PHILIP. "How Mac Changed the World." *Time*. January 31, 1994: 93–94.

ELMER-DEWITT, PHILIP. "Making Babies." *Time*. September 30, 1991: 56–63.

ELMER-DEWITT, PHILIP. "A Revolution in Making Babies." *Time*. November 5, 1990: 76–77.

ELSON, DIANE and RUTH PEARSON. "Nimble Fingers Make Cheap Workers: An Analysis of Women's Employment in Third World Manufacturing." *Feminist Review*. Vol. 7, 1981: 87–107.

ENGLAND, PAULA and IRENE BROWNE. "Trends in Women's Economic Status." *Sociological Perspectives*. Vol. 35, 1992: 17–51.

ENGLISH, CAREY W. "Is Your Friendly Computer Rating You on the Job?" *U.S. News and World Report*. February 18, 1986: 66.

EVANS, FRANCES. "Managers and Labourers: Women's Attitudes Toward Reproductive Technology." In *Smothered by Invention*. Edited by Wendy Faulkner and Erik Arnold. London: Pluto Press, 1985: 109–127.

EWEN, STUART. *Captains of Consciousness: Advertising and the Social Roots of the Consumer Culture*. New York: McGraw-Hill Book Company, 1976.

Extra! "Backing the Backlash: How the Press Promotes Myths About Women. Interview with Susan Faludi." Special Issue, 1992: 6–7.

EZRAHI, YARON, EVERETT MENDELSOHN, HOWARD SEGAL, eds. *Technology, Pessimism, and Postmodernism*. Dordrecht, The Netherlands: Kluwer Academic Publishers, 1994.

FACKELMANN, KATHLEEN. "Brave New Biology: Granny Gives Birth." *Science News*. Vol. 143, February 13, 1993:100.

FACKELMANN, KATHLEEN. "It's a Girl!" *Science News*. Vol. 154, November 28, 1998: 350–351.

FARAH, SAMAR. "Women Professors Still Face Hurdles." *Christian Science Monitor*. February 6, 2001: 12.

FARQUHAR, DION. *The Other Machine: Discourse and Reproductive Technologies*. New York: Routledge, 1996.

FAULKNER, WENDY and ERIK ARNOLD, eds. *Smothered by Invention: Technology in Women's Lives*. London: Pluto Press, 1985.

FAUST, SUSAN M. "Baby Girl or Baby Boy? Now You Can Choose: A Look at New Biology and No Law." *Albany Law Journal of Science and Technology*. Vol. 10, 2000: 281.

FEE, ELIZABETH. "Is Feminism a Threat to Scientific Objectivity?" *International Journal of Women's Studies*. Vol. 4, September-October 1981: 378–392.

FEINBERG, RICHARD A. " 'Man May Work From Sun to Sun But Woman's Work Is Never Done': A Short Note on Why the Issue of Household Work Is Important Socially,

Economically, and Politically." *Family and Consumer Sciences Research Journal*. Vol. 24, June 1996: 355.

FELDBERG, ROSLYN. "'Union Fever': Organizing among Clerical Workers 1900–1930." *Radical America*. Vol. 14, 1980: 53–67.

FELDBERG, ROSLYN L. and EVELYN NAKANO GLENN. "Technology and Work Degradation: Effects of Office Automation on Women Clerical Workers." In *Machina Ex Dea: Feminist Perspectives on Technology*. Edited by Joan Rothschild. New York: Pergamon, 1983: 59–78.

FELLOWS, ROGER, ed. *Philosophy and Technology*. New York: Cambridge University Press, 1995.

FEMINIST MAJORITY FOUNDATION. *Empowering Women in Business*. Arlington, VA: Feminist Majority Foundation, 1991.

FERGUSON, EUGENE. "The American-ness of American Technology." *Technology and Culture*. Vol. 20, 1979: 3–24.

FERNÁNDEZ-KELLY, MARÍA PATRICIA. "Broadening the Scope: Gender and International Economic Development." *Sociological Forum*. Vol. 4, 1989: 611–635.

FERNÁNDEZ-KELLY, MARÍA PATRICIA. *For We Are Sold, I and My People*. Albany: State University of New York Press, 1984.

FERNÁNDEZ-KELLY, MARÍA PATRICIA. "Gender and Industry on Mexico's New Frontier." In *The Technological Woman*. Edited by Jan Zimmerman. New York: Praeger, 1983: 18–29.

FERNÁNDEZ-KELLY, MARIA PATRICIA and KATHLEEN M. FALLON. "How Is Globalization Affecting Inequalities Between Women and Men?" In *Sociology for a New Century*. Edited by York W. Bradshaw, Joseph F. Healey, and Rebecca Smith. Boston: Pine Forge Press, 2001: 239–260.

FERNÁNDEZ-KELLY, MARÍA PATRICIA and ANNA M. GARCIA. "Invisible Amidst the Glitter: Hispanic Women in the Southern California Electronics Industry." In *The Worth of Women's Work: A Qualitative Synthesis*. Edited by Anne Statham, Eleanor M. Miller, and Hans O. Mauksch. Albany: State University of New York Press, 1988: 265–290.

FERREE, MYRA MARX. "Beyond Separate Spheres: Feminism and Family Research." *Journal of Marriage and the Family*. Vol. 52, November 1990: 866–884.

FERREE, MYRA MARX and PATRICIA YANCEY MARTIN, eds. *Feminist Organizations: Harvest of the New Women's Movement*. Philadelphia: Temple University Press, 1995.

FIELD, MARTHA A. *Surrogate Motherhood*. Cambridge, MA: Harvard University Press, 1988.

FINE, MICHELLE and ADRIENNE ASCH. "Who Owns the Womb?" *The Women's Review of Books*. Vol. 2, May 1985: 8–10.

FINEMAN, MARTHA A. and MARTHA T. MCCLUSKEY. *Feminism, Media, and the Law*. New York: Oxford University Press, 1997.

FINGER, ANNE. "Claiming All of Our Bodies: Reproductive Rights and Disabilities." In *Test-Tube Women: What Future for Motherhood?* Edited by Rita Arditti, Renate Duelli Klein, and Shelley Minden. London: Pandora Press, 1984: 281–297.

FISHMAN, RACHELLE. "Infertility Doctors Use Egg Donors Worldwide." *The Lancet*. Vol. 353, February 27, 1999: 736.

FLANDERS, LAURA. *Real Majority, Media Minority: The Cost of Sidelining Women in Reporting*. Monroe, ME: Common Courage Press, 1997.

FLEMING, ANNE TAYLOR. "Our Fascination With Baby M." *The New York Times Magazine*. March 24, 1987: 33–38, 87.

FLYNN, MARY KATHLEEN. "Computers: The Newest Appliance." *U.S. News and World Report*. November 29, 1993: 90–94.

FOLKERS, RICHARD. "Xanadu 2.0: Bill Gates's Stately Pleasure Dome and Futuristic Home." *U.S. News and World Report*. December 1, 1997: 87.

FORESTER, TOM, ed. *Microelectronics Revolution: The Complete Guide to the New Technology and Its Impact on Society*. Cambridge: Massachusetts Institute of Technology, 1981.

Fortune. "Saving Time With New Technology." December 30, 1991: 98–104.

FOX, BONNIE J. "Selling the Mechanized Household: 70 Years of Ads in *Ladies Home Journal*." *Gender and Society*. Vol. 4, March 1990: 25–40.

FOX, STEVE. *Toxic Work: Women Workers at GTE Lenkur*. Philadelphia: Temple University Press, 1991.

FRANKLIN, SARAH and MAUREEN MCNEIL. "Reproductive Futures: Recent Literature and Current Feminist Debates on Reproductive Technologies: Review Essay. "*Feminist Studies*. Vol. 14, Fall 1988: 545–560.

FRENKIEL, NORA. "'Family Planning': Baby Boy or Girl?" *The New York Times*. November 11, 1993: C1, C6.

FRIEDRICH, OTTO. "The Computer Moves In." *Time*. January 3, 1983: 14–24.

FRIEDRICHS, GUENTER and ADAM SCHAFF, eds. *Microelectronics and Society: A Report to the Club of Rome*. New York: New American Library, 1982.

FRÖBEL, VOLKER, JURGEN HEINRICHS, and OTTO KREYE. *The New International Division of Labor: Structural Unemployment in Industrializing Countries and Industrialization in Developing Countries*. New York: Cambridge University, 1980.

FUENTES, ANNETTE and BARBARA EHRENREICH. *Women in the Global Factory*. New York: South End, 1983.

FULLERTON, HOWARD N. "Labor Force Participation: 75 Years of Change, 1950–98 and 1998–2025." *Monthly Labor Review*. Vol. 122, December 1999: 3.

The Futurist. "Voice-Controlled Ovens and Cameras: Appliances Will Hear and Obey." July-August, 1990: 50.

GABRIEL, TRIP. "High-Tech Pregnancies Test Hope's Limit." *The New York Times*. January 7, 1996: 1, 18–19.

GARLAND, ANNE WITTE. *Women Activists: Challenging the Abuse of Power*. New York: The Feminist Press, 1988.

GARSON, BARBARA. "Manager Inside the Machine: Electronic Monitoring Is the Scourge of Today's Knowledge Workers, Who Still Consider Themselves White-Collar." *Information Week*. July 18, 1994: 36.

GILKEY, LANGDON. "The Religious Dilemmas of a Scientific Culture: The Interface of Technology, History and Religion." In *Being Human in a Technological Age*. Edited by Donald Borchert and David Stewart. Athens, OH: Ohio University Press, 1979: 73–88.

GISCOMBE, KATHERINE and ADRIENNE D. SIMS. "Breaking the Color Barrier." *HR Focus*. Vol. 75, July 1998: S9–S11.

GITLIN, TODD. *The Whole World Is Watching*. Berkeley: University of California Press, 1980.

GIULIANO, VINCENT. "The Mechanization of Office Work." *Scientific American*. Vol. 247, 1982: 148–164.

GLATER, JONATHAN. "Women Are Close to Being Majority of Law Students." *The New York Times*. March 26, 2001: A1, A16.

GLEICK, JAMES. "Reproductive Help: Widespread and Unregulated." *The New York Times*. March 11, 1987: A16.

GLENN, EVELYN NAKANO. "From Servitude to Service Work: Historical Continuities in the Racial Division of Paid Reproductive Labor." *Signs*. Vol. 18, Autumn 1992: 1–37.

GLENN, EVELYN NAKANO. *Issei, Nisei, War Bride: Three Generations of Japanese-American Women in Domestic Service*. Philadelphia: Temple University Press, 1986.

GLENN, EVELYN NAKANO. "Racial Ethnic Women's Labor: The Intersection of Race, Gender, and Class Oppression." *Review of Radical Political Economics.* Vol. 17, 1985: 86–108.

GLENN, EVELYN NAKANO and ROSLYN FELDBERG. "Degraded and Deskilled: The Proletarianization of Clerical Work." *Social Problems.* Vol. 25, 1977: 52–64.

GLENN, EVELYN NAKANO and CHARLES M. TOLBERT II. "Technology and Emerging Patterns of Stratification for Women of Color: Race and Gender Segregation in Computer Operations." In *Women, Work, and Technology: Transformations.* Edited by Barbara Drygulski Wright. Ann Arbor: University of Michigan Press, 1987: 318–331.

GOLDBERG, GERTRUDE and ELEANOR KREMEN. "The Feminization of Poverty: Only in America?" *Social Policy.* Vol. 17, Spring 1987: 3–14.

GOLDBERG, ROBERTA. *Organizing Women Office Workers: Dissatisfaction, Consciousness, and Action.* New York: Praeger, 1983.

GOLDEN, FREDERIC. "Patrick Steptoe and Robert Edwards: Brave New Baby Doctors." *Time.* March 29, 1999: 178–179.

GOLDEN, FREDERIC. "Boy? Girl? Up to You." *Time.* September 21, 1998: 82–83.

GOLDMAN, STEVEN L., ed. *Science, Technology, and Social Progress.* Bethlehem: Lehigh University Press, 1989.

GOODKIND, DANIEL. "Should Prenatal Sex Selection Be Restricted? Ethical Questions and Their Implications for Research and Policy." *Population Studies.* Vol. 53, March 1999: 49–61.

GOODMAN, PAUL. "The Morality of Scientific Technology." *Dissent.* January–February, 1967: 41–53.

GOODRIDGE, ELISABETH. "Untapped Pool of Talent." *Information Week.* April 2000: 17.

GORDON, LINDA. "Women's Freedom, Women's Power: Notes for Reproductive Rights Activists." *Radical America.* Vol. 19, November/December, 1985: 31–37.

GORDON, LINDA. "The Struggle for Reproductive Freedom: Three Stages of Feminism." In *Capitalist Patriarchy and the Case for Socialist Feminism.* Edited by Zillah R. Eisenstein. New York: Monthly Review Press, 1979: 107–132.

GORDON, LINDA. *Woman's Body, Woman's Right: A Social History of Birth Control in America.* New York: Penguin Books, 1974.

GORDON-BRADSHAW, RUTH H. "A Social Essay on Special Issues Facing Poor Women of Color." *Women and Health.* Vol. 12, 1988: 243–259.

GORMAN, CHRISTINE. "How Old Is Too Old?" *Time.* September 30, 1991: 62.

GOTTESFELD, MIRIAM B. "The Worker's Paradise Lost: The Role and Status of Russian and American Women in the Workplace." *Comparative Labor Law Journal.* Vol. 14, Fall 1992: 68–95.

GOTTFRIED, HEIDI, ed. *Feminism and Social Change: Bridging Theory and Practice.* Urbana: University of Illinois Press, 1996.

GRADY, DENISE. "How to Coax Life." *Time.* Fall 1996: 36–39.

GRAHAM, HILARY. "The Concept of Caring in Feminist Research: The Case of Domestic Service." *Sociology.* Vol. 25, February 1991: 61–78.

GRANT, NICOLE J. *The Selling of Contraception: The Dalkon Shield Case, Sexuality, and Women's Autonomy.* Columbus, OH: Ohio State University Press, 1992.

GREENBAUM, JOAN. *Windows on the Workplace: Computers, Jobs, and the Organization of Office Work in the Late Twentieth Century.* New York: Monthly Review Press, 1995.

GREENHOUSE, LINDA. "High Court Bars Some Drug Tests." *The New York Times.* March 22, 2001: A1, A22.

GREENHOUSE, STEVEN. "Report Outlines the Abuse of Foreign Domestic Workers." *The New York Times.* June 14, 2001: A20.

GREENSTEIN, THEODORE N. "Gender Ideology and Perceptions of the Fairness of the Division of Household Labor: Effects on Marital Quality." *Social Forces.* Vol. 74, March 1996: 1029.

GREENWALT, JULIE. "Thankful for Five Tiny Blessings." *People.* February 15, 1988: 92 ff.

GREGORY, JUDITH. "The Next Move: Organizing Women in the Office." In *The Technological Woman: Interfacing with Tomorrow.* Edited by Jan Zimmerman. New York: Praeger, 1983: 260–272.

GRINT, KEITH and ROSALIND GILL, eds. *The Gender-Technology Relation: Contemporary Theory and Research.* London: Taylor and Francis, 1995.

GROSSMAN, RACHAEL. "Woman's Place in the Integrated Circuit." *Southeast Asia Chronicle.* Vol. 66, 1979: 2–18.

GRUNWALD, JOSEPH and KENNETH FLAMM. *The Global Factory: Foreign Assembly in International Trade.* Washington, D.C.: The Brookings Institute, 1985.

GUENDELMAN, SYLVIA, STEVEN SAMUELS, and MARTHA RAMIREZ. "Women Who Quit Maquiladora Work on the U.S.-Mexico Border: Assessing Health, Occupation, and Social Dimensions in Two Transnational Electronics Plants." *American Journal Of Industrial Medicine.* Vol. 33, 1998: 501–509.

GUINAN, MARY E. "Artificial Insemination by Donor: Safety and Secrecy." *The Journal of the American Medical Association.* Vol. 273, March 15, 1995: 890–891.

GUPTA, SANJIV. "The Effects of Transitions in Marital Status on Men's Performance of Housework." *Journal of Marriage and the Family.* Vol. 61, 1999: 700–711.

GUTEK, BARBARA. "Women's Work in the Office of the Future." In *The Technological Woman: Interfacing with Tomorrow.* Edited by Jan Zimmerman. New York: Praeger, 1983: 159–168.

GUY, MARY E. "Three Steps Forward, Two Steps Backward: The Status of Women and Integration into Public Management." *Public Administration Review.* Vol. 53, July/August, 1993: 285–292.

GWYNN, PETER. "The First Test-Tube Baby." *Newsweek.* July 24, 1978: 76.

HACKER, SALLY. "The Culture of Engineering: Women, Workplace and Machine." In *Women, Technology and Innovation.* Edited by Joan Rothschild. New York: Pergamon Press, 1982: 341–353.

HACKER, SALLY. "Sex Stratification, Technology, and Organizational Change: A Longitudinal Case Study of AT&T." *Social Problems.* Vol. 26, 1979: 539–557.

HADDAD, CAROL J. "Technology, Industrialization, and the Economic Status of Women." In *Women, Work, and Technology: Transformations.* Edited by Barbara Drygulski Wright. Ann Arbor: University of Michigan Press, 1987: 33–57.

HANDLIN, OSCAR. "Science and Technology in Popular Culture." *Daedalus.* Vol. 94, Winter 1965: 156–170.

HARAWAY, DONNA. "A Cyborg Manifesto: Science, Technology, and Socialist-Feminism in the Late Twentieth Century." *Simians, Cyborgs and Women: The Reinvention of Nature.* New York: Routledge, 1990.

HARKESS, SHIRLEY. "Directions for the Future." In *Women Working: Theories and Facts in Perspective.* Edited by Ann Stromberg and Shirley Harkess. Mountain View, CA: Mayfield Publishing Company, Second edition. 1988: 348–360.

HARRINGTON, MICHAEL. *The Vast Majority: A Journey to the World's Poor.* New York: Simon and Schuster, 1977.

HARRIS, BEN. Unpublished. "I Have Seen the Future and It Is Down at the Moment."

HARRIS, LOUIS. "The LIFE Poll." *Life Magazine.* June 13, 1969: 52–55.

HARTMANN, BETSY. *Reproductive Rights and Wrongs: The Global Politics of Population Control.* Boston: South End Press, 1995.

HARTMANN, HEIDI. "The Family as the Locus of Gender, Class, and Political Struggle: The Example of Housework." *Signs.* Vol. 6, Spring 1981: 366–394.

HARTMANN, HEIDI. "Capitalism, Patriarchy, and Job Segregation by Sex." In *Capitalist Patriarchy and the Case for Socialist Feminism.* Edited by Zillah R. Eisenstein. New York: Monthly Review Press, 1979: 206–247.

HAZOU, WINNIE. *The Social and Legal Status of Women.* New York: Praeger, 1990.

HENDERSON, HAZEL. "Philosophical Conflict: Reexamining the Goals of Knowledge." *Public Administration Review.* January/February, 1975: 77–80.

HENIFIN, MARY S. "New Reproductive Technologies: Equity and Access to Reproductive Health Care." *Journal of Social Issues.* Vol. 49, 1993: 61–74.

HEPWORTH, MARK and KEVIN ROBINS. "Whose Information Society? A View From the Periphery." *Media, Culture, and Society.* Vol. 10, 1988: 323–343.

HESSE-BIBER, SHARLENE. "The Black Woman Worker: A Minority Group Perspective on Women at Work." *Sage.* Vol. 3, Spring 1986: 26–34.

HILTS, PHILIP. "Life Expectancy for Blacks in U.S. Shows Sharp Drop." *The New York Times.* November 29, 1990: A1, B17.

HIRSCHHORN, LARRY. *Beyond Mechanization: Work and Technology in a Post-Industrial Age.* Cambridge: Massachusetts Institute of Technology Press, 1984.

HOCHSCHILD, ARLIE with ANNE MACHUNG. *The Second Shift: Working Parents and the Revolution at Home.* New York: Viking, 1989.

HOLDEN, CONSTANCE. "Japanese Views on Science Compared to U.S. Attitudes." *Science.* Vol. 240, April 1988: 277–278.

HOLMES, HELEN B., BETTY B. HOSKINS, and MICHAEL GROSS, eds. *The Custom-Made Child?: Women-Centered Perspectives.* Clifton, NJ: Humana Press, 1981.

HOLMES, HELEN B., BETTY B. HOSKINS, and MICHAEL GROSS, eds. *Birth Control and Controlling Birth: Women-Centered Perspectives.* Clifton, NJ: Humana Press, 1980.

HONDAGNEU-SOTELO, PIERRETTE. "Regulating the Unregulated?: Domestic Workers' Social Networks." *Social Problems.* Vol. 41, February 1994: 50–64.

HONDAGNEU-SOTELO, PIERRETTE and ERNESTINE AUILA. " 'I'm Here, But I'm There': The Meanings of Latina Transnational Motherhood." In *Gender Through The Prism of Difference.* Edited by Maxine Baca Zinn, Pierrette Hondagneu-Sotelo, and Michael A. Messner. Boston: Allyn and Bacon, 2000: 279–294.

HOOKS, BELL. *Ain't I a Woman?* Boston: South End Press, 1981.

HOPKINS, PATRICK D., ed. *Sex/Machine: Readings in Culture, Gender, and Technology.* Bloomington: Indiana University Press, 1998.

HORNSTEIN, FRANCIE. "Children by Donor Insemination: A New Choice For Lesbians." In *Test-Tube Women : What Future for Motherhood?* Edited by Rita Arditti, Renate Duelli Klein, and Shelley Minden. London: Pandora Press, 1984: 373–381.

HOROWITZ, TONY. "Mr. Edens Profits from Watching His Workers' Every Move." In *Computerization and Controversy: Value Conflicts and Social Choices.* Edited by Rob Kling. New York: Academic Press, 1996: 322–325.

HOSKINS, BETTY B. and HELEN B. HOLMES. "Technology and Prenatal Femicide." In *Test-Tube Women: What Future for Motherhood?* Edited by Rita Arditti, Renate Duelli Klein, and Shelley Minden. London: Pandora Press, 1984: 237–255.

HOSSFELD, KAREN J. "Hiring Immigrant Women: Silicon Valley's 'Simple Formula.'" In *Women of Color in U.S. Society.* Edited by Maxine Baca Zinn and Bonnie Thornton Dill, Philadelphia: Temple University Press, 1994: 65–93.

HUBBARD, RUTH. "Personal Courage Is Not Enough: Some Hazards of Childbearing in the 1980's." In *Test-Tube Women: What Future for Motherhood?* Edited by Rita Arditti, Renate Duelli Klein, and Shelley Minden. London: Pandora Press, 1984: 331–355.

HUBBARD, RUTH. "The Case Against IVF." In *The Custom-Made Child?: Women-Centered Perspectives.* Edited by Helen B. Holmes, Betty B. Hoskins, and Michael Gross. Clifton, NJ: Humana Press, 1981: 259–262.

HUGHES, THOMAS PARKE, ed. *Changing Attitudes Toward American Technology.* New York: Harper and Row, 1975.

HUWS, URSULA. *Your Job in the Eighties: A Woman's Guide to New Technology.* London: Pluto Press, 1982.

IACONO, SUZANNE and ROB KLING. "Computerization, Office Routines, and Changes in Clerical Work." in *Computerization and Controversy: Value Conflicts and Social Choices.* Edited by Rob Kling. New York: Academic Press, 1996: 309–315.

IDE, THOMAS R. and ARTHUR J. CORDELL. "Automating Work." *Society.* Vol. 31, September/ October 1994: 65–72.

IKEMOTO, LISA C. "Furthering the Inquiry: Race, Class, and Culture in the Forced Medical Treatment of Pregnant Women." In *Critical Race Feminism: A Reader.* Edited by Adrien Katherine Wing. New York: New York University Press, 1997: 136–143.

"INFANTREPENEURS." *Commonweal.* Vol. 112, April 19, 1985: 228–229.

INSTITUTE FOR WOMEN'S POLICY RESEARCH. "Impact of the Glass Ceiling and Structural Change on Minorities and Women." December 1993.

INTERNATIONAL WORKING GROUP ON PREIMPLANTATION GENETICS. "Preimplantation Diagnosis: An Alternative to Prenatal Diagnosis of Genetic and Chromosomal Disorders." *Journal of Assisted Reproductive Genetics.* Vol. 16, 1999: 161–164.

IRVIN, HELEN DEISS. "The Machine in Utopia: Shaker Women and Technology." In *Women, Technology, and Innovation.* Edited by Joan Rothschild. New York: Pergamon Press, 1982: 313–319.

JACKSON, MONICA. "And Still We Rise: African-American Women and the U.S. Labor Market." *Feminist Issues.* Vol. 10, Fall 1990: 55–64.

JACOBSON, JODI. *Women's Reproductive Health: The Silent Emergency.* Worldwatch Paper 102, Worldwatch Institute: 1991.

JAMES, STANLIE M. "Mothering: A Possible Black Feminist Link to Social Transformation?" In *Theorizing Black Feminisms: The Visionary Pragmatism of Black Women.* Edited by Stanlie M. James and Abena P. A. Busia. New York: Routledge, 1993: 44–54.

"JANE." "Just Call Jane." *The Fight for Reproductive Freedom: A Newsletter from Student Activists.* Vol. 4, Winter 1990: 1–4.

JANSEN, SUE CURRY. "Gender and the Information Society: A Socially Structured Silence." *Journal of Communication.* Vol. 39, Summer 1989: 196–215.

Jet. "Why Exercise Should Be Important to Women." March 13, 2000: 46.

JONAS, HANS. "Reflections on Technology, Progress, and Utopia." *Social Research.* Vol. 48, Autumn 1981: 411–455.

Journal of the American Medical Association (JAMA). "Primary and Secondary Syphilis–United States, 1998." Vol. 282, November 10, 1999: 1715.

JURIK, NANCY K. "Getting Away and Getting By: The Experiences of Self-Employed Homeworkers." *Work and Occupations.* Vol. 25, 1998: 7–35.

KAMAL, SULTANA. "Seizure of Reproductive Rights? A Discussion on Population Control in the Third World and the Emergence of the New Reproductive Ties in the West." In *Made to Order: The Myth of Reproductive and Genetic Progress.* Edited by Patricia Spallone and Deborah Lynn Steinberg. New York: Pergamon, 1987: 146–153.

KANE, ELIZABETH. *Birth Mother: The Story of America's First Legal Surrogate Mother.* New York: Harcourt, Brace, Jovanovich, 1988.

KANTROWITZ, BARBARA. "The Butlers of the Digital Age Will Be Just a Keystroke Away." *Newsweek.* January 17, 1994: 58.

KANTROWITZ, BARBARA and PAT WINGERT. "The Norplant Debate." *Newsweek.* February 15, 1993: 37–42.

KEIGHER, SHARON M. "Reflecting on Progress, Health, and Racism: 1900 to 2000." *Health and Social Work.* Vol. 24, November 1999: 243.

KHALIL, E.M. OMAR and Jessie E. Melcher. "Office Automation's Threat to Health and Productivity: A New Management Concern." In *Computerization and Controversy: Value Conflicts and Social Choices.* Edited by Rob Kling. New York: Academic Press, 1996: 830–837.

KING, DEBORAH K. "Multiple Jeopardy, Multiple Consciousness: The Context of a Black Feminist Ideology." In *Feminist Social Thought.* Edited by Diana Tiejens Meyers. New York: Routledge, 1997: 220–242.

KLAPHOLZ, HENRY. "The Electronic Fetal Monitor in Perinatology." In *Birth Control and Controlling Birth.* Edited by Helen B. Holmes, Betty B. Hoskins and Michael Gross. Clifton, NJ: The Humana Press, Inc., 1980: 167–173.

KLEIMAN, DENA. "Anguished Search to Cure Infertility." *The New York Times Magazine.* December 16, 1979: 38 ff.

KLEINBERG, SUSAN. "Technology and Women's Work: The Lives of Working Class Women in Pittsburgh, 1870–1900." In *Dynamos and Virgins Revisited: Women and Technological Change in History.* Edited by Martha Moore Trescott. Metuchen, NJ: Scarecrow Press, 1979: 185–204.

KLING, ROB. "Computerization at Work." In *Computerization and Controversy: Value Conflicts and Social Choices.* Edited by Rob Kling. New York: Academic Press, 1996a: 278–308.

KLING, ROB. "The Seductive Equation of Technological Progress and Social Progress." In *Computerization and Controversy: Value Conflicts and Social Choices.* Edited by Rob Kling. New York: Academic Press, 1996b: 22–25.

KLING, ROB and SUZANNE IACONO. "The Mobilization of Support for Computerization: The Role of Computerization Movements." *Social Problems.* Vol. 35, June 1988: 226–243.

KOLATA, GINA. "Childbirth at 63 Says What About Life?" *The New York Times.* April 27, 1997a.

KOLATA, GINA. "Successful Births Reported with Frozen Human Eggs." *The New York Times.* October 17, 1997b: A1, A26.

KOLATA, GINA. "Clinics Selling Embryos Made For 'Adoption.'" *The New York Times.* November 23, 1997c: 1, 34.

KOLATA, GINA. "Amid Fears About a Fetal Test, Many Are Advising Against It." *The New York Times.* July 15, 1992: C13.

KRAMARAE, CHERIS, ed. *Technology and Women's Voices: Keeping in Touch.* New York: Routledge and Kegan Paul, 1988.

KRAUSS, DEBORAH. "Regulating Women's Bodies: The Adverse Effect of Fetal Rights Theory on Childbirth Decisions and Women of Color." *Harvard Civil Rights-Civil Liberties Law Review.* Vol. 26, Summer 1991: 523–548.

KRAUT, ROBERT E., ed. *Technology and the Transformation of White-Collar Work.* Hillsdale, NJ: Lawrence Erlbaum, 1986.

KUNISCH, JUDITH R. "Electronic Fetal Monitors: Marketability Forces and the Resulting Controversy." In *Healing Technology: Feminist Perspectives.* Edited by Kathryn Strother Ratcliff. Ann Arbor: University of Michigan Press, 1989: 41–60.

KYNASTON, CHRIS. "The Everyday Exploitation of Women: Housework and the Patriarchal Mode of Production." *Women's Studies International Forum.* Vol. 19, May/June, 1996: 221.

LAMPHERE, LOUISE, PATRICIA ZAVELLA, FELIPE GONZALES, with PETER B. EVANS. *Sunbelt Working Mothers: Reconciling Family and Factory.* Ithaca: Cornell University Press, 1993.

LARDNER, JAMES. "Please Don't Squeeze the Tomatoes Online: Supermarkets of the Future Have No Aisles." *U.S. News and World Report.* November 9, 1998: 51–52.

LASKER, JUDITH and SUSAN BORG. *In Search of Parenthood: Coping with Infertility and High-Tech Conception.* Boston: Beacon Press, 1987.

LAWSON, CAROL. "Celebrated Birth Aside, Teen-Ager Is Typical Now." *The New York Times.* October 4, 1993: 5.

LAWSON, CAROL. "New Birth Surrogates Carry Couples' Babies." *The New York Times.* August 12, 1990: 1, 24.

LEE, MARTIN A. and NORMAN SOLOMON. *Unreliable Sources: A Guide to Detecting Bias in News Media.* New York: Carol Publishing Group, 1990.

LEE, ROBERT S. "Social Attitudes and the Computer Revolution." *Public Opinion Quarterly.* Vol. 34, Spring 1970: 53–59.

LENT, MARGARET. "The Medical and Legal Risks of the Electronic Fetal Monitor." *Stanford Law Review.* Vol. 51, April 1999: 807–837.

LEO, JOHN. "Baby Boys, To Order." *U.S. News and World Report.* January 9, 1989: 59.

LERMAN, NINA E., ARWEN PALMER MOHUN, and RUTH OLDENZIEL. "The Shoulders We Stand On and the View From Here: Historiography and Directions for Research." *Technology and Culture.* Special Issue: Gender Analysis and the History of Technology. Vol. 38, January 1997: 9–30.

LIM, LINDA Y.C. "Women's Work in Export Factories: The Politics of a Cause." In *The Politics of Women in Development.* 1990: 101–119.

LIM, LINDA Y.C. "Capitalism, Imperialism, and Patriarchy: The Dilemma of Third-World Women Workers in Multinational Factories." In *Women, Men and the International Division of Labor.* Edited by June Nash and María Patricia Fernández-Kelly. Albany: State University of New York Press, 1983: 70–91.

LIN, V. "Women Electronics Workers in SouthEast Asia: The Emergence of a Working Class." In *Global Restructuring and Territorial Development.* Edited by J. Henderson and M. Castells. London: Sage, 1987.

LIPKE, DAVID J. "Truth Be Told." *American Demographics.* February 2001.

LONGMAN, PHILIP J. "The Slowing Pace of Progress." *U.S. News and World Report.* Vol. 129, December 25, 2000: 68.

LONG-SCOTT, ETHEL and JUDY SOUTHWORTH. "Norplant: Birth Control or Control of Poor Women?" *Extra!* Special Issue 1992: 17–18.

LORBER, JUDITH. *Gender Inequality: Feminist Theories and Politics.* Los Angeles: Roxbury Publishing Company, 1998.

LORBER, JUDITH. *Paradoxes of Gender.* New Haven, CT: Yale University Press, 1994.

LORDE, AUDRE. *Sister Outsider.* Trumansburg, NY: The Crossing Press, 1984.

LUPTON, ELLEN. *Mechanical Brides: Women and Machines from Home to Office.* New York: Cooper-Hewitt National Museum of Design Smithsonian Institute and Princeton Architectural Press, 1993.

McCARROLL, THOMAS. "Ending the Paper Chase." *Time.* June 14, 1993: 60–65.

McCLURE, LAURA. "Thinking Ergonomics." *The Progressive.* Vol. 58, August, 1994: 40–41.

McGAW, JUDITH A. "Review Essay: "Women and the History of American Technology." *Signs.* Vol. 7, Summer 1982: 798–828.

MACHUNG, ANNE. " 'Who Needs a Personality to Talk to a Machine?': Communication in the Automated Office." In *Technology and Women's Voices: Keeping in Touch*. Edited by Cheris Kramarae. New York: Routledge and Kegan Paul, 1988: 62–81.

MACINTYRE, M. NEIL. "Counseling in Cases Involving Antenatal Diagnosis." In *Antenatal Diagnosis*. Edited by Albert Dorfman. Chicago: University of Chicago Press, 1972: 63–67.

MACKENZIE, DONALD and JUDY WAJCMAN, eds. *The Social Shaping of Technology: How the Refrigerator Got Its Hum*. Philadelphia: Open University Press, 1985.

MCNULTY, MOLLY. "Pregnancy Police: The Health Policy and Legal Implications of Punishing Pregnant Women for Harm to their Fetuses." *Review of Law and Social Change*. Vol. 16, 1988: 277–319.

MALAT, JENNIFER. "Racial Differences in Norplant Use in the United States." *Social Science and Medicine*. Vol. 50, May 2000: 1297.

MALVEAUX, JULIANNE. "Will Technology Bridge the Gap Between Black and White?" *Black Issues in Higher Education*. Vol. 13, August 22, 1996: 48–49.

MANN, PEGGY. "New Help for the Childless." *Reader's Digest*. January 1986: 135–140.

MARCUSE, HERBERT. *One-Dimensional Man*. Boston: Beacon Press, 1964.

MARGOLIS, DIANE ROTHBARD. "Women's Movements Around the World: Cross Cultural Comparisons." *Gender and Society*. Vol. 7, September 1993: 379–399.

Marketing to Women. "Among U.S. Women of Child-bearing Age, 19.2% Had No Health Coverage in 1999." Vol. 14, January 10, 2001.

MARSCHALL, DANIEL and JUDITH GREGORY, eds. *Office Automation: Jekyll or Hyde?* Cleveland, OH: Working Women Education Fund, 1983.

MARSHALL, ELIOT. "Public Attitudes Toward Technological Progress." *Science*. Vol. 205, July, 1979: 281, 283–285.

MARTIN, PAUL. "Smart Houses: When Houses Take Over." *Social Issues and Health Review*. Vol. 2, No. 1, 1987: 5.

MARX, LEO. "Technology: The Emergence of a Hazardous Concept." *Social Research*. Vol. 64, Fall 1997: 965–988.

MARX, LEO. "The Idea of 'Technology' and Postmodern Pessimism." In *Technology, Pessimism, and Postmodernism*. Edited by Yaron Ezrahi, Everett Mendelsohn, Howard Segal. Dordrecht, The Netherlands: Kluwer Academic Publishers, 1994.

MARX, LEO. "Does Improved Technology Mean Progress?" *Technology Review*. Vol. 90, January 1987: 32–41, 71.

MARX, LEO. "The Machine in the Garden." *New England Quarterly*. Vol. 29, 1956: 25–41.

MATTERA, PHILIP. "High-Tech Cottage Industry: Home Computer Sweatshops." *The Nation*. April 2, 1983: 390–392.

MAYER, JACOB PETER. *Max Weber and German Politics: A Study in Political Sociology*. London: Faber and Faber, 1956.

MELYMUKA, KATHLEEN. "Wanted: A Workplace Without a 'Ceiling.'" *Computerworld*. January 24, 2000: 50–51.

MENNING, BARBARA E. "In Defense of IVF." In *The Custom-Made Child?: Women-Centered Perspectives*. Edited by Helen B. Holmes, Betty B. Hoskins, and Michael Gross. Clifton, NJ: Humana Press, 1981.

MENZIES, HEATHER. "Test-Tube Mothers Speak." *The Canadian Forum*. Vol. 72, July/August, 1993: 5–11.

MERCHANT, CAROLYN. *The Death of Nature: Women, Ecology, and the Scientific Revolution*. New York: Harper and Row, 1980.

MESTHENE, EMMANUEL. *Technological Change: Its Impact on Man and Society.* New York: New American Library, 1970.

MEYER, CHERYL. *The Wandering Uterus: Politics and the Reproductive Rights of Women.* New York: New York University Press, 1997.

MEYERS, DIANA TIETJENS, ed. *Feminist Social Thought.* New York: Routledge, 1997.

MILKMAN, RUTH, ELLEN REESE, and BENITA ROTH. "The Macrosociology of Paid Domestic Labor." *Work and Occupations.* Vol. 25, November 1998: 483.

MILLER, MICHAEL W. "Productivity Spies: Computers Keep Eye on Workers and See If They Perform Well." *Wall Street Journal.* June 3, 1985: 1, 15.

MITCHELL, SUSAN. *American Attitudes: Who Thinks What About the Issues That Shape Our Lives.* Ithaca, NY: New Strategist Publications, Inc. 1998.

MORALES, REBECCA. "Cold Solder on a Hot Stove." In *The Technological Woman: Interfacing with Tomorrow.* Edited by Jan Zimmerman. New York: Praeger, 1983: 169–180.

MORGEN, SANDRA. "'It Was the Best of Times, It Was the Worst of Times': Emotional Discourse in the Work Cultures of Feminist Health Clinics." In *Feminist Organizations: Harvest of the New Women's Movement.* Edited by Myra Marx Ferree and Patricia Yancey Martin. Philadelphia: Temple University Press, 1995: 234–247.

MORRIS, MICHAEL. "The New American Home '94: An Amazing Adaptable Showcase Proves How Far a House Can Go With Innovative Off-the-Shelf Technology." *Popular Science.* February 1994: 73–77, 83.

MORSY, SOHEIR. "Biotechnology and the Taming of Women's Bodies." In *Processed Lives: Gender and Technology in Everyday Life.* Edited by Jennifer Terry and Melodie Calvert. New York: Routledge, 1997: 166–173.

MORTON, BRIAN. "The Decline of Public Health Care." *Dissent.* Summer 1986: 269.

MOSLE, SARAH. "Letter From Vegas: How the Maids Fought Back." *The New Yorker.* February 26 and March 4, 1996: 148–156.

MUMFORD, LOUIS. *The Myth of the Machine.* 2 Volumes. New York: Harcourt Brace World, 1967, 1970.

MUMFORD, LOUIS. *Technics and Civilization.* New York: Harcourt Brace and Company, 1934.

NAHATA, RENU. "Too Many Kids and Too Much Money: Persistent Welfare Stereotypes." *Extra!* Special Issue, 1992: 12–13.

NAISBITT, JOHN. *Megatrends: Ten New Directions Transforming Our Lives.* New York: Warner, 1982.

NAPLES, NANCY A., ed. *Community Activism and Feminist Politics: Organizing Across Race, Class, and Gender.* New York: Routledge, 1998.

NASH, JUNE. "The Impact of the Changing International Division of Labor on Different Sectors of the Labor Force." In *Women, Men and the International Division of Labor.* Edited by June Nash and María Patricia Fernández-Kelly. Albany: State University of New York, 1983: 3–38.

NASH, JUNE and MARÍA PATRICIA FERNÁNDEZ-KELLY, ed. *Women, Men and the International Division of Labor.* Albany: State University of New York, 1983.

Nation. "Norplant and the Social Cleansers, Part II." July 25/August 1, 1994: 116–117.

National Catholic Reporter. "Appointment of Ethicist at Princeton Criticized." October 23, 1998: 9.

NATIONAL ORGANIZATION OF WOMEN LEGAL DEFENSE AND EDUCATION FUND, INC. "Out of the Shadows–Strategies for Expanding State Labor and Civil Rights Protections for Domestic Workers." Part I, 1997.

NATIONAL RESEARCH COUNCIL. *Computer Chips and Paper Clips: Technology and Women's Employment*. Volume 1. Report of the Panel on Technology and Women's Employment. Edited by Heidi I. Hartmann, Robert E. Kraut, and Louise A. Tilly. Washington, D.C.: National Academy Press, 1986.

NATIVIDAD, IRENE and JENNY LAUTH, eds. *Contingent Employment of Women Workers in Japan, the Philippines, and the United States*. Washington, D.C.: The Philippine American Foundation, 1999.

NEEL, K.C. "Still a Man's Club." *Cable World*. Vol. 13, January 29, 2001: 46.

NEFT, NAOMI and ANN D. LEVINE. *Where Women Stand: An International Report on the Status of Women in 140 Countries 1997–1998*. New York: Random House, 1997.

NELKIN, DOROTHY. *Selling Science: How the Press Covers Science*. New York: W. H. Freeman and Company, 1995.

NELSON, ANNE. "Women in Unions." *The American Woman 1987-88*. Edited by Sara E. Rix. New York: Norton, 1987: 232–238.

NELSON, HILDE L. "Held to a Higher Standard." *The Hastings Center Report*. Vol. 21, May/June, 1991: 2–3.

NELSON, KRISTEN. "Labor Demand, Labor Supply and the Suburbanization of Low-Wage Office Work." In *Production, Work, Territory*. Edited by Allen T. Scott and Michael Stooper. Boston: Allen and Unwin, 1986: 149–171.

NEUMANN, PETER, SOHEYLA GHARIB, and MILTON WEINSTEIN. "The Cost of a Successful Delivery with In Vitro Fertilization." *The New England Journal of Medicine*. Vol. 331, July 28, 1994: 239–243.

New Statesman & Society. "Maids for Export." December 1, 1989: 29–31.

The New York Times. "South's Prosperity Fails to Cut Child Poverty." May 5, 1988: A22.

The New York Times. "Women in Clerical Jobs Band Together to Learn 9-to-5 Rights." February 20, 1985: C9.

Newsweek. "How Far Should We Push Mother Nature?" January 17, 1994c: 54–57.

Newsweek. "The Infertility Trap." April 4, 1994b: 30–31.

Newsweek. "Contraceptive Controversy." July 18, 1994a: 65.

Newsweek. "Making Babies After Menopause." November 5, 1990: 75.

NISBET, ROBERT. *History of the Idea of Progress*. New York: Basic Books, 1980.

NIX, CRYSTAL. "Americans Find The Good Life in Guatamala." *The New York Times*. September. 10, 1987: A22.

NOBLE, DAVID. *American By Design: Science, Technology and the Rise of Corporate Capitalism*. Cambridge: Massachusetts Institute of Technology Press, 1977.

NOBLE, DAVID. "Automation Madness, or the Unautomatic History of Automation." In *Science, Technology, and Social Progress*. Edited by Steven L. Goldman. London: Associated University Presses, 1989: 65–92.

NOBLE, DAVID. Progress Without People: In Defense of Luddism. Chicago: Charles H. Kerr Publishing Company, 1993.

NOBLE, DAVID. "Social Choice in Machine Design: The Case of Automatically Controlled Machine Tools, and a Challenge for Labor." *Politics and Society*. Vol. 8, 1978: 313–347.

NORTH AMERICAN CONGRESS ON LATIN AMERICA. "Electronics: The Global Industry." New York: *NACLA's Latin America and Empire Report*. Vol. 11, April, 1977: 11–17.

NSIAH-JEFFERSON, LAURIE. "Reproductive Laws, Women of Color, and Low-Income Women." *Women's Rights Law Reporter*. Vol. 11, Spring 1989: 15–38.

NSIAH-JEFFERSON, LAURIE and ELAINE J. HALL. "Reproductive Technology: Perspectives and Implications for Low-Income Women and Women of Color." In *Healing Technology: Feminist Perspectives*. Edited by Kathryn Strother Ratcliff. Ann Arbor: University of Michigan Press, 1989: 93–117.

NYE, RUSSEL B. "The American Idea of Progress." In *The Almost Chosen People*. Edited by R. B. Nye. East Lansing, Michigan: Michigan State University Press, 1966: 1–40.

OAKLEY, ANN. *The Captured Womb: A History of the Medical Care of Pregnant Women*. Oxford: Basil Blackwell, 1984.

O'CONNOR, DAVID. "Women Workers and the Changing International Division of Labor in Microelectronics." In *Women, Households and the Economy*. Edited by Lourdes Benería and Catharine Stimpson, New Brunswick, NJ: Rutgers University Press, 1987: 243–267.

OJITO, MIRTA. "Nannies Whose Hearts Ache for Home." *The New York Times*. August 1, 1998: B1.

OLDENZIEL, RUTH. *Making Technology Masculine: Men, Women and Modern Machines in America. 1870–1945*. Amsterdam: Amsterdam University Press, 1999.

ONG, AIHWA. "Disassembling Gender in the Electronic Age." *Feminist Studies*. Vol. 13, Fall 1987a: 609–626.

ONG, AIHWA. *Spirits of Resistance and Capitalist Discipline: Factory Women in Malaysia*. Albany: State University of New York Press, 1987b.

ORBUCH, TERRI L. and SANDRA L. EYSTER. "Division of Household Labor Among Black Couples and White Couples." *Social Forces*. Vol. 76, September 1997: 301–332.

ORTIZ, VILMA. "Women of Color: A Demographic Overview." In *Women of Color in U.S. Society*. Edited by Maxine Baca Zinn and Bonnie Thornton Dill. Philadelphia: Temple University Press, 1994: 13–40.

PACE, BRIAN. "Syphilis." *JAMA, The Journal of the American Medical Association*. Vol. 284, July 2000: 520.

PAUKERT, LIBA. *The Employment and Unemployment of Women in OECD Countries*. Organization for Economic Cooperation and Development, 1984.

PAYNE, CHARLES. "Ella Baker and Models of Social Change." *Signs*. Vol. 14, 1989: 885–899.

PENA, DEVON. *The Terror of the Machine: Technology, Work, Gender, and Ecology on the U.S.–Mexico Border*. Austin, TX: Center for Mexican-American Studies, 1997.

PENA, DEVON. "Tortuosidad: Shop Floor Struggles of Female Maquiladora Workers." In *Women on the U.S.–Mexico Border: Responses to Change*. Edited by Vickie Ruiz and Susan Tiano. Boston: Allen and Unwin, 1987: 129–154.

PETCHESKY, ROSALIND POLLACK. *Abortion and Women's Choice: The State, Sexuality, and Reproductive Freedom*. Boston: Northeastern University Press, 1984.

PETCHESKY, ROSALIND POLLACK. "Reproduction, Ethics, and Public Policy: The Federal Sterilization Regulations." *Hastings Center Report*. Vol. 9, October 1979: 29–41.

PETERSON, I. "Knowing Little About How Things Work." *Science News*. Vol. 129, February 22, 1986: 118.

PETERSON, JANICE. "Public Policy and the Economic Status of Women in the United States." *Journal of Economic Issues*. Vol. 26, June 1992: 441–448.

PETIT, CHARLES. "Brave New Medicine: Wondrous Technology Could Bring Back the House Call." *U.S. News and World Report*. December 1, 1997: 82.

PION, GEORGINE M. and MARK LIPSEY. "Public Attitudes Toward Science and Technology: What Have the Surveys Told Us?" *Public Opinion Quarterly*. Vol. 45, 1981: 303–316.

PIORI, MICHAEL J. and CHARLES F. SABEL. *The Second Industrial Divide: Possibilities for Prosperity*. New York: Basic Books, 1984.

POLLARD, SIDNEY. *The Idea of Progress: History and Society.* Baltimore, MD: Penguin Books, 1968.

POLLITT, KATHA. "The Strange Case of Baby M." *The Nation.* May 23, 1987: 667, 682–688.

POPPEL, HARVEY. "Who Needs the Office of the Future?" *Harvard Business Review* . Vol. 60, November/December, 1982: 146–155.

Popular Science. "Seventh Annual Best of What's New: The Year's 100 Greatest Achievements in Science and Technology." December, 1994b: 49–65.

Popular Science. "The $30 Million Refrigerator." January, 1994a: 65–67, 87.

POPULATION CRISIS COMMITTEE. "Country Rankings of the Status of Women: Poor, Powerless and Pregnant." *Population Briefing Paper.* Washington D.C., June, 1988: 1–10.

POTT, MARTHA. "Selective Nontreatment of Handicapped Newborns." In *More than Kissing Babies?: Current Child and Family Policy in the United States.* Edited by Francine Jacobs and Margery Davies. Westport, CT: Auburn House, 1994: 179–206.

Poughkeepsie Journal. "More Women Make Leap to Corporate Boards." Wednesday, April 19, 1995: 9A.

POWELL, WALTER W. "Review Essay: Explaining Technological Change." *American Journal of Sociology.* Vol. 93, July, 1987: 185–197.

PRATO, LOU. "Women Move Up in TV Newsrooms." *American Journalism Review.* Vol. 18, November 1996: 48.

PRATT, JANE. "Home Teleworking: A Study of Its Pioneers." *Technological Forecasting and Social Change.* Vol. 25, 1984: 1–14.

PS: Political Science and Politics. "Females Match or Exceed Males in Educational Achievement." Vol. 33, December 2000: 944.

PURDY, LAURA M. "What Can Progress in Reproductive Technology Mean for Women?" *The Journal of Medicine and Philosophy.* Vol. 21, 1996: 499–514.

RAPP, RAYNA. "Feminists and Pharmacrats." *The Women's Review of Books.* Vol. 2, July 1985: 3–4.

RASMUSSEN, BENTE and TOVE HAPNES. "Excluding Women from the Technologies of the Future? A Case Study of the Culture of Computer Science." *Futures.* Vol. 23, December 1991: 1107–1119.

RATCLIFF, KATHRYN STROTHER, ed. *Healing Technology: Feminist Perspectives.* Ann Arbor: University of Michigan Press, 1989.

RECER, PAUL. "Yankee Ingenuity: Ways It Will Change Your Life." *U.S. News and World Report.* June 1981: 64–66.

REESE, STEPHEN D., PAMELA J. SHOEMAKER, and WAYNE A. DANIELSON. "Social Correlates of Public Attitudes Toward Communication Technologies." *Journalism Quarterly.* Winter 1987: 675–682.

REINELT, CLAIRE. "Moving onto the Terrain of the State: The Battered Women's Movement and the Politics of Engagement." In *Feminist Organizations: Harvest of the New Women's Movement.* Edited by Myra Marx Ferree and Patricia Yancey Martin. Philadelphia: Temple University Press, 1995: 84–104.

DOS REIS, ANA REGINA GOMEZ. "IVF in Brazil: The Story Told by the Newspapers." In *Made to Order: The Myth of Reproductive and Genetic Progress.* Edited by Patricia Spallone and Deborah Lynn Steinberg. New York: Pergamon, 1987: 120–132.

RENTELN, ALISON. "Sex Selection and Reproductive Freedom." *Women's Studies International Forum.* Vol. 15, May/June, 1992: 405–426.

Research Alert. "Women Account for Less Than 20% of Executive Positions in Fortune 500 Companies." Vol. 18, February 16, 2001: 8.

RESKIN, BARBARA and NAOMI CASSIRER. "Occupational Segregation by Gender, Race, and Ethnicity." *Sociological Focus.* Vol. 29, August 1996: 231–243.

RESKIN, BARBARA F. and HEIDI I. HARTMANN, eds. *Women's Work, Men's Work: Sex Segregation on the Job.* Washington, D.C.: National Academy Press, 1986.

RHOODIE, ESCHEL. *Discrimination Against Women: A Global Survey of the Economic, Educational, Social and Political Status of Women.* London: McFarland & Company, Inc., 1989.

RICHARDS, DONA. "European Mythology: The Ideology of 'Progress.'" In *Contemporary Black Thought: Alternative Analyses in Social and Behavioral Science.* Edited by Molefi Kete Asante and Abdulai S. Vandi. Beverly Hills: Sage Publications, 1980: 59–79.

RICHARDSON, CHARLEY. "Computers Don't Kill Jobs, People Do: Technology and Power in the Workplace." *The Annals of the American Academy of Political and Social Science.* Vol. 544, March 1996: 167–179.

RIFKIN, JEREMY. "A New Social Contract." *Annals of the American Academy of Political and Social Science.* Vol. 544, March 1996: 16–26.

RIFKIN, JEREMY. *The End of Work: The Decline of the Global Labor Force and the Dawn of the Post-Market Era.* New York: G. P. Putnam's Sons, 1995.

ROBERTS, DOROTHY. *Killing the Black Body: Race, Reproduction, and the Meaning of Liberty.* New York: Random House, 1997.

ROBERTS, DOROTHY. "The Future of Reproductive Choice for Poor Women and Women of Color." *Women's Rights Law Reporter.* Vol. 14, Spring/Fall, 1992: 305–314.

ROBERTS, DOROTHY. "The Bias in Drug Arrests of Pregnant Women." *The New York Times.* August 11, 1990: 25.

ROBERTSON, JOHN A. *Children of Choice: Freedom and the New Reproductive Technologies.* Princeton, NJ: Princeton University Press, 1994.

ROBINSON, JOHN P. and GEOFFREY GODBEY. *Time for Life.* University Park, PA: Pennsylvania State University Press, 1997.

RODRIGUEZ, REGINA. "Maternal Mortality and Morbidity: From Tragedy to Prevention." *Women's Health Journal.* Vol 35, 1990: 36–50.

ROGERS, JACKIE KRASAS. "Just a Temp: Experience and Structure of Alienation in Temporary Clerical Employment." *Work and Occupations.* Vol. 22, May 1995: 137–166.

ROLLINS, JUDITH. "Ideology and Servitude." In *At Work in Homes: Household Workers in World Perspective.* Edited by Roger Sanjek and Shellee Colen. American Ethnological Society Monograph Series, No. 3, 1990: 74–88.

ROMERO, MARY. *Maid in the U.S.A.* New York: Routledge, 1992.

ROPER CENTER AT THE UNIVERSITY OF CONNECTICUT PUBLIC OPINION ONLINE. http://www.ropercenter.uconn.edu/ipoll.html

ROSE, HILARY. "Science's Gender Gap." *The Women's Review of Books.* Vol. 2, May 1985: 5–6.

ROSE, HILARY and JALNA HANMER. "Women's Liberation, Reproduction and the Technological Fix." In *Sexual Divisions and Society: Process and Change.* Edited by Diana Leonard Barker and Sheila Allen. Tavistock, London, 1976: 199–223.

ROSEN, ELLEN I. *Bitter Choices: Blue-Collar Women In and Out of Work.* Chicago: University of Chicago, 1987.

ROSEN, MARJORIE. "Betrayal of Hope." *People Weekly.* Vol. 42, September 5, 1994: 5.

ROSENBERG, HARRIET. "The Kitchen and the Multinational Corporation: An Analysis of the Links Between the Household and Global Corporations." *Journal of Business Ethics.* Vol. 6, 1987: 179–194.

ROSS, CATHERINE. "The Division of Labor at Home." *Social Forces.* Vol. 65, March 1987: 816–833.

ROTHMAN, BARBARA KATZ. *Recreating Motherhood: Ideology and Technology in a Patriarchal Society.* New York: W.W. Norton and Company, 1989.

ROTHMAN, BARBARA KATZ. "The Meanings of Choice in Reproductive Technology." In *Test-Tube Women: What Future for Motherhood?* Edited by Rita Arditti, Renate Duelli Klein, and Shelley Minden. London: Pandora Press, 1984: 23–33.

ROTHSCHILD, JOAN. "Technology, Housework, and Women's Liberation: A Theoretical Analysis." In *Machina Ex Dea: Feminist Perspectives on Technology.* Edited by Joan Rothschild. New York: Pergamon Press, 1983: 79–93.

ROTHSCHILD, JOAN, ed. *Women, Technology, and Innovation.* New York: Pergamon Press, 1982.

ROTHSCHILD, JOAN. "A Feminist Perspective on Technology and the Future." *Women's Studies International Quarterly.* Vol. 4, 1981: 65–74.

RUIZ, VICKI. "By the Day or the Week: Mexicana Domestic Workers in El Paso." In *Women on the U.S.-Mexico Border: Responses to Change.* Edited by Vicki Ruiz and Susan Tiano. Boston: Allen and Unwin, 1987: 61–76.

RULE, JAMES and PETER BRANTLEY. "Computerized Surveillance in the Workplace: Forms and Distributions." *Sociological Forum.* Vol. 7, 1992: 405–423.

RUSKIN, GARY and ROBERT WEISSMAN. "The Cost of Commercialism." *Multinational Monitor.* Vol. 20, January/February, 1999: 9.

RUZEK, SHERYL. *The Women's Health Movement: Feminist Alternatives to Medical Control.* New York: Praeger, 1978.

SAFA, HELEN. *The Myth of the Male Breadwinner: Women and Industrialization in the Caribbean.* Boulder: Westview Press, 1995.

SAFA, HELEN. "Runaway Shops and Female Employment: The Search for Cheap Labor." *Signs.* Vol. 7, Winter 1981: 418–433.

SANJEK, ROGER and SHELLEE COLEN. "Conclusion." In *At Work in Homes: Household Workers in World Perspective.* Edited by Roger Sanjek and Shellee Colen. American Ethnological Society Monograph Series, No. 3, 1990a: 176–188.

SANJEK, ROGER and SHELLEE COLEN. "Introduction." In *At Work in Homes: Household Workers in World Perspective.* Edited by Roger Sanjek and Shellee Colen. American Ethnological Society Monograph Series, Number 3, 1990b: 1–13.

SAUNDERS, CAROL S. "Atlas of Racial Health Inequalities." *Patient Care.* May 15, 2000a: 18.

SAUNDERS, CAROL S. "Healthy Information for Minority Women. *Patient Care.* May 15, 2000b: 16.

SAVAGE, J.A. "Are Computer Terminals Zapping Workers' Health?" *Business and Society Review.* Winter 1993: 41–43.

SCALES-TRENT, JUDY. "Women of Color and Health: Issues of Gender, Community, and Power." *Stanford Law Review.* Vol. 43, July 1991: 1357–1368.

SCHARFF, VIRGINIA. *Taking the Wheel: Women and the Coming of the Motor Age.* New York: Free Press, 1991.

SCHNEIDER, DOROTHEA. "The Work That Never Ends: New Literature On Paid Domestic Work and Women of Color." *Journal of American Ethnic History.* Vol. 17, Winter 1998: 61.

SCHROETER, JAMES. "Technology and the Sexual Revolution." *Yale Review.* Vol. 62, Spring 1973: 392–405.

SCHWARTZ, JOHN. "Computers: The Next Revolution." *Newsweek.* April 6, 1992: 42–48.

SCHWARZER, ALICE. *After the Second Sex: Conversations with Simone De Beauvoir.* New York: Pantheon Books, 1984.

SCOTT, HILDA. *Working Your Way to the Bottom: The Feminization of Poverty.* London: Pandora Press, 1984.

SCOTT, JOAN W. "The Mechanization of Women's Work." *Scientific American*. Vol. 247, September 1982: 166–187.

SEAGER, JONI. *The State of Women in the World Atlas*. London: Penguin Books, 1997.

SEGAL, HOWARD. "The Cultural Contradictions of High Tech: On the Many Ironies of Contemporary Technological Optimism." In *Technology, Pessimism, and Postmodernism*. Edited by Yaron Ezrahi, Everett Mendelsohn, and Howard Segal. Dordrecht, The Netherlands: Kluwer Academic Publishers, 1994: 175–216.

SEGAL, HOWARD P. *Technological Utopianism in American Culture*. Chicago: University of Chicago Press, 1985.

SEN, GITA. "Reproduction: Policies and Politics." In *Power and Decision: The Social Control of Reproduction*. Edited by Gita Sen and Rachel C. Snow. Cambridge: Harvard University Press, 1994: 1–4.

SEN, GITA and CAREN GROWN. *Development, Crises, and Alternative Visions: Third World Women's Perspectives*. New York: Monthly Review Press, 1987.

SHAPIRO, THOMAS. *Population Control Politics: Women, Sterilization and Reproductive Choice*. Philadelphia: Temple University Press, 1985.

SHEN, CE and JOHN B. WILLIAMSON. "Maternal Mortality, Women's Status, and Economic Dependency in Less Developed Countries." *Social Science and Medicine*. Vol. 49, July 1999: 197.

SHERWIN, SUSAN. *No Longer Patient: Feminist Ethics and Health Care*. Philadelphia: Temple University Press, 1992.

SIBLEY, MUMFORD. "Utopian Thought and Technology." *American Journal of Political Science*. Vol. 17, May 1973: 255–281.

SIEGEL, JUDITH M. "Pathways to Single Motherhood: Sexual Intercourse, Adoption, and Donor Insemination." *Families in Society: Journal of Contemporary Human Services*. Vol. 79, January/February, 1998: 75.

SILVER, HILARY. "Homework and Domestic Work." *Sociological Forum*. Vol. 8, 1993: 181–204.

SILVER, HILARY and FRANCES GOLDSCHEIDER. "Flexible Work and Housework: Work and Family Constraints on Women's Domestic Labor." *Social Forces*. Vol. 72, June 1994: 1103–1119.

SILVER, LEE. "A Quandry That Isn't: Picking a Baby's Sex Won't Lead to Disaster." *Time*. September 21, 1998: 83.

SIMURDA, STEPHEN. "Shooting Star: A Crusader for Black Women's Health." *American Health*. Vol. 12, March 1993: 28–31.

SINGER, PETER. "Technology and Procreation: How Far should We Go?" *Technology Review*. Vol. 88, February/March 1985: 22–30.

SINGER, PETER and DEANE WELLS. *Making Babies: The New Science and Ethics of Conception*. New York: Charles Scribner's Sons, 1985.

SKINNER, B.F. *Beyond Freedom and Dignity*. New York: Knopf, 1971.

SMART, CAROL. "'There Is of Course the Distinction Dictated by Nature': Law and the Problem of Paternity." In *Reproductive Technologies: Gender, Motherhood and Medicine*. Edited by Michelle Stanworth. Minneapolis: University of Minnesota Press, 1987: 98–117.

SMITH, JOAN. "The Paradox of Women's Poverty: Wage-Earning Women and Economic Transformation." *Signs*. Vol. 10, 1984: 291–310.

SMITH, JUDY. "Women and Technology: What Is At Stake?" *Graduate Woman*. Vol. 75, March/April 1981: 8–11.

SMITH, MERRITT ROE. "Technology, Industrialization, and the Idea of Progress in America." In *Responsible Science: The Impact of Technology on Society.* Edited by Kevin Byrne. New York: Harper and Row, 1986: 1–30.

SMITH, MERRITT ROE and LEO MARX, eds. *Does Technology Drive History?: The Dilemma of Technological Determinism.* Cambridge: Massachusetts Institute of Technology Press, 1994.

SMITH, SHELLEY A. and MARTA TIENDA. "The Doubly Disadvantaged: Women of Color in the U.S. Labor Force." In *Women Working: Theories and Facts in Perspective.* Edited by Ann Stromberg and Shirley Harkess. Mountain View, CA: Mayfield Pub. Co., 1988: 61–80.

SNOW, RACHEL. "Reproductive Technologies: For Whom, and To What End?" In *Power and Decision: The Social Control of Reproduction.* Edited by Gita Sen and Rachel C. Snow. Cambridge: Harvard University Press, 1994: 147–151.

SOKOLOFF, NATALIE. *Black Women and White Women in the Professions: Occupational Segregation By Race and Gender, 1960–1980.* New York: Routledge, 1992.

SOLINGER, RICKIE. *Wake Up Little Susie: Single Pregnancy and Race Before Row v. Wade.* New York: Routledge, 1992.

SOLORZANO, LUCIA. "How Schools Train Kids For Tomorrow's Jobs." *U.S. News and World Report.* December 23, 1985: 47–48.

SOUTH, SCOTT J. and GLENNA SPITZE. "Housework in Marital and Nonmarital Households." *American Sociological Review.* Vol. 59, June 1994: 327.

SPALLONE, PATRICIA. *Beyond Conception: The New Politics of Reproduction.* Granby, MA: Bergin and Garvey Publishers, 1989.

SPALLONE, PATRICIA and DEBORAH LYNN STEINBERG, eds. *Made to Order: The Myth of Reproductive and Genetic Progress.* New York: Pergamon, 1987.

SPELMAN, ELIZABETH V. "Theories of Race and Gender: The Erasure of Black Women." *Quest.* Vol. 5, 1982: 36–62.

SPENDER, DALE. "The Position of Women in Information Technology–or Who Got There First and with What Consequences?" *Current Sociology.* Vol. 45, April 1997: 135–147.

SPIGEL, LYNN. *Make Room For TV: Television and the Family Ideal in Postwar America.* Chicago: University of Chicago Press, 1992.

SPIGEL, LYNN and DENISE MANN. "Women and Consumer Culture: A Selective Bibliography." *Quarterly Review of Film and Video.* Vol. 11, 1989: 85–105.

SPINRAD, R. J. "Office Automation." *Science.* Vol. 215, 1982: 808–813.

SQUIER, SUSAN. "Fetal Subjects and Maternal Objects: Reproductive Technology and the New Fetal/Maternal Relation." *The Journal of Medicine and Philosophy.* Vol. 21, 1996: 515–535.

STANLEY, T.L. "Only One of 4 Behind Camera Is Female." *Media Week.* Vol. 6, November 18, 1996: 28.

STANWORTH, MICHELLE, ed. *Reproductive Technologies: Gender, Motherhood, and Medicine.* Minneapolis: University of Minnesota Press, 1987.

STARK, STEVEN. "Housekeeping Today: Just a Lick and a Promise." *The New York Times.* August 20, 1987: C6.

STARK, WERNER. *The Sociology of Knowledge: An Essay in Aid of a Deeper Understanding of the History of Ideas.* London: Routledge and Kegan Paul, 1958.

STAUDENMAIER, JOHN M. "Perils of Progress Talk: Some Historical Considerations." In *Science, Technology, and Social Progress.* Edited by Steven L. Goldman. London: Associated University Presses, 1989: 268–298.

STAUDENMAIER, JOHN M. *Technology's Storytellers: Reweaving the Human Fabric.* Cambridge: Massachusetts Institute of Technology Press, 1985.

STAUDT, KATHLEEN. "Programming Women's Empowerment: A Case from Northern Mexico." In *Women on the U.S.–Mexico Border: Responses to Change.* Edited by Vickie Ruiz and Susan Tiano. Boston: Allen and Unwin, 1987: 155–173.

STEINBERG, DEBORAH LYNN. "Selective Breeding and Social Engineering: Discriminatory Policies of Access to Artificial Insemination by Donor in Great Britain." In *Made to Order: The Myth of Reproductive and Genetic Progress.* Edited by Patricia Spallone and Deborah Lynn Steinberg. New York: Pergamon, 1987: 184–189.

STELLMAN, JEANNE M. and MARY SUE HENIFIN. "Health Hazards in the Computerized Office." In *Office Automation: Jekyll or Hyde? Highlights of the International Conference on Office Technology.* Edited by Daniel Marschall and Judith Gregory. Ohio: Working Women Educational Fund, 1983a: 162–166.

STELLMAN, JEANNE and MARY SUE HENIFIN. *Office Work Can Be Dangerous to Your Health.* New York: Pantheon, 1983b.

STEWART MILLAR, MELANIE. *Cracking the Gender Code: Who Rules The Wired World?* Toronto: Second Story Press, 1998.

STOHS, JOANNE HOVEN. "Multicultural Women's Experience of Household Labor, Conflicts, and Equity." *Sex Roles: A Journal of Research.* March 2000: 339.

STOHS, JOANNE HOVEN. "Predictions of Conflict Over the Household Division of Labor among Women Employed Full Time." *Sex Roles.* Vol. 33, 1995: 257–275.

STRASSER, HERMANN and GUNTHER SCHLEGL. "Gemeinschaft or Gesellschaft? Two Competing Visions of Society in Werner Stark's and Max Weber's Sociology of Religion." Presented at the Meetings of the American Sociological Association, August, 1988.

STRASSER, SUSAN. *Never Done: A History of American Housework.* New York: Pantheon Books, 1982.

STURGEON, NOEL. *Ecofeminist Natures: Race, Gender, Feminist Theory and Political Action.* New York: Routledge, 1997.

SULLIVAN, ORIEL. "The Division of Housework among 'Remarried' Couples." *Journal of Family Issues.* Vol. 18, March 1997: 205.

TAEUBER, CYNTHIA. *Statistical Handbook on Women in America.* Phoenix, AZ: Oryx Press, 1996.

TAVISS, IRENE. "Notes and Queries: A Survey of Popular Attitudes Toward Technology." *Technology and Culture.* Vol. 13, 1972: 606–621.

Technology Review. "Machine Dreams: An Interview with Nicholas Negroponte." January 1992: 33–40.

TERKEL, STUDS. *Working: People Talk About What They Do All Day and How They Feel About What They Do.* New York: Pantheon, 1972.

TERRY, DON. "U.S. Child Poverty Rate Fell as Economy Grew, But Is Above 1979 Level." *The New York Times.* August 11, 2000: A10.

THOMAS, SUSAN GREGORY. "1998 Tech Guide." *U. S. News and World Report.* December 1, 1997: 66–80.

THUROW, LESTER. "Why Their World Might Crumble." *The New York Times Magazine.* November 19, 1995: 78–79.

TIANO, SUSAN. *Patriarchy on the Line: Labor, Gender, and Ideology in the Mexican Maquila Industry.* Philadelphia: Temple University Press, 1994.

TIANO, SUSAN. "Maquiladora Women: A New Category of Workers?" In *Women Workers and Global Restructuring.* Edited by Kathryn Ward. New York: Cornell University Press, 1990: 193–223.

TIFFT, SUSAN. "It's All in the (Parental) Genes." *Time.* November 5, 1990: 77.

Time. "Fertility with Less Fuss." November 14, 1994: 79.

Time. "Old Enough To Be Your Mother." January 10, 1994: 41.

Time. "New, Improved, and Ready For Battle." June 14, 1993: 48–51.

Time. "Special Issue: Beyond the Year 2000: What to Expect in the New Millennium." Fall 1992.

Time. "How a Dazzling Array of Medical Breakthroughs Has Made Curing Infertility More Than Just A Dream." September 30, 1991: 1.

Time. "Amazing Births: Babies From 'Donor Eggs.'" January 23, 1984b: 30.

Time. "The Saddest Epedemic." September 10, 1984a: 50.

Time. "Machine of the Year: The Computer Moves In." January 3, 1983: 13–39.

Time. "A Test-Tube Baby Is Not a Clone." July 31, 1978a: 65.

Time. "To Fool (or Not) with Mother Nature." July 31, 1978b: 69.

Time. "The First Test-Tube Baby." July 31, 1978c: 58–69.

Time. "Frenzy in the British Press." July 31, 1978d: 70.

Time. "Test-Tube Baby: Conceived in a Laboratory." July 24, 1978e: 47.

Tinker, Irene and Jane Jaquette. "UN Decade for Women: Its Impact and Legacy." *World Development.* Vol. 15, 1987: 419–427.

TOFFLER, ALVIN. *The Third Wave.* New York: Bantam, 1980.

TRESCOTT, MARTHA MOORE, ed. *Dynamos and Virgins Revisited: Women and Technological Change in History.* Metuchen, NJ: Scarecrow Press, 1979.

UN Chronicle. "Women Are Poorer." September, 1990: 47.

U.S. AGENCY FOR INTERNATIONAL DEVELOPMENT. "Agency Emphasizes Women in Development." *USAID Highlights.* U.S. Government Printing Office, Washington, D.C., Vol. 7, Winter, 1990: 1–4.

U.S. BUREAU OF THE CENSUS. EDUCATION. Section 4 in *Statistical Abstract of the United States: 1999* (119th ed.). Washington, D.C.: U.S. Government Printing Office, 1999.

U.S. BUREAU OF THE CENSUS. *Statistical Abstract of the United States: 1996* (116th ed.). Washington, D.C.: U.S. Government Printing Office, 1996.

U.S. BUREAU OF THE CENSUS. *We the American Women.* Washington, D.C.: U.S. Government Printing Office, September, 1993.

U.S. BUREAU OF THE CENSUS. *Women in the American Economy* by Cynthia Taeuber and Victor Valdisera. Washington, D.C.: U.S. Government Printing Office, 1986.

U.S. BUREAU OF LABOR STATISTICS. Usual Weekly Earnings Summary: First Quarter 2000. *Labor Force Statistics from the Current Population Survey.* Washington, D.C.: U.S. Government Printing Office, 2000.

U.S. CONGRESS, OFFICE OF TECHNOLOGY ASSESSMENT. *Artificial Insemination: Practice in the United States: A Summary of a 1987 Survey.* Background Paper. Washington, D.C.: U.S. Government Printing Office, August, 1988.

U.S. DEPARTMENT OF LABOR. BUREAU OF LABOR STATISTICS. *Working Women: A Chartbook.* Washington, D.C.: U.S. Government Printing Office, August, 1991.

U.S. DEPARTMENT OF LABOR. WOMEN'S BUREAU. *20 Leading Occupations of Employed Women: 1999 Annual Averages.* On line at http://www.dol.gov/dol/wb/public/wb_pubs/20/ead99.htm

U.S. DEPARTMENT OF LABOR. *Women's Bureau.* Working Women Count! A Report to the Nation: Executive Summary. Washington, D.C.: U.S. Government Printing Office, 1994: 1–4.

U.S. News and World Report. "England's Test-Tube Baby." July 31, 1978: 24.

U.S. News and World Report. "Jobs of the Future." December 23, 1985: 40–44.

U.S. Newswire. "Black Women's Health Project: Why Is Motherhood So Unsafe for Women of Color?" June 18, 1999.

VALLAS, STEVEN PETER. "New Technology, Job Content, and Worker Alienation: A Test of Two Rival Perspectives." *Work and Occupations.* Vol. 15, May 1988: 148–178.

VALLI, LINDA. *Becoming Clerical Workers.* Boston: Routledge and Kegan Paul, 1986.

VALVERDE, MARIANA and LORNA WEIR. "Regulating New Reproductive and Genetic Technologies: A Feminist View of Recent Canadian Government Initiatives." *Feminist Studies.* Vol. 23, Summer 1997: 419–431.

VANEK, JOANN. "Household Technology and Social Status: Rising Living Standards and Status and Residence Differences in Housework." *Technology and Culture.* Vol. 19, July 1978: 361–375.

VAN ZOONEN, LIESBET. "Feminist Theory and Information Technology." *Media, Culture, and Society.* Vol. 14, 1992: 9–29.

VOLK, STEVE and AMY WISHNER. "Electronics: The Global Industry." *NACLA Report on the Americas.* Vol. 11, April 1977: 1–25.

WAGAR, W. WARREN. *Good Tidings: The Belief in Progress from Darwin to Marcuse.* Bloomington, IL: Indiana University Press, 1972.

WAGNER, CYNTHIA. "Enabling the Disabled: Technologies for People With Handicaps." *The Futurist.* May-June 1992: 29–32.

WAGNER, MARSDEN. "IVF: Out-Of-Date Evidence, Or Not." *The Lancet.* Vol. 348, November 23, 1996: 1394.

WAJCMAN, JUDY. "Delivered Into Men's Hands? The Social Construction of Reproductive Technology." In *Power and Decision: The Social Control of Reproduction.* Edited by Gita Sen and Rachel C. Snow. Cambridge: Harvard University Press, 1994: 153–175.

WAJCMAN, JUDY. *Feminism Confronts Technology.* University Park, PA: The Pennsylvania State University Press, 1991.

WALLIS, CLAUDIA. "The New Origins of Life." *Time.* September 10, 1984: 46–53.

WALTHER, VIRGINIA and ALMA YOUNG. "Costs and Benefits of Reproductive Technologies." *Affilia.* Vol. 17, Summer 1992: 111–122.

WARD, SHEILA, IEDA POERNOMO SIGIT SIDI, RUTH SIMMONS, GEORGE B. SIMMONS. "Service Delivery Systems and Quality of Care in the Implementation of NORPLANT in Indonesia." Report prepared for The Population Council, New York. February 1990: 1–77.

WEBER, MAX. *The Protestant Ethic and the Spirit of Capitalism.* Translated by Talcott Parsons. New York: Charles Scribner's Sons, 1958.

WEBSTER, JULIET. *Shaping Women's Work: Gender, Employment and Information Technology.* London: Longman, 1996.

WEEDON, CHRIS. *Feminism, Theory, and the Politics of Difference.* Oxford: Blackwell Publishers Inc., 1999.

WERNEKE, DIANE. "Effects of New Technologies on Women's Employment." *News Report.* October 1984: 16–19.

WERNEKE, DIANE. *Microelectronics and Office Jobs: The Impact of the Chip on Women's Employment.* London: International Labour Office, 1984.

WESTLEY, LAURIE and JANICE DE GOOYER. *Women's Work: Undervalued, Underpaid.* National Commission on Working Women, Washington, D.C.: U.S. Government Printing Office, 1982.

WHELEHAN, IMELDA. *Modern Feminist Thought: From the Second Wave to Post-Feminism.* New York: New York University Press, 1995.

WHICKER, MARCIA LYNN and JENNIE JACOBS KRONENFELD. *Sex Role Changes: Technology, Politics, and Policy.* New York: Praeger, 1986.

WILLIAMS, ROSALLIND. "The Other Industrial Revolution: Lessons for Business from the Home." *Technology Review.* July 1984: 31–40.

WINNER, LANGDON. "Technology Today: Utopia or Dystopia?" *Social Research.* Vol. 64, Fall 1997: 989–1017.

WINNER, LANGDON. "Electronic Office: Playpen or Prison." In *Computerization and Controversy: Value Conflicts and Social Choices.* Edited by Rob Kling. New York: Academic Press, 1996: 83–84.

WINNER, LANGDON. "Social Constructivism: Opening the Black Box and Finding It Empty." *Science as Culture.* Vol. 3, Fall 1993: 427–452.

WINNER, LANGDON. *The Whale and the Reactor: A Search for Limits in an Age of High Technology.* Chicago: University of Chicago Press, 1986.

WINNER, LANGDON. *Autonomous Technology: Technics-Out-of-Control as a Theme in Political Thought.* Cambridge: Massachusetts Institute of Technology Press, 1977.

WINNER, LANGDON. "On Criticizing Technology." *Public Policy.* 1972: 35–59.

WIN News. "Commission on the Status of Women." Vol. 26, Spring 2000: 2.

WIN News. "Counting Women's Unwaged Work." Vol. 19, Autumn 1993: 78.

Women and Health: Mainstreaming the Gender Perspective into the Health Sector. New York: United Nations Publication, 1999.

WOMEN'S INTERNATIONAL NETWORK NEWS. "Counting Women's Unwaged Work." Lexington, MA.: *WIN News,* Vol. 19, Autumn 1993: 78.

WOOTTON, BARBARA H. "Gender Differences in Occupational Employment." *Monthly Labor Review.* Vol. 120, April 1997.

Working Woman. "Science and Technology." November–December, 1996: 41.

WORLD HEALTH ORGANIZATION. *Removing Obstacles to Healthy Development. WHO Report on Infectious Diseases.* New York: WHO, 1999.

WORLD HEALTH ORGANIZATION. *World Health Day Highlights Scandal of 600,000 Maternal Deaths Each Year.* New York: World Health Organization, 336 Press Release, April 1998.

WORLD HEALTH ORGANIZATION. *"Women's Health: Across Age and Frontier."* Geneva, Switzerland: 1992.

WRIGHT, BARBARA DRYGULSKI. "Introduction." In *Healing Technology: Feminist Perspectives.* Edited by Kathryn Strother Ratcliff. Ann Arbor: University of Michigan Press, 1989: 13–22.

WRIGHT, BARBARA DRYGULSKI, ed. *Women, Work, and Technology: Transformations.* Ann Arbor: University of Michigan Press, 1987.

YANOSHIK, KIM and JUDY NORSIGIAN. "Contraception, Control, and Choice: International Perspectives." In *Healing Technology: Feminist Perspectives.* Edited by Kathryn Strother Ratcliff. Ann Arbor: University of Michigan Press, 1989: 61–92.

YOUNG, GAY. "Gender Identification and Working-Class Solidarity among Maquila Workers in Ciudad Juarez: Stereotypes and Realities." In *Women on the U.S.–Mexico Border: Responses to Change.* Edited by Vickie Ruiz and Susan Tiano. Boston: Allen and Unwin, 1987: 105–128.

YOUNG, MARGOT E. "Reproductive Technologies and the Law: Norplant and the Bad Mother." In *Families and Law.* Edited by Lisa McIntyre and Marvin Sussman. Binghamton, NY: The Haworth Press, 1995: 259–281.

ZAMBRANA, RUTH E. "A Research Agenda on Issues Affecting Poor and Minority Women: A Model for Understanding Their Health Needs." *Women and Health.* Vol. 12, 1988: 137–160.

ZIMMERMAN, JAN. *Once Upon the Future: A Woman's Guide to Tomorrow's Technology.* New York: Pandora Press, 1986.

ZIMMERMAN, JAN, ed. *The Technological Woman: Interfacing With Tomorrow.* New York: Praeger, 1983.

ZIMMERMAN, JAN. "Technology and the Future of Women: Haven't We Met Somewhere Before?" In *Women, Technology, and Innovation.* Edited by Joan Rothschild. New York: Pergamon Press, 1982: 355–367.

ZINN, MAXINE BACA and BONNIE THORTON DILL. "Theorizing Difference from Multiracial Feminism." In *Gender Through the Prism of Difference.* Edited by Pierrette Hondagneu-Sotelo and Michael A. Messner. Boston: Allyn and Bacon, 2000.

ZINN, MAXINE BACA and BONNIE THORTON DILL. "Theorizing Difference from Multiracial Feminism." *Feminist Studies.* Vol. 22, Summer 1996: 321–331.

ZUBOFF, SHOSHANA. *In the Age of the Smart Machine: The Future of Work and Power.* New York: Basic Books, 1988.

Index

❖ ❖ ❖ ❖ ❖ ❖